# THE
# POSTWAR
# WORLD

*an introduction*

Peter Lane

B. T. Batsford Ltd   London

For Christopher Dominic, Mary Bernadette, Clare Veronica,
Anthony Paul, Simon Benedict, Peter Iltydd, Damien Patrick
and Gerard Mostyn, and in memory of Anne Elizabeth who
saw much less than they did and will.

© Peter Lane 1987
First published 1987

Typeset by Deltatype Lecru, Ellesmere Port, Cheshire
and printed in Great Britain by
Biddles Ltd
Guildford and Kings Lynn

Published by B. T. Batsford Ltd
4 Fitzhardinge Street, London W1H 0AH

ISBN 0 7134 5493 8 (cased)
ISBN 0 7134 5494 6 (limp)

# Contents

# Preface

As its title suggests, this book is intended as an introduction to world history since 1945, providing a basic knowledge of some of the major developments which have taken place in the postwar world and an understanding of the context in which these occurred. It is intended both for the general reader seeking to know how the problems of our day have come about, and for the student pursuing a first course of study in preparation for examinations at school or at college. It does not claim to offer novel perceptions or original scholarship; it is not as interpretative nor as analytical a work as that which would be needed by a third year under-graduate, but it will, I hope, point students to more detailed and specialized studies, enabling them to understand these the better for having read this introductory guide.

A reviewer of a companion volume, *Europe Since 1945*, wrote that in that book he 'perceived the mind of an examiner'. If he would allow the addition of 'and teacher', I would plead guilty. I am grateful for the experience I have gained from teaching International Affairs at a variety of graduate institutions, and to the students from so many nations who have provided me with fresh insights into the history of their own countries – Benin, Iran, Iraq, Japan, Jordan, Korea, Lebanon, Saudi Arabia, Singapore, Spain, Syria, Thailand, Venezuela and others have become much more than 'geographical expressions' to me as a result of this contact. The many maps (aids for the geographically illiterate), cross references throughout the text, and the detailed index are intended to help future students.

It is possible to perceive, with varying degrees of clarity, certain developments that have taken place since 1945, when some people looked forward optimistically to closer international cooperation (Chapters 2 and 16). Others, however, realized that East–West relations, soured by wartime experience, would develop into that Cold War which plagued the immediate postwar world (Chapters 1, 2, 3 and 17). We can now see that this 'war' did not end in 1953–4; it has continued to dominate international affairs since then, although the degree of frigidity has changed from time to time, with talk of détente and disarmament (Chapters 18 and 19).

We can now see that, in a sense, the years 1971–3 marked a watershed in world history, with Brandt's *Ostpolitik* helping to solve the German problem, while making it more possible for East and West to engage in talk of détente (Chapters 18 and 19). At that time, too, the USA was recognizing the need for a withdrawal from Vietnam (Chapter 15), accepting the reality of the postwar world which she could no longer hope to dominate as she had done until then (Chapter 6). Clear evidence of the link between international affairs and domestic development can be found in the decline of the US economy, which may also be dated from that period.

1972–3 marked the start of a relatively short period during which the OPEC countries (Chapter 9) seemed to have gained control of the world's economy. Their use of their power was particularly influenced by the still unresolved Arab–Israeli dispute (Chapters 8–9). However, we have also seen, in 1985–6, a decline in the relative power of OPEC, although the Arab–Israeli problem remains as troublesome as ever.

If the OPEC states seem to have risen and fallen in power, Japan and the ASEAN states (Chapters 13 and 14) provide clear evidence of the unbroken rise of economies in the Pacific Basin, with Japan deserving of treatment as a superpower in all but military strength. The several countries in western Europe, having lost their empires (Chapters 8, 10, 11, 12, 14 and 15), have sought a new role in the creation of the EEC (Chapter 4), while the satellites in eastern Europe have become increasingly restless (Chapter 3) and dissatisfied with their communist lot. In the Soviet Union, too (Chapter 5), there is clear evidence that even state leaders have lost whatever faith they may have had in Marxist–Leninism and, like China's new leaders (Chapter 7), are looking for new ways of revitalizing a decaying economy.

There has been a similar loss of 'faith' within the former colonial territories, where leaders once claimed that, if only free of the imperial yoke, their countries would grow economically and socially. Unhappily, nationalism has all too often turned into tyranny, more so, perhaps, in Africa (Chapters 8–11) than in Asia (Chapters 12–15), although even there the examples of Cambodia (Kampuchea), Vietnam, Pakistan and Bangladesh are chilling reminders of man's inhumanity to man.

So, too, is the failure of the rich world to provide sufficient aid and help for the poorer countries, occupied by about two-thirds of the world's population (Chapter 20). In spite of the creation of international agencies dedicated to helping these countries to develop, much publicized rhetoric, and a superfluity of Commissions, Committees and Reports, the fact is that in 1985–6 the poorer countries paid over to the rich some five times what they received from them in aid in that financial year: 'To everyone who hath shall be given, and given abundantly; but as for him that hath not, even what he hath shall be taken from him.'

In 1972 commentators spoke or wrote of 'a new golden age . . .' in which '. . . peace had descended on the earth'. We have seen how those hopes were falsified in the 1970s and early 1980s. It may be, then, that the gloom which is currently fashionable, may one day be seen to have been misplaced. For the sake of my children and grandchildren, I hope so.

A final point. I am only too well aware that as 1986 comes to an end and 1987 looms afar off, events to come may overturn many of the judgements reached in this book, and that some, at least of the unfinished business recorded here may have been concluded. I hope that the kind reader will understand that this is inevitable.

*Peter Lane, September 1986*

# Acknowledgements

For permission to quote passages of some length, the author and publishers would like to thank the following:

Macmillan, *The End of the Day*, Harold Macmillan
Hodder and Stoughton, *The Best of Cameron*, James Cameron
Holt, Reinhard and Winston, *Palestine or Israel,* Jon Kimche
Weidenfeld and Nicolson, *The Memoirs of Israel Sieff*
Pan Books, *North-South: A programme for survival*
Andre Deutsch, *Singapore: Its Past, Present and Future,* A. Jossey
Hutchinson, *Memoirs*, G. F. Kennan
*Le Monde*
*Paris Match*
*Time*
*The Guardian*
*The Times*
*The Sunday Times*

# 1

# The Second World War, 1939–45

## Its significance

Now tell us all about the war,
And what they fought each other for.

Robert Southey, After Blenheim

John Churchill, newly-created first Duke of Marlborough, led the Allied troops to victory at Blenheim in 1704. Eighteenth-century wars, according to Southey, were relatively simple matters: why else invite someone to 'tell us all about' one? In 1945 Winston Churchill, a descendant of the great Marlborough, led the British people to victory in the Second World War. This war, however, must be seen as particularly complex in its causes, its development and its effects.

Some historians argue that two wholly separate wars were fought between 1939 and 1945: the first in Europe and along the coast of North Africa; the second in the Far East. As to the first, most would agree with Sir Llewellyn Woodward: 'The Second World War was Hitler's war. He planned it, began it, and ultimately lost it.' During that war, Hitler was variously supported by Italy, Romania, Bulgaria and Hungary. Opposed to him were Britain, France – before her occupation – and, after 1941, the Soviet Union and the USA. The Far Eastern War had its roots in the blueprint for world conquest drawn up by the Japanese Prime Minister, Tanaka, and put before the Japanese Emperor in 1928. In his 'Memorial' Tanaka wrote, 'If we want to control China . . . we must first crush the United States . . . conquer China . . . the remainder of the Asiatic nations . . . India . . . and even Europe.' In 1937 the Japanese launched their attack on China, a prelude to their bombing of the US base at Pearl Harbour in December 1941. This raid, and Hitler's bravado support for his Axis ally, ensured US participation in the first of the 'two wars'.

The European War ended in May 1945, but the Far Eastern War continued until August 1945, when the two atomic bombs were dropped on Nagasaki and Hiroshima. By then some 60 million people had died in a 'total war' which involved civilian populations to an unprecedented degree, leading to economic dislocation on a massive scale (Document 1.1). This period saw governments extending their roles within the social and economic life of nations, and the growth of a demand in Allied countries for a 'brave new world', of which the Beveridge Report (1942) was the symbol. In postwar Europe, governments deliberately turned away from the economic and social policies which had made the thirties a decade of depression and want. Internationally, too, the war had its effects. The devastated nations of Europe found themselves dwarfed by the two superpowers, the USA and the USSR, and incapable of withstanding anti-imperialism in Asia and Africa.

The war saw the growth of international cooperation among allied nations determined to defeat the Axis powers. That cooperation had postwar repercussions. In the 1920s and 1930s the nations of the world had become increasingly introverted, their policies tending to deepen the world's economic crises. Wartime discussions led to the creation of the International Monetary Fund and the World Bank, and to the General Agreement on Tariffs and Trade, all aimed at encouraging the development of international trade. Along with the United Nations Organization, these agencies were the product of wartime plans for the promotion of a better world.

## The initial stage: September 1939–June 1940

'Our enemies are little worms: I saw them at Munich.'

Adolf Hitler

On 1 September 1939, 56 German divisions attacked Poland. The German air force controlled the skies, and the Poles were quickly defeated in a *blitzkrieg* for which they were ill-equipped. Rapid thrusts by motorized and tank divisions, supported by air power, put the railway system out of action and destroyed the Polish air force. Resistance was heroic but futile; the Poles had no motorized divisions, and relied on cavalry charges to halt the invaders. Fighting ceased at the end of September, and Poland was partitioned, shared between Germany and the Soviet Union – which had invaded eastern Poland in mid-September.

Although Britain and France declared war on Germany on 3 September, they took no direct action in support of their Polish ally. French generals, secure (as they thought) behind the Maginot Line, were unwilling to take the offensive, while the British army was too small to be really effective, despite the relative weakness of the German defensive line (the Siegfried Line). Hitler himself did not launch an attack in the west; he may have hoped for peace once Poland was defeated, and his generals warned him that the army was not strong enough to attack France (Document 1.3).

This 'phoney war' was to last for eight months, despite the Russian invasion of Finland in November 1939. Britain and France negotiated with Sweden, aiming to send troops to aid the Finns. Norway would have been an essential staging point for these Allied troops, but in the event they were never sent, and Finland was left to resist heroically until March 1940.

By then, Hitler feared that the Allies might decide to seize Norway, a country of particular importance to Germany: its port of Narvik was one of the main outlets for Swedish iron ore exports to Germany. Britain had already tried to interfere with this trade, by mining Norwegian waters. In February 1940 British warships chased the German vessel, *Altmark*, into a Norwegian fjord and rescued three hundred British prisoners. So, on 9 April 1940 German forces invaded Denmark and Norway. Although British and French troops arrived a few days later, they were unable to dislodge the Germans, and, in spite of a temporary success at Narvik, Allied troops were forced to withdraw from Norway. The country was finally conquered by the Germans in June 1940.

Germany was now assured of her iron ore supplies, while the German navy had the use of ports from which to launch attacks on Britain's transatlantic trade lines. The short-lived campaign in Norway had shown the incompetence of the Chamberlain government. As Churchill put it, 'The troops lacked aircraft, anti-aircraft guns, tanks, transport and training. There were neither snow-shoes nor skis – still less skiers [in] this ramshackle campaign.'

On 4 April 1940, Chamberlain had assured the British people that 'Hitler has missed the bus'. The German conquest of Denmark and Norway was Hitler's answer to this claim. On 10 May, Chamberlain was forced to resign, and Churchill formed an all-party coalition government. On the same day, Hitler's forces invaded Belgium, Holland and Luxembourg, bypassing the Maginot Line on their way to France. Dutch resistance collapsed after four days of heavy fighting, which included the bombing of Rotterdam and the use of parachute forces to capture salient points in the Dutch defences. On 20 May, German forces reached the Channel ports on the north coast, driving British, French and Belgian troops towards Calais and Dunkirk. Between 26 May and 4 June, some 300,000 Allied troops (mainly British) were evacuated from the beaches at Dunkirk, leaving the French to bear the brunt of the German attack.

On 10 June, Mussolini too declared war on France and Britain. Paris fell to Hitler's forces on 14 June, and a new French government, led by the First World War hero, Marshall Pétain, asked for an armistice. This was dictated by Hitler on 22 June, in the same railway carriage in which the Germans had signed the armistice in November 1918. Northern France, including Paris and the Atlantic ports, were to be occupied by Germany, and the French were to pay the occupation costs. The rest of

France, its capital now at Vichy, was to be administered by the French. The Vichy government kept control of the French navy, but in July much of it was destroyed at Oran by the British navy: this was because the French refused to sail to any Allied or neutral ports, and, if employed by the Germans, the French fleet would have tilted the balance of naval power in favour of the Axis alliance.

## The Battle of Britain, July–September 1940

'Never in the field of human conflict was so much owed by so many to so few.'

Churchill, 20 August 1940

Given the British superiority at sea, Germany had to gain control of the air if a cross-channel invasion (Operation Sealion) was to succeed and Britain forced to make peace.

Between 10 July and 7 August, German aircraft attacked British coastal convoys and vital inland targets, including some cities, while river estuaries were mined. At the onset of this battle, Germany had about 2600 aeroplanes, more than twice the number available to the Royal Air Force, but an unexpected loss of aircraft in the fighting led to a switch in German tactics. Between 8 and 23 August, there were large-scale attacks on RAF airfields and radar stations, which might have succeeded in crippling the RAF. However, Goering, commander of the German Luftwaffe, switched forces and from 24 August to 6 September, launched attacks on factories and certain military targets. During this period Germany lost over 1000 aircraft. The final phase of the Battle of Britain (7–30 September) saw huge raids by massed German squadrons which, again, suffered heavy losses at the hands of the RAF. These raids were then called off, the Germans returning to the bombing of airfields and to night raids on London and other cities (Document 1.2).

## Mussolini and the extension of the war

'This whipped jackal who, to save his own skin, has made of Italy a vassal state of Hitler's Empire, is frisking by the side of the German tiger with yelps not only of appetite – that could be understood – but even of triumph.'

Churchill in the House of Commons, April 1941

In April 1939 Italian forces overran Albania as Mussolini took advantage of the German seizure of Bohemia to stake out his claims to a Balkan Empire. In October 1940, when Italian troops invaded Greece, they were themselves defeated by Greek forces, which then invaded Albania. Mussolini appealed to Hitler, who arranged alliances with Hungary, Romania and Bulgaria, ensuring food supplies as well as stepping-stones for the passage south. In April 1941 German forces invaded Yugoslavia and Greece. Some 60,000 British troops, with-

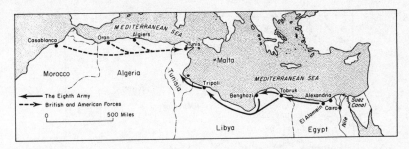

1.1 The war in the African desert

drawn from North Africa to help defend Greece, were soon driven both from the mainland and from the island of Crete. By the end of May 1941 the Balkan region was under Axis control. Meanwhile, the fluid war in North Africa (Fig. 1.1) provided Britain with a series of victories and defeats during 1940 and 1941. Britain drew some comfort from a victory over the Italian forces in Ethiopia, and from the destruction of a large part of the Italian fleet at the battles of Taranto (November 1940) and Matapan (March 1941).

## Operation Barbarossa, 1941

'The year 1941 will bring the completion of the greatest victory in our history.'

Hitler's New Year message

'This war with Russia is a nonsensical idea to which I can see no happy ending.'

Field Marshall von Rundstedt, May 1941

In August 1939 the Nazi–Soviet Pact had amazed the world, thrown non-Soviet communists into confusion and convinced anti-communists of Stalin's lack of all principle. However, in the autumn of 1940, Hitler, already in control of much of western Europe, planned an invasion of the Soviet Union.

There were ideological, economic and military reasons for this projected attack on an ally: Hitler wanted to destroy both Bolshevism and its heartland among the Slav people, whom he believed to be 'sub-human', fit only to work for German industry and Empire. A successful attack on the USSR would bring access to the wheat-belt of the Ukraine and the oil fields of the Caucasus, as well as providing that *Lebensraum* (living space) which Hitler claimed was essential for the growth of the 'new' Germany. Victory would also allow closer links with Germany's ally, Japan. With most of Europe and the Soviet Union under control, Hitler would be able to effectively ignore Britain and the USA, while launching attacks from new bases in the USSR on Africa, the Middle East (with its oil supplies) and India.

**1.2** German advances into the Soviet Union, 1941–2

Hitler's generals were opposed to the planned invasion, outlined to them in 1937 (Document 1.3). Hitler overrode their objections, and also vetoed a General Staff plan for a simple campaign in which the army would have struck at Moscow. Instead, he insisted on a five-pronged drive against Leningrad, Moscow, the Ukraine, Stalingrad and the Crimea. He was convinced that Stalin's forces would provide only weak opposition: the purges of the 1930s had led to the execution or imprisonment of many Soviet generals; Russia's industrial base was unlikely to be strong enough to provide the armaments needed for modern warfare; moreover, her attack on Finland (p. 16) provided evidence of incompetence and inefficiency. Hitler assured von Rundstedt, commander of the forces attacking the Ukraine, that 'You only have to kick in the door and the whole rotten structure will come crashing down.'

The invasion, planned for spring 1941, was delayed when Hitler sent troops to bail out Mussolini in Albania, but on 22 June 1941, 153 German divisions (some 3.5 million men) with 3500 tanks, supported by 5000 aircraft, drove into the Soviet Union. (Figure 1.2). Initially they enjoyed only success: important cities such as Riga, Smolensk and

Kiev were captured as the various prongs of the attack extended into Russia. However, they failed to capture Leningrad and Moscow, and were hampered by the rains of October and the frosts of November and December, when temperatures fell to minus 30 degrees Celsius. By the spring of 1942 no further progress had been made in the north and centre, so Hitler decided to concentrate on a drive to seize the oil-fields in the Caucasus.

## Japan attacks the USA

'A member of the embassy was told by my Peruvian colleague that . . . a surprise attack on Pearl Harbour was planned by the Japanese.'
US Ambassador in Tokyo to Roosevelt, 27 January 1941

The surprise attack did not, in fact, take place until 7 December 1941. Until then, the USA remained neutral while aiding the British war effort (p. 30).

The Japanese particularly wanted to gain control of Britain's Malaya and Burma, with their rubber, oil and tin resources, and of the oil-producing Dutch East Indies. Japan had been at war with China since 1937, and following the fall of France in May 1940 she persuaded the Vichy government to allow Japanese troops to occupy French Indo-China. There, Japan set up military bases from which to launch attacks on the British and Dutch colonies.

The USA was already providing aid to the Chinese, and in the summer of 1941 Roosevelt demanded the withdrawal of Japanese forces from Indo-China. While negotiations were going on, he placed an embargo on oil supplies to Japan (26 June 1941). Then, in October 1941 the aggressive General Tojo became Prime Minister of Japan. He was determined both to withstand US demands for the withdrawal of Japanese troops, and to push through the plans laid out in Tanaka's Memorial (p. 15).

While negotiations were slowly proceeding in Washington, the Japanese air force attacked the US naval base at Pearl Harbour on 7 December 1941, which Roosevelt described as 'a date which will live in infamy.' The US naval and air forces were almost completely destroyed, giving the Japanese control of the Pacific. By May 1942, Malaya, Singapore, Burma, Hong Kong, the Dutch East Indies, the Philippines and the US islands of Guam and Wake had been captured by the Japanese (Fig. 1.3).

Japan's attack encouraged Hitler to declare war on the USA. He need not have done so, and the USA might then have concentrated its attention on the war against Japan in the Pacific. As it was, Germany was now faced with the industrial power of the USA, together with the vast resources of the USSR and the British Commonwealth; this alliance ensured that the longer the war lasted, the less chance there was of that swift knock-out blow upon which Hitler relied.

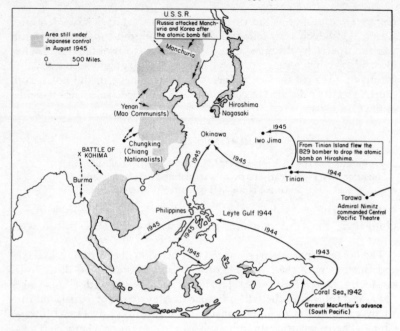

Area still under
Japanese control
in August 1945

0        500 Miles.

U.S.S.R.

Russia attacked Manch-
uria and Korea after
the atomic bomb fell.

Manchuria

Yenan
(Mao Communists)

Hiroshima
Nagasaki

Okinawa

1945

Iwo Jima

From Tinian Island flew the
B29 bomber to drop the atomic
bomb on Hiroshima.

BATTLE OF
X KOHIMA

Chungking
(Chiang
Nationalists)

1945

1945

1944

Burma

Tinian

Tarawa
Admiral Nimitz
commanded Central
Pacific Theatre

Philippines

Leyte Gulf 1944

1945

1944

1945

1943

1945

Coral Sea, 1942

General MacArthur's advance
(South Pacific)

**1.3** The defeat of Japan

## Turning points: summer 1942–summer 1943

'This is not the end. It is not even the beginning of the end. But it is,
perhaps, the end of the beginning.'
                    Churchill, 10 November 1942, on the Battle of El Alamein

In the Pacific, the Japanese advance was halted in May 1942 when the
USA won a naval action in the Coral Sea, to the south of New Guinea,
where US and Australian troops prevented the total conquest of the
island itself (Document 1.4). More importantly, in June 1942,
American dive-bombers, launched from aircraft carriers, sank two
Japanese carriers with all their planes, weakening the Japanese and
providing the USA with a lead in numbers of carriers and aircraft. Since
carrier-based air power was the key to success in the Pacific, US forces
were able to begin their recovery of the Pacific Islands, starting in
August 1942 when they landed in the Solomons. The costly and slow
process of 'island hopping' was to continue throughout 1943 and 1944.

In Russia, the German advance had been halted in the summer of
1942, in the face of strong Soviet resistance in Leningrad, Moscow and
Stalingrad (Fig. 1.2). Hitler had previously assured the Germans that, at
Stalingrad, 'The Russians are finished. In four weeks they will

collapse.' However, here, as in Moscow and Leningrad, the Russians held out, and the Battle of Stalingrad is remembered as one of the greatest siege-battles of all time. The Russians, fighting street by street, were helped by the severe weather, and by Hitler's refusal to allow the tactical retreat suggested by his commander, von Paulus. In January 1943, von Paulus surrendered, along with some 100,000 survivors, thus shattering the myth of German invincibility, and boosting Soviet morale. The surrender also encouraged the counter-attacks which forced the Germans to lift their siege of Leningrad and retreat from their position west to Moscow.

In North Africa, Rommel's Afrika Korps had driven the Allies from Libya in 1942 (Fig. 1.1). Pushing on into Egypt, they were eventually checked in August 1942, at Alam-el-Halfa. The new British commander, Montgomery, having built up an armoured force outnumbering Rommel's, launched a counter-attack at El Alamein. Within two weeks, the 60,000 men and 500 tanks of the Afrika Korps had been pushed back about seventy miles into the desert; Rommel never took the offensive again. On 8 November 1942 the Anglo-American First Army landed in Morocco, and by the spring of 1943 Allied troops had retaken the whole of North Africa.

## Victory in the west, July 1943–May 1945

Allied troops landed in Sicily on 10 July 1943, quickly capturing the island. This caused the downfall of Mussolini, dismissed by King Victor Emmanuel as Allied troops crossed to the Italian mainland, taking Naples and forcing Mussolini's successor, Badoglio, to sign an armistice. However, Hitler rushed troops to Italy, rescued Mussolini and fought to save Rome, which did not fall to the Allies until June 1944. Further north, the Germans built new defences, where the Allies were delayed until the following spring.

On 6 June 1944 the Allies landed on the Normandy beaches, where, aided by inventions such as PLUTO, and developments such as the Mulberry Harbour, a million men were landed within a month. In spite of heavy losses inflicted by the retreating Germans, Paris was liberated on 25 August, and the whole of France cleared by the end of September. In spite of a German counter-attack in the Ardennes, in the winter of 1944, the Allied advance was maintained. The Rhine was crossed in March 1945, placing Germany under attack from both east and west.

The Russians had begun their advance in the summer of 1943, driving the Germans from the Ukraine. By the end of 1944 they had freed Romania and Finland; Hungary surrendered in January 1945, and Poland was freed in February, when the Russians also entered Germany. In late April 1945, Berlin was besieged and Hitler trapped. On 30 April he committed suicide, leaving his successor, Admiral

Doenitz, to agree to an unconditional surrender, on 7 May. On 8 May
1945 VE Day was celebrated. Victory in Europe had been achieved.

## The defeat of Japan

In 1944, US forces were 'island hopping' northwards in the Pacific. A
major naval victory as Leyte enabled General MacArthur to retake the
Philippines. At the same time, British troops were pushing into Burma;
Rangoon fell in early 1945, and Burma was liberated. MacArthur then
captured the island of Okinawa, from where air attacks could be
launched on Japan itself. However, the process of capturing individual
islands was a costly one; the Japanese fought to the bitter end in every
case. The Allies were therefore faced with the possibility of losing
millions of men in a fight to retake South-East Asia, and to invade
Japan.

Then on 6 August 1945, the USA dropped the first atomic bomb on
Hiroshima, killing 84,000 people; three days later a second bomb was
dropped on Nagasaki, killing a further 40,000 people. Defending his
controversial action, President Truman claimed to have saved millions
of Allied lives. Critics claim that Japan was on the verge of surrender
before these new weapons were used, and some argue that Truman
wanted to hasten the end of the war, preventing the Soviet Union
(which had promised to enter the war against Japan) from gaining
further territory or the right to share in the occupation of Japan. In the
event, Japan agreed to an unconditional surrender on 14 August 1945,
although the final capitulation was not signed until 2 September.

## Why did the Axis powers lose the war?

'. . . they became stretched out far beyond their basic capacity for
holding their gains. For Japan was a small island state with limited
industrial power. . . . Italian incompetence was a constant drain on
Hitler's resources.'

B. H. Liddell-Hart, military historian

Initially, Germany and Japan had swept all before them; of the major
Axis powers, only Italy was incompetent and unsuccessful. The
aggressors had developed sophisticated war machines, and often had
the advantage of surprise (in, for example, their attacks on Russia and
Pearl Harbour). Above all, they were ruthlessly efficient. Until 1943,
the Allies seemed only capable of reacting to Axis strategy and tactics,
rather than initiating their own.

With the benefit of hindsight it is clear that by 1943 the Axis powers
had overreached themselves. Hitler, for example, took on the might of
the Soviet Union before ensuring the defeat of Britain; he had also
voluntarily declared war on the USA in December 1941. This decision
to 'spread the war' may have reflected an underestimation of his
enemies. Hitler, as we have seen, had a contempt for the western Allies

(p. 16), and for the 'rotten structure' of Russia (p. 20). The Japanese, too, may have thought that, after Pearl Harbour, the pleasure-loving Americans would be either unwilling or unable to undertake a war.

In fact, the combined resources of the USA, the USSR and the British Commonwealth were so great that the longer the war lasted, the less chance the Axis powers had of victory. A shortage of raw materials – rubber, cotton, nickel and, after mid-1944, oil – meant that an Axis victory depended upon a quick success. British resistance after June 1940 ensured that this was never achieved.

Britain's ability to resist was due, in large measure, to the role played by the Royal Navy. The British fleet protected merchant ships carrying food and other supplies, and fought off the challenge of the German submarines and surface raiders; it also blockaded German ports, and ferried Allied troops to the fighting in North Africa, Italy and western Europe. The Navy had been forced to learn painful lessons before it could play this leading role; its leaders had failed to accept the importance of air support in naval operations, and had therefore provided too few aircraft carriers. Naval defeats in Norway, Crete and Malaya were a direct result of enemy air superiority. However, the Allies learned their lesson: victories at Taranto and Matapan were due to the efforts of planes from the carrier *Illustrious*; US victories in the Pacific were again due to carrier-based aircraft and, later, to heavy bombers flying from recaptured islands.

The RAF saved Britain during the summer of 1940 (p. 18), but it was unable to prevent the subsequent heavy bombing of civilian targets. In time, however, the pendulum swung: Allied control of the air allowed the dropping of agents and supplies behind enemy lines, the destruction of Axis shipping and, from 1942, the almost continual bombing of Germany. In North Africa, the RAF hindered the flow of supplies to Rommel, and attacked his forces from the air. Later, the RAF dropped parachutists to aid the landings in Sicily and Normandy.

Meanwhile, the Axis powers made a series of tactical errors. Firstly, the Japanese failed to appreciate the role of the aircraft carrier, and instead produced battleships. Secondly, Hitler failed to provide the means for a successful winter campaign in the Soviet Union, but became obsessed with the idea that the Germans must not retreat. Thirdly, perhaps his most serious mistake was to concentrate on the production of V-rockets instead of the jet aircraft which might have provided Germany with air superiority in 1944 and 1945.

## Documentary evidence

### Document 1.1
*Wartime devastation and its effects*
Even during the war, attention was given to planning for the relief of battle-

worn areas in Europe. A United Nations Relief and Rehabilitation Administration was formed in 1943 to provide temporary relief. Most of the assistance provided by UNRRA went to central and eastern Europe. By June 1947 it was clear that more than temporary relief was needed, and General George C. Marshall, US Secretary of State proposed a plan to aid European recovery. This is an extract from the report prepared by ministers from 16 European countries in response to Marshall's invitation for a survey of their needs.

'To sum up, the difficulties of the participating countries at the end of a war fought over three continents were due to the following main causes:

  (i) Physical devastation and disruption in Western Europe and in the principal food and timber producing zones of Eastern Europe which, together with the dislocation of the European transport system, caused a temporary paralysis of production in Western Europe, including Germany;

 (ii) Prolonged interruption of international trade, which occurred simultaneously with the loss of income from merchant fleets and foreign investments, led to the exhaustion or diminution of dollar funds in the sixteen countries at a moment when many vital needs could be met only from dollar sources;

(iii) Human strain and exhaustion resulting from six years of war or enemy occupation;

 (iv) Internal financial disequilibrium which is the inevitable result of a long war;

  (v) In South-East Asia, the shortage in the supply of food and raw materials which were vital to the European economy, both for direct consumption and as earners of dollars;

 (vi) The abnormal increase of population in certain areas resulting from the war-time movement of peoples.

The scale of destruction and disruption of European economic life was far greater than that which Europe had experienced in the first World War. Industrial production in Belgium, France and the Netherlands was reduced to between 30 and 40 per cent of pre-war, and in Italy to only 20 per cent; production of bread grains fell to only two thirds of pre-war; 300,000 freight cars had been destroyed out of a total of 2,000,000, and 800,000 freight cars were damaged. The devastated countries had to start again almost from the beginning.'

(Committee of European Economic Cooperation, *General Report*, HMSO, 1947, vol. I, pp. 3–8)

## Document 1.2

*The Battle of Britain, 1940*

The 'Battle of Britain' of which Churchill told the Commons did not in fact begin until 10 July (see p. 18).

'18th June, 1940: The Prime Minister, Mr Churchill: . . . What General Weygand called the 'Battle of France' is over. I expect that the Battle of Britain is about to begin. Upon this battle depends the survival of Christian civilization. Upon it depends our own British life and the long continuity of our institutions and our Empire. The whole fury and might of the enemy must very soon be turned on us.

Hitler knows that he will have to break us in this island or lose the war. If we can stand up to him all Europe may be free and the life of the world may move forward into broad, sunlit uplands; but if we fail then the whole world, including the United States, and all that we have known and cared for, will sink into the abyss of a new dark age made more sinister, and perhaps more prolonged, by the lights of a perverted science.

Let us therefore brace ourselves to our duty and so bear ourselves that if the British Commonwealth and Empire lasts for a thousand years men will still say, "This was their finest hour".'

(*Parliamentary Debates, House of Commons (fifth series)*, 1940, vol. 363, cols. 60–1)

## Document 1.3

*Hitler's plans for Lebensraum*

On 5 November 1937 Hitler called a meeting of his leading military advisers and outlined for them his plans for the conquest of other countries. The details of the meeting were kept by Hitler's adjutant, Colonel Hossbach, and the following is an extract from the *Hossbach Document*:

'The Fuhrer then stated: The question for Germany is where the greatest possible conquest can be made at lowest cost. . . . If the Fuhrer is still living, then it will be his irrevocable decision to solve the German space problem no later than 1943–5. . . . It must be our first aim, in every case of entanglement by war to conquer Czechoslovakia and Austria simultaneously. . . . The Fuhrer believes that England and perhaps also France, have already silently written off Czechoslovakia. . . . Feldmarschall von Blomberg and Generaloberst von Fritsch . . . repeatedly pointed out that we should not run the risk that England and France become our enemies. . . .'

## Document 1.4

*The Battle of the Coral Sea, May 1942*

The Japanese successes in the Pacific were eventually checked by the Allied fleets in the summer of 1942. There were three years of bitter fighting still to come, but the Battle of the Coral Sea was a turning point in the war.

'*Friday, 15th May 1942*:
The Battle of the Coral Sea has resulted in the destruction of a number of Japanese warships and transports. Details of Allied losses are not yet known, but the general belief is that they are considerably smaller than those of the enemy. The curious thing is that it seems at least doubtful whether the surface naval craft ever got within range of each other. The destruction of the ships may have been carried out by aircraft. Experts refer to this action as one of the most important which has yet taken place in this war.

It's encouraging that the Japanese have lost so many naval and mercantile vessels, for they can't replace them as Britain and America can; and as their aggressions depend on sea transport, sooner or later they must come to an end.

Burma has fallen, but no move of a major kind has taken place this week. The Battle of the Coral Sea may have been preparatory to an attempted invasion of Australia.'

(Anthony Weymouth, *Journal of the War Years*, 1948, vol. II, pp. 115–16)

## FURTHER READING

ARNOLD-FORSTER, M., *The World at War*, Collins, 1973
BLUMENSON, M., *Mark Clark*, Jonathan Cape, 1985
CALDER, A., *The People's War*, Jonathan Cape, 1969.
DEUTSCHER, I., *Stalin*, Penguin, 1972
FITZGIBBONS, C., *The Blitz*, Macdonald, 1957
IRVING, D., *Hitler's War*, Hodder and Stoughton, 1977
KHRUSHCHEV, N., *Khrushchev Remembers*, vol. I, Penguin, 1977
LIDDELL-HART, B. H., *History of the Second World War*, Cassell, 1970
SMITH, D. M., *Mussolini*, Weidenfeld and Nicolson, 1981
SPEER, A., *Inside the Third Reich*, Weidenfeld and Nicolson, 1971
TAYLOR, A. J. P., *The Second World War*, Hamish Hamilton, 1975

# 2

# The effects of the war and of wartime conferences

Some of the consequences of the war were inevitable. Technological development enabled heavy bombing to take place, leading to massive destruction of economic assets (Document 1.1), as well as the loss of many lives. Less foreseeable, but almost as inevitable, were the effects of particular Japanese victories; the British and Dutch were never able to recover their domination over their Asian colonies after the war.

However, no one could have foreseen the wartime upsurge in the demand for social reform within the Allied countries. This demand was encapsulated in the Beveridge Report (1942), and in the Resistance Charters of anti-Nazi forces in occupied Europe. Nor could anyone have foreseen the rapid industrial growth of the USA, and the spread of communist power in eastern Europe – results of the war which, with the level of hindsight, may appear to have been inevitable.

Allied leaders, meeting at wartime conferences, reached decisions and agreed policies which were to have dynamic effects in the postwar world. Plans were drawn up for the creation of the UNO (Chapter 16), for the division of Europe into Soviet and western spheres of influence, and for the partitioning of Germany by the Allies. The German problem was to remain at the heart of East–West relations until the 1970s, one of the long-term effects of wartime decision-making.

## The Atlantic Charter, August 1941

'The President . . . and Mr Churchill . . . make known certain common principles in national policies . . . on which they base their hopes for a better future for the world.'

*Joint Declaration*, or Atlantic Charter, August 1941

Despite President Woodrow Wilson's efforts, the USA had never become a member of his brain-child, the League of Nations. Reverting to her traditional isolationist policy, the USA played little part in world affairs after 1919, and before the Second World War. This was in spite of the Japanese attack on China, Mussolini's war with Abyssinia and Hitler's repudiation of the Versailles Treaty. Reinforcing US isolationism, the Neutrality Act (1935) forbade the sale of munitions and the lending of money to warring countries. Many Americans thought that they had been trapped into going to war in 1917, in defence of loans made to Britain and France. Even when Germany invaded Poland in 1939, Roosevelt promised the Americans that they would not become involved in the European war.

In August 1940 Britain stood virtually alone against Germany, and although the British will to resist was great, weapons were in short supply. Roosevelt and many Americans saw their destiny and that of Britain as closely linked. The Neutrality Act, was therefore amended to allow the supply of arms to Britain, and the 'Cash and Carry' plan agreed, allowing Britain to buy arms in America provided that they were paid for in cash, and carried away in British ships.

By November 1940 Britain had sold most of its investments in the USA to raise the dollars needed to buy these arms. Churchill later wrote: 'It was plain that we could not go on any longer in this way' – for the supply of British-held dollars would soon run out.

Hitler's military success eventually led the US Congress to authorize the spending of millions of dollars on US rearmament, and American industry laid the foundations of its postwar growth. Roosevelt then persuaded Congress to amend the Neutrality Act, allowing America to give Britain 50 First World War destroyers in return for the use of military bases on certain British-held islands. In December 1940 the President outlined the Lend-Lease scheme, by which the USA 'loaned' arms to Britain for the duration of the war, to be returned, if unused at the end of the war. If, in the meantime, they were used, this would benefit the USA, because, said Roosevelt, 'the best defence of the US is the success of Great Britain in defending itself . . . we should do everything possible to help'. The Lend-Lease Act (March 1941) was later extended to apply to the USSR and China, making the USA the 'arsenal of democracy' – and an industrial giant.

In January 1941 Roosevelt spoke of 'four freedoms' for which, he said, Britain was fighting: the freedom of speech and worship, and the freedom from want and from fear of other countries. In August 1941 Roosevelt and Churchill met on the US warship, *Augusta*, based off Newfoundland. Here, in the first wartime 'summit', they discussed the Lend-Lease scheme, and the probability of Japan becoming involved in the war. They also discussed the feasibility of the development of an atomic bomb, and drew up a Joint Declaration, the 'Atlantic Charter' (Document 2.1), in which, perhaps unwittingly, they laid the basis for a great deal of postwar development. Notably, the Charter stressed the rights of colonial peoples to self-government, and the need for all nations to cooperate in the raising of living standards throughout the world, and in the establishment of some international organization which might lead to peace and disarmament.

## The Anglo–US 'special relationship'

'Lend-Lease . . . the most unsordid act in the history of any nation, transformed the whole position.'

Churchill

Postwar claims made about the 'special relationship' ignore the jibe that the British and Americans are two peoples divided by a common language. Certainly, during the war, Roosevelt said that there was 'no doubt in the mind of Americans' that the USA and Britain were united in the fight against tyranny. And if Americans admired the stead-fastness of the British, some even volunteering to serve in the British forces before December 1941, the British for their part were conscious of America's generosity and capacity to respond to Churchill's request, 'Give us the tools. . . .'

After Pearl Harbour, the relationship became even closer. In December 1941 Churchill met Roosevelt in Washington, where they both agreed to give priority, above all else, to the war against Germany, and set up the machinery for united action at economic, diplomatic, political and military levels, so cementing the 'relationship' with a web of friendships in a variety of fields. However, even at this early stage, there was disagreement about the establishment of the 'second front' demanded by Stalin. Roosevelt, General Marshall and the influential Harry Hopkins wanted an invasion of France, even in March 1942, while Churchill argued, successfully, for the invasion of North Africa (Fig. 1.1) and the build-up of forces over a long period prior to an invasion of mainland Europe. Some Americans thought Churchill more concerned about Britain's position in Egypt, the Middle East and India than with the needs of Europe. US antipathy to imperialism always tended to blur US perceptions of British policies and to mar the 'special relationship'.

The Americans accepted the argument for Operation Torch and the invasion of Morocco. This, in turn, angered de Gaulle, the leader of the Free French forces, who was not invited to share in the discussions, although Morocco was a French colony. He feared that the Anglo-Saxons would run the world in their own interest, ignoring the rights of other powers to a say in international affairs. In the 1950s and 1960s, de Gaulle was to be a thorn in the flesh of British and US politicians, his postwar repayment for what he saw as wartime insults.

Churchill and Roosevelt met again in January 1943 at Casablanca, Morocco. Here they agreed on the invasion of Italy – Churchill having persuaded Roosevelt that this would be a relatively easy way into the 'soft underbelly of Europe'. Events, however, were to prove otherwise. At Casablanca, too, Roosevelt announced the terms for the end of the war: 'Unconditional surrender'. The British Cabinet had already discussed this principle, and overridden Churchill's plea that Italy be excluded from this demand. Roosevelt wanted to assure Stalin that the western allies would not make a separate peace with Germany. At the same time, he hoped to ensure that there would be no postwar German haggling over peace terms.

### East and West in alliance, 1941–5

'[The signatories] agree to act according to the principle of not seeking territorial aggrandisement for themselves and of non-interference in the internal affairs of other States.'

The Anglo–Soviet Treaty, May 1942

Following the German invasion of the Soviet Union and Japan's attack on Pearl Harbour, the USA, USSR and Great Britain joined together as the 'Big Three' in the anti-Axis alliance. Contacts were made and agreements signed that would have been unimaginable in 1939, and which were to have major effects on postwar development.

In December 1941 negotiations were started which eventually led to the Anglo–Soviet Treaty of May 1942. Churchill wanted this treaty to incorporate Soviet territorial claims within eastern Europe, arguing it would be better to agree such claims while the USSR still depended on western aid, rather than to leave negotiations until the end of the war when Russia might be in a stronger position. Roosevelt would not allow the recognition of such territorial claims, which would run counter to the Atlantic Charter (Document 2.1) endorsed by Stalin in January 1942. Later developments were to show the worthlessness of Stalin's wartime acceptance of 'not seeking . . . aggrandisement'.

Churchill and Stalin, and Roosevelt's delegate, Harriman, met in Moscow in August 1942 to inform Stalin of the discussions between Roosevelt and Churchill which had taken place in December 1941. The 'Big Three' leaders met next in Teheran, in November 1943, where they agreed to coordinate the opening of a second front in the west with Soviet attacks from the east. They also agreed to the formation of a postwar organization to preserve peace, and to a Soviet declaration of war against Japan to be given at some suitable moment. This first meeting of the world's capitalist and communist leaders may have seemed the basis of an unlikely 'alliance', but Roosevelt left the conference confirming that he had at least as high a regard for Stalin as he did for Churchill. More significantly, he felt that he understood the Soviet leader better than Churchill did: 'I think I can handle Stalin personally better than either your Foreign Office or my State Department.' Subsequent developments were to show how ineffective Roosevelt had been, and how naive his optimism actually was.

In October 1944 Stalin and Churchill met to work out an agreement on 'spheres of influence' in eastern Europe. Churchill proposed that the Soviet Union should have 90 per cent control of Romania, that Britain should have 90 per cent control of Greece, and that both countries should share control over Yugoslavia and Hungary. This bilateral

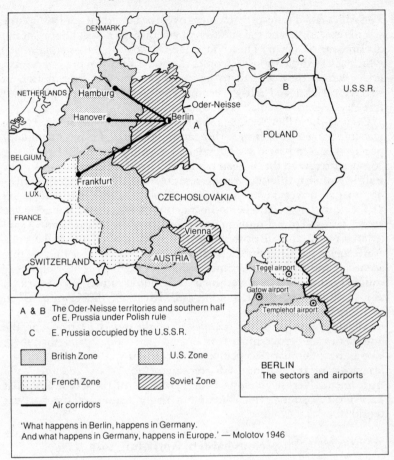

**2.1** Divided Germany and divided Berlin

disposition of millions of people was contrary to both the Atlantic Charter and the 1942 Anglo–Soviet Treaty. Allied behaviour at the second meeting of the 'Big Three', in Yalta (February 1945), confirmed the nature of this world of *realpolitik* in which Stalin and Churchill were at home, and where Roosevelt was at a disadvantage.

At Yalta (Document 2.2), the Allies agreed to divide Germany into four zones following her surrender (Fig. 2.1). They also agreed on plans for the punishment of war criminals, the payment of reparations for war damages, and on German demilitarization. A conference was planned, to be held at San Francisco to launch the United Nations Organization; the principles of the Atlantic Charter were reaffirmed; and plans were made to liberate conquered nations and Axis satellites.

The Allies failed to reach agreement over the boundaries of Poland, the size of reparations and the question of whether the Soviet Union should declare war on Japan. They issued the *Declaration on Liberated Europe*, which asserted the right of peoples to choose the form of government under which they wished to live, and promised the restoration of sovereign rights and self-government to re-conquered peoples, with free elections to take place as soon as possible.

Even as the Allies were signing this Agreement, the Soviet Union was imposing a puppet government on Poland and using its military power to extend its own boundary westwards, with Poland being compensated with the Silesian region of what had been Germany. The Polish Stalinist, Bierut, was responsible for the new Communist-dominated government of Poland, (which came into effect on 31 December 1944, and he co-operated with Marshall Zhukov in the arrest, trial and imprisonment of the leaders of the Polish Home Army (March 1945). Some British politicians attacked the terms of the Yalta Agreement, but Churchill defended Stalin's apparent violations of that accord: 'I know of no government which stands to its obligations more solidly than the Soviet government. I decline absolutely to embark on any discussion of Russia's good faith,' he told the Commons on 27 February 1945.

Allied acceptance of the changes wrought by Soviet troops in the boundaries and government of Poland persuaded Stalin that there would be a similar acceptance of further Soviet violations of the principles of the Atlantic Charter, the 1942 Treaty and the Yalta Agreement. Here were sowed the first seeds of the Cold War, that East–West hostility which became a major feature of the postwar world.

## Suspicions harden, April–July 1945

'What is to happen to Russia? Like you I feel deep anxiety . . . an iron curtain is drawn upon their front.'

Churchill to Truman, May 1945

The Yalta Conference has been described as the high tide of allied cooperation and understanding. When the Allied leaders next met, at Potsdam in July 1945, much had changed: Roosevelt's death (12 April) had brought the inexperienced Truman to the leadership of the USA; Germany had surrendered; Britain had held a General Election, after which Attlee replaced Churchill as Prime Minister, and as Britain's representative at Potsdam.

The Potsdam Conference revealed a cooling-off in relations. Truman and Churchill, and later Attlee, were annoyed by the Soviet occupation of Germany to the east of the Oder–Neisse line, which had led to this region being run by the Communist-dominated Polish government, and to the expulsion of some five million Germans, contrary to the principles of the Yalta Agreement. On the other hand, Truman did not inform Stalin about America's successful testing of the atomic bomb; this was hardly the way in which to treat an 'ally', particularly when Churchill was informed about it.

Truman went to Potsdam in July 1945 with his own firm ideas about Soviet policy and intentions. The State Department had already presented him with a memorandum outlining its suspicions of Soviet aims, and Truman told his top advisers that 'our agreements with the Soviet Union had so far been a one-way street . . . [that] could not continue.' Some 'doves' in the US government suggested that America should disregard Soviet violations of the Yalta Agreement on the grounds that 'Russia was being more realistic than we were in regard to their own security', by imposing their control over eastern Europe. Some 'hawks' argued that 'Russia had been under the impression that we would not object if they took over all eastern Europe . . . we had better have a showdown with them now, rather than later'. Leahy, one of Roosevelt's advisers at Yalta, admitted that 'he had left Yalta with the impression that the Soviet government had no intention of permitting a free government . . . in Poland'. This was a harsh reflection on Roosevelt's belief that he understood Stalin, and could handle him.

Truman's own comments on Potsdam show that he held a different view: '. . . the personal meeting with Stalin enabled me to see at first hand what we and the West had to face in the future. I was not altogether disillusioned to find now that the Russians were not in earnest about peace. . . . Russian foreign policy was based on the conclusion that we were heading for a major depression, and they were planning to take advantage of our setback.' In January 1946 Truman wrote to his Secretary of State, that '. . . Russia intends an invasion of Turkey. . . . Only one language do they understand – "How many divisions have you?" . . . .I'm tired of babying the Soviets.' By then, as we shall see in Chapter 18, the Cold War was well under way.

## Planning for the post-war world economy

'We need a central institution to aid and support other international institutions concerned with the planning and regulation of the world's economic life.'

John Maynard Keynes, April 1943

The industries of Britain and the USA produced a flow of materials for the war effort. Everyone who wanted a job had one, and a shortage of labour led to the industrial conscription of married women in Britain. Millions of families had 'never had it so good'. In the 1920s and 1930s both American and Britain had suffered from a trade recession originating in the problems in the balance of payments which faced most countries after 1919. Many countries adopted a 'beggar my neighbour' policy of tariffs and import-cutting, as they sought a favourable balance of payments. Since one country's imports are another one's exports, countries were in effect exporting unemployment.

Following the discussions which led to the Lend-Lease Act (p. 30), British and American representatives considered some of the problems that would face the postwar world. John Maynard Keynes, adviser to the British Treasury, led the British team in discussions which lasted until 1944. The US team was led by Harry Dexter White, an Assistant to the US Secretary of the Treasury, Henry Morgenthau. Keynes and White shared a common aim: they both recognized the need to provide the machinery to help international economic cooperation and development. They differed only with regard to the nature and power of the agencies which they hoped to set up. In the event, the USA being the more powerful nation, White tended to get his way.

By July 1944 agreement had been reached on the establishment of the International Monetary Fund (IMF) and the International Bank for Reconstruction and Development (the World Bank), both of which were formally put into operation on 7 December 1945. Members of the IMF would each have a quota, expressed in dollars, which determined their voting rights and subscriptions (to be paid partly in gold and partly in the members' own currencies), as well as their borrowing rights against the Fund (limited to one-quarter of the subscription). The IMF was intended to provide additional international liquidity; countries with temporary difficulties in their balance of payments could borrow from the Fund, and so would not have to adopt the restrictive policies which had deepened the recession in the inter-war years. The IMF would be, in effect, a banker to its members, lending them the currencies that they needed. Keynes wanted the IMF to have the right to create some 30 billion dollars of new money to finance postwar development. White saw that if Keynes had his way, most of this 'new money' would be spent in the USA, the only country able to supply the goods needed by the war-torn world. This would have had an inflationary effect on the US economy, so the IMF remained restricted in its creative activities. The IMF could give more help, for example, to Britain (which paid a large subscription) than to Zambia (with its smaller subscription), and it is therefore not surprising that many people in underdeveloped countries today see the IMF as 'a rich man's club'.

Keynes and White also differed in their opinions about the need for borrowing countries to make good such deficits within five years. Keynes claimed that this would prove too short a term, and that its rigid application would compel the IMF to force borrowing countries to impose domestic and international restrictions on development – the negation of their original aim. In the end, White got his way, and the agency was provided with powers which allowed it to impose restrictive policies on borrowing countries.

The World Bank obtains its funds from sales of stock to member countries, and from the issue of bonds in world financial centres. It is empowered to lend either directly to governments or, as it does more frequently, to private firms and institutions guaranteed by particular governments. In either case, the Bank aims to furnish capital for reconstruction, supplementing private investment and encouraging the expansion of the world's resources, especially in Third World countries (Chapter 20). It differs from the IMF in that it makes only long-term loans, and provides borrowing countries with a series of advisory and liaison services as further non-monetary aids to development. One of its major drawbacks is its stipulation that loans must show a profit; this prevents the World Bank from lending as much or as freely as some developing countries might wish. These countries see the Bank as an unduly conservative, profit-oriented organization, but it has, none-theless, helped many countries, and played, to a certain extent, the role which Keynes and White assigned it.

In September 1943 British and US representatives met in Washington to discuss the need for greater freedom of trade in the postwar world, one of the key points in the Atlantic Charter. They noted that free trade would succeed only if the USA and Britain adopted domestic policies aimed at ensuring full employment; this would in turn ensure a growth of world trade, allowing free trade to be more easily adopted by other countries.

However, in spite of the 'special relationship', the negotiations revealed major differences in the trade policies of the two countries. The USA was in favour of as much free trade as possible, despite an already higher-than-average tariff level, and demanded an end to the British system of Imperial Preference, which linked the members of the Commonwealth. Not surprisingly, Britain opposed the breaking of these links, which covered some fifty per cent of Britain's foreign trade.

The discussions were still going on when the war ended. With a Labour government in power in Britain, and the abrupt end of Lend-Lease, British politicians and economists were acutely aware of a dollar shortage and the need to expand British trade. This made them even less willing to agree to the dismantling of the Imperial Preference system.

The wartime negotiators had hoped to create an International Trade Organization, empowered to devise principles of commercial policy designed to expand multilateral and non-discriminatory world trade. In 1947–8 some fifty-seven nations were represented at a UN Conference in Havana. Here the Charter of the ITO was devised, to come into operation after twenty or more of the signatory nations had ratified it. The optimists hoped that along with the IMF and the World Bank this agency would form one of the three legs of 'a stool of postwar growth'. However, too few nations ratified the Charter, and the ITO was still-born. In its place the world had to accept the terms of the General Agreement on Tariffs and Trade (GATT) which was negotiated at

Geneva in 1947. This incorporated the key commercial principles which the ITO was then discussing: non-discrimination in trade, negotiated reductions in tariffs, and gradual elimination of non-tariff barriers to trade. Since 1947 there has been some progress under GATT, although, in the 1980s, there is strong evidence that the developed countries of the West are considering protectionist measures, as a counter to the successful incursion into the world's economy of less developed or newly developed countries (Chapter 20).

## Documentary evidence

## Document 2.1

*The Atlantic Charter, August 1941*

The USA had moved closer to Britain, particularly after the Lend-Lease Act. This process was taken a stage further when Churchill and Roosevelt drew up the Atlantic Charter, outlining their ideas for postwar development.

'The President and the Prime Minister deem it right to make known certain common principles on which they base their hopes for a better future for the world.

First, their countries seek no aggrandisement, territorial or other.

Second, they seek no territorial changes that do not accord with the freely expressed wishes of the people concerned.

Third, they respect the right of all peoples to choose the form of government under which they will live; and they wish to see sovereign rights and self-government restored to those who have been forcibly deprived of them.

Fourth, they will endeavour to further enjoyment by all States of access, on equal terms, to the trade and raw materials of the world needed for their economic prosperity.

Fifth, they desire to bring about the fullest collaboration between all nations in the economic field with the object of securing for all improved labour standards, economic advancement and social security.

Sixth, after the final destruction of Nazi tyranny, they hope to see established a peace which will afford to all nations the means of dwelling in safety within their own boundaries, and which will afford assurance that all men may live out their lives in freedom from fear and want.

Seventh, such a peace would enable all men to traverse the high seas and oceans without hindrance.

Eight, they believe all nations, for realistic as well as spiritual reasons, must come to the abandonment of the use of force . . . they believe, pending the establishment of a wider and permanent system of general security, that the disarmament of such nations is essential. They will likewise aid all other practicable measures which will lighten for peace-loving peoples the crushing burden of armaments.'

(Joint Declaration by the President of the USA and Prime Minister Churchill, August 1941)

# Document 2.2

*Roosevelt presents the Yalta Agreement to Congress*

Roosevelt reported optimistically to Congress. However, even before the 'Big Three' met in February 1945 at Yalta, Stalin had imposed a communist-dominated government on Poland which never had, and never would have, the 'free elections' on which Roosevelt placed such great store.

'There were two main purposes in this Crimea Conference. The first was to defeat Germany with the greatest speed. The second was to continue to build the foundation for an international accord that would give some assurance of lasting peace. . . .

There have been instances of political confusion and unrest in these liberated areas, as in Greece or in Poland, and there may be more. Worse than that, there began to grow up queer ideas of 'spheres of influence' incompatible with the basic principles of international collaboration. If allowed to go unchecked, these developments might have had tragic results. . . .

It is fruitless to try to place the blame for this situation on one particular nation or another. It is the kind of development that is inevitable unless the powers of the world continue to work together and to assume joint responsibility for the solution of problems that may endanger the peace of the world.

We met in the Crimea, determined to settle this matter of liberated areas. . . . The Three Nations have agreed that the political and economic problems of any liberated area are a joint responsibility of all three Governments. They will join together, during the temporary period of instability, to help the people of any liberated area to solve their own problems through firmly established democratic processes.

One outstanding example of joint action was the solution reached on Poland. The Polish question was a potential source of trouble and we came to the Conference determined to find common ground for its solution. And we did – even though everybody does not agree with us, obviously.

Our objective was to create a strong, independent and prosperous Nation. To achieve that objective, it was necessary to provide for the formation of a new government much more representative than had been possible while Poland was enslaved. There were two governments, one in London, one in Lublin – practically in Russia. Accordingly, steps were taken at Yalta to reorganize the existing Provisional Government in Poland on a broader democratic basis, so as to include democratic leaders now in Poland and those abroad. This new reorganized government will be recognized by all of us as the temporary government. . . . However, the new Polish Provisional Government of National Unity will be pledged to holding a free election as soon as possible on the basis of universal suffrage and a secret ballot.

Throughout history Poland has been the corridor through which attacks on Russia have been made. Twice in this generation, Germany has struck at Russia through this corridor. To ensure European security and world peace, a strong and independent Poland is necessary to prevent that from happening again.

The decision with respect to the boundaries of Poland was a compromise. I did not agree with all of it, but we did not go as far as Britain wanted, in certain areas; we did not go as far as Russia wanted, in certain areas; and we did not go as far as I wanted, in certain areas. It was a compromise. The decision is one

under which the Poles will receive compensation in territory in the North and the West for what they lose in the East. The limits of the western border will be permanently fixed in the final Peace Conference.'
(Roosevelt to Congress, February 1945)


## FURTHER READING

ARMSTRONG, D., *The Rise of International Organisations*, Macmillan, 1982
BEST, G., *Nuremberg and after*, Reading University, 1984
BULLOCK, A., *Ernest Bevin: Foreign Secretary*, Heinemann, 1983
FEIS, H., *Between War and Peace: The Potsdam Conference*, OUP, 1960
FEIS, H., *From Trust to Terror: The Onset of the Cold War, 1945–50*, Blond, 1970
LUARD, E., *The Management of the World Economy*, Macmillan, 1983
MEE, C. I., *Meeting at Potsdam*, Andre Deutsch, 1973
POSTAN, M. M., *An Economic History of Western Europe, 1945–64*, Methuen, 1967
SCAMMELL, W. M., *The International Economy Since 1945*, Macmillan, 1982
THORNE, C., *Allies of a Kind: The USA, Britain, and the War against Japan*, OUP, 1979
TOLSTOY, N., *Victims of Yalta*, Hodder and Stoughton, 1977
DE ZAVAS, A. M., *Nemesis at Potsdam*, 1979

# 3

# Eastern Europe

## The Soviet Union gains power in eastern Europe

'The Soviet régime and the Popular Democratic régimes are two forms
of one and the same system.'

Georgi Dimitrov, Prime Minister of Bulgaria

Soviet troops liberated most of eastern Europe on their way through to
Germany. As the Nazis were driven out, Stalin tried to set up a uniform
system of communist government in the 'liberated' states, reducing
each to the level of a satellite or colony. What was the reason for this?
How did the countries of eastern Europe develop under this system?
How, when and where did their peoples express anti-Soviet feelings,
and how did the Soviet government cope with them? These are some of
the questions examined in this chapter.

Poland and Czechoslovakia were officially at war with Nazi
Germany and were therefore considered 'allies' when they were
liberated by the Red Army. Romania, Bulgaria and Hungary, on the
other hand, had sided with the Nazis and were treated as 'enemies' by
the Soviet 'liberators', as was Germany itself. Albania and Yugoslavia
received little or no Soviet help in their anti-Nazi struggles; they owed
their liberation almost entirely to their own partisans, who, for a time at
least, allowed their countries to be drawn into the Soviet system of
'empire'.

As the Red Army drove westwards, it brought with it sections of the
Soviet secret police (NKVD), as well as politicians who had taken
refuge in Moscow before or during the war. These 'Muscovites'
included Dimitrov (Bulgaria), Rakosi (Hungary), Ulbricht (Germany)
and Gottwald (Czechoslovakia). In Moscow they had learned that
national loyalties were meaningless, and that they owed their allegiance
only to the world-wide interests of the communist movement, of
which the Soviet Union was the standard bearer. They were quite
prepared to be Stalin's puppets. Gomulka (Poland), Rajk and Kadar
(Hungary), and Tito (Yugoslavia) represented a local breed of
communist, always suspect to Stalin, but nevertheless ready to
welcome the Red Army.

Soviet suspicion of the West, part of the continuum of Russian history, lay behind Stalin's determination to create an 'empire' in eastern Europe, a *cordon sanitaire* between the Soviet Union and what was perceived to be an anti-Bolshevik, capitalist West. (See p. 265 and Document 2.2). Western leaders saw the matter differently. Referring to the extension of 'Soviet influence and control', Churchill noted that 'this is certainly not the Liberated Europe we fought to build up' (Document 3.1). Some historians view this expansion of Soviet power as of a piece with traditional Russian policy: 'since the foundation of the Kiev state in the ninth century, Russia has been expanding . . . [and] has come to regard the outside world as made up of deadly enemies. The Russian state has become paranoiac . . .' (*The Times*, April 1980). Some influential observers saw Stalin's expansionism as part of the communist drive for 'world revolution', so their call for anti-Soviet policies had ideological overtones. Such observers did not see Stalin's policies as part of a Russian continuum; if they had, they might have employed traditional diplomatic policies, aimed at bringing Stalin to the bargaining-table, as, surprisingly, Churchill tried to do in October 1944 (p.32). This ideological opposition to Stalinism led to a hardening of western attitudes, and contributed to the development of the Cold War (Document 17.2).

## Imposing communist control, 1945–53

'We can persuade rivals in our coalitions to slice off opposing parties: these "salami tactics" will, in time, leave us in complete control.'
                                 Mátyás Rakosi, Hungarian communist leader

The invading Red Army imposed a communist-controlled government on Poland in spite of the Yalta Agreement (Document 2.2), the promises contained in the Atlantic Charter (Document 2.1), and the Declaration on Liberated Europe (p. 34). In other 'liberated' countries, events took a different course. In Romania, Bulgaria and Hungary, coalition governments were formed. Socialists of various hues, including representatives of Peasants' Parties, and even Monarchists, joined Communists to form what Tito called 'People's Democracies'.

Initially there was some support for the communists within these countries; they had often led pre-war resistance to right-wing dictatorships, and they benefitted from the welcome given to the liberating Red Army. However, when elections were held in Hungary, in 1945, the Communists gained only a minority of the votes, in spite of the activities of police, secret agents and a controlled media. This served as a warning to other communist leaders who ignoring the Yalta articles on free elections, adopted the Rakosi 'salami tactics'.

Rakosi and Laszlo Rajk, wartime leader of the communist resistance forces in Hungary, agreed to join a coalition government provided that they could nominate their supporters to key positions, thus ensuring control of the police, press and radio. The Smallholders' Party (who gained four times as many votes as Communists) made these concessions, only to find that their control was whittled away 'slice by slice' until Rakosi became leader of a Stalinist government whose secret police were a major cause of the Hungarian rising of 1956 (Document 3.2).

In Romania, the liberating Red Army retained King Michael as Head of State, and appointed a Provisional Government in which the Communist leader, Gheorgiu-Dej, and the 'Muscovite', Anna Pauker, were leading ministers. Dej who was not a 'Muscovite' had to show himself to be more loyal to Stalin than the Stalinists themselves. His Communist-dominated Democratic Front purged itself of 'nationalists', forced King Michael to abdicate (December 1947), and named Romania a People's Republic. Between 1950 and 1952, a series of party purges saw the death or imprisonment of Pauker and other 'Muscovites' who had shown 'nationalist' tendencies.

On 30 April 1945 Walter Ulbricht flew from Moscow to take charge of the Soviet zone of occupied Germany. In October 1946 free elections held in East Berlin gave the Communists less than 20 per cent of the votes, even fewer than they had won before Hitler came to power. The depredations of the Red Army, the Soviet asset-stripping in the eastern zone, and the Polish seizure of Silesia led Germans to resent Ulbricht's hard line government. It was maintained in power, nonetheless, by the Red Army and a ruthless secret police force.

In Yugoslavia, resistance to the Germans had been led by the Moscow-trained Tito, General Secretary of the Yugoslav Communist Party since 1937. After 1943 he received aid from the western allies advancing through Italy, but none from Stalin, who tried, but failed, to organize a breakaway Muscovite Communist Party in opposition to Tito. Elections in 1945 were followed by the abolition of the monarchy and the setting up of the Federal People's Republic of Yugoslavia, with a constitution based on that of the Soviet Union. Very much a hardliner, Tito had a secret police force who purged his critics and imprisoned dissidents.

In 1947 Stalin called the leaders of the eastern European Communist parties to Warsaw, where they set up the Communist Information Bureau (Cominform). Zhdanov, speaking for Stalin, argued that the USA was trying to gain control over Europe. He claimed that the Truman Doctrine (p. 265) and the Marshall Plan (p. 271) were 'twin forks' of a US policy which had to be opposed by communists both in eastern Europe and worldwide. Stalin and Zhdanov had been alarmed by 'nationalist' statements made by communists like Gomulka (Stalin's nominee as Polish leader), who hoped that Poland would develop its own brand of national communism; 'Our democracy is not similar to the Soviet system,' he declared. Western observers viewed the Cominform, and Zhdanov's statements, as confirmation of their fear that the Soviet Union wanted to exercise an iron control over their satellites.

In October 1947 Tito took part in the Warsaw conference which established the Cominform, whose headquarters were to be in Belgrade. He opposed, however, the notion that the Bureau should coordinate communist activities throughout Europe, claiming instead that every country had the right to choose its own 'road to socialism'. For this Gomulka-like heresy, Stalin had Tito expelled from the Cominform. In addition, he stopped Soviet aid to Yugoslavia and forced the satellite states to break off relations with the independent Tito, who then accepted aid from the West. In 1953 Tito even made a state visit to Britain, the only communist leader free enough to do so.

If, in Cold War terms, Yugoslavia was a 'defeat' for Stalin, he gained a 'victory' in Czechoslovakia in 1948. Before 1939 this liberal democracy had been the most industrialized state in eastern Europe. During the war, Czech communists had played a part in the anti-German resistance movement and had welcomed the 'liberating' Red Army. In 1945 President Benes, conscious of the presence of that Army and eager to gain Soviet economic aid, agreed to help the Czech Communist Party to gain increased power. He banned the popularly-supported Agrarian Party, accepted the communist Gottwald as Prime Minister, and enabled other communists to take charge of the police, radio, press and armed forces. Early in 1947 Benes allowed a purge of the Social Democratic Party, which brought a communist to its leadership.

In 1947 Stalin insisted that no satellite should accept Marshall Aid. The communist-dominated Czech government was divided over the issue, with even communists arguing that it would be possible to accept aid without joining any western 'club'. Gottwald insisted on following the Stalinist line; several ministers resigned, allowing the promotion of more hardliners, which led to student demonstrations against the government's anti-western policies. In March 1948 the government postponed elections, fearing the return of an anti-communist majority. Benes, increasingly the prisoner of the Left, rejected popular demands for the dismissal of the Communists who instead sent strong arm gangs to occupy the offices of non-communist ministers. Jan Masaryk, the son of the founder of the Czech state, 'fell from the window of his ministry' and died. In May 1948 the elections were held, but voters were given a single list of candidates for whom they could vote. The Communist-controlled National Front gained an overwhelming victory. Benes resigned and Gottwald became President. The Communists had taken over Czechoslovakia (Document 17.3).

Gottwald then proceeded to purge the Party, as part of a Stalinist attack on 'Titoism' throughout eastern Europe. Dimitrov, who had called for talks with Tito, died in suspicious circumstances in 1949. Gomulka and Dej were dismissed from their posts as First Secretaries;

Pauker (Romania), Rajk (Hungary), Slansky and Clementis (Czechoslovakia) were executed; Prime Minister Nagy of Hungary escaped only because he was in Switzerland when his arrest was announced – he resigned by telephone.

All these leaders were replaced by less well known Soviet nominees, trusted Stalinists who, like Ulbricht, were prepared to subordinate their countries' interests to those of the Soviet Union. In 1949 Stalin set up the Council for Mutual Economic Assistance (COMECON), the Soviet answer to the Marshall Plan and the OEEC (p. 60). Under Comecon, the Soviet Union would provide technical and industral aid to further the development of the satellites' economies. They, in return, had to be run for the benefit of the Soviet Union's own development. As imperialism came under pressure in Africa and Asia, it was being imposed on eastern Europe.

## Khrushchev's restless empire, 1953–68

'We demand socialism with a human face'

Dubcek, January 1968

Stalin died on 5 March 1953; Gottwald on 14 March of the same year. Their almost simultaneous deaths signalled a series of anti-Soviet risings in eastern Europe. Workers at the Skoda car-works in Pilsen, Czechoslovakia, rioted in demand of greater freedom and better living standards, tired of their country's role as the Soviet Union's milch cow. Their strike was quickly crushed by the police and armed forces. One uprising in East Germany was longer-lived. In May 1953 the East German government announced that, while wages were to remain unaltered, every worker had to produce 10 per cent more than in the previous year. This increase in 'norms' led to a strike by East Berlin building workers (16 June 1953). The workers marched in demand of 'bread and freedom', and on 17 June led some 100,000 demonstrators, carrying banners with anti-Soviet and anti-Communist slogans. When military police failed to disperse the crowds, Soviet tanks were brought up and the streets cleared. News of the Berlin rising led to demonstrations in over 300 towns throughout East Germany. The unpopular government did not bring the country back under control until the end of June, and even then it was only with the aid of Soviet troops and armoured units.

The events of June–October 1956 were even more serious. In February 1956 Khrushchev made his attack on Stalin (p. 78). The Poles, traditionally anti-Russian, took advantage of the uncertainties caused by this historic event to demonstrate their anti-Soviet nationalism and demand improved living standards. On 28 June, car workers in Poznam began a strike, in the course of which their demands became increasingly political, changing from requests for higher wages to more radical demands, such as 'Free Gomulka' and 'End the Communist

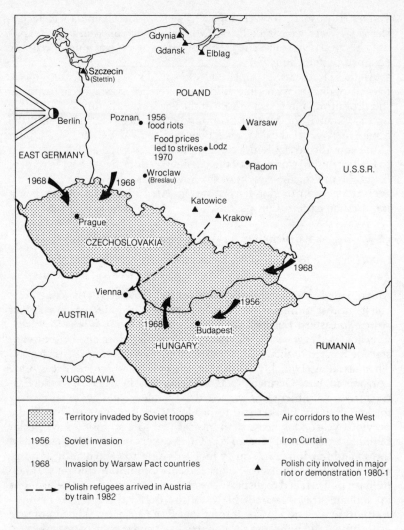

**3.1** The 'restless empire' from which Yugoslavia had escaped, and in which
Soviet military force was used to ensure policital uniformity

government'. Demonstrators fought with police, troops and armoured
units until the Soviet government prompted its Polish puppets to make
concessions. Gomulka was restored as Party Secretary and allowed to
initiate a more 'liberal' régime, although he was careful not to try
disengaging Poland from the Warsaw Pact, signed in 1955.

News of the Polish uprisings led to similar developments in
Hungary, where the Stalinist Rakosi had executed hundreds of
opponents and imprisoned thousands in concentration camps. The

Hungarians fought to demand freedom from Soviet control, an improvement in living standards and a change of government. The Soviet authorities ordered immediate concessions: Rakosi was deposed, Nagy restored to office and Cardinal Mindzenty, in prison since 1950, released. When the demonstrations continued, Nagy was forced to seek further concessions, requesting that Soviet troops be removed from Hungary. Perhaps foolishly, he also hinted at Hungary's possible withdrawal from the Warsaw Pact.

Nationwide demonstrations persisted (Document 3.2) until 26 October, when Soviet troops moved in (Fig. 3.1) and forced Budapest into submission after a month-long battle during which some 20,000 Hungarians were killed. A further 200,000 Hungarians fled to the West, and Nagy took refuge in the Yugoslavian Embassy. His successor, Janos Kadar, offered him safe conduct and freedom, but he was kidnapped, taken to the USSR and later executed. The restoration of Soviet control was overseen by Andropov, who, like Khrushchev, took a Stalinist view of dissidents such as Nagy (Fig. 16.2).

Khrushchev learnt some lessons from the Polish and Hungarian uprisings. He allowed eastern European governments to provide their 'subjects' with more consumer goods, hoping to lessen their anti-Soviet hostility. He also decreased Russian control over the satellites. In 1962 Khrushchev suggested that each state should concentrate on producing a particular commodity; the Hungarians, Romanians and Poles objected to this pro-Soviet rationalization and demanded that they be allowed to develop their economies as they wished. Khrushchev did not press his views, and in Hungary, for example, Kadar was allowed to adopt a form of controlled capitalism, leading to a rise in living standards unusual in a communist country.

In Czechoslovakia, the last satellite to become fully communist, Gottwald and Novotny had imposed a Stalin-like control over the state. Over 1600 people, many of them former communist ministers, were executed in a series of purges (1949–51), and, in spite of the Pilsen strike, Czechoslovakia remained an obedient satellite. There was no uprising in 1956, and although the policies of Gottwald (who died in 1953) were denounced and some prisoners freed, Novotny retained an iron control over Czechoslovakia. However, many Czechs resented the Soviet domination of their economy; it seemed senseless to them that their steel industry had to use poor-quality Siberian iron ore, when it could otherwise have imported high-quality Swedish ore. Non-communists from all racial groupings resented the restrictions on personal liberty, the press censorship, the loss of freedom of speech, and the activities of the brutal secret police. The Slovak population, for its part, resented the political and economic power enjoyed by Novotny and other Czechs.

In January 1968 Alexander Dubcek, a Slovak, replaced Novotny as First Secretary, and a resistance hero, General Svoboda, became

**3.2** A portrayal of a Soviet tank's role in the suppression of the riots by Polish workers in Poznam, 1956

President. The new government took a more liberal line on workers' demands for more consumer goods, and on intellectuals' demands for more freedom of expression and an end to censorship. In the 'Dubcek Spring' a new programme was adopted: the Party would no longer dictate policy; industry would be decentralized, factories run by workers' councils, and independent cooperatives encouraged in agriculture. Greater freedom was offered to trade unions, and to people wanting to travel abroad (the frontier with West Germany was thrown open immediately). There would be freedom of speech, and even the formation of non-communist political parties. Dubcek believed that even if other parties were formed, the Communists would win popular approval and retain control. He assured the Soviet Union that he would not withdraw Czechoslovakia from the Warsaw Pact, but claimed the right to negotiate trade treaties with the West.

In August 1968 troops from the Soviet Union, Poland, Bulgaria and

East Germany invaded Czechoslovakia and put its main cities under Soviet control, in spite of some resistance (Fig. 3.2). Dubcek was arrested, his supporters removed from office and an anti-Dubcek government formed under the pliant Husak. There would be no 'socialism with a human face'.

## The Polish problem, 1970–86

'No goals, no future, no hope, no joy.'

From a Polish pop-song

In December 1970 the Polish government announced rises in the price of food, fuel and clothing, ranging from eight to 60 per cent. For many Poles this was the last straw. While heavy industry produced goods which nobody wanted, everyday consumer goods were in short supply. Food shortages and rationing, the result of low output from collective farms, were facts of life. The price rises were the signal for rioting in Gdansk and other industrial centres, where there was heavy fighting between rioters and the police and army.

The Soviet Union forced the Polish First Secretary, Wladyslaw Gomulka, to resign, and allowed his successor, Edward Gierek, to cancel the price rises and authorize large wage increases. Under Gierek younger people came to power; industry was allowed some freedom from Soviet control, and western firms invited to open factories in Poland. In the short term, there was a rise in real wages and an increase in industrial and agricultural output. However, in 1976 the government tried to increase the price of basic goods: rioting forced Gierek to backtrack, and an uneasy calm prevailed.

In October 1978 the Polish Cardinal, Wojtyla, was elected Pope, becoming John Paul II. His election encouraged anti-Soviet Polish workers to form free trade unions, under the general heading of Solidarity, to demand greater freedom, higher wages and improved working conditions. The Solidarity campaign dominated Polish life between 1978 and 1982, and, because of the popularity of John Paul II, won major headlines in the western press.

The majority of Poles are Catholics, their devotion to the Church having grown rather than diminished since 1945. In the 1950s the most outspoken critic of the Soviet-controlled government was Cardinal Wyszynski, who was imprisoned from 1953 to 1956. In 1970–71 he encouraged Polish priests to act as local catalysts for anti-communist feelings, and use their pulpits, schools and presses to encourage demands for democracy and condemnation of the brutally repressive treatment of dissidents.

With the formation of Solidarity, the Church became even more outspoken, its priests sharing platforms with leaders such as Lech Walesa (Document 3.3), and its churches used as centres for the open expression of anti-Soviet and nationalist feelings. This created a problem for the Soviet Union and the Polish government. How far could they go in allowing the Church the freedom it demanded – to preach, teach and publish. In the Stalin years the Catholic Church had been the focus for anti-Soviet feeling in other satellite states: Mindzenty (Hungary) and Beran (Czechoslovakia) were just two of the Church leaders arrested and imprisoned. In the 1980s the Soviet government has been unwilling to take such a hard line, fearing a national uprising in Poland, and the high political cost of suppressing the Polish Church while talking détente to the West.

In the winter of 1981 the Soviet government forced Gierek to make way for the Polish General, Jaruzelski, as Prime Minister. He was told to impose martial law and suppress Solidarity, many of whose leaders were arrested or driven into hiding. Jaruzelski had been Minister of Defence in 1968, when Czechoslovakia was invaded; he knew that in spite of détente the Soviet Union would, in the last resort, intervene to crush a successful nationalist movement. Army, police and secret services combined to hound Solidarity leaders; harsh treatment was meted out to dissidents, and a ban imposed on public demonstrations. The death of Wyszynski, and the appointment of the more pliable Glemp as head of the Church, marked the onset of a new, if uneasy, phase in Church–State relations.

In July 1984 the General relaxed some of the worst features of martial law, and in November 1985 stepped down as Prime Minister, retaining real power as President. In the hope of continued peace, he approved the sacking of most of his former ministers. However, personnel changes will not end a situation where young couples have to wait 15 years for an apartment, where rationing is still the norm, and where it remains to be seen whether or not western bankers will continue to extend the credits needed to finance industrial development.

## The roads ahead

'. . . the basic purpose of Communist strategy remains constant through every change of leadership; only the tactics vary.'

Khrushchev, May 1958

'. . . goulash Communism . . .'

From Mao's attack on Khrushchev

In 1954, shortly after becoming Soviet leader, Khrushchev declared that if the Soviet régime could not produce enough consumer goods, people 'will not believe that Communism is a good thing, no matter what you tell [them]'. Subsequent unrest in the 'empire' has proved the truth of this. Many disturbances have originated in workers' discontent with economic and social conditions. Only after expressing anger at low wages, shortages of consumer goods, and food rationing have such protestors gone on to demand freedom of speech and political liberty.

East Germany remains the satellite most true to Stalinist principles, under Erich Honecker, who succeeded Ulbricht on his death in 1971. It is a state particularly in need of Soviet support, for its people can easily compare their lot with that of West Germans. It took the hardest line against Czechoslovakia in 1968, fearing that success of an anti-Soviet régime there would lead to similar calls for reform within East Germany.

However, there were some changes in domestic policy in the sixties. In 1962 Ulbricht permitted a more flexible economic policy, and East Germans showed that they could work as hard as West Germans. By 1985 they had the highest living standards of any country in eastern Europe; the East Germans are well-fed and well-housed, and one in three families owns a car. With western aid, notably from West Germany, East Germany has become the world's ninth leading industrial power. It remains a loyal satellite: when cruise missiles were deployed in West Germany, Honecker obeyed Soviet orders and called off a much-desired visit there.

Romania has developed along more independent lines. In the late 1950s the Stalinist Gheorghiu-Dej refused to follow the dictates of COMECON: he wanted to develop Romania rather than have it remain a supplier of oil and food to other Comecon states. He received financial aid from China and, surprisingly, France, visiting Paris and Peking in 1964 – a mark of his independence.

Nicolae Ceausescu, who succeeded Gheorghiu-Dej in 1965, has continued along this independent path. In 1967 he opposed proposals for the invasion of Czechoslovakia, and refused to allow Romanian troops to take part in the operation in 1968. In 1980–81, alone among Warsaw Pact countries, he refused to put military pressure on Poland; again, in 1984, while the other satellites obeyed Soviet orders and pulled out of the Los Angeles Olympics, Romania sent her team.

Nonetheless, Ceausescu has maintained a Stalin-like grip on the country, which still has a low standard of living. There have been no popular uprisings, and no signs of any Solidarity-type movement. Ceausescu has encouraged 'a cult of personality' which allows followers to greet him as 'Supreme Personality', 'the polyglot genius' and 'the Titan among Titans'. Rigidly adhering to Stalinist principles of centralized planning and the building of heavy industry, he has thrust his country back into the dark ages: private cars are banned in Budapest; restaurants have to close at 6 p.m.; and farmers have been urged to give up tractors for horses and oxen. Shortages are endemic: butchers' shops are open for only a few hours a week; 'economic police' patrol the streets to ensure that no one uses anything stronger than a 40 watt bulb, and that homes are kept no warmer than 54 degrees Celsius. While Romania's economic position forces Ceausescu to remain close to the Soviet Union, Moscow still hopes that his present cancer may allow the emergence of a more amenable leader. However, Ceausescu has promoted his son and his wife as potential successors, in a dynasty

which many Romanians fear will succeed only in extending the decline
and fall of the economy.

By contrast, Hungary has developed its own form of 'goulash
Communism' since 1956. Although Kadar has maintained a strong grip
on the country, there have been no further uprisings. After he
persuaded the Soviet Union to end its pillaging of Hungary's economy,
and increase its development aid, real income rose by 36 per cent
between 1956 and 1963. In 1965 Kadar introduced a new programme
designed to increase productivity and output, and create more trade
with the capitalist West. In 1984, the West was responsible for over half
of Hungary's foreign trade. State investment was made on the basis of
profitability, foreign investment encouraged, and peasants allowed to
spend more time on their private plots (which in 1984 contributed some
39 per cent of Czechoslovakia's total agricultural output).

The régime has succeeded – in Khrushchev's terms. Living standards
are higher than in most other satellite states; shops are stocked with
food and clothes; streets are crowded with privately-owned cars, and
restaurants filled with prosperous workers and their families. Kadar
encourages private initiative, self-improvement and self-enrichment;
workers work overtime and professional people run private practices.
Kadar's 'people's capitalism' may provide the model for Gorbachev as
it may be the model on which Mao's successors have based their reform
of China (Chapter 7). As yet, Hungary has not provided evidence to
support Kissinger's theory that a prosperous people will demand
political reform.

## Documentary evidence

Churchill was not the first to use the term 'iron curtain'; nor was his speech at
Fulton (Document 3.1) the first occasion on which he himself used it (p. 34).
However, that speech gave great publicity to the vivid description of eastern
Europe's isolation. Churchill also refers to the harsh nature of 'totalitarian
control' being imposed throughout the East. His references to Czechoslovakia
and Berlin may seem ironic in view of subsequent events. The Hungarian
uprising showed the unpopularity of the Stalinist system; it failed in view of the
severe repression subsequently inflicted by the 'liberal' Khrushchev with the aid
of his henchman, Andropov, another future leader of the Soviet Union.

## Document 3.1

### The 'Iron Curtain'

'A shadow has fallen upon the scenes so lately lighted by the Allied victory.
Nobody knows what Soviet Russia and its Communist international organisation intends to do. . . . From Stettin on the Baltic to Trieste in the Adriatic, an
iron curtain has desended across the Continent. Behind that line lie all the
capitals of the ancient states of Central and Eastern Europe. Warsaw, Berlin,
Prague, Vienna, Budapest, Belgrade, Bucharest and Sofia, all these famous

cities and the populations around them lie in what I must call the Soviet sphere, and all are subject . . . to Soviet influence . . . [and an] increasing measure of control from Moscow. Athens alone . . . is free to decide its future at an election under British, American and French observation. . . . The Communist parties, which were very small in all these Eastern States . . . have been raised to pre-eminence and power far beyond their numbers and are seeking everywhere to obtain totalitarian control. Police governments are prevailing in nearly every case, and so far, except in Czechoslovakia, there is no true democracy. . . .

An attempt is being made by the Russians in Berlin to build up a quasi-Communist party in their zone of Occupied Germany by showing special favours to groups of left-wing German leaders. At the end of fighting last June, the Americans and British Armies withdrew westwards, in accordance with an earlier agreement, to a depth at some points of 150 miles upon a front of nearly 400 miles . . . to allow our Russian allies to occupy this vast expanse of territory which the Western Democracies had conquered. If now the Soviet Government tries, by separate action, to build up pro-Communist Germany in their areas, this will cause new serious difficulties in the British and American zones, and will give the defeated Germans the power of putting themselves up to auction between the Soviets and the Western Democracies . . . this is certainly not the Liberated Europe we fought to build up. Nor is it one which contains the essentials of . . . peace.'

(Winston Churchill at Fulton, Missouri, March 1946)

## Document 3.2

### *The Hungarian Uprising, 1956*
'Soviet tanks, the Hungarian Army and security forces are tonight gaining the upper hand in the struggle for Budapest. . . . The rising began yesterday with student demonstrations demanding the return of Nagy as Prime Minister. Great crowds swelled the demonstrations far into the night, and firing began. Mr Nagy, who was deposed last year from office for his 'Titoist' leanings, was swept into power again as a result of last night's demonstrations.

Reports reaching Vienna speak of 2000 dead and uncounted injured in Budapest alone, where Soviet tanks today fired at random into houses suspected of harbouring rebels. Machine-gun fire went on all day, and Soviet jet fighters swept the city, seeking to locate rebel strongholds. The curfew imposed last night was extended until 6 a.m. tomorrow 'to safeguard the peace-loving population'. Shops were closed and traffic banned from the streets, which were given over entirely to tanks, armoured cars and ambu-lances. . . . In the suburbs rebels attacked factories and succeeded in capturing a number. . . . Insurgents also occupied one of the studios of Budapest radio, but surrendered on being promised an amnesty.

. . . Budapest demonstrators . . . eventually succeeded in removing the 24-feet high statue of Stalin from its pedestal. . . . In the early hours of today demonstrators procured blowlamps and burned through the base of the statue, and amid great shouts of joy sent the statue tumbling to the ground. . . . During the three-and-a-half hours it took to saw through the legs of the statue, the crowd chanted: 'We want back our church' . . . the little church that used to occupy the site on which the statue was erected. [One] eye-witness was impressed by the . . . 'passive attitude' adopted by the Hungarian police and troops. Unless demonstrators were armed and threatening, the police and

troops ignored them. Many soldiers had removed the communist emblems
from their caps.'

(*The Times*, 25 October 1956)

## Document 3.3

*Lech Walesa and John Paul II: Polish heroes*

Poland was the first satellite to be brought within the Soviet ambit and
geographically it is the most proximate to the communist centre. In spite of
over forty years of Communist rule, it remains capable of producing anti-
Soviet heroes.

'You see here two giants, two Poles who in a miraculous way appeared in the
glare of history. These two who until recently were virtually unknown
brighten our Earth as it stands on the verge of despair. They appeared in the
East, heroic but poor – their only weapon their strong faith, both struggling
against the folly and threat of all the enemies of Man . . . in a peaceful crusade
aiming only at gathering the support of all people of good will against the
assault of barbarity. Here is the modest metal worker from Gdansk, applauded
today as a real King of Poland, Lech Walesa, and the former actor from
Krakow, elected Pope in 1978, the only unquestioned leader of the twentieth
century, Karel Wojtyla, who became John Paul II . . . Wojtyla – Walesa –
engaged in the same contest. They both know it. Just as they know that their
meeting has real historical meaning: each of them in their way is the
personification of hope, not only for the countries of Eastern Europe, enclosed
in the dehumanized communist ghetto, but also for the whole West, paralysed
by fear and resignation, more preoccupied to satisfy its selfish needs and its own
safety than to listen to the powerful summons of love in the souls of every
individual. The summons that cannot remain without an echo, that at the sight
of the smallest spark of hope is ready to renew itself. . . . Here are these two
men, and how exceptional they are! . . . What luck for mankind, what luck for
every man. How fortunate that their meeting has come to pass.
(Robert Setrou, *Paris Match*, 23 January 1981)

## FURTHER READING

ACZEL, T., *Ten Years After: Hungary 1956*, McGibbon and Kee, 1966
ARNOLD-FORSTER, M., *The Siege of Berlin*, Collins, 1979
AUTY, P., *Yugoslavia*, Thames and Hudson, 1965
BOYES, R. and MOODY, J., *The priest who had to die*, Gollancz, 1986
BROWN, A. and GRAY, J., *Culture and Political Changes in Communist States*,
    Macmillan, 1977
BRUS, W. and MATEJKA, H., *The Economic History of Eastern Europe, vols 2 and
    3*, Clarendon Press, 1985
CHAPMAN, C., *August 21: The Rape of Czechoslovakia*, Cassell, 1968
COHEN, I. and WARWICK, P., *Political Cohesion in a Fragile Mosaic; The
    Yugoslav Experience*, Westview Press, 1983
CZCZESIAK, E., et al., *The Book of Lech Walesa: a collective portrait by Solidarity
    members and critics*, Penguin, 1982
FISCHER-GALATI, S., *Eastern Europe in the 1980s*, Croom, Helm, 1981

FRANKLAND, M., *Khruschev*, Penguin, 1966
GRAHAM, L. S., *Rumania: A Developing Socialist State*, Westview Press, 1982
KHRUSHCHEV, N., *Khrushchev Remembers*, Penguin, 1977
MIKES, C., *The Hungarian Revolution*, Andre Deutsch, 1957
PIPES, R., *Soviet Strategy in Europe*, Macdonald and Janes, 1976
RACHWALD, A. R., *Poland between the Superpowers*, Westview Press, 1983
SCHARF, C. B., *Politics and Change in East Germany*, Westview Press, 1984
SCHÖPFLIN, G., ed., *The Soviet Union and Eastern Europe*, Muller, Blond and White, 1986
SEJNA, J., *We Will Bury You*, Sidgwick and Jackson, 1982
URBAN, G. R., *Euro-Communism*, Temple Smith, 1978

# 4

# The Growth of Unity in Western Europe

## Europe in 1945

'What is Europe? A rubbish heap, a charnel house, a breeding ground for pestilence and hate.'

Churchill, writing in 1947

In 1939 Europe was the centre of world affairs. Some of its member-states still controlled vast empires, and its politicians decided whether there was to be war or peace. By 1945 Europe had become a devastated no man's land, caught between the two superpowers whose leaders would determine whether there was to be war or not, with the USA dominating the western world – economically, socially and politically.

While Europe takes up only two per cent of the world's land surface, it contained ten per cent of the world's population in 1945. Its peoples were collectively the most literate in the world, as well as the most experienced in trade and industry, with a shared cultural background. Taken together, the various states were capable of forming the richest and most powerful bloc in the world; acting independently, they would remain a collection of semi-important or unimportant states, squeezed by the superpowers. In May 1945 some 25 million Europeans were living in refugee camps, or in the cellars of bombed-out buildings; commerce, industry and communications had been almost destroyed; Europe was indeed 'a rubbish heap'. No single country was in a position to rebuild on its own; Europe would only recover, if at all, if every country cooperated, and acted, in Churchill's words, as 'the European family'.

In every country in western Europe people from every part of the political spectrum called for closer cooperation between the various states. Some even pondered the creation of a united federal Europe, along the lines of the United States of America. These 'federalists', or 'maximalists', wanted a greater degree of unity than did the 'minimal-ists', who admitted the need for functional cooperation (on trade and defence for example), but wanted each state to retain the greatest possible degree of sovereignty within the 'union', in whatever form it took, giving to that 'union' the minimum of power and control over national affairs.

## The Council of Europe: a political path to unity?

'We're not making a machine, we're growing a living plant, and we must wait and see until we understand what this plant turns out to be. Nevertheless, we've lit a fire which may blaze or may go out . . . the members may glow and then one day they may spring to light again.'

Churchill, at Strasbourg, 1949

In 1945 Britain was economically and politically the leading European power. Unconquered by Hitler, she had, for a time, stood alone against him, providing a home for governments-in-exile and aiding resistance movements. Even after losing office in July 1945, Churchill remained the outstanding European statesman of his day, his speeches receiving world-wide attention, as shown by the reaction to his 'Iron Curtain' speech in 1946 (p. 52). Later in the same year, at a gathering in Zurich, Churchill called for the creation of 'the European family . . . with a structure under which it can dwell . . . a kind of United States of Europe.' The 'federalists' thought that they had found their leader, and the campaign for a federal Europe gained momentum. Under Churchill's aegis, the International Committee of the Movement for European Unity was set up in 1947, organized by Churchill's son-in-law, Duncan Sandys. In May 1948 the first Congress of Europe met at the Hague, where Churchill again championed the federalist cause. A plan was produced for a European Parliament, which the 'federalists' hoped would be a true Parliament, its members directly elected by the people. Others, notably the Labour government in Britain, would not agree to the creation of such an important body. What powers might it demand? Would it become too powerful a rival of the national parliaments? Would it lead to the creation of a European Cabinet – a government of Europe?

The result was the creation, in May 1949, of the Council of Europe. Its members were appointed by national parliaments and not directly elected, which limited its possible scope. It was to meet only three or four times a year, at Strasbourg, and had no control over legislation; power remained with the national parliaments, making the Council itself little more than a debating chamber. Its original members were Belgium, Denmark, France, Ireland, Luxembourg, the Netherlands, Norway, Sweden and the UK. These were later joined by Greece, Iceland and Turkey (1949), West Germany (1951), Austria (1956), Cyprus (1961), Switzerland (1963) and Malta (1965).

It may seem strange, in view of later history, that in 1949 France led the call for a federal Europe. In May the socialist Guy Mollet, addressing the Council of Europe, took up Churchill's reference to the 'European family': 'It is indeed a family gathering which we are holding here; but there are all kinds of family gatherings. They may be funerals as well as births. It is for us to decide whether we are here to bury Europe, or to give birth to Europe. I beseech you, my dear colleagues, to let it be the birth of the United States of Europe which we are celebrating today.' It was not to be, and the 'federalists' had to look for some other method of bringing unity to Europe.

## A military road to unity: a European Defence Community?

'Churchill himself proposed the creation of a United European Army under a single Minister of Defence. I think he felt that he might be that Minister of Defence.'

Lord Boothby

Churchill made his proposal for 'a European army under a unified command in which we would all bear a working and honourable part' while he was still leading the Opposition in Britain in 1950. Some Europeans thought that he was making a major commitment to some form of European unity. However, he only ever spoke in general terms on this subject, and, as the future would show, his aim was the association of governments rather than of peoples. Moreover, Churchill always saw Britain as being the centre, if not quite the hub, of three overlapping circles – the USA, the Commonwealth, and Europe – and he refused to give priority to any one over the other two.

By 1950 the British Labour government had taken some steps down the 'functionalist' road to cooperation, thus pleasing the 'minimalists' while encouraging the 'federalists', who hoped that the experience might teach even the British that federation was desirable. In 1947 Britain and France signed the Treaty of Dunkirk, agreeing to take joint action in the event of any aggressive threat from Germany, still the perceived threat to Europe's peace. In this Treaty the two governments also agreed to constant consultation on economic matters of joint concern, making the Treaty more than a military pact. In March 1948 Britain and France were joined by the three Benelux countries, who had already set up a customs union which abolished internal barriers to free trade between Belgium, Holland and Luxembourg, and which later led them to agree to the free movement of capital and goods between their three states. In the Treaty of Brussells (March 1948) the two Dunkirk powers and the three Benelux states promised mutual help if any member came under attack. They also agreed to hold quarterly meetings between their Foreign Ministers, and to establish a Permanent Military Committee as well as several economic and social sub-committees aiming to further the idea of a Western European Union.

The creation of the Brussels organization was stimulated by the Czech crisis (p. 44), and in 1948–9 the Berlin crisis (p. 267) led to the creation of the North Atlantic Treaty Organization (NATO), in which the five Brussells powers were allied to seven other nations, including the USA. For the 'federalists', NATO was a major step; the Alliance had an integrated political structure, and its members agreed to put a portion of their national forces under international command. Each country in effect ceded a part of its national sovereignty to a supranational authority. If the NATO members were prepared to do this for a military end, they might be persuaded to cede even more for other ends, perhaps learning to surrender sovereignty completely.

In September 1950 the USA agreed to create a defence force in western Europe, to give more power to NATO, but only on condition that there was a German contribution to this force. Pleven, the French Prime Minister, was uneasily aware of the speed of German recovery, and of the logic of the US argument that rich West Germany should contribute to the West's defence against the Soviet threat. Nevertheless, like most other Frenchmen, he was fearful of Germany, and felt that he could not persuade French voters to accept German rearmament, even as part of the price to be paid for security in western Europe.

By September 1950, negotiations were well under way for the creation of the European Coal and Steel Community (p. 61), and Pleven sought to apply the same principle to defence, proposing the creation of a European Defence Community (EDC) which would have a European army including West German troops. Following the return of the Conservatives to power in Britain (February 1951), the 'Europeans' in Churchill's Cabinet supported this concept, and gave encouragement to Pleven and his Foreign Minister, Schuman. However, more powerful British voices, notably Eden's, rejected the idea of Britain becoming a part of the proposed EDC. Following Britain's refusal, the French cabinet rejected its own idea, fearing that Germany might become the dominant power in a non-British 'Europe'. The USA therefore proposed the withdrawal of its forces from western Europe, and the 'Atlanticist' Eden spent much of 1954 persuading the Benelux states, Italy and West Germany to agree to German rearmament as an essential condition of any US agreement to keep her forces under NATO control. The French Prime Minister, Mendès-France, gave his assent to this, but only on condition that Britain agreed to station four army divisions in Europe, as well as its Tactical Air Force, for as long as the European powers wished. Eden was thus forced to make the commitment to Europe which he had been unwilling to make earlier to promote the EDC. By the spring of 1955, the Western European Union (of Britain, France, West Germany, Italy and the Benelux states) had come into being, allowing West Germany to become a member of NATO, to control her own conventional weapons and to undertake rearmament. West Germany now had the national army which she would have been denied if the EDC had been established, but this 'functionalist' scheme failed to lead to much further development of the ideal Europe.

## The first economic step to 'Europe': the ECSC

'The pooling of coal and steel production should immediately provide for economic development as a first step in the federation of Europe. . . .'

The Schuman Plan, 1950

Following the offer of Marshall Aid in 1947 (p. 271) sixteen countries set up the Organization for European Economic Cooperation (OEEC) to apportion the aid among its members, and find a method of liberalizing trade and encouraging the growth of industrial and agricultural production in western Europe. By 1953, trade between OEEC members had doubled, and along with GATT (p. 37) the Organization could claim some of the credit for the speedy recovery enjoyed by western Europe after the war. 'Federalists' welcomed the fact that this 'functionalist' organization had a permanent administrative staff and a number of specialist advisory committees, who dealt with cooperation in trade, agriculture, power supplies, fisheries and transport.

West Germany joined the OEEC in 1955; Spain in 1959. In 1961 the eighteen members of the OEEC were joined by the USA and Canada, when the Organization for Economic Cooperation and Development was set up to replace the OEEC. The OECD's aims were more outward-looking than those of its predecessor, and its members (the world's leading industrial nations) proposed to offer aid to developing countries and to assist the economies of less highly-developed member states by providing financial stability and encouraging world trade.

Robert Schuman was Prime Minister of France from November 1947 to July 1948 while negotiations were going on to set up the OEEC. Perhaps more importantly, he was Foreign Minister from July 1948 to January 1953 when the OEEC was established, the Council of Europe formed and the first discussions held about the proposed EDC. He was greatly influenced by Jean Monnet, who had prepared the wartime plans for the reconstruction of postwar France, and headed the commission set up in December 1945 to modernize and re-equip French industry. He also developed the 'Monnet Plan', which within five years enabled France to outstrip its pre-war industrial level.

It was Jean Monnet who worked out the details of the 'Schuman Plan' for the pooling of the coal and steel industries of western Europe, and it was fitting that Monnet served as the first president of the European Coal and Steel Community from 1952 to 1955. France's Foreign Minister, Schuman, presented Monnet's scheme to the other states of western Europe in 1950, by which time many Frenchmen were alarmed at the speed of West Germany's recovery. Would a fully revived Germany again pose a threat to France? Could the desired German recovery take place without a revival of West German heavy industry? Would that industry be used to provide the means for German re-militarization? These were the questions many Frenchmen asked themselves.

Monnet's scheme provided for the integration of German heavy industry with that of France, Belgium, Luxembourg, Italy and, he hoped, Britain. However, when Schuman put the plan forward in May 1950, Britain turned it down. The Labour government, on the threshold of nationalizing Britain's iron and steel industry did not wish to see it pass under the control of the sort of supranational authority proposed by Monnet and Schuman. The latter's plan made it clear that he and Monnet were aiming at more than an economic agreement, for it would place the coal and steel industries of many states 'under a common higher authority . . . whose decisions will bind France, Germany and other member countries . . . [in] the first concrete foundations of the European federation which is indispensable to the preservation of peace.'

The European Coal and Steel Community was established by the Treaty of Paris (April 1951) signed by France, West Germany, Italy and the three Benelux countries – 'the Six'. This treaty set up Europe's first supranational body, the High Authority, consisting of nine experts appointed by the six governments for a period of six years, with Monnet as president. At their headquarters in Luxembourg the members of the High Authority were not responsible to their respective governments, but were to think as 'members of the Community', as 'Europeans' and not, for example, as Germans or Frenchmen. Their role was to encourage the coal and steel industries within the member states, by eliminating tariffs and other restrictions hampering free trade in these industries, and by favouring a free labour market within the six countries.

A Permanent Secretariat administered the Authority's decrees, and a Court of Justice (of seven international lawyers) interpreted the Authority's decisions. A Consultative Assembly, made up of repre-sentatives of the six countries, already met at the Council of Europe. This Assembly could pass on recommendations to the High Authority, which it also had the power to dismiss, but only with the approval of two-thirds of the Assembly's members. The Foreign and Economic Ministers of the six member states worked closely with the Authority; in their Council of Ministers they could discuss, but not block, Authority decisions, which were also discussed by a Consultative Committee of 51 delegates representing employers and workers in heavy industry.

Under Monnet's leadership, the Authority helped old-fashioned firms to modernize, and stimulated the output of coal and steel. Not everyone had his vision of a wider 'Europe'. Most delegates to Authority bodies, brought up in the tug-of-war economic negotiations of the inward-looking thirties, found it difficult to understand why the 'little group of Frenchmen around Monnet disagreed among themselves just as much as with other delegations'. How, wrote a Dutch delegate, could one negotiate one's nation's special interest in an orderly fashion if even Monnet and his French colleagues had no clear view of the national interests they wished to defend? Nonetheless, Monnet's methods slowly caught on, and delegates learned to try to find solutions for common problems instead of simply defending a particular national interest. Delegates soon found that this was a liberating and exhilarating experience, so Monnet succeeded in creating out of 'hard-boiled negotiators, a group of ardent Europeans'.

Under Monnet's guidance, the Authority also widened its scope to take into account other problems, such as those associated with, for example, the free movement of workers among member states, and their housing and social security benefits, about which supranational decisions had to be made. In eastern Europe, some Communist leaders used a 'salami technique' to slice away layers of opposition to a Communist take-over. Monnet adopted this 'salami technique' to persuade politicians, industrialists and workers to agree on particular matters, and thus, perhaps unwittingly, learn to think as 'Europeans'.

The Authority had the right to interfere in the economic life of the member states: it could close down a section of an industry in one country and invest heavily in another country, guided by 'European', not national, interests. Until 1956, it stimulated coal output to meet a growing demand. Then, however, coal was hit by competition from cheap oil and natural gas. The Authority tried to lessen the hardship caused by falling coal production by providing aid in areas hit by the closure of uneconomic pits. In the 1970s and 1980s the Authority provided similar help to areas affected by the fall in demand for European steel, and British workers benefitted from such aid. In 1967 the ESCS was merged with the EEC, which Britain joined in 1973, its High Authority losing some of its independence as a planning force following its integration into the Community for which it had been the prototype.

## The European Economic Community: a major stride towards 'Europe'?

'Determined to establish the foundations of an ever closer union among the European peoples . . . [we] have decided to create a European Economic Community . . . to promote a harmonious development of economic activities, the elimination of customs duties, a common agricultural policy [and] a common transport policy.'

From the Treaty of Rome, 25 March 1957

In 1955 the members of the ECSC, delighted by its success, decided to examine ways of enlarging this economic union. The war had ended ten years before, but, as the debates over the proposed EDC had shown, there was still a real fear of a German recovery: Franco-German hostility had a long and bitter history, and one of the main aims of the 'Europeans' – perhaps even their main aim – was to create conditions which would make it impossible for these two countries to go to war against each other again. It was fortunate for the 'Europeans' that many of the leading statesmen in ECSC countries at the time had been born in what had once been the Kingdom of Lotharingia, created in the break-up of Charlemagne's empire, separating the French Kingdom of Charles and the German Kingdom of Louis. Lotharingia ran from modern Belgium to modern Italy, and for centuries the French and Germans had fought to gain control of this region, which contained, among much else, Alsace-Lorraine, the Ruhr and Rhine valleys and the birthplaces of Spaak (Belgian Foreign Minister, 1955), Adenaeur (West German Chancellor), Schuman and Monnet, and de Gasperi (Prime Minister of Italy).

One of the benefits which followed on from closer European cooperation was the signing of the Treaty of Franco-German Friendship on 22 January 1963. Now, in 1986, a war between these two traditional enemies is almost unthinkable. A thousand years of history has been buried by the EEC.

Paul-Henri Spaak headed the committee established to work out plans for a wider economic union. His committee held its initial meetings at Messina in Italy, to which, as we shall see, Britain sent a low-level delegate. The committee examined 'the possibilities of expanding their existing Community [the ECSC] into an economic association based upon free trade, joint social and financial policies, the abolition of restrictive trading practices, and the free movement of labour and capital.' Its report was debated by the member states of the ECSC, who then agreed to sign the Treaties of Rome on 25 March 1957, setting up the European Economic Community.

The immediate aims of the EEC were the creation of a customs union (and the abolition of all tariff barriers by 1967, leading to a free movement of capital, labour and goods within the Community); the creation of a uniform and low external tariff on imports into the Community; the creation of a central authority empowered to interfere in the social and economic policies of member states, ensuring that there were no hidden tariffs or subsidies to aid a country's industry; and, finally, the development of supranational structures which it was hoped would pave the way to political unity (Document 4.2).

The 'high authority' of the EEC is the European Commission. Initially this had nine members, appointed by the governments of the 'Six', to which they owed them no responsibility, but with the accession of new members, the number of Commissioners has since grown. So too has the scope of the Commission's work, and each Commissioner now has, as it were, a 'portfolio' or area of responsibility – Agriculture, Transport, Finance and so on – giving the Commission the semblance of a European Cabinet. The Commission's first chairman was the former German Foreign Minister, Walter Hallstein. He made it clear that the EEC was 'in politics not economics or business', a view which was to bring him into conflict with the 'un-European' ideas of de Gaulle (Documents 4.1 and 4.2), and also alarm others, including the British, who retained a Churchillian vision of three interlocking circles representing USA, Europe and the Commonwealth, with Britain as the hub.

Commission decisions have to be ratified by the Council of Ministers, to which member states send their relevant ministers, depending on the issues being discussed. There is also a Court of Justice, whose members once formed the Court of Justice of the ECSC and Euratom; the merger of these two Communities with the EEC in 1967 saw the creation of a European Community of which the EEC was merely a part. The EEC also had a Parliament (sometimes confused in the popular mind with the Council of Europe). Until 1978, members of this Parliament were nominated by their national parliaments, who tended to send unimportant figures to serve in Europe: real power, it was thought, lay in the national parliament. Since 1978 there have been direct elections to the European Parliament, and some prominent domestic parliamentarians have chosen to stand for election to this European house. It is possible that in time more will do so, leading the demand for an increased role for this democratically elected House. The Parliament can dismiss the Commission, which is also bound to consult it about Commission plans and decisions, and it can question both the Commission at large and individual Commissioners. The 'European' nature of the Community is emphasized by the creation of supra-national blocs, with members of right-wing parties from various countries sitting and voting together, as do the members of the various socialist and centrist groups.

The founding of the EEC in 1957 created a 'domestic' market of some 175 million people for industrialists, who were also enabled to use Europe's resources more efficiently. An Investment Bank with an initial fund of 1 billion dollars was set up to help the development of more backward regions of the EEC such as southern Italy, and declining industrial areas such as the Ruhr and southern Belgium. A Common Fund was established to help ease the movement of labour across borders and provide migrant workers with social security benefits, while an Overseas Development Fund was set up to invest in the foreign dependencies of the 'Six'.

Trade between the 'Six' increased rapidly: by 1960 it was 29 per cent above its 1957 level. Trade barriers were lowered more quickly than had been originally intended, leading to a fall in prices which further stimulated trade and encouraged a rise in living standards. the EEC was largely responsible for the economic growth of West Germany, France and Italy in particular, and for the fact that the German *mark* became one of the world's leading currencies, to which the world's bankers turned for help during crises in 1968, 1974, 1978 and in 1985–6.

The Treaties of Rome emphasized that there had to be a common agricultural policy, but negotiations for this were long and bitter. France, for example, saw the EEC as a market in which its inefficient farmers could sell their output; politicians in West Germany, Holland and Italy, as well as France, had to take more account of the farming vote than did those in Belgium or Britain where agriculture is responsible for only some 5 per cent of the labour force. Farmer-dominated politicians had to ensure that the EEC brought as much gain to their agricultural sectors as it brought to the industrial sector as a whole.

The basic provisions of the Common Agricultural Policy were: (i) free trade within the Community; (ii) common prices for most commodities; (iii) protection by minimum import prices for European-produced commodities through imports levied on agricultural imports; (iv) the purchase, by the Community, of any surpluses so as to guarantee the prices paid to farmers; (v) the storage of such surpluses at Community expense, or their diversion to export markets through export subsidies.

The CAP guarantees farmers an agreed price for their output, that price being agreed at annual reviews by the Ministers of Agriculture of the member states. This encourages farmers to maximize their incomes by increasing output, and since prices are fixed to suit the more inefficient farmers, the more efficient become increasingly richer while producing vast surpluses of output. This has led to the creation of 'mountains' of meat, grain, butter and fruit, and 'lakes' of milk and wine, all held in expensive storage, accounting for about half of the CAP's budget, which itself accounts for about two-thirds of the Community's annual budget. Many people complain that the CAP 'tail' wags the EEC 'dog' (Document 4.4). ·

### Britain and the EEC: reluctant 'converts'?

'Britain sent an official from the Board of Trade . . . told to make the Europeans understand that if they were up to their supranational tricks they could not expect Whitehall to take them seriously.'
Nora Beloff, *The General Says No*, 1963

In spite of Britain's non-participation in the ESCS, she was invited to take part in the Messina talks in 1955–6. While other countries sent leading ministers, outstanding economists and other 'European-minded' delegates, Britain sent a second-level civil servant who was instructed to let the 'Europeans' know that Britain welcomed the idea of a customs union (and an enlarged market for her manufactured goods), but that she opposed anything beyond this. Britain had to consider her Commonwealth commitments and the Imperial Preference system, accounting then for some 48 per cent of British exports, which would have to be dismantled if the common external tariff proposed by the 'Europeans' was accepted. She also claimed that her own agricultural support system was superior to the one proposed by the French, which, if accepted by Britain, would force her (as a member of the Community) to pay massive levies to the CAP budget, as a food-importing country (Document 4.3).

Apart from these economic arguments against British membership, there were strong objections raised by those who (rightly) feared a loss of national and parliamentary sovereignty if Britain joined 'Europe', whose supranational Commission could impose rules on member states. It is strange that it was the Labour leader, Gaitskell, who argued that membership would require the rejection of 'a thousand years of British history'; chauvinism and isolationism were powerful forces in Britain, even after the Suez debacle of 1956 (p. 122).

As soon as the Treaties of Rome were signed, Britain proposed the setting up of a free trade area inside which there would be no internal tariff barriers; this would ensure increased trade and industrial development, but would exclude the free trading of agricultural goods, and have none of the supranational organizations created by the EEC. Britain proposed that the EEC be treated as a single member of such a free trade area, which would have provided free access for British goods into Europe while allowing the maintenance of the Commonwealth system and Britain's agricultural support scheme. British sovereignty would have remained almost intact.

It came as a surprise to Britain that some Europeans saw this proposal as a selfish device for ensuring access for British goods into Europe while denying European farmers access to the British market. Other Europeans saw the proposal as a plot to divide Germany (which might have been attracted by the notion of a tariff-free British market) from France, with its concern for agriculture. In general, other countries saw Britain's plan as an opportunistic attempt to have the best of all possible worlds, while seeking incidentally to damage the European movement. In 1958 the EEC rejected the British idea; this led to the creation of the European Free Trade Area (EFTA) consisting of Britain, Norway, Sweden, Denmark, Portugal, Austria and Switzerland. EFTA was formally established in December 1959; its population was much smaller and less wealthy than that of the EEC, and its member states formed a less natural and less compact unit. In fact, EFTA was very much a second-best alternative. It enjoyed a limited success, but there was an increase in trade between its members. It was clear however that even this success depended on the health of the British economy, the largest in the Association, and that, in spite of EFTA, British trade with the EEC grew more quickly (in spite of tariffs) than her trade with other EFTA countries. It was also soon apparent that, whatever the benefits of EFTA to its members, the benefits of membership of the EEC were far greater: its member states grew richer more quickly, and their peoples enjoyed a more rapid rise in living standards.

In 1961 the Macmillan government, alarmed at the decline in Britain's relative economic position, adopted a French-style planning system (the National Economic Development Council), and proposed to set up a National Incomes Commission to stem the rate of wage increases. It is not surprising therefore that in 1961 the government also set out to gain entry to the EEC, which it might have joined much earlier. Nonetheless, Macmillan still wanted to get as much of the best of all worlds as possible. His negotiator, Edward Heath, tried to persuade the EEC states to accept Britain's right to safeguard her special interests in Commonwealth trade, and to adjust the infant CAP to suit the British position. This angered the Germans, who wanted British membership as a counterweight to the French, and de Gaulle (Documents 4.1 and 4.2), who might have welcomed British support for his 'non-European' position, but who resented British attempts to change the rules of the 'club' they wanted to join.

Macmillan's behaviour ensured a French rejection of the British application. Having visited de Gaulle (Document 4.1), he went to Nassau to meet President Kennedy, who offered Britain the Polaris sea-to-ground missile in return for British endorsement of the US scheme for a Multilateral Nuclear Force, a NATO fleet of Polaris-armed ships and submarines, with mixed crews and mutual vetoes on the use of nuclear weapons. Macmillan saw this agreement as a triumph, confirming the 'special relationship' between the USA and Britain. De Gaulle saw it as merely a confirmation of his suspicion that Britain was a pawn in the US attempt to influence European affairs, which would weaken his own ability to control the EEC (Document 4.2). On January 14 1963 he announced his veto of Britain's application; he also vetoed a further application in 1967, although the Labour government, under Wilson, had made it clear that it was more amenable to compromise than the Macmillan government had been in 1961–3. De Gaulle seemed to take pleasure in the continued decline in Britain's position: 'The British people can no doubt see more and more clearly . . . [her] national personality . . . put in jeopardy in the face of the enormous power of the United States, the growing power of the Soviet Union, the renascent power of the continental nations, the new power of China, and the growing centrifugal movement apparent within the Commonwealth. The serious economic, financial, monetary, and social difficulties with which Britain is grappling make her feel this day after day. From all this emerges a tendency to look for a framework, even a European one, which would help her to save and safeguard her own substance, allow her to play a leading role again, and

"I suspect you of driving under the influence of America."

**4.1** In opposing British entry into the EEC in 1968, De Gaulle gained revenge for the 'insults' which he thought he had received from the British and the Americans during the Second World War

relieve her of part of her burden.' This would not, he implied, occur at Europe's expense (Fig. 4.1).

Britain's entry into the EEC was eventually secured from 1 January 1973. After de Gaulle's resignation in 1969, his successor, Pompidou, made it clear that he supported a British application. Heath, now Prime Minister and a committed 'European', negotiated British entry, and Ireland, Denmark and Norway followed, although the latter rescinded its entry after an anti-EEC vote in a national referendum. Many people in Britain demanded a similar referendum, hoping for a similar result. In 1975 the Labour government held this referendum, which confirmed by two to one the electors' support for Britain's continued membership of the EEC, twenty years after the fateful talks at Messina.

## Still concerned with unity?

'. . . we are coming under another sovereignty – that of Europe and the Council of Ministers.'

Lord Denning, 31 July 1986

Jean Monnet, 'the father of Europe', and Schuman learned by experience that there were distinct national attitudes towards the 'European idea'. The majority of spokesmen from West Germany, France (before de Gaulle), Italy and the Benelux states supported some form of federal Europe; their cooperation in the ESCS had persuaded 'the Six' that unity was both possible and desirable. On the other hand, the majority from Britain and the Scandinavian countries favoured only 'functionalist' cooperation and a looser confederation.

Hallstein, the first president of the Commission, hoped to see the economic road to bring about the political unity which many 'Europeans' wanted. De Gaulle's accession to power in 1958 put an end to hopes of achieving a 'United States of Europe'. In April 1962 he proposed that the only form of collaboration should be through meetings of heads of states. In May 1962 he denounced the idea of a supranational Europe, and talked of 'a Europe of the nations': 'I do not believe that Europe can be a living reality without France and her Frenchmen, Germany and her Germans, Italy and her Italians.' (Document 4.2). He would have found an 'anti-European' ally in Britain – if he had allowed her to join the EEC (Document 4.1). De Gaulle was quite prepared to wreck the Community in defence of French interests. In the autumn of 1961 he ordered the French team to quit the EEC if they did not negotiate the agricultural agreement needed to suit French farmers; he got his way, and in January 1962 the ill-fated CAP was agreed. In 1965 de Gaulle withdrew all French representatives from the EEC as a result of the sale of French surplus wheat to the USSR. When Hallstein claimed that the Commission, not the Council of Ministers, had charge of the agricultural budget, de Gaulle attacked this attempt to enlarge the powers of the Commission and, in September 1965, announced his refusal to allow France to be 'ruled by some sort of technocratic body of elders, stateless and responsible to no one'. Again, de Gaulle got his way, and the Commission's powers were not increased; the Council of Ministers, in which each member had a veto to be used to safeguard national interests, remained the powerful organ which de Gaulle and the 'non-Europeans' wanted it to be.

The long-term effects of de Gaulle's victory in the debate over the CAP in 1961–2, along with his downgrading of the Commission in 1965, have become increasingly evident in the 1980s. We have seen France seeking to limit the importation of cheap wine from Italy and lamb from Britain, even refusing entry to these products, although this is in breach of Community law. 'Nationalism rules' it seems. The cost of maintaining the CAP has continued to rise, along with inflation and the cost of storing the surpluses (Document 4.4), and in 1980 Britain protested about her contribution to the Community budget – £1209 million in 1980, compared to £669 million from West Germany and only £13 million from France, although both these countries had more prosperous economies than Britain. This discrepancy was due to the way in which contributions were calculated, partly by a levy on the duties received by each country from non-EEC imports. Since Britain imports more than other EEC countries, her contribution was therefore greater, and was largely used to pay for the inefficient CAP. Margaret Thatcher took a leaf out of de Gaulle's book and refused to make the payments, forcing the Community to re-examine the method of fixing the contributions, reducing Britain's to a total of £1346 million over the years 1981–4.

This unseemly wrangling was a far cry from the harmony which had prevailed in the ESCS, which Monnet, Schuman and Hallstein hoped would guide the development of the EEC. Yet Britain was not the only complainant, as was seen when the fear of Community bankruptcy forced the Commission and the Council of Ministers to re-examine the CAP. Such a reconsideration had become all the more urgent following the entry into the EEC of Greece (January 1981), Spain and Portugal (January 1986). Their relatively poor, and mainly agricultural, economies put further strain on the CAP budget in particular, and on EEC finances in general, which may lead to new 'mountains' – of oranges, olives and lemons – and even larger 'lakes' of wine. In 1985–6 the EEC lowered the quotas of wheat and milk for which it would pay farmers, but not to the point where the CAP problem would be solved. In April 1985 the Agriculture and Finance Ministers hammered out an agreement on the 1985–6 budget. All ten nations agreed that belt-tightening was necessary, but disagreed about whose belt should be tightened first or most. West Germany resisted a proposed cut in cereal prices, fearing the anger of Bavarian farmers; Italy and Greece opposed the planned 6 per cent cuts in fruit and vegetable quotas; Ireland demanded to be excluded from any cuts in quotas of milk.

In this self-seeking manner the Ten crippled their own decision-making process, but had the sense to realize that things could not be allowed to go on in this way. A special committee was set up under the Irish Senator, James Dooge, to study ways of streamlining procedures. The Dooge report proposed the limiting of the veto to the most fundamental questions, so that other issues would be decided either by simple majority votes or 'qualified majorities'. These proposals have been encapsulated, for the British, in the European Communities (Amendment) Bill which is to be debated in Parliament in the autumn and winter of 1986. Supporters and critics alike agree that this is a most important amendment to the Treaties of Rome, aimed at making 'concrete progress towards European unity', conferring on the Council of Ministers a right to 'exercise directly implementing powers', and bringing within the single jurisdiction of the EEC matters which hitherto were considered to be the exclusive concern of national parliaments. The Dooge proposals would increase the powers of the Commission and, according to a House of Lords committee, 'increase the extent of Community Law and the areas subject to Community Law, weaken the position of the UK Parliament and shift the balance of Parliamentary responsibility from the member states to Strasbourg'. It is too soon to say whether the various national parliaments will support such developments, which would have pleased Monnet, Schuman, Hallstein and the other 'Europeans', while angering Macmillan, de Gaulle and the 'statists'. It is somewhat ironic that the Dooge committee was set up following the near collapse of the EEC under the weight and cost of agricultural surpluses – themselves the result of the de Gaulle-inspired CAP.

## Documentary evidence

Britain might have helped to establish the EEC by taking an active part in the Messina talks (1955–6). Instead, she set up the EFTA, hoping, some Europeans thought, to stifle the EEC at birth. When she applied to join the Community (1961–3), de Gaulle had returned to power in France, imbued with a 'hatred of the Anglo-Americans' as a result of real or imagined wartime insults, and determined to restore the greatness of France (Document 4.1). He vetoed British applications in 1963 (Document 4.2), and again in 1967. With Heath as Prime Minister in 1970, Britain made a fresh application for membership, in spite of the opposition of many MPs (Document 4.3), finally joining the Community in 1973. The shortcomings which critics had pointed to, notably in the CAP, have become even more noticeable in the 1980s (Document 4.4), and have still to be tackled if the Community is to make further progress.

## Document 4.1

*Macmillan on de Gaulle, 1961*

'The Emperor of the French (for he is now an almost complete autocrat, taking no notice of any advice and indeed receiving little of independent value) is older, more isolated and far more *royal*. He is well informed, yet remote. His hatred of the 'Anglo-Americans'. is as great as ever. He talks of Europe, and means France. The France of Louis XIV (as regards its religion, boundaries, and power), of Napoleon (as regards the fanatical loyalty of its Army). He allows a little of Napoleon III, as regards the management of a so-called Parliament. The tragedy is that we all agree with de Gaulle on almost everything. But his pride, his inherited hatred of England (since Joan of Arc), his bitter memories of the last war; above all, his intense vanity for France – she must dominate – make him half welcome, half repel us.'

(Diary, 29 November 1961)

## Document 4.2

*Macmillan meets de Gaulle, December 1962*

'We then turned to the Brussels negotiations. I made a strong plea for their rapid conclusion. Britain had fully accepted the Treaty of Rome. The main Commonwealth objections had been overcome, subject to some particular points. Of course the Government had taken risks, but anything was better than that a Europe already divided by the Iron Curtain should be split up a second time into the Six and Seven. From the political even more than from the economic point of view, a united Europe was essential to the growth of European ideals.

The General's reply was discouraging. He doubted the value of the Common Market as a political organization; it was an economic agreement and no more. It was true that the Treaty of Rome had envisaged political development, but it had failed even to make a start. The truth was the European countries did not dare do anything without the United States. Moreover, if Britain joined, then Norway, Denmark, Ireland, Portugal, perhaps even Spain, would want to be included. Perhaps one day something might be worked out, but only gradually. In the Six, France could say 'no' against even the Germans; she could stop policies with which she disagreed, because of the strength of her position. Once Britain joined and all the rest joined the organization, things would be different.'

(H. Macmillan, The End of the Day, Macmillan, 1973)

## Document 4.3

*A British case against joining, 1971*

'In the atmosphere of release, almost euphoria, which seems to prevail in Western Europe since the departure of General de Gaulle, there is a real danger of people failing to notice how little the underlying realities have changed. I hear much clamour arising about a directly elected European parliament and there will be those who will be foolish enough to take up the cry for want of thought, [but] until the inhabitants of different parts of Europe are so penetrated with a sense of common interest, the attempt to create an elected assembly would be foredoomed to ridicule. For the foreseeable future, under the common agricultural policy, Britain would subsidize Continental farmers through taxes [while] the power of decision and regulation is necessarily removed from Parliament and vested in a Community institution.'

(J. Enoch Powell, The Common Market: the Case Against, 1971)

## Document 4.4

*Pluses and minuses, 1981*

'The Common Agricultural Policy has always been more inward-looking. Its

aims are mainly to sustain Community farmers' incomes, to increase productivity and therefore improve European self-sufficiency in food, and to stabilize
prices and quantities in agricultural markets. The CAP has certainly helped to
raise production, but in recent years large unforeseen surpluses of certain
products together with inflation have brought the EEC's agricultural policies to
a state of crisis.

The Community has fostered free trade policies towards both industrial and
developing countries. One major step was the total abolition of tariffs with
seven members of the former EFTA. Agreements have also been signed with
Canada, the USA, [and] Japan. . . . Over the years special relationships have
also been established with several developing countries, mostly former colonies
of Belgium, France, Italy and the Netherlands.'

(A Report on the EEC prepared by European banks, 1981)


## FURTHER READING

ARBUTHNOTT, H. and EDWARDS, G., eds., *A Common Man's Guide to the
Common Market*, Macmillan, 1979
BELOFF, N., *The General Says No*, Penguin, 1963
CAMPS, M., *European Unification in the Sixties*, New York, 1967
COOMBES, D., *The Future of the European Parliament*, PSL, 1979
FELD, U. J., *The European Community in World Affairs*, Washington, 1976
HALLSTEIN, W., *United Europe: Challenge and Opportunity*, London, 1962
HOLLAND, S., *The Uncommon Market*, Macmillan, 1979
HU, Y. S., *Europe under Stress*, Butterworth, 1982
KITZINGER, U. W., *The Challenge of the Common Market*, 1982
LAQUEUR, W., *A Continent Astray: Europe, 1970–78*, 1979
LODGE, J., *Institutions and Policies of the European Community*, Frances Pinter,
1983
MARQUAND, D., *Parliament for Europe*, Cape, 1979
MAYNE, R., ed., *Western Europe*, Muller, Blond and White, 1986
TUGENHADT, C., *Making Sense of Europe*, Viking, 1985
TRACEY, M., *Agriculture in Europe*, Granada, 1982
TWITCHETT, C. and K., eds., *Building Europe*, Europa Publications, 1982

# 5

# The Soviet Union

## Government and people

'. . . Russia . . . a riddle wrapped in a mystery inside an enigma.'
Churchill, in a broadcast talk, 1 October 1939

'The Communist Party of the Soviet Union is the leading guiding force
of Soviet society and the nucleus of its political system.'
Brezhnev, introducing the 1977 Constitution

It is difficult for outsiders to understand the country which Churchill
technically misnamed 'Russia'. Russia is only one of the 15 Union
Republics in the Soviet Union, each a supposedly voluntary member of
a Union from which they are, in theory, free to secede. The treatment
of Soviet dissidents, and of Hungary (1956) and Czechoslovakia (1968),
suggest that such independence is inconceivable.

The 1977 Constitution named the 15 Republics, some of which
contain other autonomous republics and/or Regions. The Russian
Soviet Federative Socialist Republic, the most densely populated and
largest of all, contains ten National Areas. While Brezhnev stressed the
dominant role of the Party, formal power under his 1977 Constitution
belongs to non-Party political organs (Fig. 5.1). *The Supreme Soviet*,
'the highest representative body of the people and the supreme state
authority', consists of two Chambers: the Soviet of the Union has
about 740 members and the Soviet of Nationalities has 32 members
from each of the National Areas – about 630 members in all. Delegates
to these Chambers are nominated by local Party-controlled organizations, and elected as the sole candidates for each constituency. They
meet only for a few days each year, and simply approve items presented
to them by the Party Secretariat.

The Supreme Soviet elects the *Praesidium* of 30–40 members, all of
whom are major figures in either the Party or the government, or in
both. The Praesidium Chairman is the President of the Soviet Union,

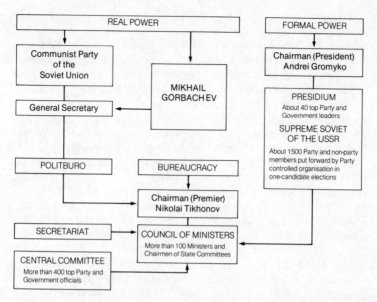

**5.1** The theory and practice of the Soviet political structure

currently Andrei Gromyko, latterly Foreign Minister and ally of Gorbachev. The Praesidium is in session throughout the year; it issues decrees and interprets the constitution, but has no control over the more important *Council of Ministers*, consisting of some 100 Ministers and Chairmen of State Committees, whose Chairman is the Prime Minister. Yet the power of this Council is more apparent than real, for it is supervised by the *Politburo* of the Party.

The basic organ of the Party is the *local cell*, a handful of members in a given unit within the army, or an institution or factory. Each cell elects a representative to its *town committee* (or 'soviet') which elects representatives to a provincial soviet, and so on until one reaches the *Party Congress*. This meets every five years or so, electing a *Central Committee* to run the Party and the country. This Central Committee, made up of some 400 top Party officials, generals, judges, editors and others, elects the Politburo of 15 or so members, whose names will have been presented to the Committee by the *General Secretary of the Party* (now Gorbachev), who is free to sack members of this small body which is, in almost every sense, his creature.

Lenin devised this 'democratic centralist' system, which is nominally democratic since the people (at the base), elect representatives in the Party and State systems, and centralist since each lower body has to obey the decisions made by higher bodies. The Politburo controls all other organizations, and is itself controlled by the General Secretary, who has the powers of a dictator, or, in Russian terms, a Tsar.

There are three other powerful forces in the system. The first, *the Army*, saved the Soviet Union from Nazi conquest; it is the bulwark against threats from the West, and its leaders serve in the Council of Ministers, the Central Committee and the Politburo. Khrushchev called its leaders 'metal eaters', consuming some 17 per cent of national industrial output, using men, materials and machinery which might have been otherwise used to raise Soviet living standards. The generals are suspicious of Gorbachev's calls for economic reform, and any proposals for decreased military expenditure or détente (Chapter 19).

A second powerful force is the *KGB*, the acronym since 1953 for the 'secret branch' of the police, formerly known as the OGPU and the MVD. Its leaders have always been men of power, as they are the only people who know everything about everyone else. Its millions of 'working' members are particularly feared by the people because of its history of torture, murder, secret arrests, and imprisonment without trial. One of its leaders, Andropov, became General Secretary of the Party, and his successor is now in the Politburo.

The third 'force' is the huge *state bureaucracy*, consisting of the millions who work in Soviet ministries and industries. Sixty-four Federal ministries administer the USSR; 23 State committees run various enterprises, and 50 others are in charge of separate industries. These central committees are replicated in the 15 Republics and 20 autonomous Republics and have their models at provincial and local level. Over a million people work in the central committees and ministries; no one knows how many work in the lower reaches of officialdom. This cumbersome system makes it difficult to implement reforms or to end the corruption resulting from the persuading officials to ignore regulations, sometimes in the name of efficiency. Andropov died before his attack on the system and its corruption had got under way; Gorbachev, Andropov's heir in many ways, knows that reform is essential if there is to be economic improvement. The forces of inertia, and of opposition to change, may yet prove too strong for him.

### Stalin's last years, 1945–53

'An ungainly dwarf, one of the cruellest figures in history, convinced he was carrying out the will of history.'

> Djilas, *Conversations with Stalin*, 1965

Stalin had imposed the democratic centralist system on the Soviet, and led the Union through a series of Five Year Plans in the 1920s and 1930s, only to see much of Soviet industry destroyed in the 'Great Patriotic War' after 1941. A fifth Five Year Plan, launched in 1946, aimed at the reconstruction of a shattered economy, gave priority to heavy industry and neglected agriculture and the consumer industries. It succeeded: by 1950 heavy industrial output was 40 per cent above its 1940 level, and new industrial centres had been built and old ones restored, although people still lived in the ruins of their old homes or crowded together in blocks of ungainly flats.

In the 1930s Stalin had killed thousands of once loyal Bolsheviks, putting millions more in concentration camps. After 1945, he and his ally Zhdanov (p. 43) attacked racial groups which had co-operated with the Germans in 1941; millions of Crimean Tartars and the Kalmuks were exiled to distant regions of the Union. Stalin also attacked intellectuals, artists, dramatists and musicians, who were accused of 'cosmopolitanism' or 'slavishly imitating western patterns'. This anti-Western attitude was in the 'Slavophil' tradition of pre-1917 Russia, and in this, his savage cruelty and his paranoia towards the outside world Stalin was 'the logical culmination of the Russian political tradition', and under the Soviet system he was able to be even more Tsarist than the Tsars.

In February 1953 the pace of Stalin's purges increased, with attacks on Jews, including the doctors who had treated Zhdanov in his final illness in 1948, on Beria and other leaders of the secret forces who 'knew too much', and on Party chiefs, such as Khrushchev, whom Stalin saw as over-ambitious heirs apparent. Molotov, a member of the Politburo, was unable to save his Jewish wife from arrest; Malenkov came under threat. One US correspondent noted: 'It was apparent that Russia stood on the brink of a reign of terror beside which that of the 30s would seem trivial.' Stalin died on 5 March 1953, ending the purges but leaving an uncertain leadership in charge of one-sixth of the world's population.

## The Khrushchev years, 1953–64

'Even today you'll find those who think that Stalin's way was the only right way to build Socialism. . . . A personality cult is like a religion. For centuries people have been dreaming, "Lord help and protect us." People are set in their ways and continue to believe in God despite evidence to the contrary.'

*Khrushchev Remembers*, 1971

Millions of Soviet citizens mourned the death of the 'little father' who had ruled for so long. However, the clique of Party leaders, grateful to be alive, determined that there would be no more personality cults like that which had surrounded Stalin, and similar to that developed around Mao in China (p. 107). With no obvious heir apparent, the Politburo decided to share power: Malenkov was named First Secretary and Chairman of the Council of Ministers; Marshall Voroshilov became Chairman of the Praesidium; Khrushchev became Senior Party Secretary and Marshall Zhukov Minister of Defence.

Many westerners thought that Malenkov would emerge as the new leader. He was seen as 'smiling', 'chubby-cheeked' and 'liberal', his history as Stalin's ally forgotten. All subsequent Soviet leaders have received this initial approval by western 'liberals', eager it seems to appease the unappeasable.

Khrushchev and Malenkov united to arrest Beria, who was tried in
secret and executed, thus removing the danger of a KGB-inspired
assumption of power. Serov, Khrushchev's ally, became head of the
KGB. Malenkov proposed a series of 'liberal' reforms, including an
increased production of consumer goods, more freedom for peasants to
work on their private plots for sale at a profit, and a relaxation of the
censorship of films, books and the press.

In September 1953 Malenkov ceded one of his posts and Khrushchev
became Party Secretary. During the next two years he persuaded
'Stalinists' such as Voroshilov and Molotov that Prime Minister
Malenkov was going down a wrong ('liberal') path. He won the
support of Army chiefs by showing that concentration on consumer
goods weakened the nation's ability to produce weapons, and the
support of the bureaucracy by arguing that Malenkov's economic
reforms would have unwelcome social and political repercussions. In
February 1953 he and his allies moved against Malenkov: Marshall
Bulganin became Prime Minister, and Khrushchev's companion, in a
'K and B' duopoly. As a sign of the changing times Malenkov was
neither executed nor imprisoned.

At the Twentieth Party Congress (1956), Khrushchev, spurred by
Mikoyan's criticism of the Stalin they had both served slavishly, made
his outspoken attack on the former leader. He condemned the Stalinist
cult of personality, revealed details of the injustices and stupidities of
the purges (in which he had played a major role), criticized Stalin's
conduct of the Second World War, conceded that Tito and Gomulka
were right and that there were roads to socialism other than Stalin's,
and suggested peaceful coexistence with the West.

Following the unrest resulting from the speech, notably in Hungary
(p. 46), Molotov, an old Party 'faithful', and Malenkov, who still had
supporters in the Politburo, claimed that Khrushchev's 'foolish' speech
had caused it. They tried to force him from office, but Khrushchev, like
Stalin in the 1920s, had filled key positions with his supporters, and also
had the powerful backing of Marshall Zhukov and the armed forces.
Molotov and Malenkov were dismissed as 'anti-Party collaborators',
which left Khrushchev in a strong position, despite his consciousness of
the power of the Central Committee, which supported him against the
'collaborators'.

Khrushchev now developed some of Malenkov's policies, concen-
trating on the build-up of light industry producing consumer goods,
and trying to overcome the inertia of the bureaucracy by creating 100
Regional Economic Councils with the power to organize local
industries. This new tier of 'economic government' added yet one more
level to the Soviet bureaucracy, all the more cumbersome in that the
areas covered by the Economic Councils had nothing in common with
existing provincial or district regions of the Union.

Khrushchev encouraged managers to make their industries profitable and to link wage levels with productivity; he started a vast housing scheme and was responsible for the improvement in living standards illustrated by the following table, which shows that, in spite of Khrushchev's work, the USSR lagged far behind the USA.

*Ownership of consumer goods per thousand people*

|  | 1955 (USSR) | 1966 (USSR) | US (1966) |
| --- | --- | --- | --- |
| Radios | 66 | 171 | 1300 |
| TV sets | 4 | 82 | 376 |
| Refrigerators | 4 | 40 | 293 |
| Washing machines | 1 | 77 | 259 |

Khrushchev rashly promised that the Soviet Union would outstrip the USA within a few years, but although the Soviets put the first spacecraft into orbit (1957) and sent Gagarin on the first manned orbit of the earth (1961), the technological and industrial base of the USSR was neither large enough nor sufficiently developed to allow even an approach to American levels of production and productivity.

Nor were Khrushchev's much vaunted agricultural reforms a success. His 'Virgin Lands' scheme (started in 1954) involved the cultivation of huge areas in Siberia and Kazakhstan. Elsewhere, peasants on collective farms were allowed to sell the produce of their private plots, but the government paid higher prices for the produce of the collective farms to provide incentives for higher output. Between 1953 and 1962, grain production rose from 82 million tons to 147 million tons. Thereafter, the record was one of continued failure. In 1963 grain output fell to 110 million tons, the result of the failure of the Virgin Lands plan: too much of the new land was of poor quality, on which too little fertilizer was used while the dusty top soil was eroded in dust storms. The collectivized system was proven to be less efficient than the capitalist system, and the USA and Canada were asked to sell grain to a Soviet government anxious to avoid famine.

At first, Khrushchev's economic reforms were matched by political changes: a reduction in the activities of the secret police, a relaxation of press censorship and more freedom to travel abroad. In foreign affairs, too, Khrushchev presented a 'more acceptable' face (Chapter 17). However, there was little substance in the apparent changes in Soviet foreign policy: Hungary was not allowed to find its own 'road to socialism' in 1956; in 1961 Berlin was again the scene of a major confrontation; in 1962 the Cuban crisis threatened world peace. In Khrushchev's domestic policies change was also merely superficial. Khrushchev did not tolerate dissidents, or students who called for more liberalism, or Jews or other racial minorities. The labour camps of the Gulag Archipelago were almost as full under him as they were under Stalin; the framework of secret policing, imprisonment without trial and the harsh treatment of dissidents remained intact, making it easier for Brezhnev to revert to Stalinism in the 70s.

While attacking Stalin in 1956, Khrushchev did not explain how the Marxist–Leninist system could have produced such a powerful monster; nor did he try to dismantle the system which had produced Stalin and been perfected by him, although Khrushchev knew that it led to inefficiency in industry and agriculture; he was unwilling or unable to allow the development of initiative and freedom which might have lessened that inefficiency, fearing that this would have anti-Communist political repercussions.

In October 1964, while he was on holiday, the Central Committee voted Khrushchev into retirement, and in spite of his last-minute attempt to get the motion put aside, he fell from power. He had quarrelled with Mao (p. 106), had pursued a disastrous policy in Cuba (p. 278), annoyed some Soviet leaders by his extrovert (some said 'clownish') behaviour when abroad, and alarmed the 'metal eaters' with the 'consumer goods' policy which left the army weaker than it wished to be. The catalogue of charges brought against him by the Central Committee was, however, as much a condemnation of the system as of Khrushchev. If he was that much of a failure, how had he held on to power for so long?

## The Brezhnev years, 1964–82

'Improvement in the well-being of working people is a more and more urgent requirement for our economic development.'

Brezhnev, 1971

As in 1953, so in 1964 the Politburo shared out power more widely: Kosygin became Prime Minister while Brezhnev, Secretary-General after Khrushchev's fall, gave up the Presidency in 1965 to allow Podgorny to join a triumvirate of rulers.

The new leaders followed Khrushchev's economic and industrial policies, although they abolished the Regional Economic Councils and reverted to a more centralized management of the economy. In September 1965 Kosygin proposed a series of Khrushchev-like reforms aimed at profitability and economic efficiency. Enterprises would be able to use part of their profits as bonus payments to workers, while managers would be allowed more freedom. However, the pervading bureaucracy blocked these modest reforms. Moreover, the demands of the military ensured that the proportion of heavy industry within the overall national product rose from 68 per cent, under Stalin to 72 per cent under Khrushchev, and to 74 per cent under Brezhnev in 1979. This larger share was taken from an economy that was already slowing down: the rate of industrial growth had fallen from an average of 8 per cent in the 1950s to 3.7 per cent in 1980, while the target for the 1981 Five Year Plan was the lowest since 1945.

In 1979 the Central Committee called for an implementation of Kosygin's 1965 reforms, a sign of the chasm between proposal and reality. In 1980 Kosygin was replaced by Tikhonov, an elderly protégé of the octogenerian Brezhnev. Tikhonov told the 26th Party Congress of the unhealthy state of the economy, which was still declining despite western investment in mining, car production, chemical and other industries. Western 'aid' took the form of the provision of components and new factories, with technical help and credit provided by banks or governments. Between 1972 and 1976 the USSR borrowed over $11 billion; by 1980 this debt had more than doubled so that the cumulative debt of all the Communist countries was over $80 billion.

Khrushchev tried but failed to solve the agricultural problem. So, too did Brezhnev, by providing increased investment. A combination of bad weather, peasant inefficiency and bureaucratic mismanagement ensured that the grain crop of 1972 was even lower than that of 1970. Soviet buyers bought grain on the world markets, thus driving up prices in 1972 and 1973, and adding to the West's inflationary problem. In 1975 the harvest was 65 million tons lower than planned; without western aid there would have been a major famine in the Soviet Union.

Brezhnev might have wished to imitate the Hungarians by allowing peasants greater freedom; the bureaucrats would have none of it – until 1977 and yet more poor harvests. In 1981 restrictions on ownership of livestock were lifted, and banks encouraged to provide loans for the private farmers who were now allowed to increase the size of their holdings. In 1985 the forty million workers on collective farms were unable to provide for Soviet need, so, under Gorbachev, the USSR has to rely on the less than four million working on profitable US farms.

Brezhnev may have been Khrushchev-like in his economic policies; in other ways he was more of a Stalinist. Rebellion was put down in Czechoslovakia (1968); praise was heaped on the memory of Stalin and his ideological ally, Zhdanov; dissidents were attacked inside the Soviet Union as ruthlessly as they were under Stalin. In his disregard for the promises made at Helsinki in 1975 (p. 289). Brezhnev was as cynical as previous Soviet leaders. Eager to accept western aid, he yet refused to tolerate criticism of his record over human rights, insisting that 'the class struggle between the two systems will be continued'.

## Gorbachev's inheritance

'Gorbachev represents a complete break with earlier generations.'
                    Denis Healey, British Labour spokesman
'. . . the fact [is] that the source of our conflict with the Soviet Union . . . is the character of the system itself . . . intolerant, aggressive and expansionist.'
            G. Urban of Radio Free Europe, in the *Wall Street Journal*

Brezhnev died in November 1982 after a long period of ailing government. His successor, Andropov, was the repressor of Hungary in 1956 and head of the KGB from 1967–82. Western commentators saw him giving a 'new, liberal face to the system'; he 'liked western films and whisky'. Andropov died in February 1984; it is impossible to say whether he would have been 'liberal'. Certainly he wished the system to be more efficient and productive. He proposed a series of reforms which, in aims and methods, were similar to those of Khrushchev and Kosygin. As head of the KGB he knew of the corruption rife in the system; in speeches and articles he drew attention to, and tried to weed out, the large number of Party bureaucrats involved in illegal activities. He also tackled the problem of alcoholism, responsible for much absenteeism, shoddy work and a low level of productivity.

Andropov's reforming zeal was a reflection of the failure of the sixty-year-old system, and indicated the anxieties of the leaders with it; party ideologues wanted a more efficient system so that they could claim that communism delivered the goods; some bureaucrats wanted greater efficiency, which would justify their existence; dissidents too wanted increased productivity, if only to provide better living standards for the oppressed Soviet people. Above all, the leaders of the armed forces demanded an improved economic performance, which alone could guarantee increased quantities of modern weaponry.

Andropov knew that, *per capita*, the Soviet Union consumed one-third of the goods and services consumed in the USA and only a half of the goods and services consumed in most eastern European countries. The grain crop having failed, again, in 1983–4 the USSR had to import 52 million tons of grain (one-sixth of their total requirement) from the USA and other 'capitalist' countries. In 1983 the GNP of the USA rose by almost 7 per cent; that of the USSR by only 2.6 per cent. Khrushchev's boast of outstripping the Americans seemed ever more improbable; the danger was rather that the Soviet Union would soon become a Third World state with First World weaponry.

Andropov died in February 1984. His successor, Chernenko, was seventy-three, an 'old hand' and a former protégé of Brezhnev. He imitated his mentor by claiming more power for himself, becoming President and Chief of the Defence Ministry as well as Party Secretary. However, he had neither the drive nor the inclination needed to pursue the necessary reforming policies. His 'reign' was seen to be a stop-gap, providing time for others to assimilate Andropov's views. When Chernenko died in March 1985, Gorbachev was quickly installed as Party Secretary.

Once again, western commentators saw 'newness' and 'liberalism', comparing Gorbachev and his 'glamorous wife' with the still-mourned Kennedys. His speeches, and his impromptu discussions with people when on walkabouts in factories and state farms, showed that he meant to carry on where Andropov had left off. He called for industrial efficiency, a doubling of living standards by the year 2000 (more modest than Khrushchev's aims) and the weeding out of corruption. He dismissed some ageing members of the Politburo, along with the younger Romanov, who might have been a rival, and replaced them with his own supporters. He reorganized the bureaucracy at both regional and district levels, allowing younger and more ambitious men to take charge. If Gorbachev remains in better health than Andropov and Chernenko he may stay in power for many years, and change the face of the Soviet Union (Document 5.1). On the other hand, the inertia of the bureaucracy and the system's inability to accept economic and social change may prove too strong a force to overcome.

## Documentary evidence

Successive leaders of the Soviet Union have tried to reform the agricultural and industrial sectors. Their failure to enforce the much-needed reforms is evident from Gorbachev's speeches, and from the Soviet-based statistics in the following document. Brezhnev and his successors have sought western aid as a means of improving their domestic economy; in spite of this, the USSR continues to decline. There is little evidence, yet, that Gorbachev will succeed, largely because economic reform would probably lead to demands for social and political reform.

## Document 5.1

*Gorbachev's problems, the West's dilemma*

'The Soviet Union is not economically capable of maintaining the military machine at anything like parity with the US. Nevertheless the Soviet leadership has a profound vested interest in trying to maintain the pretence that it is co-equal militarily with the US. It wants, in the words of Marshall Ogarjov, to expose "the historical futility of the capitalist system because the correlation of forces in the international arena has changed irreversibly" in favour of Communism. This is intended to induce in the West that there is no point in resisting Moscow's might. Of course, such a belief cannot be sustained if the real evidence shows that the Soviet system of economic centralism, corruption and Party control is collapsing under the strain.

That is the reality which faced Gorbachev. The choices may not be so obvious to him as they appear to be to those in the West who have been able to callibrate the inexorable decline in Soviet achievements. One must not expect the Soviet bureaucracy to tell its leaders too many painful truths. Andropov's impatience with Soviet performance derived from his long tenure as head of the KGB – the best informed man in the entire system. Gorbachev does not have the knowledge of Soviet failure which would have come to a man who had looked over everybody's shoulder for fifteen years.

The decline in Soviet standards of living and economic performance is pervasive, not just in agriculture, but in all aspects of industry, public health, life expectancy, housing. . . . It seems a mockery to have to take so seriously as a military power a country with such a wretched performance for its people. In 1981 Soviet housing still did not meet the minimum standards for health and decency set by the government in 1928. 30 per cent of the urban population still live communally, sharing with strangers, or in crowded factory dormitories. Deaths from acute alcohol poisoning stand at 16 per 100,000, a figure quite outside the range of other world experience (more than 88 times the US figure of 0.18 for instance). Food is rationed, and the incidence of measles, according to published Soviet statistics, is now so high that it stands fractionally below the level at which epidemiologists attribute the problem to mass malnutrition. Infant mortality is rising. Life expectancy is falling. Recent issues of Soviet medical literature say that five of the seven key communicable diseases are out of control: polio, diphtheria, scarlet fever, whooping cough and measles.

In the 1960s Khrushchev predicted that the Soviet Union would catch up with the US by 1980. The fact that this prophecy now looks so pitiable can be derived from the decisions taken at the 23rd Party Congress in March 1966 which meant that the Brezhnev era was distinguished by a persistent rise in military spending. A CIA report in 1983 calculated that the Soviet defence costs were by then 25 per cent higher than those of the US, though borne on the back of a crippled economy. Within that economy only the military has been allowed any kind of priority.

This system is not capable of absorbing or exploiting the full potential of the information revolution of which the SDI is such a symbolic pinnacle. The second, third and fourth computer revolutions which are engulfing the advanced economies, are based on the dispersion of this technology into millions of decentralized work stations which can only thrive in an open society where a myriad individual random decisions are taken every day. In the Soviet system knowledge is power. Can the Party contemplate such a surrender of its central control as would be necessary for the economy to benefit at all from this computer revolution? There is no evidence from Gorbachev's past that he will be prepared to dismantle or weaken the apparatus which maintains him in power. But if he does not, Russia's decline will continue. The gap between the illusion of superpower status abroad and the reality of third world economic conditions at home will widen.

For the West this contradiction also presents a choice between helping the Soviet system to overcome its difficulties while still according it the respect due to a major military power, or intensifying the pressure by opening up the technology gap between East and West so that the Soviet Union cannot avoid recognizing its decline and taking appropriate decisions.

At that stage it will be open to Gorbachev and his Party to decide whether their system is capable of reform without loss of control or whether it is better to maintain control at home even though that means declining influence abroad. It will be a painful decision which they will try to avoid taking. What the West has to do is to bring home to the Soviet leadership that there will be no external solution to their dilemma. The Soviet system cannot escape from its contradictions by diversionary threats elsewhere. That will require strong nerves in the West. It will not be helped by any attitude which appears susceptible to whether Gorbachev smiles or frowns. Neither response is historically significant compared to the underlying forces at work in Soviet society. It is that system which is at bay, which must change, or contract, before we can sleep soundly in our beds.'

(*The Times*, 22 April 1985)

# FURTHER READING

BROWN, A. and KASER, M., *The Soviet Union Since the Fall of Khrushchev*, Macmillan, 1975

BROWN, A. and KASER, M., *Soviet Policy for the 1980s*, Macmillan, 1983

CONQUEST, R., *The Great Terror*, Macmillan, 1968

CONQUEST, R., *Kolymann: The Arctic Death Camps*, Macmillan, 1978

DANIELS, R., *Politics and Society in the USSR*, Weidenfeld and Nicolson, 1970

DUMORE, T., *Soviet Politics, 1945–53*, Macmillan, 1984

EDMONDS, R., *Soviet Foreign Policy, 1962–73*, OUP, 1975

HOSKING, G., *A History of the Soviet Union*, Collins/Fontana, 1985

DE JONGE, A., *Stalin and the Shaping of the Soviet Union*, Collins, 1986

KHRUSHCHEV, N., *Khrushchev Remembers*, Penguin, 1971

LANE, D., *Politics and Society in the USSR*, 1978

MCCAULEY, M., ed., *The Soviet Union after Brezhnev*, Heinemann, 1983

MEDVEDEV, R., *Khrushchev*, Basil Blackwell, 1982

MOONEY, J. P., *The Soviet Superpower*, Heinemann, 1982

MUNTING, R., *The Economic Development of the USSR*, Croom Helm, 1983

RUBENSTEIN, A. Z., *Soviet Foreign Policy since World War II: Imperial and Global*, Prentice-Hall Int., 1983

SHORT, P., *The Dragon and the Bear: Inside China and Russia Today*, Hodder and Stoughton, 1982

SOLZENITSYN, A., *The Gulag Archipeligo (1918–56)*, Fontana, 1974

ZINOVIEV, A., *The Reality of Communism*, Gollancz, 1984

# 6

# The United States of America

## The Truman years, 1945–52

'Dewey defeats Truman.'

*Chicago Tribune* headline on the morning
after the 1948 Presidential election

Harry Truman, a surprise choice as Vice-Presidential candidate in 1944, was 'bewildered and shocked' when he succeeded Roosevelt on 12 April 1945. Nonetheless, he quickly put his stamp on the domestic and foreign policies of a country where industries had expanded greatly during the war, where workers enjoyed huge increases in wages, where trade unions had become stronger and more militant, and where black people and other racial minorities, having got jobs easily during the war, became more conscious of the need for social and political change.

At the end of the war there was a widespread desire for a return to 'normalcy', ranging from demands to 'bring the boys home' to calls for the abolition of wartime controls such as those exercised by the Office of Price Administration. Meanwhile, the unions were determined to build on their newly-won power. In 1946, prices rose by 100 per cent; unions demanded large wage increases and threatened nation-wide strikes. Truman wanted to draft strikers into the armed forces, making a strike a treasonable action; Congress refused to pass the Bill, but Truman still lost the support of many workers.

In September 1945 Truman announced his 'Fair Deal' programme, proposing an extension of social security policies, a National Health Service, maternal and child benefits, an old age pension scheme, higher minimum wages, slum clearance and full employment. The Republican-dominated Congress threw out this programme and, over Truman's veto, pushed through the Taft-Hartley Act (1947) which aimed to weaken union power by abolishing the closed shop, and imposing a 60-day 'cooling-off' period before a strike could be called; the President was also empowered to impose a further 90-day ban if a strike threatened the national interest.

Truman was expected to lose the 1948 Presidential election. His party was divided, with the southern Democrats opposing his ideas on civil rights for blacks (p. 88), and the liberal Democrats, led by Henry Wallace, demanding more radical policies. Truman's rival, Tom Dewey, leading a Republican Party which had won the 1946 Congressional elections, promised that when elected he would implement most of the 'Fair Deal' programme. In a surprise move, Truman recalled Congress in July 1948, saw the Republicans reject his programme, and called Dewey's bluff. He campaigned for the support of workers angered by the Taft-Hartley Act, of blacks eager for civil rights, and of those who sympathized with the apparent underdog President. In spite of pollsters' forecasts, Truman defeated Dewey and helped his Party to win control of both Houses of Congress. One problem was the tendency of right-wing and anti-black southern Democrats to vote with the Republican minorities in an attempt to block Truman's proposed reforms.

In 1949 Truman presented Congress with the semi-socialist 'Fair Deal' programme. He proposed changes in civil rights and un-employment benefits, aid to farmers, price controls, federal aid for education, a repeal of the Taft-Hartley Act, and tax reductions for the less well-off. Congress approved some of this, allowing an extension of the social security system, an increased minimum wage and a Housing Act, which provided 810,000 cheap houses by 1955. But Truman could not push through the rest of the programme, and after the 1950 Congressional elections his position worsened when Republicans gained seats, although they failed to win control of Congress. These elections showed the effects of McCarthy's campaign (p. 89) and the hysteria surrounding the trial of Alger Hiss, as well as fear of Truman's 'creeping socialism' and opposition to his stand against Stalin (p. 265)

## The Eisenhower years, 1953–60

'I thought what was good for our country was good for General Motors and vice versa.'

Charles Wilson, ex-President of General Motors, and a member of Eisenhower's Cabinet

In the 1952 Presidential election, the Democratic candidate was the liberal-minded intellectual, Adlai Stevenson, while the Republicans had chosen the war hero, Eisenhower, whom some Democrats had wanted as their candidate in 1948, indicating the widespread support he enjoyed. The campaign was fought on the issues of Korea (p. 268), Communism and corruption. In the right wing atmosphere of the time, Eisenhower won with a large majority.

In foreign affairs Eisenhower followed Truman's policies (p. 274 and Document 18.2). In domestic affairs he was a moderate, offering no 'Deal', but allowing Roosevelt and Truman's legislation to stand. His

policies aimed to cut government spending, reduce taxation and
encourage private enterprise. He cut the spending power of agencies
such as the Tennessee Valley Authority, lessened company taxation,
and handed over US atomic energy plants to private corporations. The
end of the Korean War (p. 269) allowed temporary cuts to be made in
military spending and taxation, freeing both men and materials. This
contributed to a fall in world prices of raw materials, and began a period
in which real purchasing power rose sharply.

By 1960 industrial output was three times that of 1939, and
agricultural output up one-third compared with 1952. The USA was a
prosperous country, with one car for every three people and a
widespread ownership of other consumer goods. However, the
economy suffered from inflation and unemployment, and, in spite of
presidential hopes, increased taxation was necessary to subsidize a
continuing rise in military spending. In 1959–60 this was higher than it
had been during the Korean War, a reflection of US determination to
match the USSR, while maintaining a strong presence abroad and
sustaining allies and 'friends' throughout the world. This rise in
spending was also the result of the increasing cost of the technology
demanded by the military and provided by industry in what Eisenhower condemned as the 'military-industrial complex'.

Eisenhower's presidency saw the development of the Civil Rights
movement among black people, and the fall of McCarthy. In 1953
black Americans, in northern and southern states, were literally
second-class citizens, disenfranchised by a poll tax and by literacy and
property qualifications. Forced to take the worst jobs and housing,
black people were entitled to 'separate but equal facilities' which,
although separate, were certainly never equal. In terms of schools and
public facilities such as lavatories and transport, black people were
disadvantaged throughout the US. During the war, black servicemen
had served in segregated units, but in Europe, where there was little
official segregation, they had enjoyed a status denied them in their own
country.

In 1946 Truman set up a Civil Rights Committee, whose report he
presented to Congress in February 1948 when he proposed legislation
to end the poll tax and literacy tests as qualifications for the franchise.
By decree, Truman ended segregation in the armed forces, and banned
discrimination in federal employment and in hotels in the District of
Colombia. In 1951 he banned the awarding of defence contracts to
firms practising discrimination, strengthened the civil rights section of
the Justice Department, and appointed one black as Governor of the
Virgin Islands and another to a federal judgeship. Also in 1951 the
Supreme Court demanded the ending of segregated dining facilities on
inter-state trains and tried to force southern states to increase the voting
registration of blacks. Congress would not pass the legislation
proposed by Truman, nor was public opinion prepared to support him.

White voters in the southern states 'bolted' from their traditional loyalty to the Democrats to support a 'States Rights' or 'Dixiecrats' party, led by Governor Strom Thurmond of South Carolina, preparing to fight the 1948 presidential election.

Between 1952 and 1960 there was a marked improvement in the legal position of the 18 million black Americans as a result of federal intervention in the affairs of states practising segregation, and a determined campaign by blacks and white sympathizers. The influence of independent Asian and African countries, and several decisive rulings made by the Supreme Court, also encouraged the government to try and ease the racial problem. A Civil Rights Act (1957) set up a commission to investigate the denial of voting rights to blacks. Another Act (1960) ruled that help should be given for blacks seeking to register as voters, but this remained largely ineffective. More importantly, in 1954 the Supreme Court ruled that, in education, 'the doctrine of 'separate but equal' had no place. Separate educational facilities were recognized as inherently unequal, and the 17 States with no integrated school systems were ordered to provide one 'with all deliberate speed'. Eisenhower supported the ruling, which was resisted in the south as an interference with State rights, and sent federal troops to Little Rock, Arkansas, to enforce the law when the Governor refused to allow 17 black students to enrol in a white-only school.

In 1955 blacks in Montgomery, Alabama, protested at segregation on public buses. Led by Rev. Martin Luther King, they boycotted the system and forced the authorities to end the practice of providing separate seating for blacks. This led to protests against 'white-only' drug stores, hotels and libraries. The moderate and non-violent policy of the King-led Civil Rights Movement slowly gained supporters in both Democratic and Republican circles, although in 1960 only a minority of blacks were registered as voters.

The success of Senator Joseph McCarthy had its origins in the traditional American fear of Communist subversion which had flourished in the 1920s and again after 1945. In 1946 Truman allowed a hunt for 'Communists in government service', and three cases seemed to justify his fears of 'reds in government service'. Alger Hiss, a high-ranking official in the State Department, was found guilty of passing secrets to Soviet agents in the 1930s; two US citizens, Julius and Ethel Rosenberg, were executed for disclosing atomic secrets to Soviet agents in the 1940s; Klaus Fuchs, a British atomic physicist, was found guilty (in Britain) on a similar charge. Churchill's 1946 'iron curtain speech' (p. 52), the Truman 'doctrine' of 1947, the Czech coup in May 1948 and the Berlin crisis of 1948–9 (p. 267) all contributed to the growth of anti-Communist feeling in the USA. With the onset of the Korean War in 1950, many Americans were persuaded that Stalin was intent on world conquest. It is not surprising, perhaps, that McCarthy, Nixon and other right-wingers gained a good deal of support at this time.

Congress reacted to growing hysteria by passing the Internal Security Act (1950), putting restrictions on all known Communists. This encouraged McCarthy to begin his bizarre hunt for communist sympathizers. Between 1949 and 1954 he used the Un-American Activities Committee as a platform on which he could bully witnesses, and publicly discredit organizations, universities, politicians and officials by claiming (without proof) that they were, or had been, members of, or supporters of, the Communist Party or communist-led movements. McCarthy was supported by the Churches for opposing atheistic Communism, and by the public for his apparently 'brave' stand against traitors in public places. He drove many people from public office and private employment, and forced the government to decree (1951) that civil servants could be dismissed if there was 'reasonable doubt' of their loyalty.

Eisenhower's victory in 1952 was due in part to McCarthy's popularity, and the consequent public perception of Democrats as 'soft on Communism'. In 1953 McCarthy became chairman of the Senate's Permanent Committee of Investigation. He had the atomic scientist, Oppenheimer, sacked from his government post on the flimsiest of evidence; he organized the burning of 'subversive books' written by US writers, and persuaded the press, publishers and the film industry to practice an unofficial 'anti-communist' censorship.

In 1954 McCarthy overreached himself by accusing Senators of being Communist sympathizers and Army commanders of being 'reds'. Sanity was restored when TV commentators showed him at work cross-examining Army generals. Increasingly 'confused and ridiculous', McCarthy was evidently becoming a drunken bully. Public opinion changed as, under the TV lights, McCarthy was transformed from a hero into something of a villain and buffoon. As public opinion changed, the Senate found the belated courage needed to condemn one of its own members removing him from his chairmanship in 1954. He died in 1957, but by then McCarthyism had led to the investigation of nine million people, many thousands of whom had lost their jobs, and had created an atmosphere of suspicion which lingered on.

## The Kennedy–Johnson years, 1961–8

'The nation has man's first opportunity to create a Great Society . . . [of] success without squalor . . . [and] open the doors of learning, of fruitful labour and rewarding leisure . . . to everyone.'

President Lyndon B. Johnson

In the 1960 Presidential election, the Democratic candidate was John F. Kennedy, whose millionaire father had been Ambassador to Britain in the 1930s and opposed US entry into the war. As Senator for Massachussetts, in whose capital, Boston, his Irish–American supporters had their political base, Kennedy had kept a craven but politically understandable low profile during the McCarthy period, his brother, Robert, having worked on McCarthy's team. During the election campaign he overcame the problem of anti-Catholic bigotry which many thought would lead to his defeat by Richard Nixon, the former Vice-President. Nixon had entered the House after winning an election in California against an opponent whom he described as a subversive liberal, indistinguishable from a communist. An active member of the House Un-American Activities Committee, Nixon played a major role in the Hiss case, and supported McCarthy.

Kennedy won by a narrow majority, achieved only as a result of polling irregularities in Cook County, Illinois, controlled by Catholic Mayor Daley of Chicago. Kennedy's election was seen as 'the passing of the torch' to a new generation. With a young, intellectual Cabinet he promised to tackle domestic problems such as unemployment, inflation, urban poverty and the position of black Americans; he produced plans for a health service for old people, a Bill for slum clearance and an extension of social security for the unemployed. The Republicans, allied with right-wing Democrats, ensured that none of this passed into law. In the 1962 mid-term elections the Republicans made significant gains, worsening Kennedy's position.

With his brother Robert as Attorney-General, Kennedy ventured into the field of civil rights, but accomplished little (pp. 95–6). Abroad, he enjoyed high prestige as a 'liberal': the Peace Corps of young volunteers provided assistance in underdeveloped countries; the Alliance for Progress (1961) with Latin American countries aimed at increased economic cooperation and a rise in living standards; the 'Kennedy Round' of tariff cuts provided opportunities for a growth in world trade, benefitting both developed and underdeveloped countries. (His confrontations with Khrushchev and Castro are examined on pp. 277 and 278; his intrusion into Vietnam on p. 239).

Kennedy was assassinated in Dallas on 22 November 1963 and Vice-President Johnson replaced him at the White House. A former leader of the Democrats in the Senate, and a more astute politician than Kennedy, Johnson used the sympathy which followed Kennedy's death to push through the social legislation he had proposed. Johnson had always been a dedicated social reformer, ready to call for a 'Great Society'. His Development Act (1964) provided for the rebuilding of inner city areas; a Social Security Act provided 'Medicare' for old people; another Act raised the minimum wage. He assigned federal money to an expansion of the education system, and began the process of providing federal aid for the unemployed.

In 1964 Johnson won a crushing victory over the Republican, Barry Goldwater, following which he pushed through a Civil Rights Bill (p. 94). However, his extension of US involvement in Vietnam (p. 240) led to a distortion of the US economy (Fig. 6.1), as well as causing much anger, fanned into violence by the anti-war movement. Johnson

### The Train Robbery

**6.1** A cartoonist's view of the effect of the Vietnam War on the 'Great Society' which Johnson hoped for

decided not to stand in the 1968 election, hoping that his withdrawal would allow for the 'binding together' of a divided nation.

### Nixon's domestic policies, 1968–74

'It is not the critic who counts, nor the one who points out how the strong man stumbled. . . .'

Theodore Roosevelt

Nixon, who defeated Vice-President Humphrey in 1968, will be remembered as much for his success in foreign affairs as for the Watergate scandal. His almost total involvement in the wider world meant that he spent little time on domestic matters. His Council for Urban Affairs succeeded, nonetheless, in improving conditions in the inner cities, where there was now less violence. Although Nixon wanted to cut public expenditure, and reduce the 'poverty programme' inherited from Johnson, social security benefits were increased, and Medicare extended to disabled people under the age of 65.

In spite of huge government spending on arms and space research, unemployment figures rose to over four million; partly because of the Vietnam War (p. 242), inflation continued to rise, which led Nixon to impose an unpopular freeze on wages and prices – a surprising move for a 'free market' Republican President to make.

Nixon won a massive victory over Senator McGovern in the 1972 elections, but suffered as it became clear that he had attempted to pervert justice by shielding supporters who had engineered a break-in at the Democratic headquarters in the Washington Watergate building. As more and more of his senior officials were tried, found guilty and sentenced, Nixon resisted calls for his resignation. In August 1974, however, he was forced to step down, and since his Vice-President, Agnew, had already been found guilty of financial malpractice and had resigned, the former leader of the House, Gerald Ford, became President.

## Effects of the US involvement in Vietnam

'The rules of economics are not working the way they used to . . . even high unemployment may not suffice to check the inflationary process.'
Arthur Burns, 29 July 1971

The causes and course of US involvement in Vietnam will be found on p. 239. Here we can examine some of the domestic effects of that war.

From the outset, 'liberals' had opposed US participation in Vietnam; as involvement grew, so too did the extent of opposition (Documents 15.2 and 15.3). Students, opposed to a war in which they might have to fight, led anti-war demonstrations in which they clashed with anti-riot police. 1968 saw the growth of a world-wide students' movement which, in the US in particular, had an anti-war bias and which became increasingly politicized as students demanded the right to 'participate' in their own education, to write courses to be studied, to judge their teachers' abilities and to share in college and university government.

Black Americans, already active in the Civil Rights Movement, were also supporters of the anti-war campaign. Many blacks refused to serve in a war from which they would have to return to an unequal status; many joined one or other of the Black Power groups; in the 1968 Olympics, black athletes gave Black Power signs from the victors' rostrum to draw attention to their frustration.

Liberals, students, radical Democrats and blacks combined to raise the level of violence, and drove Johnson to withdraw from the 1968 Presidential race, won by the anti-communist, Nixon, who made a humiliating peace with Vietnam to halt the wave of anti-war violence.

The war in Vietnam had other, perhaps more serious, effects. In 1961 Eisenhower had warned that spending on arms consumed half of the nation's budget, and already employed 10 per cent of the labour force. Khrushchev condemned his military leaders as 'metal eaters'; Eisenhower, while conscious that much of the USA's prosperity was due to military spending, saw the dangers of the 'unwarranted influence of the military-industrial complex'. One effect of high spending on arms was a rise in the rate of domestic inflation. Another was a rise in the US deficit in its balance of payments. Ever since 1944 the dollar had been the world's key currency; others had parities fixed in relation to it, and through its convertibility into gold (at $35 per ounce) it linked the IMF system (p. 36). Until 1960 the dollar maintained this strong position, and slight deficits in the US balance of payments provided the world with an adequate supply of dollars. In the 1960s US deficits rose alarmingly, and continued to rise under Nixon, from $9.8 billion in 1970 to $29.8 billion in 1971 to over $10.2 billion in 1972. These deficits were caused by grants to overseas allies, direct investment overseas by US firms, and, above all, by military expenditure in Vietnam.

These deficits were matched by dollar surpluses in the balance of payments account of Japan, West Germany and some lesser countries. In 1971 Nixon asked these creditor countries to revalue their currencies to help improve US balances; they refused, so in August 1971 Nixon was forced to devalue the dollar by 8 per cent in gold terms and impose a 10 per cent surcharge on imports into the USA. By 1973 it was clear that these small changes had failed: in February, the US was forced into a further devaluation (to $42.2 per ounce of gold) while in March 1973 the world's finance ministers put an end to the system agreed in 1944. Currencies no longer have a parity fixed to the dollar, but 'float' in response to monetary forces. This ended an era during which the US had dominated world economic affairs, and marked a stage on the road of relative decline which runs on into the 1980s as other economies have assumed increasing importance (Figure 13.1).

## The Civil Rights Movement, 1960–86

'I have a dream that one day on the red hills of Georgia the sons of former slaves and the sons of former slave owners will sit down together at the table of brotherhood . . . that my little children will . . . live in a nation where they will not be judged by the colour of their skin but the content of their characters.'

Martin Luther King, 28 August 1963

By 1960 black Americans were more vocal in their demand for civil rights legislation and for political action to implement existing

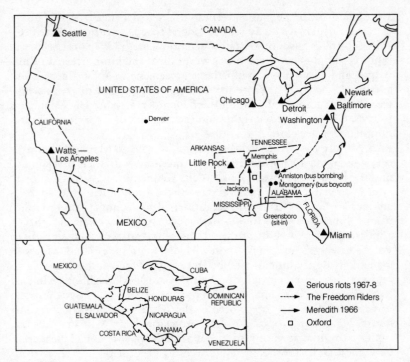

**6.2** The USA faced problems at home as well as in South America

legislation. Their leaders pointed out that, in spite of the 1954 Supreme Court decision, southern schools were still largely unintegrated, and that in five states there were no integrated schools at all.

Younger, more radical leaders, impatient with the conservative leadership of organizations such as the National Council for the Advance of Coloured People, formed the Congress for Racial Equality (CORE) to express their demands. Many had taken part in the black exodus from the south to the industrial north where, in spite of an economic improvement in their lives, they faced social problems in the decaying inner city areas.

Kennedy took a few small steps to assuage black anger: he appointed black judges, the first black Ambassador and the first black commander of a US warship. At the same time, Robert Kennedy used his power as Attorney-General to help blacks to register as voters. In 1961 radical blacks joined James Farmer's Freedom Riders, crossed state borders by 'bus and defied waiting-room regulations (Fig. 6.2). At Anniston, Alabama, white reactionaries burned buses – and blacks. In 1962 James Meredith, a Mississippi black who had served in the US Air Force, tried to become the first black to enter the University of Mississippi. White students joined in the anti-Meredith riots, during which several people were killed. Since the state governor refused to use state troops or police to restore order, Kennedy sent in federal troops to protect Meredith.

White police in southern states used brutal methods against black and white civil rights' workers; many were killed, and more arrested. White judges and juries gave sympathetic treatment to whites accused of anti-black crimes. The same attitude was reflected in Congress, where Republicans combined with southern Democrats to hold up Kennedy's proposals regarding civil rights and the cleaning of slums in the black-dominated inner cities.

In August 1963 King led the Washington Peace March (Document 6.1) which, via TV, provided many Americans with their first sight of dignified, educated black spokesmen. Kennedy (assassinated shortly after the March) and Johnson saw these spokesmen as moderates anxious to head off the violence preached by younger, more radical blacks. Johnson's Civil Rights Acts (1965) gave blacks equal rights of admission to cinemas, theatres and shops, and guaranteed their right to vote. However, governors, police chiefs, state judges and whites in general made it difficult, if not impossible, for southern blacks to register and claim their rights under the Act. On March 8 1965 King led blacks in Selma, Alabama, on a voter-registration march: two thousand were arrested as they tried to enter the white-only door of the court house. King then proposed to lead protestors from Selma to the state capital to dramatize the injustice, but Selma's Mayor banned the march. Governor Wallace ordered state forces to prevent the marchers from leaving Selma, while they were attacked by whites determined to keep blacks in their subordinate position (Document 6.2).

Liberal support for the moderate King gave no satisfaction to the majority of blacks who took matters into their own hands in the inner cities. Some joined the Black Muslims demanding a separate state for US blacks; others joined Black Power movements, threatened armed revolt and took part in urban rioting of the kind which destroyed the black Los Angeles suburb of Watts, and which swept 'like a string of firecrackers' across the USA, flaring up in Chicago, New Jersey, Detroit and other cities.

In an effort to appease black anger, Congress approved more civil rights legislation; millions of dollars were provided for job-creation schemes, welfare relief and training programmes for black teenagers. New houses, medical centres and hospitals were built in inner city areas; more blacks went to college, entered the professions, joined the security services, and became politicians. Their success helped defuse a dangerous situation, but white anger at black success was reflected in the assassination of King, while Black Power leaders argued that whites would either 'kill off' or 'buy off' what they saw as 'dangerous blacks'.

For many whites, the most significant move by pro-black legislators was the attempt to integrate city schools. Black children were taken by bus from their deprived areas to white suburbs and white schools; white children from these same suburbs were then 'bussed' to inner city schools to provide an element of integration. Anti-bussing riots and white-led boycotts increased tension in many cities and led Nixon to halt the process.

1985 marked the twentieth anniversary of King's Selma March (Document 6.2), and it is clear that there have been many improvements in the lives of black people since 1965. Blacks, nonetheless, are still relatively deprived: between 1975 and 1985 black unemployment rose to 15 per cent, twice that of whites; in inner cities, 80 per cent of black teenagers fail to find jobs in their first year after school. Reagan promised, in 1981, a 'commitment to equal treatment of all citizens.' Much still remains to be done.

## Domestic politics since Watergate, 1976–86

'I have my veto pen drawn and ready for any tax increase that Congress might even think of sending up. And I have only one thing to say to the tax increasers. Go ahead – make my day.'
Reagan to the US Business Conference, March 1985

Ford and his Democratic successor, 'Jimmy' Carter, faced a Congress which, having 'overthrown' a strong President in 1974, was more than willing to stand up to weaker men. Carter found it impossible to push through proposals for the tackling of urban poverty and unemployment. At the same time, the US economy was affected by the increased price of oil. (p. 135). Its balance of payments moved into ever increasing deficits, while inflation rose from 4 per cent in 1976 to 10 per cent in 1979.

Carter's popularity declined, largely because of the perceived weakness of his foreign policy in a period which saw the USSR gain more influence in Africa (p. 165) and invade Afghanistan (p. 146), while US forces failed to free the hostages held in the US Embassy in Teheran (p. 142). In 1979 the Republican Ronald Reagan promised a tougher foreign policy, and this helped sweep him to victory in the 1980 Presidential election.

Liberals mocked Reagan as 'an ageing actor' and 'an amiable dunce', unfit to govern a troubled USA whose economy was under increasing attack from the more efficient economies of Japan and West Germany (Figure 13.1). In 1980–81 Reagan tackled the problem of inflation by cutting federal spending (other than on the armed forces), and by trying to achieve balanced budgets. Since this caused even greater unemployment and increased racial tension, Reagan adopted more liberal policies after 1981. There were increases in budget deficits as the government spent more than it collected in taxes. Unemployment began to fall as people spent more money, but much of this was spent on imports, leading to even greater deficit in the balance of payments. Deficits in the internal budget and the external balance were covered by borrowing from abroad, which was made easier by high US interest rates. This, however, ensured that US export prices were high due to the strength of the dollar, which pleased exporting countries but angered US industrialists and workers, who were unable to compete with overseas producers, and whose industries went into decline.

In spite of his expansion of the money supply, and his budget deficiting, Reagan has seen the US economy drift into decline, as the following figures show:

| | % quarterly changes in | | Budget deficit | Trade deficit |
|---|---|---|---|---|
| | Industrial output | GNP | billion $ | billion $ |
| 1983 | 11.1 | 3.5 | | |
| | 13.4 | 9.0 | | |
| | 18.4 | 4.0 | 210 | 70 |
| | 11.0 | 6.0 | | |
| 1984 | 14.0 | 9.8 | | |
| | 7.0 | 4.0 | | |
| | 4.0 | 3.5 | 190 | 125 |
| | −0.6 | 1.5 | | |
| 1985 | 2.0 | 2.0 | | |
| | 1.0 | 1.0 | 210 | 150 |
| | 1.0 | 1.0 | | |
| | 1.0 | 1.0 | | |
| 1986 | 0.5 | 3.0 | | |
| | −2.9 | 1.1 | 200 (est.) | 130 (est.) |

To date, President and Congress have failed to agree on policies aimed at curbing the deficits at home and abroad. Meanwhile, the value of the dollar continues to fall, to almost 2 German marks (from 4 in 1971) and to 150 Japanese yen (from 270 in 1985), making the USA the world's leading debtor. World bankers may yet decide to call a halt to overseas lending to a declining economy. Whatever happens in the US will have major effects on other economies.

## Documentary evidence

The Washington Peace March (Document 6.1) put President Kennedy in a difficult position. There was a threat of increased racial violence if King was unsuccessful, and white racists in the southern states were using illegal and brutal methods to halt black progress. In March 1985 some of those who took part in the 1965 march in Selma looked back in wonder (Document 6.2). Times had changed.

## Document 6.1

*The Great March for Freedom, August 1963*

'Tomorrow the thousands gathered for the Civil Rights protest will advance on Washington in the most enormous civil demonstration ever known. Over the months it has been sporadic – Alabama, Mississippi, Tennessee; the dismal humiliating contests over schools and States rights. Now it has become national, universal; the open demands at last for a square deal for the American coloured man everywhere in the land of the free.

From tomorrow nineteen million semi-citizens will have formally insisted through their physical symbols in Washington that they must have the vote where now they have it not, and the right to work and to send their children to school, and that this future shall not be years away but tomorrow. For a nation that has shuffled the immense problem under the rug for so long, the experience is astonishing, even unnerving.

President Kennedy could well have done without the embarrassment of a Freedom March; his Administration has dragged their feet over Negro rights as long as they could; this troublesome business is the canker at the Democratic Party's soul. Now, he must make like a liberal even if it chokes him. He is committed; the blacks have committed him. But his Civil Rights legislation is hopelessly stalled in Congress. Perhaps he hopes the 200,000 multi-coloured faces will force the diehards' hands and save not only the Government's face but the integrity of the USA, now at stake. Consequently we have the situation most piquant to anyone British, adjusted to the inflexibility of Tory rule, of a Government responding to a basic challenge by embracing its principles and snatching the words of freedom from its mouth, making it clear that if you can't like them, you join them – and perhaps use them.

The March is pledged to non-violent aims with the minimum of partisan politics. But the problem remains; if the March is too peaceful, dull, inconclusive, many Negroes will be resentful; if the multitude is too stimulated, there may be terrible trouble. Here is the test for those Negro leaders who have advocated negotiations and non-violence as the way to promote the black man to a decent way of life. When nothing happens, they will be denounced by the extremists. If there is violence, there will be a bitter price to pay. Can the USA afford to let the world know that ten per cent of the population have lost faith in democracy, and can no longer accomplish anything through peaceful means?'

(James Cameron, *Daily Herald*, 28 August 1963)

## Document 6.2

*Selma, twenty years on*

'Selma (pop. 27,264) has a restful Southern ambience these days. Edwin Moss, 69, was an Army combat veteran and one of the few blacks who was registered to vote in the town 20 years ago. Have things changed? "You're looking at one change," said Moss. He was the first black ever appointed as a registrar in Dallas County. Though the totals are distorted because people who have died or

moved away have not been removed from the rolls, by last November Selma
had 10,069 registered blacks, almost catching up the 12,137, white voters.

[On Sunday 7 March 1965 600 blacks and a few whites gathered at the Brown
Chapel African Methodist Episcopal Church in Selma to prepare for their
March. Among the crowd was Jesse Jackson. Opposing the March was the
Mayor, Joe Smitherman.] As both sides seemed to anticipate, the Selma march
would become a turning point in the civil rights movement, prompting
Congress to pass the Voting Rights Act, eliminating literacy tests and leading to
the end of poll taxes, which discriminated against blacks. Last week [March
1985] a crowd of 1800 people, mostly black, gathered in front of the same
church to re-enact the march. Nattily dressed in a blue blazer, Jackson noted
some changes; "Twenty years ago, we could not drink water from a fountain
when we were thirsty. We could not use the rest room when we had the need."
Yet Jackson declared, "we stand here today because of unfinished business."
Wilbert Thigman, a municipal worker who bears a scar on his arm as a result of
the 1965 march, said conditions in Selma are much better now. A job then, he
recalled, meant "50 a day and ten hours a day. You can get a lot more money
now." Selma was once altogether totally dependent on agriculture, mostly
cotton. Now, observed Smitherman, still the mayor twenty years later, "there
are 65 different sorts of manufacturing operations here." But Dallas County
suffers a 15 per cent unemployment rate . . . the adult black employment rate is
about 30%.

[Dale Ross, then aged 10, watched his father among the mounted force
obstructing the marchers.] "My father told me it would be history in the
making," Ross recalled last week, "and it was. That was a different time then.
I'm glad to see blacks got all their rights. It's something to be proud of."
Smitherman agreed. "We look back on it now, and we were wrong. Every
American ought to have the right to vote."

As the anniversary march crossed the Pettus bridge, black and white Selma
police officers and state troopers held back the traffic. Blacks constitute 35% of
the Selma police department and 45% of the fire department. Two of Selma's
six councillors are black. A black woman, Jackie Walker, was elected tax
collector last fall, the first of her race to win a countywide election since
Reconstruction. Walker died in an auto accident on Feb. 1. Selma's minority
community is waiting to see if the white county commissioners will appoint
another black to take her place.

[In March 1965 black marchers were attacked with bullwhips.] "What
happened was unjust," said Selma Librarian Patricia Blalock. "Some people
reacted badly. But I think you should give the town another chance. We've
tried to change." To the Rev. Frederick Reese, a Selma black leader who had
invited King to check out the city's denial of voting rights in the first place, the
20-year evolution has been "miserably slow." Now the principal of the
Eastside Junior High School, Reese pointed to two private white academies that
have opened since the public schools began to integrate in 1965. "There is
toleration," he said. "Toleration is a step forward from the past, but real racial
harmony has not been achieved." '

                                                      (*Time* March 18 1985)

## FURTHER READING

AMBROSE, S. E., *Eisenhower, The President: vol. 2, 1952–69*, Allen and Unwin, 1984

BUCHAN, A., *The USA*, OUP, 1971

CARMICHAEL, S., and HAMILTON, C. V., *Black Power: The Politics of Liberation in America*, Cape, 1968

CHESTER, L., et al., *An American Melodrama: The Presidential Campaign of 1968* Andre Deutsch, 1969

COOKE, A., *A Generation on Trial*, Rupert Hart-Davis, 1950

FURLONG, W. L. and SCRANTON, M., *The Dynamics of Foreign Policymaking*, Westview, 1984

GOLDMAN, E. F., *The Crucial Decade – and After*, Alfred A Knopf, 1981

HODGSON, G., *In Our Time: America from World War II to Nixon*, Macmillan, 1977

ISSEL, W., *Social Change in the United States*, Macmillan, 1985

JOHNSON, L. B., *The Vantage Point: Perceptions of the Presidency, 1963–69*, Weidenfeld, 1972

KING, MARTIN LUTHER, *Why We Can't Wait*, New America Library, 1964

LATHAM, E., *The Meaning of McCarthyism*, D. C. Heath, 1973

NEUSTADT, R. E., *Presidential Power: Political Leadership from FDR to Carter*, Wiley, 1980

NIXON, RICHARD M., *The Memoirs of Richard M. Nixon*, Arrow Books, 1979

PARMET, H. S., *JFK: The Presidency of John F Kennedy*, Penguin, 1984

PURVIS, H. and BAKER, S. J., eds., *Legislating Foreign Policy*, Westview, 1984

ROVERE, R. H., *Senator Joe McCarthy*, Harper and Row, 1973

SCHLESINGER, ARTHUR M., (JR.), *Robert Kennedy and His Times*, Andre Deutsch, 1978 *A Thousand Days*, Andre Deutsch, 1965

SORENSEN, T. C., *Kennedy*, Hodder and Stoughton, 1965

TRUMAN, H. A., *Memoirs, vols 1 and 2*, Signet Books, 1965

WHITE, THEODORE, *The Making of the President, 1960*, Cape, 1965

# 7

# China

## The End of the Civil War, 1945–9

'On the side of the Kuomintang is a group of reactionaries opposed to every effort I have made to influence the formation of a coalition government. There is a liberal group who have turned to the Communists in disgust at the corruption evident in government. The dyed-in-the-wool Communists distrust completely the leaders of the KMT.'

General Marshall, Report to US Congress, September 1947

Chiang Kai-shek had tried to destroy the small Chinese Communist Party between 1927 and 1936, ignoring the Japanese occupation of Manchuria (1931) and her subsequent preparations for an attack on China proper. The threat of an army mutiny forced Chiang into an uneasy truce with Mao's Communists in 1936 and it could be said that he led a united China in the war against Japan which began in 1937, and became a part of the Second World War in December 1941 (p. 15).

When Japan capitulated in August 1945, Chiang ordered Japanese troops in China to surrender their weapons to his men only. Meanwhile, Chiang's allies flew his troops to occupy cities in North and East China. However, in the countryside many peasants welcomed the liberating Red Army which they knew had fought more vigorously than Chiang's. Hoping to persuade Chiang and Mao to cooperate, Truman sent US General Stilwell to see both leaders. He reported that the KMT (Kuomintang) was marked by 'corruption, neglect, chaotic economy, taxes, hoarding, black market, trading with the enemy . . .' while Mao sought 'reduction in taxes, rents and interest, increases in production and standard of living . . .'. Stilwell was recalled and his replacement, Marshall, endeavoured to bring the two sides together – in vain.

In June 1946 Chiang launched a full-scale attack on Communist strongholds in Central China. Superficially he had every chance of success: while Stalin did little for Mao, Chiang was aided by the US. Internationally recognized as one of the 'Big Four' Allied leaders, Chiang also controlled China's industrial centres. However, his dictatorial methods and his inefficiency angered Chinese intellectuals, while the raging inflation encouraged by his corrupt government angered businessmen; patriots remembered his reluctance to fight with Japan, while peasants recalled their ill-treatment by his troops. Moreover, Chiang's army was disloyal: his men often went over to the Communist side, or sold supplies to their supposed enemies.

Mao, on the other hand, had won the peasants' support by his anti-landlord and progressive policies, introduced in Communist-held areas; intellectuals admired the honesty of his government, which also gained the support of businessmen and patriots.

In June 1946 Chiang ordered a three-pronged attack against Shantung, Yenan and Manchuria regions, claiming that the Reds would be defeated in six months. The Communists retreated from Yenan, bypassing the government armies, and made their way to the south where they set up a base in the Tapeh mountains, controlling the route to the north along the Yangtze and threatening the rich river valley. Mao then built up a peasant army using weapons supplied by the USSR, or surrendered by KMT forces. By January 1949, Mao controlled every city north of the Yangtze. On 31 January he captured the old capital, Peking, and invaded the region south of the Yangtze, driving government armies into Nanking and Shanghai. There, inflation destroyed the savings of the middle classes, and KMT troops roused more opposition by their reign of terror. In the countryside, the breakdown of Chiang's government led to the re-emergence of government-by-warlords, and the Red Army was welcomed by peasants suffering under their cruel yoke.

Nanking and Shanghai were captured in April and May 1949, and while Chiang held out temporarily in Canton, Mao went to Peking where, on 1 October 1949, he inaugurated the People's Republic of China. In December Chiang fled to Formosa, in Taiwan, and Mao held undisputed control over a long-suffering country.

### Establishing the Communist system, 1949–58

'Let a hundred flowers bloom, let a hundred schools compete.'

Mao, 1957

'The purges affected more communists than non-communists and reached as high as provincial governors. Thousands of party members were denounced for 'rightism', one million put on probation.'

Edgar Snow, *The Other Side of the River*, 1963

Mao wanted to end corruption in the public services, reverse the economic decline of the past forty years, modernize China, make sweeping reforms in land-holding and agriculture, and create a

Communist state in which living standards would rise. For this he needed the agreement and help of millions of non-communist technicians and officials, so he proceeded cautiously. The nationalization of heavy industry, public utilities and banking got under way, and the property of leading KMT figures was seized. Mao's Three-Anti Campaign (against corruption, waste and inefficiency) began in August 1951 and won the support of middle-class intellectuals and officials. This was followed by a Five-Anti Campaign against bribery, tax evasion, fraud, theft of state property and betrayal of economic secrets. Women were completely emancipated, education extended to children of every class and Europeans deprived of all their former privileges, their investments seized by the government.

With 80 per cent of the people engaged in farming, progress in agriculture was a prerequisite for other reforms. Mao's agriculture reforms proceeded slowly, and sometimes barbarically. The Land Reform of June 1950 forced landlords to give land to their former peasants, a process which quickened during the first months of the Korean War (p. 268). Partly out of revenge for past injustices, and partly from fear that landlords might be counter-revolutionary, millions of landlords and richer peasants were killed in 1950–1, along with many foreign priests and missionaries, as well as Chinese suspected of being only 'faint-hearted' supporters of the new régime.

In 1952 Mao launched his first Five Year Plan for industry and agriculture, aiming at increasing the output from heavy industry as a base for future development. Private industry in these sectors was abolished, workers forced to work harder for no extra reward and slow workers, critics and absentees punished. China's output of coal, steel, electricity and oil doubled as Soviet capital and technicians provided the aid promised in the Russo–Chinese Treaty of February 1950, and in the commercial agreement signed with Russia in April 1950. However, China's output remained relatively small. Having started from a low base, a 'doubling of output' meant less than it would have done in Britain (which produced 20 million tons of steel in 1957) or the USA (100 million tons in 1957). China, despite its size, produced a mere five million tons of steel in 1957.

Industrial progress depended on development in the agricultural sector, where increased output would save foreign currency previously spent on food imports, pay for imported foreign technology and ensure food for China's masses. Mao had seen the disastrous outcome of Stalin's efforts to force the pace of agricultural change; he proceeded more slowly. In 1951 communist officials went to the countryside to persuade peasants to join Mutual Aid Teams of about ten families, each retaining its own land but all pooling their animals, equipment and labour. This led to an increased output but created a group of richer peasants, likely to be individualistic and therefore not communist-minded. In 1953 representatives were sent to persuade Mutual Aid

Teams to form cooperatives whose land would be sown and harvested in one operation, under the control of a cooperative committee who would decide which crop was to be grown, what work each person had to do and where a crop would be sold. Profits would be shared among cooperative members.

This led to a sharp increase in output and, for the first time, China was free of famine. Moreover, the peasant was being weaned off the notion of private ownership and cautiously introduced to the notion of communal ownership. In 1955 Mao's officials went to the cooperatives to encourage (or force) peasants to form collective farms on which private property was abolished and peasants paid simply for the work they did. The peasants resisted; they had been taught their right to property (1950–2) and had enjoyed the benefits of individual work (1952–5). Peasant uprisings against efforts to drive them into collectives forced the government to break the farms into smaller units, and ask the peasants to organize their work within the framework of a Party plan for the overall collective. Peasants were also allowed private plots for growing vegetables or raising a few animals. These concessions, plus the threat from an ever-present Red Army, ensured that by 1957 almost all land had been collectivized.

By 1957 many radicals criticized Mao's relative conservatism: they wanted more rapid communization, and opposed Mao's efforts to placate the non-communist officials and intellectuals, upon whom Mao knew China relied. The radicals viewed these groups as potentially counter-revolutionary, because of their western education and training. The outbreak of the anti-Stalinist movement in Hungary in 1956 had alarmed Mao, so in 1957 he initiated a nationwide debate, in the belief that, given their freedom, everyone would come to see the rightness of his policies. Within a few weeks the volume of criticism (on issues such as inflation, shortages of food and consumer goods) had worried Mao, who feared that the debate might lead to a critique of the entire communist system. A few months after the first mention of 'a Hundred Flowers' the debate was abruptly closed. The more important critics were punished by imprisonment, death, or exile to the country-side for re-education.

## The Great Leap Forward, 1958–66

'The transition from collective ownership to ownership by the people as a whole may take less time in some places and longer – five or six years – in others. Differences between workers and peasants, town and country and mental and manual labour will gradually vanish. Chinese society will enter into the era of Communism.'

CCP, Central Committee, 1958

In 1958 Mao introduced the Second Five Year Plan, better known as 'the Great Leap Forward,' intended as a short cut to increased industrial production and the creation of a system of communes in the country-side. This was his response to the radical demands of Liu Shao-chi and others of the 'impetuous' school, whose importance was reflected in the elevation of Liu to the Presidency in 1958 as successor to Mao, who still remained Chairman of the Party.

For industry, the Plan proposed an annual increase in output of 30 per cent, an indication of China's backwardness and need to catch up with the West. Labour was mobilized and women set free to take industrial jobs; local and small industries were set up as adjuncts to larger, state-owned units to provide peasants with an introduction to industrial work. People in both town and country were encouraged to set up 'backyard furnaces' so that 'every man' became a steel producer. This, one of the most publicized items in the Plan, was a failure as most 'backyard' steel was of poor quality.

The establishment of communes was particularly significant. Here the driving force was the need for more food to support the increasing population and to pay for essential imports. The existing 750,000 collectives were formed into 24,000 communes, each covering about 10,000 acres. Private plots were abolished and communal dining-rooms, dormitories, nurseries and schools provided. Each commune had its own welfare scheme and local government. One million townspeople were forced into the countryside to work on these communes; crops were sown on previously unused areas and the 1958 harvest was forecasted to be 375 million tons. In fact, only 250 million tons were harvested in 1958, and in 1959–61 a series of floods and droughts made matters worse. In 1962 only 175 million tons were harvested and China had to import grain from Canada and Australia. Perhaps Mao's scheme was too ambitious; certainly, the teams sent to supervise it were incompetent, and responsible for the inefficiency, crudity and brutality with which it was implemented. Their behaviour, and the failure of successive harvests, increased the resentment of the peasants who had been deprived of their private plots and who cared little about communally-owned equipment or animals.

By 1960 it was clear that the Great Leap had failed in town and country alike. Mao accepted the need to allow peasants to own some land, and although the commune survived as an element in society and government, the small team reappeared as the basis of the rural economy. Mao had hoped to inspire people with the concept of constant revolution; the pragmatic Prime Minister, Chou En-lai, and the 'rightist' General-Secretary, Deng Tsiao-ping, wanted to attend to China's pressing needs and to ignore this concept. Unlike Mao, they saw the health of the economy as more important than party ideology.

Also by 1960, the traditional hostility between Russia and China (p. 275) was reflected in the personal animosity of Mao for Khrushchev; while Mao condemned Soviet 'revisionism', he was himself condemned for his un-Soviet attempt to find a Chinese 'road to socialism' by way of the Great Leap Forward. The Sino-Soviet dispute became public at the 22nd Soviet Party Congress (1960), and soon afterwards the 1400 Soviet technicians working in China were withdrawn, technical and financial aid ended and China's faltering attempts at modernization further hampered.

## The Cultural Revolution, 1966–76

'The great Cultural Revolution is only the first; there will inevitably be many more . . . it is possible for a capitalist restoration to take place at any time.'

Mao, in the *Peking Review*, June 1967

Mao, with his notion of 'continuing revolution', was opposed by Chou, Deng and others more concerned with the practicalities of economic development. Mao feared that after his death these pragmatists would follow a Khrushchev-like line of accommodation to the West and to Chinese individualism. He also feared the inevitability of a western attack and suspected that a generation which had experienced neither the Long March nor guerrilla war would not be spiritually strong enough to defend China.

In 1966 Mao and his Defence Minister, Lin Piao, launched what became known as the Cultural Revolution, aiming to expel from office the pragmatic technicians and bureaucrats who were relatively uninterested in ideology. They were helped by a breakdown in the educational system in 1966 which forced the authorities to postpone for a year all entries into universities and other centres of tertiary education. This left millions of young people with seemingly nothing to do, and Mao urged them to form themselves into 'Red Guards' and undertake an ideological crusade against 'revisionism' (Fig. 7.1). Mao himself went on a well-publicized 'Great Long Swim' in the Yangtze to show that, aged 72, he was still strong enough to lead. His numerous sayings were published as a 'Little Red Book' which became the revolutionaries 'bible'.

The aim of the Red Guards, as published in the *Shanghai Press* on 18 August 1966, was to 'rid the country of the Four Olds: old cultures, old customs, old habits and old ways of thinking'. By not defining 'old', it was left up to individual Red Guards or rival groups to decide on courses of action. Teachers, university professors, journalists, religious leaders and Party officials all suffered at the hands of rampaging mobs. President Liu was expelled from the Party and Deng was forced to resign. Trains were commandeered, and workers forced to listen to hours of pro-Mao speech-making or to take part in 'anti-revisionist' demonstrations. Meanwhile, the economy almost ground to a halt. Lin Piao provided Mao with the support of the armed forces, and ensured that Chou, who held on to office as Prime Minister, was powerless to intervene as nine-tenths of his government were driven from office,

**7.1** A Cultural Revolution poster depicting a Red Guard waving the anti-Maoist book, *The Dismissal of Hai Jui*, while other anti-Maoist authors are driven off by the battering ram

arrested, imprisoned, sent to the countryside for re-education or killed.

In 1971 Lin Piao appeared to be on the point of using the army to halt the excesses of the Revolution which he had initiated. His proclamation as Mao's heir may have whetted his appetite; alternatively it may have led others to suggest to the paranoiac Mao that Lin was plotting his overthrow. Whatever the reason, Lin fled from China, only to be killed in an aircrash in Mongolia, along the route to the Soviet Union (Document 7.1). His flight led army commanders in China's seven military regions to act against the Red Guards. Severe fighting took place in cities and communes as both sides exacted revenge, and industrial workers, anxious to halt the decline in their living standards, battled with the Red Guards.

The Cultural Revolution may be said to have ended in 1973, when the army finally drove the young back in to the classrooms. Deng, arguing that China needed collective leadership to save itself from the excesses of Maoism, and Chou, with the remnants of the bureaucracy and 'functionaries' who ran the economy, were back in positions of power. Deng became Deputy to Prime Minister Chou in 1973, although Mao's younger, and radical, wife managed to have him driven from office in January 1976 following Chou's death. For a short time

Madam Mao and her Red Guard 'Gang of Four' tried to drive China back into revolutionary turmoil. Mao's death (September 1976) deprived them of his powerful support and they were arrested. The army put down pro-Maoist risings in various provinces, although fighting went on until 1977 and millions were killed. Deng Xiaoping ('the weathervane of the Revolution') came back to power and quickly showed that he was the real ruler of China, which he determined to set on new and very un-Maoist paths.

## Deng Xiaoping's China, 1976–86

'. . . we have wasted twenty years.'
General Secretary Hu Yaobang, *Outlook*, February 1985
'. . . there are no fundamental contradictions between a socialist system and a market economy.'
Deng, *Time*, 4 November 1985

Deng's career has signalled the state of play in China. Dismissed as General Secretary during the Cultural Revolution, he was sent in to internal exile as a 'Capitalist-roader'. In and out of power (1973–6), he was politically rehabilitated in 1978, and, while others hold the leading positions of President, Prime Minister and Party Secretary, Deng is obviously the *de facto* leader. He introduced the broad and dramatic reforms which decentralized decision-making and placed more reliance on market forces. In September 1985 he consolidated his position by retiring many of China's ageing leaders and promoting younger men to positions of power.

Mao had appreciated the dominant role of China's peasants, the 'water' in which the 'fish' of his guerrilla army moved. Once in power, he tried to increase agricultural output as the prerequisite for industrial change. Deng too appreciates the role of the peasant, and his first reforms were in land-holding and agriculture. Peasants, allowed larger private plots, were encouraged to produce food for sale in the open market, to make profits and to keep what they made. The result has been a sharp increase in food output (up eight per cent annually since 1978) and in peasant incomes (from some $67 in 1978 to about $155 in 1985). To further encourage the peasant, the state has built new housing in the countryside in which the newly-rich can install the consumer goods which their rising incomes allow them to buy.

In February 1985 Party Secretary Hu blamed 'radical leftist nonsense' for China's failure to meet the economic goals set after the 1949 revolution, saying that China could 'never again afford' notions such as 'the Great Leap Forward' and the 'Cultural Revolution'. He highlighted China's embracement of a new economic philosophy stressing incentive and reward. With pragmatists rather than ideologues in charge, there has been a push to develop foreign trade, to expand industry and to woo foreign investment. The result has been an impressive rise in output – up 13 per cent in 1984 compared to an annual growth rate of 1.4 per cent during the years of the 'Leap', and 5 per cent during the Cultural Revolution.

The new philosophy is illustrated by the Four Special Enterprise Zones and the fourteen coastal port areas (including Shanghai) which have a battery of special tax privileges and a relative degree of autonomy. One zone, Shenzen, close to Hong Kong, attracted $800 million of foreign investment during 1985 and has promises of another $3.2 billion. In Shanghai, along with a flourishing black market in imported goods, there is a huge entrepreneurial class catering for the city's hunger for consumer goods, and some 12,000 private businesses within the city's limits. Some foresee Shanghai as the leading city of the Pacific Ocean; its industrial output already equals that of Taiwan, and its exports one-sixth of all China's goods.

Not everyone is as optimistic as Deng (Document 7.2). Some economists wonder if China has the resources to meet the dual demands of a developing economy and a booming consumer market. Others question the use of child labour and the conditions of life in the teeming cities, where thousands sleep in the streets and millions are crammed into tiny rooms. Nationalists are concerned at the inroads made by Japanese goods and investment; will China become a Japanese satellite, and 'yen imperialism' achieve more than armies?

Party ideologues, influential even in Deng's China, fear that the freedom given to managers and businessmen may lead to demands for political and social freedoms. Some are disturbed by the demand by the China Writers Association for 'creative freedom', by growth in university courses allowing discussion on moral and philosophical issues, and by the new growth of Christianity. The peasant bureaucrats who have run the government apparatus since 1949 feel threatened by economic reforms, by the emergence of a new managerial technocracy, and by the promotion of intellectuals, 'the stinking ninth category' in Mao's league.

In April 1985 Prime Minister Zhao Ziyang told the National People's Congress, the nominal legislature, that the government was to re-introduce some economic controls, relaxed in 1984, because of the boom in wages, prices and credit, and an upsurge in 'unhealthy practices' including bribery, profiteering and lavish bonuses to certain workers. The enthusiastic applause which greeted Zhao's hard-hitting presentation was a reminder that China's future may, again, be an uncertain one.


### Documentary evidence

The optimism of the activist (Document 7.1) is at odds with what happened during the Cultural Revolution, which 'wasted twenty years', and which, having been instigated by Lin Piao, ended by condemning him as a 'revisionist'. Deng (Document 7.2) was humiliated during the Revolution but now, with like-minded colleagues, he seeks to improve China's economic conditions.

## Document 7.1

*Mao's Red Guards versus Confucius and nature*

'Since the start of the Great Proletarian Cultural Revolution we peasants have destroyed fetishes, freed our thinking, and we are now combatting hailstorms. I am a member of the commune's hailstorm prevention group. Under the leadership of Chairman Mao we labouring people can create miracles if we keep to the socialist road. In Minshien County, hailstorms as big as eggs damage crops and kill farm animals. In the old society during the hailstorm season landlords put up signs saying, "May God bless us and bring good weather" and extorted sacrifices from us. They preached the reactionary theory of Confucius that everything was decided by heaven. Under Mao we have become masters of our own destiny. We don't believe in God or heaven and we've taken up the fight against hailstorms. In 1970 a group surveyed all the mountains in the commune and mapped out three main routes along which stormclouds usually move. We built three defence lines across the routes, set up thirty-nine gun emplacements and organized a hailstorm protection group. Whenever storm-clouds gathered we fired the guns to disperse them before hailstones formed. This lessened the damage from hailstorms. By 1973, the county had over 700 hailstorm prevention emplacements with more than 4000 weapons. A threatening hailstorm is greeted by thunderous volleys from all the mountain tops in a people's war against heaven. Under Mao the people's strength can triumph over nature. Today we must carry on the movement to criticize Confucius and thoroughly repudiate Lin Piao's counter-revolutionary revisionist line.'

(Chen Yu-ching, Wentou Commune, Kansu Province)

## Document 7.2

*Deng Xiaoping's views, November 1985*

*'Can a free market economy co-exist with a socialist state?*

The question is what method we should use to develop the social forces of production in a more effective way. In the past the old approach was to go for a planned economy. But we have found that if we engage only in planning, the development of socially productive forces is delayed. So if we can combine planning and the market economy, I think it will help to emancipate the forces of social production. What we have done is to adopt the useful things under the capitalist system. We have been pursuing the policy of opening up to the outside world and combining the market economy and the planned socialist economy. Now it seems a correct policy. Has it violated the principles of socialism? I think not.

*On preserving the socialist system*

As long as public ownership plays a dominant role in our country, I think polarization can be avoided. There will be differences when different regions and peoples become prosperous. Some will become prosperous first, others later. The regions that have become prosperous will help the regions that have not. That's what I mean by common prosperity.

I think only when the economy has become developed and the life of the people has improved and the culture and education level raised, can the negative phenomena be eliminated in the end. It's almost seven years since we decided to start the reforms. If you want to tell whether the lives of the people are improving, you should find out what's happening in the countryside, where 80% of the people live. As you know, after the foundations of New China, the per capita income remained at the level of $20 for a long time. That's below the poverty level. It means that the people didn't have enough to eat or wear. But the reforms in the countryside took off and had results within three years. What we do in the reforms in the countryside is emancipate the productive forces and bring into play the enthusiasm of the peasants. If you want to bring the initiative of peasants into play, you should give them power to make money. That's why we put an end to the communes and introduced the responsibility system in production.

*On opposition to his economic programme.*

When we started introducing reforms in the countryside there were people who were not in favour. In the first two years, a third of the regions of China were still not enthusiastic and were left behind in starting reforms. They waited a year; when they found that other regions were doing well and starting reforms, they started to catch up. Our approach is not to force people to do anything . . . practice shows them that their approach is not right.'

(*Time*, 4 November 1985)

## FURTHER READING

BROWN, C., *China, 1949–75*, Heinemann, 1976

CHOUDHURY, G. W., *China in World Affairs: The Foreign Policy of the PRC Since 1970*, Westview, 1983

CHENG, N., *Life and Death in Shanghai*, Grafton, 1986

HINTON, H., ed., *The People's Republic of China*, Westview, 1979

KUO, PING-CHIN, *China*, OUP, 1971

GARVER, JOHN W., *China's decision for rapproachement with the United States, 1968–71*, Westview, 1983

GINSBURG, N. & LALOR, B. A., eds., *China: The 80s era*, Westview, 1984

MACFARQUHAR, R., *The Origins of the Cultural Revolution*, OUP, 1983

MITCHINSON, L., *China in the 20th century*, OUP, 1970

MOSELEY, G., *China: Empire to People's Republic*, Batsford, 1968

ROBINSON, J., *The Cultural Revolution*, Pelican, 1969

SALISBURY, H., *The Long March: The Untold Story*, Macmillan, 1985

SHAMBAUGH, D. L., *The Making of a Premier; Zhao Ziyang's Provincial Career*, Westview, 1984

SHORT, P., *The Dragon and the Bear: Inside China and Russia Today*, Abacus, 1982

SOLINGER, D. J., ed., *Three Visions of Chinese Socialism*, Westview, 1984

TARLING, N., *Mao and the Transformation of China*, Heinemann, 1977

VERTZBERGER, Y., *Misperceptions of Foreign Policymaking: The Sino-Indian Conflict 1959–62*, Westview, 1983

WANG, GUNGWU, *China and the World since 1949*, Macmillan, 1984

WU, TIEN-WEI, *Lin Biao and the Gang of Four*, Southern Illinois Univ. Press, 1983

# 8

# North Africa and the Middle East, 1945–67

## The background, 1914–45

'The history of the Middle East between 1918 and 1969 is a history of the undoing of the Peace Conference of 1919.'

Jon Kimche

During the First World War the British promised, through T. E. Lawrence, to help the Arabs to gain their independence from Turkey, arranging with France a mutual division of Arab lands and, in the Balfour Declaration (1917), promising 'the establishment in Palestine of a National Home for the Jewish people'. At the Peace Conference in 1919 Britain was given Iraq, Palestine and Transjordan as Mandates, while France received Lebanon and Syria, where they deposed Feisal after he had declared himself 'King of Syria and Palestine' in 1920. The British allowed him to become King of Iraq (1921) having already named his brother, Abdullah, as Emir of Transjordan.

Anglo–French manipulation of this region was in line with the process in which French power was extended over Morocco, Algeria and Tunisia while Britain gained control of Egypt and, by various treaties, most of the Gulf States (Figure 8.1). Only Saudi Arabia escaped European control, Britain and other powers recognizing Ibn Saud as King of Hejaz and Nejd, which he renamed the Kingdom of Saudi Arabia.

In the British Mandate of Palestine, the inter-war years saw an increase in Jewish immigration, the development of Arab hostility and outbreaks of violence by both groups. Britain tended to take the Arab side, mainly to maintain influence in other oil-producing Arab states in the region. During the Second World War, Arab lands in North Africa were fought over (Figure 1.1); Britain occupied Iraq (1941) and a joint Anglo–Soviet invasion of Iran overthrew the pro-German Reza Shah, installed his son as ruler and maintained control until 1946 (p. 148).

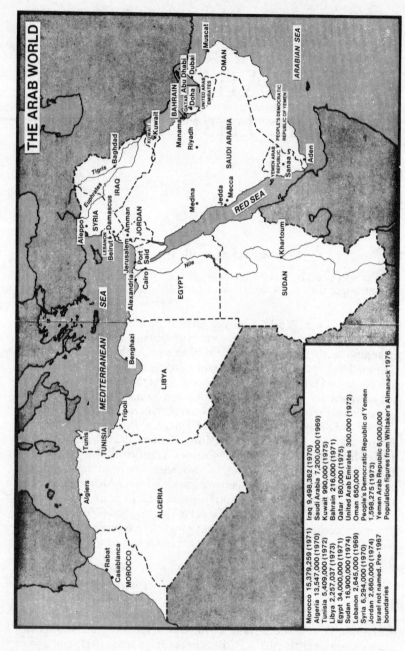

8.1 The Arab World

THE ARAB WORLD

ARABIAN SEA

Muscat
OMAN
Abu Dhabi
Dubai
UNITED ARAB EMIRATES
QATAR
Doha
BAHRAIN
Manama
Kuwait
KUWAIT
Riyadh
SAUDI ARABIA
PEOPLE'S DEMOCRATIC REPUBLIC OF YEMEN
YEMEN ARAB REPUBLIC
Sanaa
Aden
Baghdad
Tigris
Euphrates
IRAQ
Aleppo
SYRIA
Damascus
Beirut
LEBANON
Jerusalem
Amman
JORDAN
Port Said
Cairo
Alexandria
Mecca
Jedda
Medina
RED SEA
Nile
Khartoum
EGYPT
SUDAN
MEDITERRANEAN SEA
Benghazi
Tripoli
LIBYA
Tunis
TUNISIA
Algiers
ALGERIA
Rabat
Casablanca
MOROCCO

Morocco 15,379,259 (1971)
Algeria 13,547,000 (1970)
Tunisia 5,409,000 (1972)
Libya 2,257,037 (1973)
Egypt 34,000,000 (1971)
Sudan 16,900,000 (1974)
Lebanon 2,645,000 (1969)
Syria 6,294,000 (1970)
Jordan 2,660,000 (1974)
Israel not named. Pre-1967 boundaries

Iraq 9,498,362 (1970)
Saudi Arabia 7,200,000 (1969)
Kuwait 990,000 (1975)
Bahrain 216,000 (1971)
Qatar 180,000 (1975)
United Arab Emirates 300,000 (1972)
Oman 650,000
People's Democratic Republic of Yemen 1,598,275 (1973)
Yemen Arab Republic 6,000,000
Population figures from Whitaker's Almanack 1976

## Britain and the Arabs, 1945–8

'The Arab lands are a complete and indivisible whole; all efforts are to be directed towards their independence in their entirety and unified.'

Islamic Conference, 1931

In 1945 British policy was dominated by three main considerations: control of Middle Eastern oil resources, essential to the British economy; control of the Suez Canal and the Gulf States, and friendly relations with Arab states in general, to ensure the link with British interests in Asia and Australasia; the threat of Soviet aggression, typified by Stalin's attempt to seize Azerbijan in 1946 (p. 265).

In October 1945 Britain helped to establish the Arab League (Egypt, Iraq, Syria, Lebanon and Saudi Arabia) principally as an obstacle to Soviet progress. Its members saw the league in different terms. Some looked for 'a Great Arabia' in which 36 million Arabs sharing a language and a culture would be united. Others concentrated on the need for a more vigorous anti-Jewish policy in postwar Palestine (Document 8.1).

With the end of the war, and the evidence of the Holocaust and concentration camps in Nazi Europe, there was world-wide sympathy for the Jews. However, Britain ignored appeals for increased immigration into Palestine until the flow of illegal immigrants angered the Arabs, whom the British wanted to placate and who saw the new arrivals as agents of US and British imperialism. As their settlements came under attack, some Jews formed the Hagannah Defence Force; others, more militant, formed illegal groups such as Irgun to wage guerrilla war on Arab terrorists and the British 'occupying forces'.

In 1946–7 Britain was preparing to withdraw from India (Chapter 12) and Greece (p. 265), and reconsidering her position in Palestine. Bevin tried to get Arabs and Jews to accept the notion of a binational state but Arab intransigence in the face of Jewish terrorism caused this proposal to fail. In the autumn of 1947 Britain announced that in May 1948 she would hand over the Palestinian Mandate to the UNO, which accepted a resolution for a partitioned Palestine; the Jews were to be allowed a, small, independent state, and Jordan was to be enlarged to include the rest of Palestine. The Arabs refused to accept this; as the guerrilla war intensified, Britain withdrew (14 May 1948), the UNO officially recognized the state of Israel (Document 8.2) and the Arab League declared war.

## The first Arab–Israeli War, 1948–9 (Figure 9.1)

'Give the Jews the lands of the Germans who oppressed them. Amends should be made by the criminals and not by innocent bystanders.'

Ibn Saud to Roosevelt, February 1945

Truman recognized the state of Israel immediately, Stalin a little later, but the armies of five Arab states soon marched to obliterate it. Egyptian armies attacked the main Israeli forces below Tel Aviv; Jordan's army (trained and commanded by the British) advanced on Jerusalem; Syria, Saudi Arabia and Iraq prepared for war. The Jews were surrounded, outnumbered, and, it seemed, doomed.

However, then as later, Arab rhetoric outstripped practice, and self-interest was more influential than hatred of Israel. Syria did little, the Lebanese less; Iraqi armies retired as soon as the real fighting started, and Egypt's armies arrived too late to affect the outcome of the war. Jordan, meanwhile, was more concerned with the enlargement of the new Kingdom of Jordan than with Arab nationalism. In June–July 1949 a UN mediating team, led by the Swedish Count Bernadotte, organized a truce, but this quickly broke down. The Israelis, united and determined, helped by the skills of British-trained officers and inspired by the dream of a homeland, inflicted a series of defeats on the disunited Arabs whose armies were badly led and who lacked any sense of coordination.

By the end of 1948 the fighting was almost over and Palestine and Jerusalem partitioned by the verdict of arms. In February 1949 an armistice was signed between Israel and four Arab states (but not Iraq). Israel had gained more territory than she had been allotted in the UN partition plan. She had also gained the hostility of the Arabs, humiliated in war and witnesses of the flight of over one million Palestinian Arabs to refugee camps in Syria, Jordan and Egypt.

## The Eastern Arabs, 1949–56

'A new era of friendly relations based on trust [and] cooperation exists between Egypt and Britain.'

> Nasser at the signing of the
> Anglo–Egyptian Agreement, July 1954

In July 1941 Allied troops invaded *Syria* and drove the pro-Vichy officials from the Mandate. Independence, promised in 1939, was proclaimed on 1 July 1944, but French officers in Syria were reluctant to accept this, and did not leave until April 1946 after bitter fighting in Damascus. After several coups had overthrown governments, Shishakli seized power in 1949 and reigned as a dictator until 1954. His downfall marked a return to parliamentary government and reflected the growth of the Ba'ath Pan Arab movement aiming at 'freedom, unity and socialism' and 'one Arab nation with an eternal mission'. Ba'ath groups were formed in other Arab states, stimulating Arab nationalism with particular anti-western overtones.

Allied forces also occupied *Lebanon* in July 1941. In 1943 de Gaulle, leader of the Free French movement, agreed to transfer political power to the Lebanese on 1 January 1944. Lebanon's population was divided on religio-political lines, between Christians and Muslims; inside each camp were rival groups whose leaders were as much intent on gaining control of a particular camp as on asserting the power of that camp against its religious rival. Stability depended on a compromise by which a succession of Maronite Christians held the presidency, while a Sunni Muslim was Prime Minister and a Shia Muslim the Speaker of Parliament. An uneasy peace was achieved by agreement among factional leaders, who grew rich from the commercial development of 'the Switzerland of the Middle East', and from smuggling drugs through the ports they controlled.

*Transjordan*, economically poor, was nonetheless politically important. Emir Abdullah ruled under a British Mandate and in the 1948 War sought to gain control of the West Bank of the Jordan, as well as Jerusalem. With the armistice (p. 116) he gained territory on the West Bank and in Jerusalem. Arab nationalists suspected him of being 'soft' on Israel, while radicals disliked his personal government. He was assassinated in July 1951 and, after an interregnum, his grandson Hussein became King in August 1952. Some Jordanians thought that this British-educated ruler was too much influenced by Glubb Pasha, the English commander of the Jordanian Arab Legion. Some of Hussein's critics were influenced by the Syrian Ba'ath; others by Nasser (see below), who spoke of an Egypt-dominated Arab nation. In March 1956, to assuage his critics, Hussein sacked Glubb, only to find that this whetted Nasser's appetite.

Early in 1949 *Saudi Arabia* revised its oil concession with the Arabian–American Oil Company which agreed to hand over 50 per cent of its net profits from selling Saudi's crude oil. This stimulated the non-Arab, but Muslim, government of *Iran* to ask the Anglo–Iranian Oil Company for a similar agreement. Since the Company refused even to negotiate, the Persian Prime Minister, Mussadeq, nationalized the company's property (Document 9.3), evicted the British from the giant Abadan refineries and won his case at the International Court of Justice (p. 253). Britain thought that Iran would be unable to run the oil industry since no foreign company would market the oil. In 1953 Mussadeq was driven out by a CIA–British coup, supported by Persians concerned at the near-bankruptcy of their country. An American-dominated consortium of oil companies agreed to run Iran's industry, paying the government 50 per cent of net profits. National pride was satisfied and Britain's influence had suffered a blow.

*Egypt* had no oil; nor, after the 1948–9 war, did it have any pride in its soldiers or politicians. In July 1952 a clique of army officers, led by General Neguib, overthrew the corrupt King Farouk; then, in 1954 Colonel Nasser set Neguib aside and assumed power, setting himself several major aims. To free Egypt from the remnants of British control, Nasser negotiated the withdrawal of the 90,000 British troops stationed along the Suez Canal, the last of whom left in 1955. To provide better living standards, a series of reforms took land from the rich for use by the peasants, and reforms were initiated in education, housing and health provision. To develop Egypt's economy, Nasser courted foreign aid and planned the new High Dam at Aswan to control the Nile, providing better irrigation for farmers, as well as hydro-electric power for industry. To unite all Arabs in one nation he formed United Arab Republics with one or other of his neighbours in 1958 and 1963, only for them to break up in disarray.

The 'conservative' Kings of Saudi Arabia, Iraq and Jordan were opposed to Nasser's socio-democratic views; the USA and Britain feared that he would be a Soviet puppet, while France was angered by the effect of Nasser's teachings in Algeria (p. 120). In 1955 the pro-western Feisal of Iraq joined Turkey and Pakistan in a Mutual Defence Pact; Britain and Iran also joined this Baghdad Pact in 1956. The USA, already arming Turkey and Pakistan, provided members of the Baghdad Pact with military and economic aid. Nasser condemned the agreement and attacked Feisal, the only Arab member of this anti-Soviet organization, so weakening Arab support for Feisal's projected Iraqi–Syrian Union. Nasser signed a counter-alliance with Syria and Saudi Arabia, and soon appeared to be more 'Arabian' than Feisal.

## North African independence, 1945–62

'From today, France considers that in Algeria there is only one category of inhabitants, only complete Frenchmen, having the same rights and duties. . . . Algérie Française.'
President de Gaulle, in Algeria, June 1958

During the nineteenth century, Turkey, 'the sick man of Europe', was unable to maintain control over her North African Empire. France colonized Algeria (1830–60) and established a protectorate over Tunisia (1881); between 1905 and 1912, France and Spain established protectorates over both south and north Morocco, and in 1911–12 Italy annexed the region which she called Libya.

In 1939 French rule over its Maghreb states was assured; thousands of Europeans had settled; these *colons* dominated professional and commercial life and farmed the best land; French-trained Arabs, while seeking civil rights and better conditions for their people, did so on French terms, seeming to accept the permanence of French rule, the dominance of French culture and the principles of the French Revolution – liberty, equality and fraternity. Few expected to fight for that liberty.

In Morocco, young Arab nationalists had presented a reform programme to France (1934) which, although rejected, was supported by the enlightened Sultan Muhammad V, further strengthening the nationalist movement. The Bey of Tunisia, however, did not support the dynamic nationalist party formed by Habib Bourguiba in 1934, and acquiesced when the French imprisoned Bourguiba (1938–42). In

Algeria, the Partie Populaire Algérienne sought political, economic and social reform, while Arab intellectuals, led by Ferhat Abbas, asked that Muslims be given civil and political equality with the French *colons*. The latter thought, as did Italian settlers in Libya, that Europeans would remain in control while the colonies developed, with native populations always having a subordinate place.

After a see-saw war with the Axis powers (Figure 1.1), the Allies gained control of North Africa in 1943. A British administration in Libya held discussions with Allied and Italian leaders, who proposed various schemes for the division of Libya between the European powers. These schemes were condemned by the Arab states, and finally defeated at the UNO in December 1951 when the leader of the Senussi became constitutional monarch, as King Idris.

The French hoped for a return to the *status quo* in the Maghreb. However, many Arabs were mindful of the French defeat by the Germans, encouraged by the Atlantic Charter (Document 2.1) and Roosevelt's anti-colonial views, by the creation of UNO and the granting of independence to Syria and Lebanon with British and US support, and by the formation of the Arab League (Document 8.1). A new Arab attitude was reflected in the manifesto which Abbas presented to the Allied authorities, claiming independence for Algeria (Abbas himself had once argued that Algeria's future lay in assimilation by France). The French made some concessions: in 1944 French citizenship was extended to certain qualified groups of Arabs, as Abbas had demanded in the 1930s, and in 1946 Arabs were allowed to elect 15 Deputies to the French National Assembly and seven Senators to the Council of the Republic.

However, French *colons* and soldiers were less progressive, as was shown at Setif in May 1945 when police attacked an Algerian march held to celebrate the Allied victory in Europe. Algerian soldiers, who had fought for the Allies, carried an Algerian flag, which angered the *colons*. The attack by the police was followed by anti-European demonstrations in which about one hundred Europeans were killed. In French reprisals about 10,000 Muslims were killed, in an event still commemorated in the Algerian Republic as the day on which Algerian independence became inevitable.

In Tunisia, Bourguiba refused to collaborate with the Germans who released him from prison in 1942. His offer to cooperate with the French after the Allied victory was rejected, so he fled to Cairo to campaign for Tunisian independence. In 1950 France offered the Tunisians internal self-government, to be achieved in stages. A Tunisian government, formed by Bourguiba's party, negotiated some increases in its power and a reform of civil service regulations, allowing more Tunisian recruitment. The 180,000 French *colons* then persuaded the French government to slow the pace of reform, and Bourguiba and other leaders were arrested. This led to a guerrilla war in which both sides employed terrorist tactics, ending only when France recognized Tunisia's righ to independence in July 1954. In June 1955 Bourguiba signed the Franco-Tunisian Conventions, which ensured internal self-government while safeguarding French interests in the country.

In Morocco, French officials and soldiers resisted nationalist demands and the French government's attempts to arrive at an understanding with the Arabs, who had the support of the Arab League, the Afro-Asian bloc in the UN, the liberals in France and Sultan Muhammad V. The *colons* depended on the support of the army, resentful after the humiliations of Indo-China (p. 238). They also tried to win the support of the conservative and traditionalist Berber tribesmen, until nationalism spread to the villages and the Berbers joined the city-based rebellion. The French then deposed Muhammad V, replacing him with an elderly and malleable cousin, which confirmed the deposed Sultan's position as a symbol of nationalism. An Arab terrorist campaign forced the French to bring back Muhammad V in 1955, when France signed an agreement ending the protectorate and recognizing the independence of Morocco. At the same time, the Spanish government agreed to the incorporation of its zone within the independent Kingdom of Morocco. This led Bourguiba to demand full independence for Tunisia, which was granted in March 1956. Bourguiba formed a new government, deposed the Bey and installed himself as President of independent Tunisia, a position he holds at the time of writing.

French reluctance to give independence to Tunisia and Morocco was motivated by fear of what might happen in Algeria, where in 1945 de Gaulle rejected Abbas's proposal for an Algerian Republic in which French and Arab would be treated equally. De Gaulle would agree only to a decree that equal opportunities would be available to those Arabs who could 'get on', and to the establishment of an Algerian Assembly of 120 representatives elected by Muslims, to which, however, he gave no real power.

In November 1954 the National Liberation Front (FLN) started its war against France, aided by Egypt and the Soviet Union, and also supported by the Arab League and the Afro-Asians in the UNO, where French colonialism received short shrift. In 1955 the UN proposed that Algeria become fully independent; the French reply took the form of a more intense anti-FLN campaign. Millions of French soldiers were sent to fight the war which became increasingly barbarous as both sides used terrorist tactics. By May 1958 it was clear to all except the die-hard French that Algeria would gain its independence. The army, led by Indo-China veteran General Salan, led an army revolt against the Fourth Republic, which led to de Gaulle's return to power. In spite of his right-wing supporters, the hope of the army and his own policy in Algeria in 1945, de Gaulle opened negotiations with the rebel leaders. This led the *colons* and soldiers to form the Organisation de l'Armée Sécrète (OAS), a terrorist organization aimed at preventing the

Algerian independence and overthrowing de Gaulle's Republic. De
Gaulle ruthlessly suppressed the OAS before signing the 1962 agreement which ended the fighting in Algeria, where Ben Bella was
installed as the first President of the Algerian Republic.

## The Suez Crisis, 1956

'Nasser's got to go, It's either Nasser or me. I don't care if there's chaos
[and] anarchy in Egypt. I want Nasser destroyed.'

Eden, quoted by Anthony Nutting

The Suez Crisis (July–November 1956) involved a complexity of
personalities, issues and nations. It was dominated by Nasser playing
many of his chosen roles – the Arab nationalist providing refuge and aid
for Algerian and Tunisian rebels, the anti-Israeli seeking revenge for
1948–9 by buying arms from Czechoslovakia (which ensured US
hostility), and the socialist reformer looking for $1.4 billion to build the
Aswan High Dam. Britain and the USA had agreed to provide some of
the money to this dam, and to act as guarantors for Egypt's loan from
the World Bank for most of the rest. The US cotton-growing lobby
opposed this aid, which would allow more Egyptian cotton to be
grown. They gained the important support of Dulles after Nasser made
the Czech arms deal, and he persuaded Britain to join in the withdrawal
of both the aid and the World Bank guarantees. The anti-communist
Dulles (Document 18.1) wanted to cut Nasser down.

Eden was a weak successor to Churchill as British Prime Minister.
His position was worsened by a post-election recession (1955–6), by his
inability to repress the Cyprus rebellion, and by continuing right-wing
criticisms of his earlier negotiations with Nasser, which led to the 1954
Agreement and the withdrawal from the Suez bases. The beleaguered
Eden came to see Nasser as a threat to Britain's oil supplies and (as Arab
leader, social reformer and world figure) as a latter-day model of Hitler
or Mussolini, whose progress Eden had failed to halt when he was
Foreign Secretary in the 1930s. He had also clashed with Dulles, the
third important character in the Crisis, during the negotiations which
ended the Indo-China war in 1954 (p. 238). Some see in Dulles's role in
1956 a desire for revenge on Eden, and perhaps on the French, who
were hostile to Nasser and willing to arm Israel prior to what became
the second Arab–Israeli War.

In July 1956 Nasser, deprived of western aid for his dam project,
announced the nationalization of the Suez Canal Company, claiming
that its revenues would finance the building of the dam. The French, as
part-owners of the canal, wanted to attack Egypt; 'Nasser must
disgorge,' agreed Dulles, in what Eden perceived as support of
preparations for war. Secret meetings were held, at which France,
Britain and Israel coordinated their plans. Israel hoped for a victory
which would end the terrorist attacks from the Gaza Strip and open the

port of Aqaba which Egypt had closed to Israeli shipping (Document 8.2).

Following a secret agreement, Israel attacked Egypt on 29 October, three days after an Anglo–French fleet sailed from Malta. On 30 October Britain and France sent an ultimatum to both Israel and Egypt, demanding a withdrawal of forces ten miles either side of the canal, which benefitted Israel only. On 31 October Anglo–French forces bombarded Egyptian airfields and ports, although troops did not land until 5 November. By 6 November British forces had taken Port Said and were advancing down the canal.

This attack angered Eisenhower, then in the middle of his presidential campaign; he refused to take Eden's telephone calls, and allowed US monetary authorities to organize a run on the pound. The USSR, busily engaged in Hungary (p. 78), joined with the USA in condemning Britain and France at the UN. Arab countries, both pro- and anti-Nasser, threatened to cut off western oil supplies, while Nasser sank 40 ships in the canal to make it unusable.

The weight of hostile opinion forced Britain and France to accept a ceasefire on 7 November, and a UN peace-keeping force was moved in to police the frontier between Israel and Egypt. Far from toppling Nasser, the Anglo–French campaign had raised his prestige, as even Iraq condemned Britain's action and proposed her eviction from the Baghdad Pact. Jordan too rejected her British links, denounced her treaty with Britain and joined the Egyptian–Syrian alliance of 1955, to which, by now Saudi Arabia and the Yemen also belonged. Nor was the canal safeguarded; it was rendered useless until Nasser allowed it to be cleared, when, to Anglo–French surprise, he then proved that the Egyptians could run it. The Americans who helped bring the crisis about by withdrawing aid for the Aswan High Dam, ended the day by supporting Nasser, although it was the Soviet Union which claimed the credit for the eviction of the western forces and undertook to finance the dam, thus increasing Soviet influence in the region.

## An uneasy peace, 1956–67

'The existing vacuum in the Middle East must be filled by the United States before it is filled by Russia.'

Eisenhower, 1 January 1957

With Nasser triumphant and both the Soviet Union and the USA involved in Middle Eastern affairs, the region took on some of the aspects of the Cold War (Chapter 17), with Arab governments dividing into two camps. Only Lebanon welcomed the 'Eisenhower Doctrine' (p. 274) and US aid. In conservative Jordan there were anti-US riots by people who, having rid themselves of British control, were unwilling to let their country become a US satellite. In Syria, the small, but influential, Communist Party persuaded the government to sign economic and military agreements with the USSR (1957); this alarmed the Americans and angered the leaders of the Syrian Army and of Ba'ath, who did not intend to join either side in the Cold War. Ba'ath leaders asked Nasser to form a Union between Syria and Egypt, preferring even Egyptians to communists. Nasser reluctantly agreed, and a United Arab Republic was proclaimed on 1 February 1958, with Yemen becoming loosely attached to the Union in March.

This Union of radical Arab states led the Hashemite Kings of Iraq and Jordan to form the Arab Federation which the USA hoped that Saudi Arabia, opposed to Nasser, might join. In March 1958 the ruling council of Saudi princes forced King Saud to concede more power to his brother, Feisal, who was more pro-Egyptian and less pro-western than Saud.

The fragile political balance in the Lebanon was threatened in 1958 when President Chamoun tried to alter the constitution to gain for himself a second six-year term. He was opposed by Nasserite Lebanese Muslims who, with the aid of the Syrians and the USSR, began a civil war. While the USA pondered this Soviet threat, Feisal of Iraq and his pro-western Prime Minister, Nuri, were murdered in a military rising (July 1958) led by officers including some communists. The short-lived Arab Federation was also brought to an abrupt end, providing Britain with an excuse to send in forces to buttress Hussein of Jordan, who was threatened by rebels similar in outlook to those who had killed Feisal. The USA also intervened, sending troops to aid Chamoun.

The Iraqi dictator, Kassem, took his country out of the Baghdad Pact, which then moved its headquarters to Ankara. He also imprisoned his second-in-command, Aref, who favoured an Iraqi–Egyptian Union. Kassem disliked Nasser personally and, in any event, saw the development of Iraq as more important than some pan-Arab movement. Nor did Nasser's UAR bring him much comfort; he and the Ba'ath had little in common beyond a superficial socialism. The influx of Egyptian officials into Syria, and Nasser's insistence on applying Egypt's social and economic reforms in Syria, caused severe strains in the Union. The individualistic and large Syrian middle class, although divided into squabbling factions, was united in its hostility to the Egyptians. Syrian politicians, whom Nasser had tried to force into a single party, along with merchants and businessmen who disliked his socialism, and army officers and civil servants resentful of Egyptian appointees, united to support a right-wing revolution which ended the Union in 1961. Jordan, Iraq, Saudi Arabia and the western powers immediately recognized the new anti-Nasser government, viewing the dissolution of the Union as a sign of a decline in Nasser's prestige.

## The Arabian Peninsular, 1962–71

'Arabia should be at leisure to fight out it's own fatal, complex destiny.'

T. E. Lawrence

In 1950 Ibn Saud signed a new agreement with Aramco (p. 117) which ensured that his huge Kingdom became the richest of Arab states. In spite of certain vacillations in the policies of the inefficient and corrupt King Saud (1953-64), the Kingdom enjoyed friendly relations with the USA, although it remained hostile to the US client-states, Iran and Israel. Traditionally hostile to the Hashemite Kings of Jordan and Iraq, it tended to support any Nasserite movements against these kings, although in 1957 Saud sent troops to defend Hussein of Jordan, and welcomed US involvement in Lebanon.

In 1958, Saud was forced to cede increased power to the Crown Prince, Feisal (p. 123), whose 'austerity programme' rescued the Kingdom from the bankruptcy which threatened as a result of the profligate spending of Saud and other princes. In 1960 some of these supported Saud when he took power again; their subsequent behaviour, as much as their flirtation with Nasserite notions of socialism, led to Feisal's coup in 1964 and the abdication and exile of Saud. Nasser tried to organize a Princely revolt against Feisal – who drove the malcontents from the Kingdom.

In 1959 Britain set up the South Arabian Federation of Arab Emirates for the hinterland of the Crown Colony of Aden, which itself acceded to the Federation in January 1963, hoping that, when given its independence, it might join the Commonwealth. Saudi Arabia opposed these plans for an imperialist presence in the Peninsular, but was more concerned by anti-royalist developments in neighbouring Yemen (shown as North Yemen in Figure 9.2), which had been loosely attached to the United Arab Republic in March 1958. In October 1962 Nasser-aided rebels tried to overthrow the cruel rule of the Imam and set up a republic; Feisal supported the royalists in their struggle, and Nasser soon had 50,000 troops involved in a war which he could not win and which was costly in terms of time, money and prestige. In August 1965 Nasser and Feisal negotiated an agreement to end the fighting; the Yemenis were to form a coalition government until a plebiscite, to be held in 1966, would decide the political future of the country. However, Egyptian troops remained in Yemen until after the 1967 Arab–Israeli War; the civil war went on until 1970, when a republic of North Yemen was set up with leading royalists in the government.

Nasser also provided aid to nationalists in Aden, opposed to British plans for a Federation inside the Commonwealth, and encouraged by the republican revolt in the Yemen to start a terrorist campaign against the British forces. The British (Labour) government was unwilling to provide the troops requested by the right-wing sheiks until order had been restored in Aden, from where the last British soldiers were withdrawn in November 1967. The former colony, and its hinterland, was established as the People's Republic of South Yemen (later the People's Democratic Republic of the Yemen), aided by the USSR and China.

While Britain was withdrawing from the south, plans were made for a similar retreat from power on the eastern coast, along the Persian Gulf. Under a series of nineteenth-century treaties, Britain was responsible for the defence of the seven Emirates there. In 1968 and 1971 discussions were held, aimed at setting up a Federation of those states and Bahrain. The talks failed, but in February 1972 the seven Emirates joined together as the independent United Arab Emirates. Their main income comes from the oil of Abu Dhabi, for which, since 1971, Britain has had no legal responsibility.

## The path to war

'If someone throws stones at a neighbour's window he should not . . . complain if the owner comes out and beats him with a stick.'
Feisal's comment on Nasser's policies, 1964–7

In February 1963 Kassem of Iraq was overthrown in a coup led by Ba'athists who installed Nasser's alley, Aref, in power. However, he quickly showed himself hostile to the Ba'ath and so to Syria, itself in turmoil. The Syrian Ba'ath party had been dissolved in 1959, after the Syrian–Egyptian Union, but its leaders had allied with a group of Army officers led by General Jedid, a member of one of Syria's principal communities, the Alawi, who were distrusted by the Orthodox Sunni Muslims, the Druzes and the Christians. The Alawai–Ba'ath alliance was a fragile one; while they shared an antipathy to parliamentary government, the atheistic Marxism of the Ba'ath antagonized the religious Alawi. Between 1963 and 1966 the Alawi community was divided, with General Jedid leading supporters against General Assad, who was overthrown in 1966 by a coup in which Jedid, supported by the Ba'ath, called for national unity in the face of supposed threats from Israel. Feisal of Saudi Arabia, Hussein of Jordan and the Palestinians demanded Arab support for Syria, now the carrier of the anti-Israeli banner; this annoyed Nasser who saw himself losing one of his roles.

Some one million Palestinians had fled from Israel in 1948–9. After the second Arab–Israeli War (1956), forty different Palestinian resistance groups were in operation, the best organized being the Palestinian Liberation Organization (PLO), led by Yassir Arafat and financed by the Arab oil states (and probably the Soviet Union). It provided food for refugee camps in Arab countries, set up schools and publishing-houses as well as industrial bases. It ran military training courses and in January 1965 established a military wing, Al Fatah, which, from bases in Jordan, made guerrilla attacks on Israel with help and encouragement from the Syrian Ba'ath.

The PLO was set up at a meeting of Arab states called by Nasser, at Christmas 1963. He had seen a new projected Egyptian–Syrian Union collapse following the 1963 coup, and feared the creation of an Iraqi–Syrian alliance against him. He welcomed, therefore, the split in the

Iraqi Ba'ath party and Aref's search for union with Egypt. This was small satisfaction when the Arab world was bitterly divided between radicals and conservatives, between east and west (with Bourguiba accusing Nasser of interfering in affairs in the Maghreb) and between radicals themselves, as Iraq, Syria and Egypt vied for the leadership of Arab radicalism.

In January 1964 an Arab summit saw its leaders united with regard to the Israeli scheme for the diversion of the River Jordan, by which water would be taken from the Galilee to the Negev desert. Israel claimed that the volume to be pumped would not exceed the quota proposed in a UN plan (1955) for the apportioning of the waters of the Jordan, and would not leave the lower reaches of the river unduly salty. Arab states had rejected the 1955 plan and in 1964 rejected Israeli arguments, although Israel had almost completed the necessary engineering works and was preparing to operate the scheme later in 1964. At their 1964 Summit, Arab leaders agreed to the diversion of two of the Jordan's tributaries in Lebanon and in Syria; the danger of war was real.

Nasser persuaded the other leaders to create a unified Arab High Command, under an Egyptian general, to ensure that Syria did not start a war against Israel. Syria, Lebanon and Jordan refused to allow Egyptian troops to be stationed on their soil, while Hussein increasingly feared that the PLO might become a separate state within Egypt which might threaten his throne. Feisal of Saudi Arabia, at war with Nasser in the Yemen, visited the Shah of Iran and Hussein as he tried to set up a royalist bloc, and ordered arms from the west. In December 1965, addressing the Iranian Majlis, Feisal called for 'Islamic unity against subversive and alien influences from outside', a coded reference to Egypt and to Arab socialism.

In February 1966 the radical wing of the Ba'ath party seized power in Syria, and while its members had little love for Nasser they had a deep hatred for the Arab Kings and for Israel. In November 1966 Nasser made yet another agreement with the volatile Syrians, which committed him to Syria's defence without giving him control over her military policies. A few days later three Israeli soldiers were killed by a mine explosion near the Jordanian border and Israel made a retaliatory raid into the West Bank. Palestinians there rose in revolt against Hussein's ineffectiveness, spurred on by Syria and the PLO. Although Nasser was silent, it was against him that Hussein launched the bitterest attacked once he had regained control, accusing Nasser of hiding behind the UN Emergency Force in the Sinai while provoking Israeli attacks on relatively weaker states such as Jordan, Lebanon and Syria. He pointed out that, in spite of having the largest Arab army, Egypt had not closed the Straits of Tiran to Israeli shipping (open since the 1956 War) in revenge for the diversion of the Jordan waters. Nasser, Hussein suggested, was 'a paper tiger'.

This challenge could not be ignored, but it could not have come at a worst time. Saudi Arabia was withdrawing support for the joint schemes agreed at the 1964 Summit; the United Military Command was ceasing to function; 'conservatives' and 'radicals' were at logger-heads, while Israel threatened reprisals against Syria if guerrilla attacks continued to be launched from that country.

Nasser, already suffering from an illness that was to prove fatal, and under pressure from outside Egypt, asked U Thant, UN General Secretary, to withdraw the UN forces from the Sinai. When they had left, Nasser announced the closing of the Straits to Israeli shipping (Document 9.1). Two weeks later, Hussein went to Cairo to sign a defence pact with Eygpt; he then allowed Iraqi troops to move into Jordan. Everything indicated an Arab attack on Israel.

## Documentary evidence

Many Arabs saw the immigration of Jews into Palestine as part of a western plot to dominate the region; the Arab League spokesman (Document 8.1) ignored the fact that both the USA and Britain had supported the Arab case at the time of partition (Document 8.2), and that Britain continued to support that case until 1956. It was only after Nasser had threatened western interests that opinion turned in favour of Israel. Even then, Britain and the USA were at odds in 1956. Only in the 1960s did the USA become anti-Arab, although the politicians (President Johnson and Secretary Rusk) seemed to follow different policies from those pursued by the CIA (Document 8.3).

## Document 8.1

*The Arab case against Jewish immigration, 1945*
'Our brother has gone to the West and come back a Russified Jew, a Polish Jew, a German Jew, an English Jew with a different conception of things, Western, and not Eastern. That does not mean that we are necessarily quarrelling with anyone who comes from the West. But the Jew, our old cousin, coming back with imperialistic . . . materialistic ideas and trying to implement them first by British pressure and then by American pressure, and then by terrorism on his own part – he is not the old cousin, and we do not extend to him a welcome. The Zionists, the new Jew, wants to dominate, and pretends that he has a particular civilizing mission to a backward degenerate race in order to put the elements of progress into an area which has to progress. Well that has been the pretension of every power that aimed at domination. The excuse has always been that the people are backwards and that he has a mission to put them forward . . . the Arabs simply say "No." We are not reactionary and backward. Even if we are ignorant, the difference between ignorance and knowledge is ten years at school. We are a living, vitally strong nation, we are in our renaissance; we are producing as many children as any nation. We still have our brains. We have a heritage of civilization and spiritual life. We are not going to allow ourselves to be controlled either by great nations or small nations or dispersed nations.'

(Abdul Rahman Azzam Pasha, Secretary-General of the Arab League to the
Anglo–American Committee of Enquiry on Palestine, 1950)

**Document 8.2**

*A Jewish view of the establishment of Israel, 1948*

'This is not the place to embark on an indictment of the British policy towards Palestine between the two world wars but I must say that it had led to such bloody chaos that the British had nothing more to offer by 2 April 1947 than to throw in their hand and ask for the future of Palestine to be placed on the agenda of the UN. As a result the UN General Assembly established a committee on Palestine which recommended partition. In place of the Mandate, Palestine should be divided, part going to existing Arab states, the remainder becoming an independent Jewish state which would include the Negev [and the port of Aqaba]. For this it would be essential to get American and Russian support and a two-thirds majority in the Assembly. US policy was to keep on good terms with the Arabs to get oil. Weizmann broke through the [US] barrier which stood in the way of the foundation of the State of Israel. The US State Department, having decided very reluctantly to accept partition, decided that the Negev, with its all important port of Aqaba should go to the Arabs [although] Weizmann pointed out to Truman that unless the Jews had Aqaba, their sea lines could be cut off from the East by the Egyptians closing the Suez Canal or the Iraquis blocking the Persian Gulf. On 29 November the UN resolved that the Mandate would end "not later than 1 August 1948 . . . Independent Arab and Jewish States . . . should come into existence." On 14 May the Mandate ended. At 4 p.m. David Ben Gurion read Israel's Proclamation of Independence. At 5.15 p.m. the USA recognized Israel as an independent country.'

*(The Memoirs of Israel Sieff)*

**Document 8.3**

*The twin policies of the USA, 1967; an Arab view.*

'Officially, the Americans were correct in every way. They went along with the UN, with the British and French and endeavoured to find an international solution. But they were convinced that the UN would remain ineffective, and that all the British might succeed in doing was to get the Americans involved in a conflict in the Middle East.

In secret talks which they had with Israel's military and secret intelligence chiefs, the Pentagon and the CIA were satisfied that Israel could well take care of the situation as long as the great powers did not intervene. The Israelis were, therefore, informed on two distinct levels of the American position. [Politicians] Johnson and Rusk played their version of the Middle East charade with [Foreign Minister] Eban but did not realize that Eban was taking it all seriously and was unaware of the other half of the American proposal. [CIA chief] Helms told his Israeli colleagues that Israel would have to conjure up all her inner strength to withstand pressures from outside. Even the Americans might find it necessary to join in these pressures, for they had to protect themselves against the suspicion of collusion – and they could do so only by ensuring that there was no collusion. But – and this was conveyed to [military intelligence chief] Yariv rather than spelled out in so many words – if Israel wanted to have tangible results this time, she would have to be solid as a rock and not weaken before, during or after the actual military encounter.'

(Jon Kimche, *Palestine or Israel: The Untold Story of Why We Failed*)

## FURTHER READING

ABIT, M., *Power and Politics: Conflict in Arabia*, Cass, 1974

COHEN, M. J., *Palestine and the Great Powers, 1945–1948*, Princeton University Press, 1982

DODD, C. H. and SALES, M., *Israel and the Arab World*, Routledge, 1973

HOLDEN, D. and JOHNS, R., *The House of Saud*, Pan Books, 1982

HITTI, P. K., *The History of the Arabs*, Macmillan, 1970

HORNE, A., *A Savage War for Peace; Algeria, 1954–62*, Macmillan, 1977

HUREWITZ, J. C., *Middle East Politics: The Military Dimension*, Westview, 1984

KIMCHE, J., *Palestine or Israel: The untold story of why we failed*, 1973. *The Second Arab Awakening*, Holt, Reinhard and Winston, 1970

LAFFIN, J., *The Dagger of Islam*, Sphere Books, 1979

MANSFIELD, P., *The Arabs*, Penguin, 1983

ODDELL, P. R., *Oil and World Power*, Penguin, 1981

NUTTING, A., *Nasser*, Constable, 1972

PERETZ, D., *The Government and Politics of Israel*, Westview, 1984

RANDAL, J., *The Tragedy of Lebanon*, Chatto and Windus, 1983

SACHAR, H., *A History of Israel*, Blackwell, 1977

SAID, E., *The Question of Palestine*, Routledge, 1980

THOMAS, H., *The Suez Affair*, Weidenfeld and Nicolson, 1967

# 9

# Israel and the Islamic World, 1967–86

## The third Arab–Israeli War, 1967

'Our goal is clear – to wipe Israel off the map.'

Aref of Iraq, June 1967

'We consider any country aiding Israeli aggression against the Arabs [as] aggression against us. To *jihad* . . . Islamic peoples.'

King Feisal, Riyadh, 6 June 1967

Once the UN force left Gaza, Nasser closed the Gulf of Aqaba; Syria, Jordan and Lebanon massed troops along the borders with Israel, and Saudi Arabia and Algeria prepared to join them (Document 10.1). Dayan, Israeli Minister of Defence, decided that attack was the best form of defence. On 5 June a series of air strikes destroyed the Eygptian airforce on the ground and put out of action most other Arab airfields; Israeli troops rushed to take the Gaza Strip, the whole of Sinai, Jerusalem, the West Bank and the Golan Heights (Fig. 9.1).

On 8 June Hussein asked for an armistice (Feisal's troops arrived on 9 June); on 10 June Egypt and Syria accepted a UN cease-fire proposal. Israel rejected UN guidance, proposing to hold on to the Sinai, the east bank of the Canal, the Golan (from which Syrians had shelled Israeli settlements) and the West Bank, including Jerusalem. Israel felt safer with her shorter frontiers easier to defend, and her forces better strategically placed on the Golan and Canal.

Sporadic fighting continued as the UN peace mission went to police the Canal, closed by the debris of 'the Six Day War'. In November 1967 the UN Security Council passed a resolution (242/67) requiring Israel to withdraw from its recent conquests and advocating a settlement to include Arab recognition of Israel and a fair deal for Palestinians. Israel rejected this resolution, which was reluctantly supported by Arab countries. In 1968–9 there was fresh fighting on the Suez front and Israeli air raids into Egypt itself. Meanwhile, the Soviet Union stationed men and missiles in Egypt. The UN Ambassador, Gunner

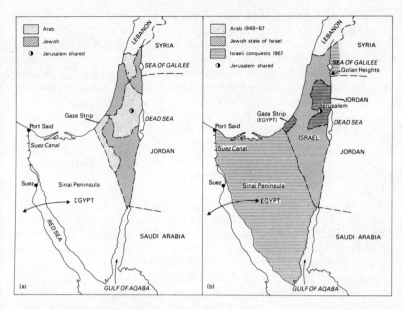

**9.1a** The United Nations plan for the division of Palestine, 1948

**9.1b** The expansion of Israel, 1948–67

Jarring, negotiated with Israel and Egypt, and the fighting finally ended. The USA proposed that Israel should withdraw from the Sinai and the Golan, while Egypt should recognize the state of Israel. Both the Israelis and the Palestinians disliked the plan; Nasser, under guidance from Moscow, reluctantly accepted it, but the proposed Israel–Egypt negotiations were called off once Egypt moved missiles into a proposed 'standstill zone'.

It was clear that Israeli determination and ability were more effective than Arab rhetoric and division. Nasser's dream of an Arab nation was further away than ever when he died on 29 June 1970, while negotiating an end to the civil war in Jordan.

## The PLO versus Jordan, 1968–71

> 'Why is it right for a Jew born in Chicago to immigrate to Israel, whereas a Palestinian born in Jaffa is a refugee?'

In 1968 some 1.7 million Arabs lived in the enlarged Israel, and 2 million refugees had fled their homeland. Arafat's PLO (p. 125) claimed to represent Palestinian interests, although many other groups, some consisting of less than ten men, also claimed that role. Three such groups were united by Habash in the Popular Front for the Liberation of Palestine, claiming that since Arab armies had failed, Palestinians would have to do it for themselves, using terrorist tactics. While these policies clashed with those of the politically-oriented Arafat, the PLO was still blamed for almost every anti-Israeli action. Yet even Habbash's terrorism failed to satisfy those who formed the Marxist Popular Democratic Front for the Liberation of Palestine.

All these groups had bases in Lebanon and Jordan from which to launch terrorist attacks on Israel. In November 1969 Nasser patched up a quarrel between Palestinians and Lebanese Christian paramilitary groups which was threatening to become a civil war. He supported the various anti-Israeli groups, while Cairo radio praised the terrorists who hijacked Israeli and other planes, many of which were flown to Jordan and blown up.

Hussein had accepted 250,000 refugees and allowed the PLO and other groups to wage a guerrilla war on Israel from Jordanian bases. In March 1968 PLO guerrillas together with the Jordanian Army fought the Battle of Karama against an Israeli invasion force seeking revenge for terrorist attacks. However, by September 1970, Hussein's anti-Palestinian advisers persuaded him that the PLO was becoming 'a state within the state' provoking Israeli attacks on Jordan. Relations between the PLO and the Jordanian Army broke down; a civil war ensued, during which the PLO did not receive the aid promised by Iraq, and Syrian intervention was only brief and ineffective. The Jordanians inflicted heavy casualties on the PLO before Nasser brought Arafat and Hussein together for negotiations. These provided Arafat with 'Head of State' status, and left Hussein isolated as 'the anti-Palestinian' King. The affair ended with Hussein driving the PLO out of Jordan into new bases in Lebanon.

Some Palestinians sought revenge on Hussein for the events of September 1970. A group calling itself 'Black September' murdered the Jordanian Prime Minister in 1971; in 1972 one hundred people were gunned down at Lydda Airport; at the Munich Olympics, Israeli athletes were seized as hostages by Black September activists – all the athletes and five guerrillas were killed during a gun fight with the German police.

### Sudan and Libya: new anti-western states

Until 1955, the Sudan was an Anglo–Egyptian condominium which Egypt hoped to draw into its 'sphere of influence'. However, the British gave Sudan its independence (1955) under a government whose anti-Arab policies led to unrest among Muslims in the south and a request for British aid to restore order. There were many short-lived governments in this restless country and, in the south, a civil war which lasted until February 1972. In May 1969 army officers led by General Nimeiry seized power and set up a left-wing, pro-Egyptian government through which Nasser hoped to extend his influence.

The anti-western trend, intensified by the Six Day War, also affected Libya, where in September 1969 the aged King Idris (p. 119) was ousted in a coup led by young Nasserite officers under Colonel Gaddaffi. He proclaimed Libya an Islamic Republic, banned alcohol and night clubs, and forced Britain and the USA to abandon their bases at Tobruk and Wheelus – the last western bases in Arab territory. While preaching a brand of 'Islamic Socialism', Gaddaffi was still an anti-Communist, although he was to use Libya's oil wealth to buy Soviet arms. Egyptian and African leaders feared that behind his call for a resurgence of Islamic fundamentalism lay the wish to create 'a Greater Mahgreb Islamic State', dominated by Libya.

Gaddaffi proposed the federation of Egypt, Libya and the Sudan, offering to aid the economic and military development of the other two states. This proposal remained a dead letter; Gaddaffi's later behaviour alarmed his neighbours as much as it angered the west (p. 155).

## The fourth Arab–Israeli War, 1973

'From the day I took office on Nasser's death, I knew I would have to fight. It was my inheritance.'

> President Sadat of Egypt

Sadat, by nature a reconciler, wanted to gain the friendship of the Kings of Saudi Arabia and Jordan, and also bring together Syria and Jordan, in dispute after the events of September 1970. However, he found himself at the head of a federation of Arab Republics (Egypt, Syria, Libya and the Sudan) under pressure from the Palestinians to act against Israel, with whom Sadat tried to negotiate. In February 1971 he offered to open the Canal to Israeli shipping if Israel withdrew from the Sinai; this offer, and UN proposals for Arab–Israeli talks, were ignored by Israel. Fearing that he would have to fight, Sadat went to Moscow in 1972, only to find that Brezhnev (now involved in détente) was unwilling to help; Sadat concluded that he and Nixon had agreed to keep Egypt in too weak a position to threaten Israel. Sadat sent his Soviet military advisers home.

The Israelis, meanwhile, were taking reprisals for terrorist actions. In February 1973 jet fighters shot down a Libyan Boeing, killing 104 people; in April 1973 Israeli commandos gunned down PLO leaders in an apartment block in Beirut. The radical Syrian government, now under Soviet influence as the Russians sought a new centre of power in the region, urged action against Israel.

On 6 October 1973, while Israel celebrated Yom Kippur (the Day of Atonement), Egyptian and Syrian forces launched a surprise attack on two fronts. The Egyptians crossed the Canal, broke through the Israeli defensive line, used SAM–7 heat-seeking missiles against the Israeli airforce and engaged in tank battles even greater than those fought in the North African desert in the 1940s. From the Golan, 1200 Syrian tanks attacked Israel; almost all of them were destroyed by airborne anti-missile weapons or by Israeli ground forces which, on 13 October, were ready to advance on Damascus. With the Golan secure, Israeli tank brigades broke the Egyptian lines in the Sinai (15 October), advanced rapidly and crossed into Egypt proper. By 24 October, the Egyptian Army in the Sinai was surrounded; the SAM missile sites were captured and the Israeli airforce was once more in control of the sky.

At the UN, the Soviet Union and the USA worked together to end the war. Henry Kissinger, the US Secretary of State, flew to see Brezhnev; the Soviet Prime Minister, Kosygin, flew to see Sadat. On 22 October, Egypt and Israel accepted a UN resolution proposing a cease-fire, the implementation of Resolution 242 (p. 130) and the convening of a peace conference. While discussions went on, Israel attacked Egyptian forces in the Sinai, prompting Brezhnev to propose that a Soviet–US force be sent as a peace-keeping unit. Nixon rejected this idea; when Brezhnev continued to support it publicly, US armed forces were put on a nuclear alert, which was cancelled on 31 October when the Soviet Union supported a second cease-fire (Document 9.2).

In January 1974 an Israeli–Egyptian disengagement was agreed; both sides withdrew and UN forces were stationed between them. An Israeli–Syrian agreement concerning the Golan was reached only with difficulty, as Israel was unwilling to withdraw from the advantageous position she had won. Kissinger failed to assuage the PLO, which refused to recognize the state of Israel and demanded her withdrawal to the pre-1967 borders. Arafat also claimed the right to speak at any peace conference, and was supported by Arab leaders including his former enemy, Hussein. In October 1974 Arafat addressed the UN General Assembly and was treated as if he were a head of state. The PLO was gaining increased recognition and a chance to recover from the humiliations of 1970.

A more important outcome of the 1973 War was the use of Arab oil as a weapon – against western supporters of Israel.

## Arab oil producers and OPEC, 1960–79

'We do not believe in the use of oil as a political weapon . . . [it is not] not . . . the best way for cooperation with the West.'
                                 Sheikh Yamani of Saudi Arabia, November 1972

Following the nationalization of Iran's oil industry (p. 117), British and US oil companies organized increased output from other countries, and drove Iran to bankruptcy. Other oil-producing nations took note and did not try to expel western companies, although they attempted to force them to increase their payments. Oil companies, resenting this 'blackmail', threatened to cut production in 'greedy' countries and to increase output elsewhere. Venezuela was one of the first countries to suffer. In 1960, aware that her oil would run out by 1990, Venezuela asked for increased payments by oil companies to pay for the development of industries which could provide employment after 1990. Oil companies reacted by threatening to cut production and revenue.

Venezuela then persuaded other oil-producing countries that, faced by united oil companies, they should themselves unite; the Organization of Petroleum Exporting Countries (OPEC) was the result. It took time for OPEC to understand its real power; in 1967 some Arab countries threatened to use their oil as a weapon against western supporters of Israel, but most were unwilling to do so.

In 1970 Gaddaffi asked British and US companies to increase their tax rate from 50 to 55 per cent, and to increase the price of Libyan oil by 30 cents a barrel; within a few weeks the companies had agreed. An Arab government could, it seems, control the companies. At the 1970 OPEC conference, Arab members pushed through a decision to limit oil supplies to the West whenever western policies offended OPEC members. In 1971 Algeria seized control of French oil companies operating there and Libya seized the assets of British companies. In 1972 the oil corporations agreed that Arab states should share the ownership and control of companies operating on their territory. They agreed to provide for a 51 per cent Arab share by 1981. More significantly in the short run, Arab pressure forced the companies to increase the price of oil by 10 cents a barrel.

When the 1973 war began, Arab states raised oil prices by a further 70 per cent and threatened to cut deliveries by five per cent each month until Israel vacated Arab territories and accepted the Palestinians' claims. Moreover, Iraq nationalized parts of certain companies, Libya talked of total expropriation, and oil prices rose sharply; by 1974 they were running at four times their 1972 levels.

Frightened western countries reduced arms supplies to Israel, hoping that their oil supply would not be cut (as Holland's was). Western economies were affected by the flow of money to OPEC, and particularly to the Arab states. Large deficits in the balance of payments led to cuts in the import of non-oil goods, which increased unemployment in exporting countries. Higher oil prices increased the rate of western inflation, already affected by the increased cost of other primary goods (such as wheat, sugar and coffee) in 1972–3. Government attempts to tackle inflation further depressed western economies and lowered the volume of world trade.

Saudi Arabia, the largest oil-producing country, tried to moderate OPEC demands. However, urged on by the Shah of Iran (for domestic reasons) and Gaddaffi (for anti-Zionist reasons), prices continually increased throughout the 1970s: in 1979 a barrel of oil (costing $1.50 in 1972) cost $35. We will study the effects of this in Chapter 20.

## The Egyptian–Israeli détente, 1975–9

'Israel will be astonished when it hears that I am ready to go the Knesset itself to talk.'

Sadat, Cairo, 9 November 1977

In 1975 Kissinger negotiated an agreement between Egypt and Israel providing for new lines of demarcation in the Suez Canal area, and for an American-staffed early warning system in the Sinai to discourage conflict there. A normal flow of traffic through the Canal was to be resumed once it was cleared of wartime debris, and in the Golan, though with more difficulty, the Syrians and the Israelis were eventually separated. To further the peace-making process, Nixon visited the Middle East himself and Sadat went to Washington.

In 1977 Menachem Begin became Prime Minister of Israel. A terrorist in 1945–8 (pp. 115), he planned to build more settlements on the occupied West Bank, although many, including Carter of the USA, condemned this as illegal. It was something of a surprise therefore when, in November 1977, the hard-line Begin invited Sadat to visit Jerusalem. Sadat had by then expelled his Soviet advisers (p. 133), imprisoned leading left-wing members of Nasser's Cabinet, and fought a 'four-day war' along the Libyan–Egyptian border to repel the forces of the fundamentalist Gaddaffi, who was angered by Sadat's lukewarm support for the PLO. Already condemned by Assed of Syria, which was now the centre of the anti-Zionist movement and a major supporter of the PLO, Sadat's acceptance of Begin's invitation led to his further condemnation by the moderate Kings of Jordan and Saudi Arabia, leaving Egypt isolated.

In his address to the Israeli Knesset, Sadat spoke of the need for a settlement. Begin repaid Sadat by going to Cairo, where he spoke of the possibility of creating an autonomous Palestinian 'entity' on the West Bank, with an Israeli military presence being maintained there for twenty years. Although critics in Israel feared that Begin might 'sell out' to the Arabs, talks between Egyptian and Israeli officials went on until September 1978, when Begin and Sadat accepted Carter's invitation to a tripartite conference at Camp David. Here, bilateral peace terms were agreed which they hoped might be the framework for a wider Middle Eastern settlement. Israel agreed to gradually withdraw her forces from the West Bank and Gaza, and to create an autonomous Palestinian 'entity' on the West Bank, with an Israeli military presence. Consideration of all other problems was deferred for five more years.

Carter tried to persuade Jordan and Saudi Arabia to support Sadat's initiative, but they joined the radical anti-Zionists in condemning Sadat's recognition of Israel and his 'betrayal' of the Palestinians. However, not even Sadat's opponents were united. When Feisal convened a meeting of Arab heads of state in 1980, among the absentee nations were anti-royalist Libya, along with Algeria, South Yemen and

Syria, which was opposed to Iraq's claim to be the leading Arab nation. By this time, events in the Lebanon (pp. 137–8) and Iran (pp. 141–2) had thrown Islamic affairs into even greater confusion. There was, it seemed, no room for the moderating voice of Sadat, who was assassinated in 1981 by anti-Zionist fundamentalists within his own armed forces.

## Lebanon, 1975–86

'A spirit of madness is passing over that war-torn country, where reason and common sense are not used, but rather suicide, blood, murder.'
David Levy, Deputy Prime Minister of Israel,
on the Lebanon, March 1985

Lebanon's cat's cradle of religious and economic communities is largely the result of its geography: two parallel mountain ranges cut Lebanon into vertical strips, themselves divided by trans-country barriers. In this grid system, separate communities still maintain individual identities – and mutual hostilities. Within two major religious groups (Muslim and Christian) there are warring factions; the Muslims are divided into the Shia (the majority), the Sunni (who tend to be richer) and the Druzes, who are descended from an eleventh-century breakaway movement with a hereditary homeland in the Chouf mountains where, under Jumblatt, they have developed left-wing tendencies. The Muslim community has become further divided by the emergence of fundamentalist groups which reject traditional leadership and war equally against Shia, Sunni and Druzes paramilitary groups. The three major Christian groups – Maronite, Greek Orthodox and Greek Catholics – are themselves riven with factional rivalries; in the majority Maronite community, the Phalange, led by the Gemayel family, fights the National Liberal Party, led by the Chamoun family. Each of these many religious groups, whether Christian and Muslim, has its own paramilitary force, ostensibly for self-defence, but in reality for increasing its own territorial, economic and political power.

Lebanon once relied on the political skills and self-interest of various group leaders; the banking and commercial centre of the Middle East, it avoided the upheavals which affected Syria, Iraq, Iran and other richer countries. In 1975 this delicate balance was upset by the actions of the PLO, following their expulsion from Jordan (p. 132), and by Israel's success in the 1973 war, which led to an increase in the number of Palestinian refugees in Lebanese camps. These were supported by left wing Muslim groups, who encouraged PLO raids into Israel and threatened the political and economic position of the dominant Maronite Christians inside Lebanon. In 1974 a minor dispute over fishing rights led to rioting by Muslim and Christian fishermen. This rapidly escalated into savage fighting between the pro-PLO Druzes and

Muslims on one side, and on the other Christian groups and the government (the government's army was, naturally, of mixed religious origins). Some Christian leaders wanted to use this fighting as an excuse to drive the PLO from Lebanon, which threatened the fragile unity of the state while providing Israel with an opportunity to intervene. Syria, with historic claims to Lebanon, opposed both Israeli intervention and the break-up of the country into separate religious 'states'. When Syria sent an army to restore peace in Lebanon, Assed of Syria came into conflict with the PLO. A left-wing Syrian army was fighting to sustain a right-wing Christian government: the Israelis could afford to merely look on.

The uneasy peace which Syria imposed on Lebanon following the civil war of 1975–6 was shattered by intra-Christian factional murders; the Lebanese government fell apart, its members forming warring Christian and Muslim groups. In the south, there was fighting between PLO and Christian forces, and Israel came under increasing attack from PLO terrorists. On 14 March 1978 Israeli troops invaded southern Lebanon, 'knocking out' PLO bases and helping the Christian leader, Haddad, to set up a semi-independent state of Free Lebanon in a largely Muslim area. Elsewhere, private armies and assassination squads pursued their factional rivalries, in spite of the presence of a UN Interim Force in Lebanon (UNIFIL), which arranged a cease-fire and then the withdrawal of Israeli forces (June 1978).

In 1980 Gemayel's Phalange gained the upper hand within the Maronite community, following a series of battles with the Chamoun-led Liberal party. This alarmed Assad of Syria, who had once intervened to help Chrisians against the PLO and Druzes, and come under pressure from other Arab states – notably Iraq, which cut off oil supplies to Syria. In 1981 Syrian forces fought the armies of the Lebanese government; this led, in 1982, to a second Israeli invasion of southern Lebanon. The Israeli armies drove through the UNIFIL lines, thrusting northwards to West Beirut where they fought a savage war against Arafat's PLO forces. Assad did not intervene to save Arafat, whom he disliked; it was left to the USA to negotiate a cease-fire (21 August 1982), which led to the expulsion of the PLO from the Lebanon.

The complexity of Lebanese politics deepened as Syrian forces now fought Christian Lebanese in the north, while accepting the humiliation of fellow Muslims in the south. Israeli forces supported the Christian armies in the south as they did in the north, where they aided Gemayel against Syria. Israeli forces were also involved in a separate 'war' against the Druzes, in their mountain heartland, since they tended to support the PLO and were vigorously opposed to Gemayel.

Following the withdrawal of the PLO, Israel agreed to retreat from the south – provided that Syria withdrew her armies from the north. Syria had now become the dominant power in Lebanese affairs, having defeated both the PLO and the Christians. Since Syria was supplied with Soviet weapons and advisers, the USA feared that Syrian success would provide the Soviet Union with a stronger influence on the region. Reagan consequently sent a US fleet and some 1500 troops to 'invade' Lebanon, claiming to act as a peace-maker. Britain, France and Italy also sent troops as part of a multi-national peace-keeping force, which came under attack from Syrian, Druzes and various Muslim armies and had to withdraw.

The weakness of Gemayel's government encouraged rival Christian groups to rebel, which in 1985 led Assad to push his occupying forces further into Lebanon to defend Gemayel (whom he had once humiliated). In the south, Israeli plans to withdraw were affected by the violent guerrilla war in which they and their Christian allies were now engaged: Shi'ite activists had now replaced the PLO as a standing threat to Israel's northern settlements.

Throughout 1986 Assad tried, but failed, to solve the Lebanese puzzle. Gemayel has refused to accept Syrian proposals for peace-and-reform, while Assad shrinks from taking over the country completely, fearing US and Israeli reprisals. Meanwhile, various paramilitary groups continue to wage terrorist war in a country which is now a mere shadow of its former wealthy self.

## The Palestine Liberation Organization, 1982–6

'The partition of Palestine in 1947 and the establishment of Israel are entirely illegal, regardless of the passage of time.'

PLO Charter, 1964

In 1974 Arafat addressed the General Assembly of the UNO (p. 134) in what now seems to have been a high tide in his influence. Although he claimed that the 1982 exodus from Lebanon was 'a victory', PLO forces had to seek refuge in eight different countries and base their new headquarters in Tunis, far from Israel – and a surprising choice, in view of Bourguiba's western stance. From here Arafat organized more terrorist attacks on Israel, including the hijacking of Israeli and other nations' planes, as part of his plan for 'driving the Jews into the sea'. In October 1985 the Israelis bombed his headquarters and forced him to seek refuge in Iraq, which he had avoided in 1982 because it was doing badly in its war with Iran (p. 142) and was hostile to Syria, whose government was already opposed to Arafat.

In 1985 Arafat tried to mend his fences with Hussein of Jordan, the Arab leader who, with Mubarrak of Egypt, most wants a peaceful settlement with Israel. He knows that the most that Israel will accept is some sort of confederation between Jordan and 'a little Palestine' on the West Bank. This would mean Palestinian subordination to Jordan but might allow the later emergence of a fully-fledged 'Palestine' if Israel became convinced that this would not harm her strategic interests.

Arafat may, have privately wished to accept Hussein's position, but equally he may be trapped by his own rhetoric and the hopes of his supporters for a 'greater' Palestine and the elimination of Israel. In 1974 Arab leaders at Rabat, gave the PLO the exclusive mandate for representing the Palestinians. In November 1985 Hussein invited Arafat to negotiate with Israel about the exchange of territory for peace, as laid down in resolution 242 (p. 130). Arafat allowed the King to make overtures on his behalf, primarily to the USA, which Arafat hoped would lead to US recognition of the PLO without the necessity of accepting resolution 242. The nature of his impossible position was illustrated when Britain agreed to receive a delegation from Jordan and the PLO in 1985, provided that the latter accepted the existence of the state of Israel. When the PLO envoys arrived in London they affirmed their opposition to resolution 242, which led the Foreign Office to cancel the proposed meeting, Arafat had fluffed a chance to advance Hussein's search for peace. This pleased some of his supporters within hard-line Arab states such as Syria (which still remains at loggerheads with Arafat and with Iraq). Arafat's apparent willingness to talk with Hussein and the USA does not please his hard-line supporters in the PLO, an organization which retains its federal structure and is riven with factional disputes. Some PLO extremists condemn Arafat as 'the Teflon Palestinian', to whom no failure seems to stick and who enjoys more than a fair share of the wealth poured into the PLO by oil-rich states.

In February 1986 an exasperated Hussein denounced Arafat for having failed to grasp the opportunity to make peace with Israel. Hopes for an Arab–Israeli peace appear to have slipped away. They could only be restored by Arafat's acceptance of resolution 242, or by his replacement with a PLO leader more willing to compromise. Neither seems likely.

## Iran and Iraq, 1968–86

In 1968 Aref of Iraq was overthrown by a military coup which installed General Hasan as President. A government was set up, dominated by the Ba'ath, whose Saddam Hussein was the brutally strong man of the new régime, which settled a long standing dispute with Iraq's Kurdish minority: in March 1970 they were promised a degree of local autonomy, following which several Kurds were admitted to the cabinet (1973) and the region of Kirkuk given its autonomy (1974).

Iraq's loyalty to the pan-Arab cause was called into dispute when 12,000 Iraqi troops stationed in Jordan declined to help the PLO in September 1970. Following the recall of these troops, Iraq tried to win back Arab support; public executions of Israeli 'spies' and other dissidents were offered as evidence of Iraqi commitment to the anti-Israeli front.

In 1979 Hussein took open control of the government after a plot by a rival clan within the Sunni establishment had been foiled. Hussein wanted to restore Iraq's position in the Gulf, where rivals Saudi Arabia and Iran (Figure 9.2) were supported by the USA, so he turned to the USSR, with whom he concluded a treaty (1972) for the supply of arms. Unlike Syria, Iraq did not become dangerously dependent on the Soviet Union; in 1975 Hussein made an agreement with France for the supply of a nuclear reactor and the setting-up of a nuclear research establishment, which particularly alarmed Israel. He also had help from Italy in the training of naval and air officers; moreover, Italy sold a number of warships to Iraq, obviously for use in the event of war in the Gulf.

Hussein also pursued domestic reforms. Major expansions in education and technical training (as an aid to industrial and agricultural development) were financed by oil revenue, which provided 98 per cent of export revenue and 90 per cent of government investment. By 1979, Iraq was the world's second largest exporter of oil.

Iraq's main rival in the Gulf was Iran, which, following the formation of the Union of Arab Emirates (p. 124), seized the islets of Abu Musa and the Tunbs in the narrows between the Persian Gulf and the Gulf of Oman, causing Iraq to break off diplomatic relations and expel Iranians from Iraq. Saudi Arabia, which also wished to control the western shores of the Gulf, connived at the Iranian seizures, which were made easier by Egypt's inability to act (following the 1967 defeat) and by Iraqi involvement in the Kurdish rebellion. Since Egypt would one day recover, and Iraq solve her Kurdish problem, the settlement in the Gulf was far from permanent.

The Shah of Iran, a member of the Baghdad Pact (p. 118), had to take account of his country's long borders with Iraq and the Soviet Union, a major importer of Iranian produce. By 1969–70 he was playing an active role in the Gulf, while using his vast oil revenues to turn Iran into a military and industrial power of major importance. In 1973 he used his power in OPEC to drive up oil prices against the wishes of the more cautious Arabs (p. 135), and Iran's annual revenue went up from $2.3 billion in 1973 to $18.2 billion in 1975.

Industrial expansion was accompanied by waste, corruption and inflation, while the rush of workers to industrial centres led to the development of shanty towns where radical politicians found ready audiences. Opposition to the increasingly tyrannical rule of a man out of touch with his people came from religious leaders, who were opposed to the introduction of western ideas into the Islamic state, and radical students. Only some supported the religious mullahs, but many demonstrated against the evident decadence of a regime which spent $2.5 billion on the celebration of a thousand years of Iranian history, liberal politicians too protested at the ruthless behaviour of the secret police (SAVAK) on whom the Shah relied.

In 1978 unarmed civilians crowded the streets to face the police and armed forces. A frightened Shah invited Shapur Bakhtiar to become Prime Minister (January 1979) but had to agree to leave the country. His departure led to the return of the aged Ayatollah Khomeini, whom the Shah had exiled in 1964. From his Parisian home, Khomeini had attacked the Shah's materialism, and called for Iran's return to the practices of Islam. Rioting demonstrators welcomed Khomeini's return (January 1979) and the flight of Bakhtiar (February 1979). Local Islamic committees, dominated by Khomeini's followers, punished the Shah's supporters and anyone suspected of 'westernization', and implemented fundamental Islamic practices. Radical supporters of Khomeini seized the US embassy in Teheran (1979), holding its occupants as hostages, to the embarrassment of President Carter, whose forces failed to free them and who was forced to pay a humiliating ransom to secure their release.

In 1980 Iraq and Iran went to war; the weakness of Iran after the Shah's fall tempted Hussein to mount an attack. Iran was now led by Khomeini, whose religious fanaticism had aroused unrest among the Shia majority over whom Hussein ruled in Iraq. Evidence that Khomeini had been involved in Shia rioting at the end of 1979, and in an unsuccessful coup against Hussein in the summer of 1980, was allied to fear that he might intrigue with Iraqi Kurds to threaten Iraq's oil interests in the Kirkuk region.

The immediate causes of the war, which broke out in September 1980, were rival claims on the Shat al-Arab waterway (Figure 9.2) which forms part of the frontier between the two countries. The Shat carries the waters of the Euphrates and Tigris Rivers into the Gulf. These rise in Iraq and along their course to the sea, are joined by the Iranian River Karun. The Shat is Iraq's only outlet to the sea, and carries Iranian traffic to Khorramshahr and Abadan. In 1969 Iraq had claimed the Shat as its own territorial water; Iran's support for the Kurdish revolt forced Iraq to accept a deal in 1975 by which the Shah stopped aiding the Kurds, and Iraq agreed that the Shat belonged equally to both countries, thus accepting 'a middle-water frontier'. In 1980 Hussein declared this agreement at an end, and claimed the whole of the Shat.

In the ensuing war, Iraq has been armed by the USSR, which led many western powers to assume that the Soviet Union would gain more power in the Gulf while she was also asserting control in Afghanistan (p. 146). However, even western-oriented Arab states such as Jordan and Saudi Arabia have supported Iraq, because they fear Khomeini's fundamentalism. Syria, Libya, Algeria, the Yemen and the PLO opposed Iraq because they want a united Arab drive against Israel. This division was revealed at the Arab summit of November 1980 (pp. 136–7).

Iraq may have hoped for a speedy victory. However, the savage war has continued, with both sides able to bomb each other's cities and launch major tank and military attacks over generally unfavourable

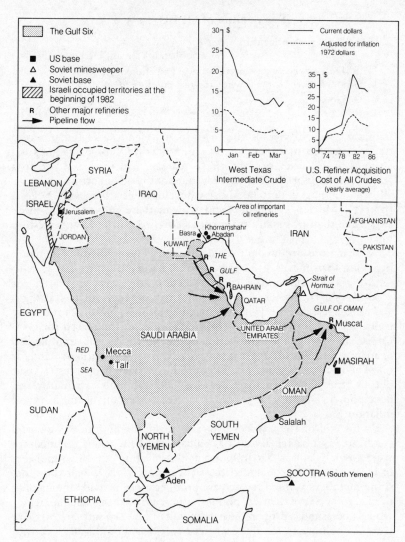

**9.2** The Gulf states rely for their wealth on their oil exports, but oil prices have fluctuated widely since 1972

ground, without being able to claim a major victory. Neutral shipping has been attacked by both sides; their oil exports have dropped so that these previously rich countries have become poorer, forcing both to rely on aid from interested parties.

## The decline of OPEC, 1985–6

'We don't want a price war.'

Sheikh Yamani, December 1985

'This [December] collapse occurred in anticipation of troubles. You can imagine what will happen when the real flooding of an already glutted market begins.'

Stockbrokers, Merrill Lynch, 1985

Increases in oil prices in the 1970s (p. 135) led to a decline in world trade, rising unemployment in the western world, business failures and an industrial deceleration which, as Yamani had predicted, led to a falling demand for oil. The vast revenues of the oil exporting countries allowed them to undertake massive development schemes; in Nigeria (p. 157), Mexico, Venezuela and Kuwait these proved to be more expensive than originally planned, as costs rose in line with western inflation.

Some nations producing oil had assumed a low elasticity of demand, believing that increased oil prices would hardly affect it. This was to ignore the effects of the trade recession, the western search for economies in the use of oil, the use of substitute fuels such as coal, gas and electricity, and the drop in demand by airlines, motorists and other users. It also showed OPEC's misjudgement of the search for non-OPEC oil sources; the exploitation of the North Sea, for example, led to an increased world supply just as there was a fall in world demand for oil. The result was that since 1981 producers have had to lessen their output, and have seen their incomes fall, although expenditure on development schemes has tended to increase, as a result of ambition and inflation.

By the end of 1985, prices had fallen from the high of $37 a barrel (1979) to $25 a barrel. Even at $25 a barrel, OPEC countries' incomes were down by at least $40 million a day. A meeting of OPEC ministers in December 1985 concluded that it was powerless to halt the slide; some members wanted to increase production to provide the income needed to preserve their economies; others warned that such increases would necessitate a drop in the production of other countries (and there were no volunteers for this sacrificial role), or would lead to further price falls.

In the Gulf, there was a slow decrease in development, leading to an exodus of foreign workers, mainly Asians, who had been drawn to the region by earlier construction work. The decline enabled Khomeini's fundamentalists to find fertile ground in the discontent affecting the 'depressed' area. Every country was affected: in 1986 Saudi Arabia sold less than half the oil sold in 1981, and its expenditure for 1985–6 was one-third less than it was in 1981–2. Four refinery projects have been shelved, and 14,000 jobs lost in its oil industry; in Bahrain, three of the off-shore banks set up to recycle the volume of petro-dollars in 1978–9 have been closed down, and others have cut their staffs; Kuwait, where the stock market collapsed in 1982–3, is now trying to shore up several banks, and reorganize a dozen bankrupt industries; the United Arab Emirates, which had a current account surplus of $10 billion in 1981, had a balance of zero in 1986.

Because 1986 proved to be a worse year than Yamani had feared when addressing OPEC in December 1985 (as can be seen in Figure 9.2) prices continued to fall until August 1986, when an OPEC agreement to cut output led to a small rise in prices. No one is sure that this agreement can hold; if it does not, prices may well fall to $5 a barrel. More significantly for the OPEC countries, the real price in oil (allowing for inflation) is now little above its 1972 level, whereas the prices paid for imports into OPEC countries have risen in real terms. When the cartel was formed in 1982, its members thought that they would be able to dictate prices and levels of supply; their experience in 1972–3 and 1979 suggested that, in the short term at least, they were right. In 1985–6 however, they have suffered what one observer described as 'the oil market's 1929; it was catastrophic'. Some believe that OPEC may recover its position of strength in the 1990s; in the meantime, they have little power to halt the downward spiral of prices and demand.

## Afghanistan and the Soviet Union, 1979–86

'We are expanding the base of the Afghan revolution.'
*Pravda*, 27 December 1985

Afghanistan has never been considered a part of the Middle East; in the nineteenth century Britain and Russia fought over it because of its proximity to India. However, the Soviet invasion at Christmas 1979 led to a Middle Eastern crisis because it brought Soviet forces within striking distance of the Persian Gulf – and western oil supplies.

In 1973 Mohammad Daud organized a coup which deposed the king, abolished the monarchy and established a republic in Afghanistan. Helped to power by a section of the communist Peoples' Democratic Party, Daud knew that his country was by international connivance part of the Soviet sphere of influence, the only non-communist state to get Soviet aid from 1953 onwards. Nonetheless, he tried to play East off against West, accepting aid from the Shah and from the USA, and persecuting the rural section of the Communist party led by Taraki and Hafizullah.

In 1978 a revolution by a section of the army installed Taraki and Hafizullah in power. Their socialist reforms angered landowners while their attitude towards Islam angered the clergy, already affected by the world-wide upsurge in Islamic fundamentalism. Widespread unrest followed, during which the US Ambassador, fifty Soviet advisers and other foreigners were killed, leading to a dispute in which the Soviet

Union encouraged Taraki to seize power. The plot failed: Hafizzullah took power after killing Taraki, but allowed himself to be tricked into asking for Soviet aid to restore order in his restless country. Soviet forces invaded Afghanistan at Christmas 1979, executed Hafizullah and installed one of Daud's supporters, Babrak Karmal, as their puppet ruler.

Brezhnev hoped for a short, successful war. Instead, his successors have fought, and Gorbachev is fighting, a costly guerrilla war which has been called 'Russia's Vietnam'. The Soviet forces face an impôssible task in fighting the guerrillas who are armed by Pakistan and at home in the mountains. Early in 1986, Gorbachev proposed an international agreement which would have allowed him to pull his forces out. Pakistan refused to sign such an agreement until the Soviets present an unequivocal and detailed plan for withdrawal; India, at odds with Pakistan for many years, agrees with her on this. Babrak Karmal, on the other hand, would not agree to a Soviet withdrawal before Pakistan had given full recognition to his government. His displacement in the spring of 1986 provided Gorbachev with the opportunity of proposing a Soviet retreat, but the withdrawal of some 7500 troops still left over 175,000 in Afghanistan, and the USA, Pakistan and India were not tempted to take up any Soviet offer. The war goes on.

## Documentary evidence

James Cameron, as a reporter, covered Arab–Israeli affairs for almost forty years after 1945. In 1967 he watched as Egypt and Israel drifted into war (Document 9.1), and in 1978 he wrote about the apparently powerful Shah of Iran (Document 9.3) who enriched himself from the increase in oil prices but whose power was much more apparent than real; his domestic policies led to his overthrow a year after Cameron's article appeared. The Shah and the King of Saudi Arabia were the props on which the USA tended to build its Middle Eastern policies. The Soviet Union, which had been pro-Israeli in 1945–7, became anti-Israeli once the new state developed into a client of the USA; in the 1950s and 1960s the Soviet Union therefore tended to support Nasser's Egypt. However, in the search for détente, the Soviet Union joined with the USA to try to impose peace in the region. That fragile détente was threatened in October 1973, when the Soviet government seemed ready to send Soviet 'peace-keeping forces' following Israeli success in the Yom Kippur war. President Nixon (Document 9.2) put US forces on a nuclear alert and there was a real danger of a Third World War.

## Document 9.1

*The Six Day War, 1967*

'The Middle East war which now seems inevitable must be recorded as the most stupid, wholly political war of all time, and yet I comprehend the folly only too well.

For all their demonstrations each side of the border, nobody really wants to fight, and to carry their attitudinizing to the point of getting painfully killed. The mad thing about the Israel–Egypt confrontation, which is a local row, is that it puts the whole world once again on the barricades, and for an issue that few understand. The blockade of the Tiran Strait means something to me; ten years ago I was with the Israeli group that 'liberated' it, which meant that the Egyptians should no longer threaten Israel's one passage to the east. To have access to the outer world is of importance to Israel. This is the issue over which Israel could go to war.

I am only too aware of Jewish impatience, chauvinism and arrogance. Nobody should know better; I was part of that early exhilarating nonsense [1947–8]. It is still fair to say that this crisis, which may embroil us all, is none of Israel's choosing. This is probably the most vulnerable state in the world, three million people surrounded by fifty million Arabs dedicated to its destruction.

At this moment Tel Aviv is a city transformed. I was here only weeks ago – it was gay then, and merry; it is not so now. The mobilization has taken away one's friends, reduced our taxi-ranks. Every citizen of Israel is in fact a soldier and every vehicle is a hostage to war, every single concern and aspect of this extraordinary society is part of a psychology that is on the defensive yesterday, today, and tomorrow. I remember it so well from the old days; one had hoped those days were done. One was foolish; they will endure for ever.

Nobody knows what will happen. We are waiting for the return of Foreign Minister Eban [Document 9.3] who has been canvassing support for Israel in the US, with three times as many Jews as Israel, [and] in London whose last public face was that of an obsequious welcome to that prince of antisemites, Feisal of Saudi Arabia.'

(James Cameron, *Evening Standard*, 28 May 1967)


## Document 9.2

### *Nixon on the Soviet threat, October 1973*

'I think it is important for you to know why the United States has insisted that major Powers not be part of the peace-keeping force, and should not introduce military forces into the Mideast.

A potentially explosive crisis developed on Wednesday [24 October]. We obtained information that the Soviet Union was planning to send a very substantial force into the Mideast. When I received that information, I ordered, shortly after midnight on Thursday morning, an alert for all American forces around the world. This was a precautionary alert to indicate to the Soviet Union that we could not accept any unilateral move on their part. At the same time, I also proceeded on the diplomatic front. In a message to Mr Brezhnev, I indicated our reasoning, urged that we not proceed along that course, and that, instead, we join in the UN in supporting a resolution which would exclude any major Powers from participating in a peace-keeping force.

As a result of the return that I received from Mr Brezhnev, we reached the conclusion that we would jointly support the resolution which was adopted in the UN. We now come, of course, to the critical time in terms of the future of the Mideast. And here, the outlook is far more hopeful. I think I could safely say that the chance for not just a cease-fire, which we have had in the Mideast for some time, but the outlook for a permanent peace is the best it has been in 20 years, for the Soviet Union and the United States have agreed that we would participate in trying to expedite the talks between the parties involved.'

(*Keesing's Contemporary Archives*, 1973)

## Document 9.3

*The repressive, but oil-rich, Shah of Iran, 1978*

'Not everyone likes the Shah as much as does Mr James Callaghan, or the Shah's methods of dealing with his dissidents, by shooting them dead in public thoroughfares when they have the impertinence to demonstrate against an oppressive and tyrannical régime. "My government has been heartened by the determination which you have shown to maintain the stability and security of Iran along the lines of your present Monarchy. We wish your government well. . . ." It somehow seemed a gratuitous piece of bootlicking. However, since Britain's trade with Iran is now worth around £2,000 million, a little fawning is doubtless in order.

What I still like to call Persia, but the Persians call Iran, is still not especially familiar ground to those who are not in the business of oil or armaments. The general image is of a sandy landscape punctuated by petroleum installations, ruled by a vastly well-to-do despot with a penchant for elegant uniforms and the marrying, and subsequently divorcing, of very attractive wives.

Having visited the country from time to time I would say that is not a wholly inaccurate definition. It is natural that almost the whole symbol of this great nation to us should be its head man, the Shah. Those who have met him describe him as well-intentioned. A benevolent despot is the phrase, though the benevolence has not been apparent of late.

The British have this curious attachment to monarchy, feeling that it represents some age-long continuity. This attribute is also fostered by the Shah. A year or two back he threw a lavish celebration to mark what was presented as a thousand years of royal rule, the implication being that the Shah is the current incarnation of a long, long line. This, of course, was a total illusion.

In October 1925 the last of the ruling Qajar dynasty was deposed after a rebellion led by Reza Khan, a soldier in the Cossack Regiment. He had himself made the Shah, the first of his line, the father of the present chap.

When the Second World War came about he made the serious miscalculation of going along with the Axis. Then, when the Germans invaded the USSR in 1941, Anglo–Soviet forces moved into Persia and booted him out. His successor, the present incumbent, very prudently switched sides.

In 1951 the Persian Parliament ordained the nationalization of the oil industry, which consisted of what is now BP. Dr Mossadiq became Prime Minister and another row broke out, during which this new Shah left the country. After the smoke died he returned. So much for the age-long lineage.

As I said, not everyone seems to share Mr Callaghan's appreciation of the firm smack of Persian Government. All over London Tube Stations are graffiti which say "Down with the Shah". All over the Paris Metro the same slogan appears. It is to be seen, in its incomprehensible bitterness, in Hamburg, Amsterdam, Rome and Bangaloree.

It is clear that there is some international orchestration of overseas Persians who do not like the Shah, and who presumably are overseas for that reason.

The security forces in Iran open fire on civilians in the street. The British

Government is "heartened by their determination". I suppose it is understandable. Oil must be much on Mr Callaghan's mind just now.'

(*Guardian*, 2 October 1978)


FURTHER READING

As for Chapter 8, plus
BAKHASH, S., *The Reign of the Ayatollahs: Iran and the Islamic Revolution*,
   Tauris, 1985
FREEDMAN, R. O., ed., *The Middle East Since Camp David*, Westview, 1984
KORANY, B. and DESSOUKI, ALI E. H., eds., *The Foreign Policies of the Arab
   States*, Westview, 1984
RAZAVI, H. and VAKIL, F., *The Political Environment of Economics Planning in
   Iran, 1971–1983*, Westview, 1984

# 10

# Africa from the Sahara to the Zambezi

## Hopes and realities – European and African

' "What's wrong with Hitler?" asked an African. "He wants to rule the whole world," said the British officer, trying to explain in terms conceivable to the African mind. "He's a German and it is not good for one tribe to rule another. Each tribe must rule itself. A German must rule Germans, an Italian, Italians, and a Frenchman, French people." ' '
Ndabaningi Sithole, in *African Nationalism*

The wartime interview must have puzzled the African: in 1945 only Ethiopia, Liberia and the Union of South Africa were strictly independent, although Egypt enjoyed a decree of autonomy. Within thirty years the whole continent was virtually free of colonial rule. Almost everywhere, black nationalists had formed political parties as vehicles for their demands for independence (Documents 10.1a and b); almost everywhere, Europeans had taken a paternal attitude towards 'their boys' (Document 10.3a) and seen independence as a (very) far-distant prospect (Document 10.1b).

Black nationalists believed that, once independent, their peoples would enjoy economic development, rising living standards, national unity, democracy, the promotion of Human Rights and Pan-African understanding (Document 10.1a). Unfortunately, most independent states have experienced waste, corruption, inefficient government and the mishandling of economic affairs, along with tribalism and civil war, and the disappearance of democracy in the face of military coups. The Belgians had hoped to provide a long period of preparation for Congo's independence (Document 10.3b). However, they, and to a lesser extent Britain, France and the other powers, were forced to allow a headlong rush to independence, leaving inexperienced peoples to grapple with the Third World problems (Chapter 20) facing most African countries. These problems frequently included a harsh climate, a shortage of water, the prevalence of disease, an over-dependence on one crop or mineral, a shortage of natural resources, a lack of an economic and social infra-structure (roads, skilled workers and technically qualified leaders) and, finally, a low per capita income, limiting the scope for self-financing economic development.

## The Gold Coast becomes Ghana

'Our economy is healthy, we have great potential . . . we are not afflicted by religious or tribal problems.'
                    Nkrumah to the National Assembly, 15 July 1953

As elsewhere in Africa, the borders of the Gold Coast were artificially created by Europeans, who ignored African history and the nature of tribal development. Within the Gold Coast's borders were four regions, each governed separately by the British Colonial administration: the 'colony' along the coast, the territory of the Ashanti, a northern region and Togoland (Document 10.1a). The country was shared by three religious groups – Muslims, Animists and Christians of various denominations. It was also socially and economically divided between feudal landowners, rural middle-class cocoa-growers, urban middle-class traders and professional people, and a working class found in towns and mining areas.

For years, Britain had governed through the agency of the tribal chiefs. A new constitution (March 1946) attempted to reconcile British interests with the claims of these chiefs, and with the radical demands for increased democracy put forward by the United Gold Coast Convention Party; this was founded in 1941 by J. B. Danquah with the support of intellectuals, small traders, journalists, skilled workers and school teachers (Document 10.1b). The 1946 Constitution proposed an African majority in the Legislative Council (21 as against ten Europeans) and the appointment of three Africans to serve on the Governor's Executive Council. Danquah's supporters pointed out that 13 of the Africans in the Legislature were to be elected by the traditionally subservient (to Britain) Council of Chiefs and only eight democratically elected. In 1947 Danquah demanded a quickening in the process of transforming the country. Kwame Nkrumah was called back from his studies in the USA to be secretary-general in the UGCCP, but quickly quarrelled with Danquah, who wanted it to be a small, moderate party; while Nkrumah wanted a mass movement to rally support for nationalist demands. In February 1948 Danquah blamed Nkrumah for organizing the anti-European riots which led to the arrests of the Party's executive. When he was released from prison, Nkrumah founded the Convention People's Party (Document 10.1b), demanding full and immediate independence for the Gold Coast.

New constitutional proposals put forward by the British in 1949–50 would still have left power in the hands of the chiefs. Nkrumah's party organized riots against these British plans and, again, he was jailed.

Under the new constitution, proclaimed on 30 December 1950, the Legislative Council became the National Assembly, consisting of 75 elected African members and a small number of members representing British interests. The Executive Council, the main instrument of government, was made up of three ex officio European members and eight Africans chosen from the Assembly. The general election of February 1951 was a triumph for the imprisoned Nkrumah's party which won 34 of the 38 rural and municipal seats and, with the support of other 'designated' members, had a majority in the Assembly. Nkrumah was released from prison to form the first Cabinet of the Gold Coast, and in March 1952 he was named Prime Minister.

Nkrumah's government faced many problems. The hostility of the chiefs, tribal rivalry, and the antipathy of the African intellectual élite to democracy, combined with British attempts to slow down the pace of the march to independence. However, Nkrumah continued to campaign for full autonomy and in 1956, at the request of the Colonial Office, he drew up a new constitution, put to the electorate in July 1956. The CCP won 72 of the 104 seats, and was therefore in a strong position to enter into negotiations with Britain. Following these, the constitution was amended to provide five regional assemblies with strong powers, and an assembly of chiefs in each region; any further constitutional changes would require a two-thirds majority in the National Parliament and a two-thirds majority in the regional assemblies. These changes being approved, Ghana became fully independent on 6 March 1957, and British Togoland was incorporated into the new state.

The first black government in Africa then set about developing its country. Provision was made for the expansion of cattle farming, fishing, forestry and related industries; water supplies were improved within villages; the Volta River Project was initiated, to produce electricity for domestic consumers and provide power for an aluminium smelter, while improving agricultural irrigation. Widespread social reforms were implemented; a programme for school building aimed to make primary education more freely available, while hospital building enabled the establishment of a national health service. At the same time, there was also a good deal of wasteful 'prestige development', in the form of new government buildings, a television and broadcasting station, and a rarely used motorway linking Accra and Toma. Private investment was encouraged, but often took the form of western-type hotels built in Accra.

To pay for these developments Nkrumah borrowed heavily. Debt repayment was always going to be difficult, but it became almost impossible when cocoa prices tumbled in the late 1950s. This led to cuts in imports, along with attempts to increase the volume of exports, and a halt to some development schemes. In the face of unemployment, inflation and evidence of waste and corruption, some Ghanaians become restless. An abortive army plot to overthrow Nkrumah (1958) led him to adopt a repressive policy; under the Preventative Detention Act (1959), Danquah and other Opposition MPs were imprisoned without trial. Nkrumah then purged his party to get rid of critics, and deported Muslim leaders who attacked the corruption of many of his ministers. In July 1960 Ghana became a Republic within the Commonwealth. Nkrumah claimed that in a plebiscite 90 per cent of the population approved of the change, following which he became increasingly autocratic. The Chief Justice was sacked for not convicting three of Nkrumah's party accused of plotting against him, the Constitution was amended to give him the power to overturn Supreme Court decisions; and a referendum was organized to approve the establishment of a one-party State.

The continuing slump in cocoa prices and the corruption involved in ministerial extravagances soon led to a major recession, during which Nkrumah turned to the Soviet Union for help. This alarmed the army, which announced Nkrumah's overthrow in February 1966 (while he was in Peking). A new democratic constitution, set up in 1969, was followed by elections. These were won by the Progress Party, led by Kofi Bassia, who set up a civilian government. However, a serious economic recession in 1971 led to further unrest, and military intervention: on 13 January 1972 Colonel Acheampong arrested the civilian administration, withdrew the 1969 constitution and proposed rule by decree through a Supreme Military Council. By 1978 his rule had also become both corrupt and incapable of coping with the country's economic problems, made worse by the increases in oil prices (p. 135). He was ousted by General Akuffo, who lasted less than a year before being overthrown by Flight Lieutenant Jerry Rawlings. After the coup, Rawlings executed both Acheampong and Akuffo, promised to end corruption, reverse the economic decline and restore civilian rule. Only the latter promise was fulfilled, and then only for a short time: after an election, Dr Hilla Limann was installed as president of a country with a collapsing economy, aggravated social tensions and little faith in politicians. It was only a short time before Rawlings reimposed military rule, a far cry from the optimism of 1953 – and an unhappy illustration of what has happened throughout post-colonial Africa.

## France and her African possessions

'Let us not take the calm which reigns in black Africa as a sign of total indifference to what is happening in North Africa.'

Gaston Déferre, 7 June 1957

'I have directed France's policy to the emancipation of peoples.'

President de Gaulle, 5 September 1960

At a 1944 Conference held at Brazzaville, the Gaullists promised more African participation in mixed Franco–African councils, as well as more decentralization and a wider franchise. In 1946 a new French Constitution created the French Union in which West and Equitorial African territories became 'Associated Territories', sending representatives to the French National Assembly and the Council of the Republic (Document 10.2). In 1956 Déferre, Minister for Overseas Territories, introduced the *loi cadre* providing a large degree of internal autonomy to these states: this included a universal franchise, elected councils and the Africanization of public services. It also meant ending the policy of integration, in favour of a freer Federation in which African countries ran their own affairs and developed their own services.

Under decrees passed in 1957, each of the twelve West and Equitorial African territories had Assemblies elected on a common roll, and Executive Councils elected by those Assemblies. With the elimination of special votes for whites, every constituency had a majority of black voters. The Rassemblement Démocratique Africain, the principal nationalist party in French West Africa, won the ensuing elections in Guinea, Soudan, the Ivory Coast and Upper Volta.

While conceding political change, France maintained an integrationist economic policy: in return for aid, and guaranteed markets in France, French African states had to serve French economic interests. Africans became increasingly dissatisfied with a system which impeded their economic growth, and prevented economic diversification. Some, among whom Sekou Touré of Guinea was the most eminent, also criticized the *loi cadre* as a device postponing independence.

In 1958 de Gaulle offered the African states a choice between independence and autonomy within the French Community (with France retaining economic control). Only Guinea chose independence; cut off from French aid, she turned to the Communist bloc for assistance. However, other states soon became discontented with French economic control. In 1959 Senegal, Soudan, Upper Volta and Dahomey decided to federate under the name of Mali, and ask for independence. Under French pressure Upper Volta and Dahomey changed their minds, while Senegal withdrew from the new federation after a few months. This left Soudan with the name of Mali, at war in 1986 with Burkina Faso (the former Upper Volta) over a mineral-rich strip along the border between two of the poorest states in Africa.

The concept of the Mali Federation was unpopular in other French African states, but led Houphet-Boigny of the Ivory Coast to form the Council of the Entente with Niger, and the detached Upper Volta and Dahomey. This obtained its independence in 1960, only to disintegrate (following coups in Upper Volta and Dahomey) in the face of suspicion within other African states that the Ivory Coast was too hostile to the charismatic Nkrumah, and too friendly to the pro-Belgian Tshombé in the Congo (p. 158).

The independence of the Entente countries in 1960 deprived the Community of any meaning, leading the French Equitorial states

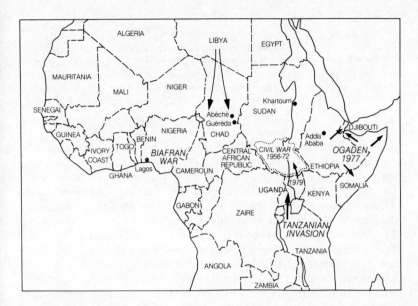

**10.1** The restless states of Central Africa

(Gabon, Chad, Ubangi-Shari and the French Congo) to produce an abortive plan for a federation, following which they too became separate sovereign states. In quest for common action, many of the former French states came to be known as the Monrovian Powers when they met with Ethiopia and other African states at Monrovia, Liberia, in 1961. They created an organization of inter-African states, a form of successor to the French Community and a forerunner of the Organization of African Unity, set up in Addis Abbaba in 1963 to promote unity and solidarity throughout the continent.

The former French states have suffered from various common post-colonial problems; these include corruption, military coups, dictatorships, tribalism and civil war. In Chad, the Arabs of the north and the Christians of the south have engaged in civil war since April 1980. Gaddaffi's attempts to defeat the rebels alarmed other African leaders who saw this as a Libyan attempt to expand southwards (see Fig. 10.1). The former French states also suffered from the oil-price increases of the 1970s, and from the effects of the world recession in which the prices of their primary products fell (Figure 14.1). Attempts to industrialize often led to an influx of rural people into growing towns, creating the problem of feeding an expanding urban population. In the search for urban popularity, many governments have tried to hold down food prices artificially, sometimes, as in Mali (1977–81), to the point where farming becomes so unprofitable that even farmers starve.

## Nigeria

'The money shop sells the Nigerian naira at N5.2 for a £. The official rate is N1.3 for a £. Bankers lend to politicians who change it into pounds at the official rate, then sell these on the open market for more naira, then turn these into sterling which they then sell. . . . You can now collect four times your entry money each time you pass "Go".'

*The Economist*, 21 December 1985

Nigeria is one of the largest and most populous countries in Africa, as well as the most potentially rich. Its fifty million people, from 150 different tribes, were brought together by the British who united the colonies of Lagos and South Nigeria in 1906, retaining a separate administration for the large agricultural north with its Islamic tribes. Even in 1945 the people of the north were socially and economically less advanced than the Yoruba of the west or the Ibo of the east, who dominated the commercial, industrial and official life of the country. The British, however, encouraged tribe-based political parties, and in 1946 created three self-governing regions in the colony, each dominated by a particular tribal group.

Nmandi Azikiwe ('Zik'), an American-educated Ibo, organized a strike of southern workers in 1945 which prompted the government to issue its federal constitution in 1946, giving each region a local Assembly with a central (federal) government in Lagos. In the Federal House of Representatives, 64 seats were reserved for the North; the West and East were allocated 34 seats each. The Council of Ministers consisted of four Ministers from each state.

In 1960 Nigeria became an independent Federal State, and in 1963 a Republic, with 'Zik' as President and a Northerner, Abubakar Tafewa Balewa, as Prime Minister. Almost immediately there was tribal unrest. Accusations of dishonesty at the 1965 elections led Balewa to order the arrest of the Yoruba leader, Awolowo, Prime Minister of the Western Region, amid accusations of election-rigging by both Ibo and Yoruba. In the rioting which followed, some 2000 people died. The unrest spread, and in January 1966 Prime Minister Balewa, Yoruba leader Akintola and the Northern Premier, the Sardauna of Sokoto, were murdered.

This political unrest was accompanied by economic recession: by 1966 inflation was running at 15 per cent, unemployment was rising and wages were below the level of the legally-fixed living wage. The Ibo general, Ironsi, led a coup setting up a military government, and promised to divide the country into many provinces, in an attempt to end regional nationalism. Northern Hausas, fearing the loss of their power, attacked Ibos living in the North and, in a new coup, the Northern General Gowon had Ironsi killed along with some 30,000 Ibos living in the North. The remaining Ibos fled to their eastern heartland, where, in May 1967, Colonel Ojukwu announced the region's secession under the name of Biafra.

During the civil war which ensued, Biafrans died from disease and starvation, as well as on the battlefield, before Ojukwu surrendered in January 1970. After the war, Gowon's government faced many problems; rising unemployment and increased tribal hatred compounded the need for a constitution to limit regional powers. Gowon reconciled the Ibo with the other tribes and persuaded them to return to their posts in other parts of the country. He then devised a constitution which divided the nation into nineteen States. In this he was helped by the increased revenue from Nigeria's oil, which provided a balance of payments surplus and allowed for industrial and commercial development.

Fearing that Gowon intended to return the country to civilian rule, a northerner, Murtalla Muhammad, organized a coup which ousted Gowon. Murtalla was assassinated within six months and power passed to General Obansanjo; he handed over power to civilians in 1979, after elections which led to a northern Muslim becoming the country's first (US-style) President. He retained his office after elections in 1983, although, by then, many people were complaining of the continuing corruption of a country affected by the economic oil-induced crisis. Increased revenues from oil in the 1970s had led Nigeria to produce economic plans based on the assumption that she would sell 3 million barrels of oil a day at the 1979 price of $35 a barrel. The fall in oil prices after 1981 (p. 144), coupled with the inflated prices which Nigeria had to pay for her capital imports, led to deficits in the balance of payments, cuts in government spending and a reduction in the level of imports. This caused a rise in urban unemployment, accompanied by increased taxation and more corruption as ministers sold scarce import licences. The rich life-style of corrupt officials and ministers was in stark contrast with the harder lives of the majority.

In December 1983 a budget proposed more tax increases and cuts in government spending. Naturally, this led to a further fall in living standards. Major-General Buhari organized the fifth military coup since independence and set up a military government which made the usual promises – an end to corruption and tribal divisions, and a restoration of the economy. Buhari failed, and yet another coup led to the establishment of a military government under General Babangida. In 1985 he was forced to ask for help from the IMF (p. 36), since Nigeria was unable to meet the interest payments on its foreign debts; the help was refused until Nigeria devalued its naira (August 1986), and imposed a severe credit squeeze on the domestic economy. Babangida faced opposition from many army officers and licence-selling officials, as well as others who gained from an overvalued currency. It remains to be seen whether he will prevail, and bring some order into the affairs of this once rich country.

## The Belgian Congo becomes Zaire

'The object of paternalist policy [Document 10.3a] is to make the native
someone who is assisted, insured and pensioned . . . a sort of vegetable.'
                                        H. Slade, *The Belgian Congo*

In the Congo there were no preparations for the independence of this
vast country with a population of about 15 million, divided into 150
tribes. Many Africans had benefitted as the colony developed,
becoming traders, merchants and skilled workmen. These *évolués*
resented the fact that they had no political or civil rights, and supported
the demands of the small African professional class, the product of the
education system, for an end to enervating paternalism (Document
10.3a) and a chance to be assimilated into the European political and
civil system. As in Algeria (p. 119) so in the Congo: Europeans refused
to change the system. Both their objections to, and the Africans'
demands for, change grew as other African states gained freedom.

In 1957 the Belgians allowed local elections to take place, but refused
to permit the formation of African political parties. Even at the local
council level, administration remained in European hands, for there
were few adequately qualified Africans. There were almost no African
army officers, graduates or senior civil servants, and certainly few
Africans with real administrative experience. In 1957–8 Patrice
Lumumba, a Post Office clerk of the Batatela tribe, founded the
Congolese National Movement demanding early independence, but
received only lukewarm support from other tribal groups. In January
1959 large-scale riots in the capital, Leopoldville, caused by rising
unemployment, turned into political demonstrations which led the
King of the Belgians to issue a statement which seemed to promise
ultimate freedom (Document 10.3a) for the Congo.

In January 1960, to almost everyone's surprise, the Belgians
announced that they would quit the Congo in June 1960; the Africans
had six months to prepare for independence. Elections were held in
which Lumumba's party was opposed by parties led by Kasavubu, the
aristocratic leader of the Bakongo; by Tshombe, a rich middle-class
*évolué* leader of the Balunda from Katanga; and by Sendwe of the
Balubakat. These, and some fifty other tribal leaders, often wanted
completely different things. Lumumba advocated a strong central
government in a loosely federated state; Kasavubu wanted an
independent state for his people or a federal state in which central
government would have limited powers; Tshombe aimed at power in
Katanga, either independently or as part of a federal Congo in which he
would have the political power to match the economic power of his
mineral-rich state.

Lumumba led the largest party in a parliament of fifty parties, and
became Prime Minister, with Kasavubu as President. Within days the
army mutinied, in an effort to replace the Belgian officers, who

remained in control, with Africans. There was also tribal violence, and the Belgians encouraged Tshombe to set up the independent state of Katanga, containing most of their valuable mines. The army mutiny made it impossible for Lumumba to deal with either the tribalism or Katanga's secession. He appealed to the UN (Document 16.3B–E), which feared that if tribalism succeeded in the Congo other African states might suffer. A UN force of some 3000 men was sent to restore order, but refused to interfere in internal political affairs which drove Lumumba to seek Soviet help against Katanga. Kasavubu, violently anti-communist, dismissed him. After unrest in the capital, Kasavubu accepted the seizure of power by ex-sergeant, now Colonel, Joseph Mobutu. His reign lasted for only six months before he was replaced by a government under Lumumba's aide, Ileo. He in turn was overthrown by another Lumumba follower, Adoula.

Throughout this restless period, attempts were made to draw together the factions led by Tshombe and Lumumba. These failed, and Lumumba was murdered by Tshombe's men, who feared a Soviet takeover of the Congo. This might have been welcomed by Gizenga, however, the leader of the Lumumbists after their founder's death. The UN refused to accept Katanga's 'declaration of independence' (Document 16.3F), but would not allow its forces to attack the Belgian-led Katangese army. There was a change of mind in September 1961, and 20,000 UN soldiers invaded Katanga, crushed the rebellion by December 1962, and forced Tshombe into exile.

Tribal violence continued after the UN forces left. In July 1964 Kasavubu recalled Tshombe and named him Prime Minister. Tribal opposition to his rule was stamped out by European mercenaries; this made him unpopular in Africa, while food shortages made him unpopular at home. In October 1965 Tshombe was dismissed, and again went into exile, condemned to death in his absence. In 1967 an aircraft in which he was flying was hijacked; he was imprisoned in Algeria, where he died in 1969.

Tshombe's fall in 1965 led Mobutu to seize power, with the active support of the USA (fearing Soviet intervention) and Belgium (concerned for its mining interests). With the aid of white mercenaries Mobutu crushed all resistance, installed himself as President and set up an autocratic government. He dismissed his white mercenaries once his power was assured, and nationalized Belgian-owned mines. Having ended Belgian influence, in 1971 he renamed the country Zaire. In 1977 Katanga was invaded by troops from Angola, in revenge for Mobutu's earlier intervention in her affairs who were supported by the USSR, resentful of US influence in Mobutu's Zaire. The Katangese rising was suppressed with the aid of troops from Morocco, Egypt, France and Belgium. Meanwhile, the country suffered from the world recession, which led to sharp falls in copper prices, as well as from drought, which required the expensive importation of food. These economic difficulties led to more political and tribal unrest. Mobutu became increasingly autocratic, and his government has been found guilty by various international agencies of the ill-treatment of thousands of political prisoners. While he assumed ever grander titles (such as 'President for Life') and amassed a personal fortune, the country and its people sank into economic decline.

## Kenya

In 1920 the East African Protectorate became the Crown Colony of Kenya. It was a major exporter of tea, coffee and sisal grown on farms owned, in the main, by Europeans, who had political privileges as well as control of the Legislative Council to which no African was appointed until 1944. Agricultural development had attracted Indian immigrants, who dominated the country's commercial life. Africans, of a multiplicity of tribes, had their best land taken from them by Land Apportionment Acts and suffered both social and economic discrimination.

The Kikuyu, the largest tribe, once relied upon their Central Association to run their affairs. Jomo Kenyatta was a delegate to the Association in 1929, and had been sent to London to form part of a Commission examining African complaints about land apportionment. He later returned to take a degree at London University, and after study at Moscow University he settled in London where in 1942 he married a white woman. He returned to Kenya in 1946 as Principal of the Kikuyu Teachers' Training College, and formed the Kenya African Union (KAU) when the Central Association was banned following unrest caused by rising unemployment, low wages and a poor standard of living. Kenyatta appealed to the white government to admit Africans into their ranks, and in 1954 six Africans were allowed to join the previously all-white Council. It was both too little and too late.

Members of the banned Kikuyu Association formed a secret society called the Mau Mau. This became a mass movement, in which Kikuyu bound themselves by terrifying oaths. In 1952 there were attacks aimed at terrorizing Europeans and the thousands of Africans working for them. The government arrested Kenyatta and 130 other leaders, but Mau Mau violence simply increased in scale and savagery. In March 1953 the government launched a war against the Mau Mau which lasted until 1960, by which time 10,000 members had been killed. In 1956 each tribe was allowed to form its own political party, although no national parties were allowed, and Africans had their first chance to elect representatives to the Legislative Assembly. A new constitution (1960) denying Africans control of the Assembly was widely condemned by a people, whose leaders were still in prison, leading to an agreement between the leaders of the two main tribes (The Kikuyu and the Luo), who formed the Kenyan African National Union (KANU) and demanded the release of Kenyatta, who was named President. He was freed in August 1961 and elected to the Council in January 1962, leading Africans in negotiations with the British over their claims to independence. In the wake of Macmillan's 'wind of change' speech (p. 180), the British seemed anxious to be rid of their colonies, even if this meant sacrificing white interests overseas. Kenyatta formed a government in April 1962 and faced tribal unrest, activity by dissatisfied Mau Mau members, industrial strikes in search of higher wages and threats of secession by Somalis in the north and Arabs along the coast. Crushing this opposition, Kenyatta proved to London that he was able to govern. In the election of May 1963 KANU won 75 per cent of the seats, and in December 1963 Kenyatta became Prime Minister and President of the independent republic of Kenya.

Seeking to overcome tribalism, Kenyatta chose ministers from more than one tribe; he also ensured that all citizens (other than Asians) were treated equally, largely in the hope that Europeans would stay on to help run the country. He made the nation a one-party state, to check the emergence of an Opposition which, under a former supporter Oginga Odinga, threatened to encourage separatism. The success of his stable government was shown in Kenya's economic performance and his continued success at elections. Kenya avoided both the financial anarchy of Ghana and the tribal warfare of Nigeria or the Congo. After Kenyatta's death in 1978, Vice-President Daniel Arap Moi took over smoothly, although he was unfortunate in that Kenya began to suffer from the effects of the oil-induced trade recession. A sharp fall in world prices for coffee and tea, which form 60 per cent of Kenya's exports, along with increased import prices, led to balance of payments deficits. A poor harvest (1978–9) led to food shortages and rising prices, and provided opportunities for corruption among ministers and officials, which Moi nonetheless crushed. Kenya remains a lone example of the successful transfer of power between empire and colony.

## Uganda

In this largely agricultural country, tribal chiefs, led by the Kabaka of Buganda, had opposed British attempts to bring Africans into the country's government. It was a sign of British commitment to decolonization that the Kabaka was exiled (1953–5), and black politicians allowed to form political parties, largely along tribal lines. In 1960 the two largest parties united to form the Uganda People's Congress, led by Milton Obote. Negotiations for independence were relatively smooth, and in 1962 Uganda became an independent nation, a federation of five states, of which Buganda was one. Obote was the first Prime Minister and the Kabaka the first President.

Obote's wish to turn the country into a one-party state led to clashes with the Kabaka; in 1966 Obote carried out a coup which deprived

Baganda of its privileges, and drove the Kabaka into exile. This Obote–Kabaka clash was but one example of tribal rivalry. It was a surprise nevertheless when in January 1971, while Obote was at the Singapore meeting of Commonwealth Prime Ministers, his army commander, Idi Amin, seized power.

Amin's rule was marked by terrorism, and by an attack on Uganda's Asians. In 1962 these Asians were allowed to retain their British citizenship, which angered Ugandans already jealous of their commercial success. Amin had seen how Kenya dealt with its Asian problem: Kenyatta insisted on a policy of Africanization which deprived Kenyan Asians of their leading positions. Thus in 1968 some 60,000 Kenyan Asians arrived in Britain with their British passports. In 1972 Amin decided that Ugandan Asians who did not take out Ugandan citizenship would be expelled. Many Commonwealth countries took in these exiles, and a great number settled in Britain, which in 1973 passed a new Immigration Act giving the government the power to refuse admittance to such refugees, even if they had British passports.

Amin's treatment of the Asians, his reign of terror and his outbursts of self praise made his régime both a laughing-stock and an object of 'liberal' attack. Nyerere of Tanzania was angered by Amin's behaviour, which gave Africa a poor image abroad; he approved of the Israeli attack on Entebbe to free hostages held by the PLO in Uganda (1976), and was appalled by the assassination of the Archbishop of Uganda, a victim of Amin's rule.

Some tribal groups shared Nyerere's hatred for Amin, whose government favoured northern Muslims at the expense of other groups and tribes. Ugandan exiles in Tanzania were encouraged to attack their homeland; border clashes between Tanzanian and Ugandan troops were followed by a full-scale attack by Nyerere's forces to help rebel tribes. Amin was defeated, and in 1979 he fled to Libya. Milton Obote, a friend of Nyerere's, was brought back to power.

Obote's rule was marked by further economic decline, along with more tribal fighting and the continuation of the terror which Amin had practised. Exports of the country's three main products (coffee, cotton and copper) have now almost ceased; medical and other services have collapsed; the currency is ruinously inflated. Whereas in 1960 there were 17 Ugandan shillings to the British pound, there are now 5000 (at the time of writing). Obote's cruel, corrupt and inefficient rule was opposed by Museveni's National Resistance Movement, which waged a guerrilla war inside a country providing another example of African politicians' failure to satisfy their people's initial hopes.

## Tanganyika (Tanzania)

Between 1920 and 1947 Tanganyika was a British Mandate, being prepared for ultimate independence. In the 1920s, politically-conscious blacks formed the Tanganyikan African Association, but received little support in a country where the majority were culturally backward, indifferent to politics and reliant on the role of the traditional and conservative chiefs. Unlike Kenya, the country was not suitable for European settlement, while its lack of economic development ensured that few Indians or Arabs were attracted to the country. Although the largest state in Africa, Tanganyika is underpopulated because of the ravages of the tsetse fly and the harsh climate.

Successive governors brought Africans into the Legislative Council but allowed the chiefs to retain some political power in a system of indirect rule. In 1947 the Council had 15 'official' members and 14 'unofficial' members, all appointed by the British government. Three of the 'unofficials' were Asians, and four were Africans. In 1954 Julius Nyerere became leader of a renamed Tanganyikan African National Union (TANU) whose manifesto was similar to that issued by Nkrumah (Document 10.1a). This aimed at the creation of a unitary state in which tribalism would be eradicated.

The British persuaded the chiefs to set up the United Tanganyikan Party; meanwhile, a committee of Europeans working in the country issued a report (1955) which attacked the notions of independence, and TANU's claims to represent 'the people throughout the countryside'. A new constitution (1955) provided for a Legislative Council of ten 'unofficial' members from each of the three main racial groups – African, Asian and European – with the government retaining control through its 31 'official' members. In 1957 ministers were made responsible to this Council, and plans were made for the election of a Parliament. In the first elections (1958) TANU won every seat, in spite of official opposition. Several Europeans stood as TANU candidates, evidence of their faith in Nyerere and also an indication of a high degree of racial harmony.

The governor, appreciating TANU's popularity, created a council of ministers to which he appointed five elected members from TANU. Nyerere, as Chief Minister, brought calm after the storms of 1958, winning the confidence of non-African minorities, and persuading the British to allow elections (1960), which he converted into a plebiscite in favour of independence. Following a series of constitutional conferences in 1961, Tanganyika became independent. Nyerere was its first Prime Minister, and all British officials were withdrawn from the council, which became the Cabinet, while the Legislative Council became the National Assembly.

In December 1962 Tanganyika was named a Republic, and in 1964 united with Zanzibar to form Tanzania. Nyerere persuaded Uganda and Kenya, already his partners in the East African Community, to draw up an economic plan (1964) under which industries were sited in each country according to Community decisions, while a Community

Services Organization controlled currency, customs, postal services, railways and harbours within the three states. The opening of the Tanganyika–Zambia Railway in October 1975 was evidence of this inter-state cooperation. It linked the Zambian copper belt to the coast, and was the largest foreign project in Africa since the Soviet Union built the Aswan High Dam (p. 122). Most of the skilled work was carried out by 15,000 Chinese technicians, demonstrating Peking's interest in Africa and its claim to be the 'real' friend to Third World countries.

Economic planning inside Tanganyika is controlled by the National Economic Development Corporation, and many industries are state owned. Health and education services have been expanded, and taxation has been used to ensure that there is no great accumulation of personal wealth. In his Arusha Declaration (1967) Nyerere declared that the country was at war, not only with neighbouring Southern Rhodesia (p. 172), but also with poverty, ignorance and disease. The way to victory, he said, lay not in foreign aid, but in hard work and self-reliance. He emphasized again that agricultural development was the first priority, enabling the country to become self-sufficient, and also promised to eliminate poverty, bribery and corruption.

Nyerere made Tanganyika a one-party state, but allowed elections to be held in which rival members of the party appealed to the voters. At each election many MPs have lost their seats, indicating at least a degree of democracy. Nyerere 'was constantly re-elected President until he retired in 1985. From 1965 onwards his was one of the 'front line' states in the guerrilla war against Rhodesia (p. 172), which brought him into dispute with Britain. As this costly war was winding down, the country was affected by the oil-price increases of 1979 which pushed up its import bill. Falls in world prices for tea and coffee (its main exports) drove down Tanganyika's foreign earnings, while the effects of the war against Amin cost Tanzania at least £1 billion. In 1980 Nyerere was forced to ask the IMF for a loan of £100 million, which many of his critics cited as proof that his high-minded ideas had not been practical. It has also been claimed that Nyerere was thwarted by corrupt TANU officials.

## The Horn of Africa

'A tragic but forgotten war rages on.'

*Time,* 13 December 1985

In 1941 British victories allowed Haile Selassie to return to the throne of Ethiopia from which he had been driven by the Italians in the 1930s. Eritrea, the former Italian Somaliland, was incorporated into an enlarged Ethiopia, so that its 600-mile coast on the Red Sea could aid Ethiopia's economic development. In 1963 a rising by Eritrean nationalists against Selassie's rule had religious overtones: the Eritreans were Muslims, and the Ethiopians Christian. The USA provided

Selassie with economic and military aid until his government was overthrown by an army coup, bringing Colonel Mengistu to power. His Ethiopian Revolutionary Council offered a radical programme promising to halt economic decline, raise living standards and pursue the war against Eritrea more vigorously.

At first, the USA continued to aid Mengistu. However, by 1977 it was clear that he was also taking aid from the Soviet Union and Cuba. The USA withdrew its help, having no wish, after Vietnam, to getting involved in a war which it could not win. Radical Arab states – Libya, Syria and Iraq – provided aid for the Eritreans, and Mengistu's case worsened in 1977 when there was a rising in the region of Somalia, centred in Mogadishu. Once again, the Soviet Union and Cuba provided the forces which enabled Mengistu to defeat the Somalis and concentrate his attention on the Eritrean theatre.

Mengistu has an army of 210,000 men, the largest and best-equipped force in Africa; the Soviet Union has spent more than $3 billion on arms for Mengistu, who has about 2000 Soviet 'military advisers'. Over 500,000 people have died in this war-torn country, partly as a result of fighting, but largely because of the famine, which is due more to persistent drought than to the war. Over 1.5 million Somalis have left Ethiopia to seek refuge in Sudan, or in foreign-supplied camps. Among the more horrific events of 1985 was Mengistu's refusal to allow food aid to reach Somali refugees. This has been seen as a ruthless, racialist strategy, very much at odds with the world-wide campaign provoked by the refugees' plight, which saw an unprecedented popular involvement in Aid for Africa (p. 304).

## Documentary evidence

The manifesto of the Gold Coast People's Party Convention (Document 10.1a) was typical of the programmes of anti-colonialist African parties generally, with its mixture of political aims, insistence on unity in diversity, awareness of the trade unions, and in its nod in the direction of Human Rights (paragraph 6 of the manifesto). The CPP's methods of winning support (Document 10.1b) were also typical, in the catalystic importance of the charismatic leader (for Nkrumah in the Gold Coast, read Kenyatta, Obote, Nyerere or others elsewhere) and in the combination of constitutional methods and violence. Note too the role of 'the schoolmasters' as important members of the Party.

The French wished to retain links with their former colonies (Document 10.2), and hoped that they would remain an integral part of the Republic. Belgian paternalism (Document 10.3a) was an extreme example of European attitudes towards Africans. Any African might be addressed as 'boy' whatever his age or education; Europeans 'knew' that 'their boys' did not support Nkrumah (Documents 10.1a and b) or Kenyatta and the rest. The riots of June 1960 surprised the Belgian government, which hastily launched the Congo into independence. Such speedy action was at odds with the ideas propounded a year before (Document 10.1b), in which the King foresaw an almost timeless continuum of Belgian control.

## Document 10.1a

*The Gold Coast People's Party Convention: Manifesto*

'1  To struggle relentlessly, using all constitutional methods available, for the achievement of "complete and immediate self-government" for the chiefs and the people of the Gold Coast.

2  To be a vigorous political vanguard in the struggle for an end to all forms of oppression and for the establishment of a democratic government.

3  To ensure and maintain complete unity of the chiefs and the people of the colony, the Ashanti, the Northern Territories and the Trans-Volta.

4  To work in collaboration with the trade union movement for the improvement of conditions of employment.

5  To work for the rapid reconstruction of a better Gold Coast in which the people would have the right to live and govern themselves.

6  To promote the political, social and economic emancipation of the people and, in particular, those who live directly by their work, whether manual or intellectual.

7  To support and facilitate the achievement of a united West Africa.'

## Document 10.1b

*A British view of the CPP*

'The CPP is a remarkable portent in African politics and deserves careful study. It has an inspired leadership and a conscious mystique. It followed, on its way to power, where it could, the path of legality; when it judged expedient, the path of violence under the name of "positive action". It has a close-knit, efficient and disciplined party organization spreading throughout the southern Gold Coast and Ashanti and even, to a much lesser extent and more recently, in the Northern Territories. Because of the inflation, it does not lack funds; it has an effective, though crudely violent, press; and a backbone of membership among the urban Africans and the schoolmasters, who carried its message into the bush villages.'

(*The Round Table*, 1952, p. 279)

## Document 10.2

*The French Constitution of 1958*

'72  All territorial units of the Republic are communes, departments, and Overseas Territories. These units administer themselves freely through elected councils and under conditions provided by law. In departments and territories, the delegate of the government has charge of national interests, administrative supervision and respect for law.

73  The legislative system and the administrative organization of the Overseas Departments may be the subject of measures of adaption required by their special situation.

74  The Overseas Territories of the Republic have a special organization taking account of their particular interests within the interests of the Republic as a

whole. This organization is defined and modified by law after consultation with the territorial assembly concerned.

75 Citizens of the Republic who do not have ordinary civil status, the only status referred to in Article 34, retain their personal status as long as they have not renounced it.

76 The Overseas Territories may retain their status within the Republic. If they express the will to do so by deliberation of their territorial assembly within the period fixed in the first paragraph of Article 91, they may become either Overseas Departments of the Republic, or, grouped among themselves or not, Member States of the Community.'

## Document 10.3a

*Paternalism in the Belgian Congo, 1959*

'The welfare state and the welfare employer, in collaboration with the Catholic missions, take care of the material and moral well-being of the native. He enjoys free medical care from the cradle to the grave. He is either housed by his employer or receives a lodging allowance or a mortgage from the public authorities. He is provided with a balanced diet and suitable entertainment. The employer automatically pays part of his salary into a savings account. His rest is guaranteed by the curfew in the areas where he lives and where the presence of European is not tolerated during the night. The formula for his happiness is studied by scientists and applied by shrewd businessmen who try to prevent him from committing misdemeanours. Only recently it was still forbidden for him to keep, let alone consume, wine or other alcohol. The films he is allowed to see are censored by a special committee. In the countryside, the programmes are either religious or educational. The newspapers, periodicals, books published for his benefit are also educational and are issued almost exclusively by the government or the missionary societies. He is not allowed to travel without permission from the administrative authorities nor without a medical certificate. He is subject to special laws, judged by special tribunals imposing special penalties; as he is subject to customary law, he cannot be brought to court by a European. Any European who disembarks in the Congo, feels and believes in his educated mission and acts accordingly, whatever his profession or trade . . . the bookseller censors the reading of his black customers. The tradesman, the grocer, the butcher "educate" their black clientele at special counters; they have trained black cashiers who in turn "educate" blacks depositing their money. Paternalism is all-pervading.'

(*Le Monde*, 7 January 1959)

## Document 10.3b

*Belgian hopes and promises, 13 January 1959*

'Message by the King:

It is our firm resolve to lead the peoples of the Congo to independence in prosperity and peace without recrimination but also without ill-considered haste.

In a civilized world, 'independence must combine and guarantee freedom, order and progress. We must give the Congo firm and well-balanced institutions, an experienced administration, a solid social, economic and financial organization, and the intellectual and moral education of the people without which democracy is both a mockery and a tyranny. We are pledged to the realization of these basic aims. We intend to consecrate ourselves to them in enthusiastic, cordial, concerted efforts with our African peoples. . . . we do not hesitate to approve and support the aspirations of our black brethren [and] . . . it must not be forgotten that, after eighty years of service, Belgium has unquestionable demands on their sympathy and loyal cooperation.

Our task as guide and counsellor must be continued while at the same time being adapted and reduced as progress is achieved. Moreover, far from imposing European solutions on them, we intend to favour original adaptations in conformity with their character and the traditions they cherish. For this purpose a large measure of decentralization, combined with a rapid extension of the electoral system and the abandonment of all discrimination between black and white, will allow the development of the various regions to take place in various ways, in accordance with their geographical, cultural and racial characteristics as well as their economic development. This is the road we have to pursue with faith and magnanimity, which we will only fulfil if, in addition to the dual exercise of will and discipline, we have a clear vision of the future prosperity of our two countries.'

(Keesing, *Contemporary Archives*)

## FURTHER READING

GAVSHON, A., *Crisis in Africa: Battleground of East and West*, Westview, 1983

HUXLEY, E., *The Flame Trees of Thika*, 1959 (on Kenya)

KAHAMA, C. G., et al., *The Challenge of Tanzania's Economy*, 1986

NAFZIGER, E. W., *The Economics of Political Instability: The Nigerian–Biafran War*, Westview, 1983

O'BRIEN, C. C., *To Katanga and Back*, Hutchinson, 1962

# 11

# Southern Africa

## British expansion

'We are the best of all races and the more of the world we possess, the better it will be for the world.'

Cecil Rhodes

In 1890 Britain had two colonies in southern Africa: the Cape Colony and Natal, hemmed in by German South-West Africa (now Namibia) and the two Boer Republics – the Transvaal and the Orange Free State, created by the descendants of Dutch settlers who left the Cape on their Great Trek (1836) because they opposed British treatment of black Africans, whom they regarded as sub-human (Document 11.2).

To prevent the possible junction of the German colony and the Boer Republics, and to provide for a British link 'from the Cape to Cairo', Britain undertook a policy of northward expansion. In 1848 she claimed Bechuanaland (now Botswana), which in 1889 was chartered to Cecil Rhodes's British South Africa Company, which was allowed to administer the Protectorate. From Bechuanaland, Rhodes pushed north; in 1896–7 he conquered the Matabele and Mashona peoples, setting himself up as 'ruler' of what was to become Southern Rhodesia (now Zimbabwe). From there he crossed the Zambezi and gained concessions from chiefs in what became Northern Rhodesia (now Zambia), and went on to add Nyasaland (now Malawi) to his 'empire', although he failed to reach copper-rich Katanga (p. 158).

In 1907 Britain assumed Protectorate rights over Nyasaland, while Northern Rhodesia became a Protectorate in 1924. By then, Southern Rhodesia had attracted white settlers, and in 1923 the British made this a self-governing colony, with the whites controlling internal affairs and the British government reserving to itself certain safeguards to protect black interests. White South Rhodesians rejected British proposals for them to unite with the four states in the Union of South Africa, preferring to retain their links with Britain and their own internal self-

government. Britain hoped, in vain, that Northern Rhodesia and
Nyasaland would form an association with Tanganyika, rather than
with Southern Rhodesia. The differences between the two Rhodesians
were shown by their respective treatment of black Africans in 1930,
when the British declared that in the Protectorates native interests were
paramount and that white settlers would not be allowed to exploit the
Africans. Southern Rhodesia defiantly passed the Land Apportionment
Act (1930) which divided the country into European Areas, Native
Purchase Areas, Unoccupied Areas and Forests; black Africans
regarded this as unjust, since the Europeans (about one-fifth of the
population) were allocated slightly more than half the land, as well as all
of the towns, while no African was allowed to own property in these
European Areas. It was clear that in Southern Rhodesia black interests
would not be 'paramount'.

In the 1930s and 1940s efforts to bring the three states into some form
of association failed, largely because of differences between Southern
Rhodesia and the Colonial Office over the issue of black interests. In
1944 a Central African Council was formed, to allow the governors of
the two Protectorates and the Prime Minister of Southern Rhodesia to
coordinate matters of common interest. This was less than some people
had hoped for, but it was to be the forum in which political leaders from
the three 'states' could meet and perhaps work towards a closer
association.

## The Central African Federation, 1953–63

'We must leave the government in the hands of civilized people.'
                              Statement by S. Rhodesian whites, 1959

In 1949 an all-white conference at Victoria Falls discussed the
possibility of a federation of two, if not three, of the territories.
Northern Rhodesia was represented by Roy Welensky, a former train-
driver and trade union official, founder of the N. Rhodesian Labour
Party, and a member of the N. Rhodesian Legislative Council from
1938 to 1953. Welensky opposed federation, fearing that Northern
Rhodesia's copper industry would be exploited for the benefit of white
Southern Rhodesians. Other Northern Rhodesian whites, envious of
Southern Rhodesians' power over their black population, hoped that in
a federation they might get similar power.

In 1951 there was a London Conference of officials from the three
territories, the Colonial Office (responsible for the two northern
territories) and the Commonwealth Office (which supervised the
affairs of S. Rhodesia). This led to another conference at Victoria Falls,
at which Africans from the two northern territories explained that
despite the economic advantages of federation they still feared government by the white supremacists of Southern Rhodesia.

In 1952 the British government called another London conference, which was boycotted by Africans from the two northern territories, although the Southern Rhodesian delegation did include two Africans – Nkomo and Savanhu. From this conference there emerged the Central African Federation of the three territories, each with its own administration and Assembly. While a Federal Government and Parliament were established, Britain retained its protective rights over the two northern territories, and decreed that the Federation would not get Dominion status without the consent of the (African) majority of the population.

The Federation came into being on 1 August 1953, with Huggins as Prime Minister and Welensky as his Deputy, in a Cabinet of six whites. Huggins formed a Federal Party with branches on both sides of the Zambezi. In Southern Rhodesia, Garfield Todd became Prime Minister and leader of the United Party; in Northern Rhodesia, Africans became increasingly politicized by leaders such as Kenneth Kaunda, another of the influential 'schoolmasters' (Document 10.1b). In 1958 Kaunda formed the Zambian African National Congress, whose manifesto resembled that issued by Nkrumah, whose Ghana had just emerged as the first independent ex-colony (Document 10.1b). Kaunda shared white suspicions that the northern copper industry would be exploited by the Southern Rhodesians, and was therefore hostile to the Federation.

There were only 9000 white settlers in Nyasaland in 1948, where the 1.7 million Africans gained a poor living in agriculture, their territory lacking both the mineral wealth of Northern Rhodesia and the rich lands of Southern Rhodesia. Africans, appointed to the Legislative Council since 1948, feared that in a federation they would come under the control of the southern whites. Their fears were expressed by the Malawi National Congress, led by Dr Hastings Banda after his return in 1958 from his medical practice in London.

Some Southern Rhodesian whites feared that cheap black labour might pour in from the north, depressing white working-class living standards. Others feared that the British would limit their freedom to handle racial problems. Most whites, however, welcomed the Federation, in which their economic and social privileges would be retained, and perhaps, enhanced. Few, if any, considered the idea of 'partnership' with the blacks, although this was written into the Constitution. they thought of blacks much as the Belgians did (Document 10.3a), and ridiculed the notion of black nationalism. Like the whites of South Africa they practised segregation, confirming the African belief that the 'Partnership' was a sham.

From the outset there was mutual suspicion between whites and blacks, and between whites in the north and their fellow whites in the south. When, Banda returned to Nyasaland in 1968 to lead an anti-federation campaign, many whites feared a Mau Mau-like guerrilla war (p. 160). Banda toured the country, whipping up anti-federation feeling; whites became increasingly convinced that violence would erupt. The Southern Rhodesian government sent 3000 troops to help keep order in Nyasaland, and called a state of emergency in its own territory. Some 3000 blacks were arrested throughout the Federation, and all African National Congresses banned. However, the British Government's Devlin Commission found no evidence of an African plan to massacre whites, and declared Banda a man of peace in what the Commission, liberal opinion in Britain and most of the world's press saw as 'a police state'.

In 1958, amid the turmoil of Banda's anti-federation campaign, Federal elections were held, and Welensky (Huggins's successor) led his Party to victory; few of the qualified Africans bothered to vote. In Southern Rhodesia, Todd's colleagues had forced him to resign because they opposed his wish to extend rights to the black majority. In the elections his United Rhodesia Party won no seats; Whitehead's United Party won most seats although a right-wing Dominion Party, led by Winston Field, won most votes.

This polarizing of opinion forced the British to set up a Commission, under Lord Monckton, to study the Federation. It reported in favour of the federal principle, but moving outside its terms of reference it argued that any member territory had the right to secede. Macmillan, the British Prime Minister, and his Colonial Secretary, MacLeod, were attacked by Welensky, although their support for the commission's findings did not assuage the anger of Banda and Kaunda. After further unrest and violence in the northern territories, a proposal was made to divide Northern Rhodesia: one part was to become a separate state under traditional chiefs, while the other was to be handed to Southern Rhodesia. This aimed to divide black opposition to white rule, but the proposal was never implemented. Nonetheless, its mere publication angered black leaders, and further threatened the continuation of the Federation.

In Britain, R. A. Butler, appointed to handle Central African Affairs, decided to wind up the Federation. By the end of 1962 Nyasaland was promised self-government and the right of secession. In Northern Rhodesia, Kaunda's party was invited to join the government, and the right to secession was agreed in 1963. The CAF officially ended on 31 December 1963.

In October 1964 Northern Rhodesia became independent Zambia, with Kaunda as the first President of a state containing 78 different tribes. Zambia's main export is copper, and fluctuations in world prices have made it difficult for the country to finance widespread development. After 1965, Zambia was a leading 'front line' state in the blacks' struggle with Smith's Rhodesia (p. 174), even though her trade depended on the rail-link through Rhodesia to the port of Beira. The building of the Tan-Zam Railway (p. 164) provided Zambia with a link to Dar-es-Salaam in Tanganyika, and freed it from reliance on Rhodesia.

In the late 1960s Vice-President Kepepwe planned to set up a separate state of Bemba in the north of the country. Kaunda dismissed him, and in February 1972 set up a one-party state to combat the separatist tendencies of tribalism. This arrangement was confirmed in elections in 1973, when the voters approved the constitution which gave Kaunda's party its privileged position. A political realist, Kaunda tried to maintain links with South Africa; while opposed to apartheid he is equally opposed to Soviet, Cuban and Chinese efforts to gain influence in newly-independent Angola and Mozambique. In 1986, however, Kaunda became increasingly critical of Botha's South African government, and led the demand for world-wide sanctions against the supremacist and racist state.

Nyasaland became independent as Malawi in July 1964, with Banda as its first President. In 1966 he named himself 'President-for-life', indicating the autocratic control which he exercises within his one-party state, of which he is also Prime Minister, Foreign Minister and Minister of Justice . . . . The intolerant and anti-Communist Banda has many of the traits of the hard-liners in the white South African government. In 1986, as he becomes frailer, the question of succession has gained attention but is nowhere near being resolved.

## From Rhodesia to Zimbabwe

'[White] obsession with independence at all costs, for the purpose of changing the constitution; is placing political considerations above the real interests of the country.'

Roy Welensky, 2 November 1964

In 1963 Winston Field's Dominion Party won the majority of seats in the Southern Rhodesian Parliament, and with the break-up of the Federation he started negotiating with Britain for independence. The British Conservative government laid down four conditions as pre-requisites for the concession of independence: unimpeded progress towards majority (African) rule; a guarantee against regressive amendments to the 1961 Constitution; an immediate improvement in African rights; the acceptance of independence by the majority of the population.

In 1964 Ian Smith ousted Field from the leadership, as white attitudes hardened towards black nationalism and Britain's supervisory role. Smith at first adopted a traditional British policy, persuading a gathering of traditional chiefs to issue a pro-Smith statement attacking the 'pretensions' of black nationalists. Few put much faith in this statement, and the election of a Labour government in Britain (1964) ensured a rigid adherence to the five conditions. When this government proposed to set up a Commission to test African feeling, the Smith government declared the country independent, under the name Rhodesia (11 November 1965). The Governor, in the name of the Queen, declared the government 'illegal', but it remained in power.

Neither the Labour government (1964–70) nor its Conservative successor (1970–4) was prepared to use force against white 'kith and kin', but under pressure from black African states, as well as from the UN and liberal opinion in Britain, the Labour government applied a series of economic sanctions against 'Rhodesia' while negotiating with the rebel, Smith. Negotiations constantly broke down; sanctions, however, which were meant to bring down the illegal régime 'in weeks not months' had some effect as 'Rhodesian' exports were blocked. As the country's financial reserves became depleted, importing became increasingly difficult. In response to this, the whites developed a wider industrial base, which freed them from such reliance on imports. 'Rhodesia' had access to export/import facilities through South Africa and the Portugese colonies of Angola and Mozambique, and many multinational companies breached the sanctions policy anyway.

In 1972 a British Commission went to see if black Africans would agree to a restoration of 'normal relations' with Smith. This Commission found that most blacks wanted the implementation of the five conditions before there was any change in relations between Britain and 'Rhodesia'. Smith's refusal to make any concessions led to the development of a guerrilla war; the government had its own security forces, most of them black, but South Africa also provided some military aid.

Initially, the Smith government managed to contain the rebels, but in 1975 Angola and Mozambique became independent (p. 177), and the whites in 'Rhodesia' and South Africa were now under pressure from a combined black mass to the north, while the guerrillas were provided with secure bases in the newly-independent states. Armed by the Soviet Union and her allies, the Zimbabwe African People's Union (ZAPU) and the Zimbabwe African National Union (ZANU) raided targets in 'Rhodesia'. ZANU was led by Robert Mugabe, a left-winger from the Shona people, who form the majority on 'Rhodesia'; ZAPU's leader was the long-time black leader, Joshua Nkomo, from the Matabele tribe, which had ruled the region before the British arrived, and whose homeland is in the south of the country. Nkomo, although rigidly nationalist, seemed more ready to negotiate than Mugabe, a doctrinaire Marxist.

In 1974–5 Smith held talks with Nkomo, whom he freed from gaol in the hope of making a deal with the apparently more malleable of the two black leaders. Negotiations broke down, however, in the face of the whites' view of the country's future. In 1975–6 the South African government shifted ground as it became more aware of the danger of hostile and politicized black opinion in the Union. At the same time, the USA, once ambivalent towards Smith (agreeing to import Rhodesian minerals despite the UN's resolutions) began to take a belated interest in African affairs, particularly in view of the growth of Soviet–Cuban influence in Angola, Mozambique and the Horn of Africa. In 1976 Kissinger declared that the USA favoured black rule in southern Africa.

Vorster, Prime Minister of South Africa, cut aid to Smith who, after meeting Kissinger, accepted the principle of 'majority rule within two years'. This spurred the guerrillas on to increased activity and quickened the rate of white emigration. Smith tried to assuage the whites, claiming that Kissinger's plan did not mean 'one man, one vote' (which it obviously did), but angered the US, the blacks and world opinion generally. In 1977 with the black Andrew Young representing the US, and David Owen representing the British Labour government, Smith came under increasing pressure in international talks, while at the same time his South African 'ally' became increasingly distanced itself from him.

Smith held new, but futile, talks with Nkomo before he reached an agreement with other black leaders (Bishop Muzorewa, the Reverend Sithole and Chief Chirau) on a power-sharing scheme. While Smith accepted 'one man, one vote', the less hard-line blacks conceded that the whites would still have entrenched rights within a new Constitution. In 1979 'Rhodesian' whites approved this agreement and elections were held in which Muzorewa's party gained a majority, making him the first Prime Minister of Zimbabwe–Rhodesia. Mugabe and Nkomo argued that, in effect, the whites remained in control; they continued their guerrilla war against the new government, which failed to introduce reforms alleviating racial discrimination and thus appeasing part, at least, of black opinion.

The Thatcher government in Britain favoured the Smith–Muzorewa deal, but under pressure from the USA and black Commonwealth leaders, and seeing the evidence of the continuing guerrilla war, Britain held talks involving Smith, Muzorewa, Nkomo and Mugabe. A new constitution was agreed upon, in which the blacks gained more power and the whites lost their entrenched and controlling position. Elections were held in which Mugabe's ZAPU won a majority of seats, so he became the new Prime Minister.

At first there were attempts to bind ZANU and ZAPU together, both providing ministers within a coalition government. This did not last, as the 7 million Shona refused to accept the privileges given to the 1.5 million Matabele. At national and local level there was discrimination against ZAPU members, including attacks on their property, often by ZANU-led police, and 'plots', uncovered by ZANU, supposedly aiming to bring Nkomo to power. Mugabe's Korean-trained brigades attacked Nkomo's people in their southern heartland as tribalism developed in Zimbabwe as it has done elsewhere. Whites too came under political and physical attack: Mugabe used his majority to end discrimination between whites and blacks but introduced discrimination against whites, who found it increasingly difficult to obtain permits for imports and development projects. White farmers were murdered by one or other of the rival 'armies' in a restless country which has also encouraged black nationalists in South Africa. Mugabe is one of the main supporters of the policy of sanctions against the Union, in which South African whites are an increasingly isolated 'tribe'.

## Angola and Mozambique

'Portugal: first in, last out.'

Press comment on Angolan independence

Portugal acquired Angola in the sixteenth century when she was one of the world's leading powers. During the nineteenth-century European 'scramble for Africa' she hoped to gain land (now Zambia and Zimbabwe) to link Angola with recently-acquired Mozambique, but Rhodes's thrust from the south (p. 169) prevented this, and Portugal was left with two widely-separated colonies.

Nationalist uprisings in the 1920s and 1930s were easily, if savagely, put down. In 1952, following the French example (p. 154), Portugal named her colonies 'Overseas Provinces of Portugal'; their government and development was an 'internal' matter, not subject to UN interference. Portugal followed a policy of assimilation, and gradually extended the franchise to 'qualified' blacks who had made social and economic progress, hoping to deprive a nascent nationalist movement of its potental leaders. However, in the 1950s large-scale Portugese immigration increased the effects of the colour bar, and led to increased black unemployment as 'poor whites' took even low-paid work.

With the independence of British, French and Belgian colonies, there was increased support for black nationalist movements within Angola and Mozambique. In February–March 1961 riots in Luanda, the capital of Angola, were ruthlessly suppressed, but followed by an invasion of Angolan refugees from Leopoldville in the north. Some 1400 Portugese and 20,000 Africans died; in the ensuing guerrilla war 170,000 black wounded took refuge in the Congo – an indication of the barbarity of the persistent war and of the inability of the Portugese to crush the nationalists. One group of nationalists formed the Popular Movement for the Liberation of Angola (MPLA) in 1956, and were supported by the Soviet Union, Cuba and other communist states. Anti-communist nationalists formed their own National Front for the Liberation of Angola (FNLA), which was supported by anti-communist groups in southern Africa who paid European mercenaries to lead the FNLA guerrillas. A third group of nationalists formed the National Union for the Total Independence of Angola (UNITA) which was supported by various western countries, including the USA.

The nationalist movement in Mozambique was united in the Front for the Liberation of Mozambique (FRELIMO), a Marxist movement supported by the Soviet Union and Cuba, who were anxious to gain a base for operations in the Indian Ocean.

The guerrilla wars in the two colonies cost about half of the Portugese national budget in 1970, and required the conscription of young people into the largest army in the country's history. The dictator Salazar was determined to hold on to Portugal's colonies, which provided valuable imports, as well as markets for exports, and living space for Portugal's growing population. When he retired in 1968, his successor and former right-hand man, Caetano, allowed free elections to take place in Portugal. During the electoral campaign there were calls for greater democracy, a liberalization of Portugese life, the release of political prisoners from gaol – and colonial freedom.

Many servicemen had become politicized during the colonial wars, and some had come to sympathize with the nationalists. The officer class, in particular, had been forced to realize that the war could not be won. In 1974 a radicalized officer, General Spinola, led a coup in mainland Portugal which overthrew Caetano. Once in power, he declared himself in favour of colonial freedom. FRELIMO took charge in independent Mozambique, but in Angola the rival groups fought for power after Portugal had announced Angola's independence in November 1975. The Soviet-backed and Cuban-led MPLA came under attack from the West-inclined FNLA and the South African-backed UNITA. By February 1976, the MPLA claimed that it controlled the country, and most nations recognized the MPLA's 'People's Republic', although a guerrilla war continued to disrupt life there. Both Angola and Mozambique became bases from which guerrillas launched attacks on Smith's 'Rhodesia', now better armed since they had access to Soviet and Cuban supplies in those countries.

## Namibia: South-West Africa

'. . . the continued presence of South Africa being illegal, South Africa is under obligation to withdraw its administration from Namibia and end its occupation of the Territory.'

UN International Court of Justice, 1971

In 1915 South African troops conquered the German colony of South-West Africa, and in 1920 the League of Nations awarded the territory to South Africa as a Mandate, to be run in the interest of its people, who were to be guided towards independence. When the UN replaced the League in 1945, South Africa promised to run the territory in the spirit of the 1920 Mandate.

The region has a population of about 950,000; most whites are immigrants from South Africa, running large farms with the help of black labour; over half the black population come from the Ovambo tribe, which has provided the basis of a nationalist movement, and supplied the majority of the workforce in the diamond and uranium mines run by multinational companies.

From 1948 onwards, hard-line governments in South Africa (Documents 11.1 and 11.2) have tried to integrate the territory into the Union, applying various anti-black Acts to Namibia, as to the Union itself. In 1960 black leaders formed the South West African People's Organization (SWAPO), with the support of Ovambo miners discontented with their pay and conditions. At first SWAPO ran a peaceful campaign, appealing to the UN to rule against South Africa, which refused to accept UN directives or to admit UN inspectors to examine the way in which the Mandate was working. South Africa forced the UN to announce the end of the Mandate in 1966, the year in which SWAPO began a guerrilla war and gained UN recognition as 'the sole authentic representative of the people of Namibia'.

In 1975–7 Vorster of South Africa held talks with representatives of white and black moderates in the territory, proposing a federal constitution as a way forward to independence. Some blacks, fearing Ovambo domination, supported these modest proposals and helped form the Democratic Turnhalle Alliance, a multi-racial group which now governs Namibia. Vorster did not invite SWAPO leaders to the Turnhalle Conference, and their response to the new government was a stepping-up of the guerrilla war.

Neighbouring black African states support SWAPO, providing it with bases for guerrilla training and with supplies. South Africa has attacked guerrilla camps in Angola, Mozambique and Zimbabwe; in 1976 hundreds of guerrillas were killed in a thirteen-day attack on bases in Angola, where Soviet advisers and arms were captured by South African forces. There was a danger that Angola might use its 20,000 Cuban and East German troops against this invading force, but they were more occupied with the Angolan civil war – in which UNITA's guerrillas fight the Marxist government.

In 1977 Britain, France, West Germany and the USA formed the Contact Group in efforts to arrange negotiations between SWAPO and the South African government. Arguing that a peaceful solution to the Namibian problem is crucial to western foreign policy, they pointed to the danger of the growth in Soviet, Cuban and Chinese influence in Africa. They realize that southern Africa is on the European trade route by sea to the East and to Australasia, by which western oil supplies arrive from the Middle East. Namibia and South Africa are of economic, political and strategic importance to the West.

## South Africa

'. . . it would be a mistake for South Africa to base her strategy on the assumption that when the chips are down the West will stand with her.'
*Edward Heath, Johannesburg, 1981*

The Union of South Africa was created in 1910 as Britain tried to win the friendship of the Boers, whom they had defeated in the second Boer War. The English colonies of the Cape of Good Hope and Natal were united with the Boer Republics of the Transvaal and the Orange Free State. A succession of Boer-led Union governments (Document 11.2) followed a policy of 'white-only government' which was supported from the outset by Britain. In 1936 blacks in the Cape lost their right to vote; there and elsewhere Asians and Coloureds were allowed to vote – but only for white representatives.

In 1948 the hard-line, Boer-dominated National Party came to power (Document 11.1) led by Dr Malan. Under Verwoerd's direction (Document 11.2) it proceeded to implement the policy of *apartheid* arguing that this would preserve the identity of blacks as much as whites. A series of acts were passed to implement this policy: a Mixed Marriages Act (1949) banned inter-racial marriage, and sexual relations between whites and non-whites were banned by the Immorality Amendment Act (1950); the Group Areas Act forced non-whites to move from inner cities to 'shanty towns'; segregation in the towns ('petty apartheid') meant discrimination in all aspects of life – sport, leisure, entertainment, travel, religion; the Bantu Education Act (1954) limited black education to that required by an unskilled working class; the Separate Universities Act (1959) tried to prevent richer blacks from enjoying higher education alongside whites.

Other acts were passed to bolster the system in which, after 1956, all blacks had to carry Reference Books ('the Pass Laws') to be produced whenever demanded by the police. A network of laws was created, under which critics of government policy could be arrested, and, if proven guilty of 'anti-government activities', be fined, imprisoned, exiled or executed. This was licensed by the Suppression of Communism Act (1950), the Criminal Law Amendment Act (1953), the Unlawful Organizations Act (1960), the Sabotage Act (1962), the Terrorism Act (1967) and the Public Services Act (1969). Under the last, the military and police security forces were coordinated, and a Bureau of State Security (BOSS) set up to weed out radicals who threatened white supremacy. Adverse publicity about BOSS's part in the death (in prison) of the African leader, Steve Biko (September 1977) led to a change of name; however, even as the Department of National Security, it remains the main arm of anti-black repression.

In 1956 the government removed Asians and Coloureds from the electoral roll. Peaceful protest against the 'Pass Laws' by 20,000 women, many of them white, were ignored, but when black demonstrators threw away their Reference Books at Sharpeville in 1960, police fired on the crowd, killing 69 blacks. At that time the African National Congress (ANC) led black opposition. Founded in 1912, its leaders had issued a Manifesto (1952) calling for support in their struggle against 'the unjust laws which keep in perpetual subjugation and misery vast sections of the population.' In the wake of the tightening of the *apartheid* screw, there were calls for the ANC to adopt more violent tactics, and start a guerrilla war. In June 1964 its leaders, including Nelson Mandela, were sentenced to life imprisonment for alleged sabotage.

By then, Prime Minister Verwoerd (Document 11.2) had been shot by a white farmer. He recovered, only to be stabbed to death in 1966. His successor, Johannes Vorster, developed the *apartheid* policy, creating ten 'racially homogeneous states' as tribal reserves, or 'homelands' for blacks. these 'Bantustans' were gradually given their independence: Transkei in 1976, Bophuthatswana in 1977, Venda in 1979, and Ciskei in 1981. None of these 'states' were recognized by the outside world. They served the government's purpose as 'homelands' to which millions of non-whites not required for work could be sent at any time, as could those without Reference Books, or passes entitling them to be in a white area.

In 1960 South Africa became a Republic and had to apply for continued membership of the Commonwealth. In 1961 this application was opposed by white Prime Ministers from Australia and Canada, and by the Afro–Asian Prime Ministers. Verwoerd withdrew the application, and South Africa left the Commonwealth. Macmillan, the British Prime Minister, had given an indirect warning to South African whites in February 1961 when he addressed the Houses of the South African Parliament, after visiting most of the former colonies to the north. He spoke of 'the wind of change' that was blowing through Africa, bringing, as it were, nationalist ships home to port.

Once South Africa was out of the Commonwealth, Britain faced increasing criticism at the UN, where there were demands for economic and arms-sales sanctions against the new Republic. Few countries applied such sanctions, preferring to trade with, and invest in, the country which produced most of the world's gold, platinum and uranium. The threat of sanctions forced the South African government to undertake industrial reform so that it became more self-sufficient in, for example, arms production.

Other forms of international protest had some effects. In 1968 South Africa refused to allow a coloured cricketer, Basil d'Oliveira, to enter the country as a member of the MCC team; the tour was cancelled. In the winter of 1968–9 British radicals tried to stop, and when they failed, to mar, the tour by a South African rugby team. Clashes during that tour led the British government to enforce the cancellation of a proposed South African cricket tour. Other Commonwealth nations followed suit; only 'rebel' teams have played in South Africa, whose cricketers have not toured anywhere. Other international sporting organizations took similar action, and South Africa was barred from almost all international sport.

Trying to win international respect, the government then allowed some relaxation of 'petty apartheid' – in as much as it affected sport.

"In South Africa we have always managed to keep politics out of sport."—Mr. Vorster

**11.1** The *Punch* cartoonist saw it differently in September 1968

White teams play against black and coloured teams; some blacks have been chosen for national sides; white schools play against black. But blacks still have few facilities, and black children in underfunded schools have poorer facilities than do whites. 'Petty apartheid' still applies once games are over, so blacks and whites are unable to drink together. The outside world sees that the effects of *apartheid* in sport cannot be removed unless the policy as a whole is swept away.

In 1978 P. W. Botha became Prime Minister, and later State President. He soon came under pressure from white businessmen in need of an educated black workforce and access to a developing black market. Botha was conscious of the growing threat from hostile governments to the north, who had aided Angola and Mozambique, and provided refuge and aid for SWAPO and ANC guerrillas, who in turn had the sympathy of most world opinion. Botha undertook what he saw as a step-by-step dismantlement of some aspects of *apartheid*, which he even claimed to oppose (Document 11.3). Job discrimination declined and firms ended the segregation of toilet, dining and other facilities in factories and offices. Some multi-racial theatres, hotels and restaurants were allowed to open. White industrialists encouraged black education and training, and in 1986 forced the government to abolish the 1959 Universities Act. Black trade unions were legalized as Botha hoped to keep the volatile black workers under control.

However, the black trade unions have created a mass movement, giving blacks a new source of economic 'clout'. This new, increasingly politicized force acts as a time bomb ticking away at the foundations of *apartheid*. In this case, and in most others, the step-by-step slicing away at *apartheid* has been an example of 'too little, too late', for the demands of blacks have increased rather than diminished over the years. Now they are more educated (and there are more Biko-like figures), and more politicized (with the funeral of every murdered black becoming a political rally at which younger people hear their views best expressed). They are better organized (by yet more extremist leaders, as the moderates are locked away) and are better supported by the outside world.

In September 1984 Botha introduced a new Constitution, providing the Republic with a three-Chamber Parliament, for Whites, Coloureds and Indians. Only people of the appropriate racial group can be elected to these Chambers, and only people of the same group may vote for them. Although the Constitution is rigged so that the wishes of the majority White Chamber will always prevail, the granting of the franchise, and of representation to two of the non-white racial groups, has served to increase resentment of the blacks.

In 1985 the Mixed Marriages Act and most sections of the Immorality Act were abolished, although mixed couples are still subject to other *apartheid* laws, governing where they live, for example. In September 1985 white business leaders from the south met black ANC leaders based in Zambia in efforts to build bridges between the two races, demonstrating their belief that the future lies with the leaders of black opinion.

Blacks see Botha as the epitome of *apartheid*; his attempts to alleviate matters are viewed as mere tinkering with a problem which will remain until there is 'one man one vote'. They see Botha's refusal to free Mandela as symbolic of his intransigence. Some liberals admire what they perceive to be a stealthy approach towards black majority rule; hard-line Afrikaaners, with the same perception, see Botha as a traitor who must be defeated. In general elections in 1981 and 1985 the right-wing gained increasing support, which may explain Botha's slightly tougher attitude towards reform and liberal opinion in 1986. The results of this may mean the isolation of the Republic, as the USA, EEC and Commonwealth threaten to unite on a policy of sanctions against the Botha régime.

In the black community there is increasing support for more violent protests. In townships such as Soweto, schoolchildren lead demonstrations (indicating the politicization of the young); terrorists have become active in all-white areas, and shops, hotels, offices and industrial areas have been bombed. It may be that the future lies in the clash between the right-wing extremists of the white 'tribe' and the more radical leaders of the black, who are, however, as divided into tribal factions in the south as they are further north.

## Documentary evidence

The system of *apartheid*, or racial separation, developed over many years (Document 11.2) was most seriously implemented following the National Party's electoral victory in 1948 (Doctument 11.1), when Verwoerd was Minister for Native Affairs (Document 11.2). He was the Prime Minister who took South Africa out of the Commonwealth, and his refusal to be swayed by outside influences has been the policy of his successors. In 1985–6 the current Boer leader, Botha, has come under attack from liberal world opinion, from black African states and, ironically, from white supremacists in South Africa who fear that his 'reforms' are the prelude to a 'sell out' to the blacks. Botha has tried to argue that, in fact, his government is opposed to *apartheid* (Document 11.3) which must surprise the African majority in his country.

## Document 11.1

*Defining, and promising to implement,* apartheid, *1948*

'The policy of separation (*apartheid*) has grown from the experience of the established European population of the country, and is based on Christian principles of justice and reasonableness. Its aim is the maintenance and protection of the European population of the country as a pure White race, the maintenance and protection of the indigenous racial groups as separate communities, with prospects of developing into self-supporting communities within their own areas, and the stimulation of national pride, self-respect, and mutual respect among the various races of the country. Either we must follow the course of equality, which must eventually mean national suicide for the White race, or we must take the course of separation through which the character and the future of every race will be protected.

Marriages between Europeans and non-Europeans will be prohibited. The State will exercise complete supervision over the moulding of the youth. The party will not tolerate interference from without or destructive propaganda from the outside world in regard to the racial problems of South Africa. Churches and societies which undermine the policy of *apartheid* and propagate doctrines foreign to the nation will be checked.

The Coloured community takes a middle position between the European and the Natives. A policy of separation between the Europeans and Coloured and between 'Natives and Coloured will be applied. No marriage between Europeans and Coloureds will be permitted. The present unhealthy system which allowed Coloureds in the Cape to be registered on the same voters' roll as

Europeans and to vote for the same candidate as Europeans will be abolished
and the Coloureds will be represented in the Assembly by three European
representatives. They will not vote on a change in the political rights of Non-
Europeans.'

(Electoral Statement by the National Party, 29 March 1948)

## Document 11.2

*Dr Hendrik Verwoerd, philosopher of* apartheid

He is extremely honest, as Hitler was honest, as Stalin was honest; they had
horrible notions, but they were not hypocrites. Since the Union of South Africa
was formed in 1910, it has had only six Prime Ministers; Botha, Smuts,
Hertzog, Malan, Strydom and Verwoerd; every one of them a Boer, every one
of them going a little farther on the path of apartheid than the one before.
Verwoerd is among the brightest of this set of granite patriots. He was
Professor of Applied Psychology at the Afrikaaner University of Stellenbosch,
a stronghold of the Boer intellectuals. For nine years he edited *Die Transvaaler*,
the chief organ of anti-British opinion in the Union. (During the visit of the
British King and Queen in 1947 his paper never mentioned it.) During the late
war with Germany the present Prime Minister was among the members of his
Government who were vigorous protagonists of the Nazi cause.

He did not enter active politics until 1948, when he was elected to the Senate,
and became Minister for Native Affairs, a key job in the Administration
dedicated to writing Native Affairs out of the Bill of Rights altogether . . . the
best mind in the Cabinet . . . passionately dedicated to the principles of
apartheid, and the definition of the Bantu as sub-human.

For this he has always invoked the authority of his Church (for he is a deeply
religious man), the Dutch Reformed Church, which long ago formally
ordained that the place of the black man is on his knees, so long as it is not in a
white man's chapel.

His election as Prime Minister was another victory for Transvaal rigidity
over Cape flexibility. He soon made it clear that he intended to abolish all
African representation from both Houses of Parliament – and did, with his
removal of the handful of Native Representatives (by law white, to be sure)
who made some small expression of the Africans' view. The next move to
which he is formally committed is the Republic. A draft Constitution is already
in existence: it renders the President of the Afrikaans Republic as 'responsible
only to God'. South Africa is to hold a referendum on this subject, and
Verwoerd has announced that he will institute the Republic whatever the result
of the referendum. He is not a man of many nuances.'

(*News Chronicle*, 11 April 1960)

## Document 11.3

*President Botha on* apartheid, *December 1985*

'If by "apartheid" is meant,
1  Political domination by any one community of any other;
2  The exclusion of any community from the decision-making process;
3  Injustice or inequality in the opportunities available for any community;

4 Racial discrimination and impairment of human dignity;
the South African government shares in the rejection of the concept.

(Quoted in *The Times*, 16 December 1985)


## FURTHER READING

DAVIDOW, J., *A Peace in Southern Africa: The Lancaster House Conference on Rhodesia, 1979*, Westview, 1984

EBINGER, C. K., *Foreign Intervention in Civil War: The Politics and Diplomacy of the Angolan Conflict*, Westview, 1983

HUDSON, M., *Triumph or Tragedy: Rhodesia to Zimbabwe*, Hamish Hamilton, 1981

LODGE, T., *Black Politics in South Africa since 1945* Longman, 1983

MANDELA, N., *No Easy Walk to Freedom*, Heinemann, 1986

MEREDITH, M., *The Past is Another Country; Rhodesia, 1890–1979*, Deutsch, 1979

WELENSKY, R., *4000 Days*, Collins, 1964

# 12

# The Indian sub-continent

## The background, 1885–1944

'The policy of HM Government is that of the increasing association of Indians in every branch of the administration and the gradual development of self-governing institutions with a view to the progressive realization of responsible government in India as an integral part of the British Empire.'

The Montagu Declaration, 1917

By August 1939, Britain had taken steps to fulfil the promises made in the Declaration issued in 1917 by the Secretary of State for India. However, the 'gradual' nature of the 'development' failed to satisfy Indian nationalists, represented by the National Congress. It roused the fears of Muslims in India, and the anger of Tories in Britain, and was accompanied by increased violence and repression in India, where Gandhi and many Congress leaders were jailed during the 1920s and 1930s.

The Indian National Congress was formed in 1885 by Indian graduates of both British and Indian Universities. Membership was by invitation only, and as membership widened Congress came to represent the interests of intellectuals, professional men, rich merchants and feudal landowners. Inevitably, it was Hindu-dominated, with only two Muslims attending the first meeting in 1885. In 1906 Muslims set up their own organization, the Muslim League, which by 1939 had persuaded the government to create Muslim constituencies, in which only Muslims voted, and only for their own candidates.

Indians had been introduced to elections by the Government of India Act (1909) which allowed for the election of 27 members of the Viceroy's 60-man Legislative Council. By 1939, much had changed: the franchise had been extended to some 35 million people voting in central and provincial elections; Government of India Acts (1906, 1919 and 1935) increased the role of Indians in the government of British

India, covering barely half of the sub-continent, the rest being ruled by Indian princes with the help of British advisers.

The 1935 Act had proposed a federal government for all India, with the princes taking one-third of the seats in a Central Legislative Assembly, and two-fifths of the seats in the Upper House; the rest of the seats were to be contested for directly. This Act proposed that a Federal Government would be set up when half the Princely States agreed to join in. They never did, and so the proposed Federal United States of India never came into being. However, the 1935 Act also provided for the election of Legislative Assemblies in each of the eleven provinces of British India, where, after the elections, governments would be responsible to the Legislatures. In the 1936 elections, Congress gained majorities in six of the eleven provinces, and was the largest single party in two others. The Muslims gained control in three provinces: Bengal, the Punjab and Sind. Jinnah, leader of the Muslim League, appealed to Nehru, the Congress leader, for Hindu–Muslim cooperation within Congress-controlled provinces. However, Congress claimed that because it had a Muslim membership it had the right to speak for all Indians, and therefore rejected Jinnah's appeal. In retaliation, Jinnah called for the creation of a separate Muslim state of Pakistan.

In September 1939 the Viceroy declared war on India's behalf, without consulting the people. In anger, Congress provincial governments resigned – although Muslim governments remained in operation. In 1942, while Japanese forces advanced towards India, the British government sent Stafford Cripps to offer India Dominion Status, with the right of secession from the Commonwealth, although this option and other internal reforms would have to be postponed until the end of the war. Nehru wanted to accept the offer, but Gandhi persuaded Congress to reject it and support his 'Quit India' campaign. The Viceroy ordered the arrest and imprisonment (without trial) of Gandhi, Nehru and other Congress leaders.

## 1944–7

'Division by creeds means the creation of political camps organized against each other . . . [and] teaches them to think as partisans and not as citizens. We regard any system of communal electorates as a serious hindrance to the self-governing principle.'
The Montagu-Chelmsford Report, 1918

In 1944 Britain appointed a new Viceroy to India, Lord Wavell, who released the Congress leaders and called them to a conference, also to be attended by the leaders of the Muslim League. The Viceroy put forward the proposals which Cripps had brought to India in 1942, and the conference was dominated by discussion of the future government of the sub-continent. This failed to heal the breach between Jinnah, the militant leader of the Muslim League who demanded a separate state for the Muslim minority, and the leaders of the Hindu-dominated Congress who hoped for an all-India government.

After the British elections of 1945, the Labour government sent three ministers, including Cripps, to India, in another vain effort to get Hindu–Muslim agreement as a preliminary to independence. Finally, Wavell called an election in August 1946, following which he invited Nehru to form a government. Jinnah, while agreeing to enter the Cabinet, called for 'Direct Action' by the Muslim League to secure a separate Pakistan once independence was achieved. The winter of 1946–7 was marked by violent clashes, and the wholesale massacre of Hindus, Muslims and Sikhs by their respective religious 'enemies'. Provincial governments, dominated by their particular religious interests, were unwilling or unable to stop the killing. Wavell declared that Britain must either stay in India for at least ten more years (and commit the resources to do so), or fix a date for withdrawal and stick to it, even if this meant handing over power to weak provincial governments. Wavell concluded that it would be impossible to create a single Indian central authority.

Prime Minister Attlee rejected this gloomy advice and replaced Wavell with Lord Mountbatten, formerly Supreme Allied Commander South-East Asia, and a cousin of King George VI. Faced with sectarian violence, and a civil war in the Punjab, along with the continual withdrawal of British troops under demobilization procedures, Mountbatten quickly agreed with Wavell's harsh alternatives. Since a Labour government would not agree to the first of these, there remained only the alternative of fixing a date for independence. On 20 February 1947 Attlee announced that Britain would leave India in June 1948, hoping that this would concentrate the minds of India's opposing factions.

## The birth of two nations, 1947

'I had to wind up the British Raj and bring India into independence . . . knowing that I would be the last Viceroy, the last of a line going back to Clive and Warren Hastings.'

Lord Mountbatten

Mountbatten had obtained from Attlee the plenipotentiary powers allowing him to act without first consulting the India Office in London. In mid-April 1947 a Conference of British Governors of the Indian Provinces told of the clashes, the danger of a complete breakdown in society, and the economic dislocation involved. By June 1947, following talks with Indian leaders (Document 12.1), Mountbatten saw that June 1948 was too remote a date for independence, in view of the risk of continued violence. He persuaded Attlee to agree to a withdrawal on 15 August 1947. Jinnah had convinced Mountbatten that India ought to be partitioned, and the Muslims given a separate state. The Hindu Gandhi, on the other hand, urged the maintenance of Indian unity, by force if necessary, – a strange request from a non-violent protester. Mountbatten, realizing the impossibility of keeping a united India, set up a commission to plan the transfer of power to two states.

There was little time to provide solutions to the various problems which this entailed, such as the question of what to do with the 562 princely states which were never part of British India. Mountbatten proposed that they be free to choose whether to become a part of India, or of Pakistan – or neither. Most of them were small, and so were forced to join one of the 'giants'. Some, notably Hyderabad, were large enough to think of independence, and the Maharajah of Hyderabad felt betrayed when India took his state by force in 1948–9. The problems concerning the princely state of Kashmir will be considered below.

A second set of difficulties, mainly technical in nature, were involved in the division of the many 'All-India' systems. Would India allow 'its' water to flow into Pakistan? And vice versa? How were the army and navy to be partitioned? The civil service was predominantly Hindu but contained people of all religions. How was this to be partitioned? Would the separate states maintain the All-India railway system?

The Commission, and the many Indians who took part in its discussions, solved most of these problems before August 1947. However, a major difficulty still remained concerning the boundaries of the two states. A boundary commission was created, in which the Hindu members 'cancelled out' the two Muslim members, leaving Sir Cyril (later Lord) Radcliffe to take a series of boundary decisions, including that which gave India access to Kashmir. The division of the Punjab meant that the Sikhs were partitioned between the two states, their holy city, Amritsar in India, being cut off from Sikhs in Pakistan. Here, as elsewhere, there was large-scale fighting; in March 1947, while the boundary commission was still being set up, Muslims wrecked Hindu bazaars in Amritsar, and burnt Hindu homes and their occupants. The warlike Sikhs attacked Muslims on the Pakistan side of the proposed boundary, while the racially-divided police took no action.

Elsewhere, fear drove millions to leave their homes and seek refuge in areas dominated by the co-religionists. Five million Hindus left West Pakistan, and were replaced by five million Muslims, while one million Hindus also left East Pakistan. Vast numbers were killed before and while making their way by train or on foot to their proposed new homeland. This orgy of violence was capped in January 1948 when a Hindu fanatic murdered Gandhi, the apostle of peace.

## Nehru's India, 1947–64

'At the strike of the midnight hour, when the world sleeps, India will wake to life and freedom.'

Nehru, 14 August 1947

More than most, Jawaharlal Nehru, India's first Prime Minister, knew that India would also 'wake' to face a series of problems. In a mainly agricultural country, millions lived below the poverty-line and thousands died each week of starvation. A 'green revolution' was necessary if India was to feed itself, avoiding the cost of importing food and allowing the purchase of the imported machinery required for India's industrialization.

India was officially a secular state, not attached to a particular religion, although the majority of the population were Hindu. Hinduism teaches people to accept their fate; Nehru had to stir these fatalists if India was to develop and provide its people with a decent standard of living. Hindu society is divided into hundreds of castes, which determine a person's job, marriage partner, political loyalty and educational opportunity. The Hindu-dominated Congress, controlled by people of higher castes, had ignored the plight of the millions of 'untouchables'. Nehru's government had to break down these traditional divisions in order that economic development could get under way. Nehru, the socialist, also had to overcome both opposition in Congress and India's traditional inertia in order to lessen the economic and social inequalities resulting from the caste system. Modernizing India also entailed providing economic and social opportunities for women, traditionally regarded as inferior.

Perhaps Nehru's greatest success was that he made democracy work in a country which had no real experience of such a system, where 80 per cent of the people were illiterate, and where some, under the influence of Stalin, wanted a revolution. While Congress won the first election, there were several Opposition groups. These included the communists, eager for a Soviet-style revolution, the Jan Sanga representing Hindu traditionalists opposed to changes offensive to their religious beliefs, and a block of MPs representing the 'untouchables', whose leader, Jagjivan Ram, demanded reforms to improve their conditions. Nor was Congress the monolith which some claimed it to be. Riven by regional differences, by caste and by economic interests, feudal landowners and millionaire mill-owners dominated a party whose members had too little contact with the great mass of their supporters.

In 1950 Nehru introduced a new, republican constitution, with a strong government in Delhi, two Houses of Parliament, provincial governments in each of the states and votes for all adults. He brought in the Untouchability Act (1955) banning discrimination against the lowest caste, who were guaranteed employment through special 'job reservations'. Not everyone accepted these changes; as late as 1980 there were riots when the Gujarat Assembly increased its 'untouchables' reservation in medical colleges to 25 per cent of places.

Nehru knew that the caste system impeded progress, as did India's lack of capital resources, which forced her to accept economic and technical aid from the Soviet bloc as well as the West. In 1951 Nehru introduced his first Five Year Plan, which concentrated on agriculture – introducing fertilizers, improving seed, stock and irrigation systems while encouraging land redistribution. Food production had increased by 20 per cent by 1956, but increases in population of two per cent a year almost wiped out the beneficial effects of this 'agricultural revolution'. The second and third Plans concentrated on industrial development; steel and cement industries were started or expanded, along with the hydro-electric schemes essential for industrial progress. By 1961 industrial output had almost doubled, although only one per cent of the population worked in industry.

Efforts were made to provide free and compulsory schooling for all children, authorities began to tackle the problem of the horrifying slums in which the majority of the urban population lived, and thousands of villages were provided with their first supply of electricity. However, despite the progress, India remained a very poor country: in 1958 the average *per capita* income was only £27 per year, the comparable figure for Britain being £425.

In 1956 Nehru introduced an intensive programme to encourage birth control. It had little success, however, in a country where many could not understand it, and where religious groups were frequently offended by such 'an interference with nature'.

Nehru kept Republican India in the Commonwealth, arguing that she would be a bridge between Europe and Asia, able to represent the interests of colonial peoples elsewhere and better placed to gain access to British aid. Hoping to act as 'an honest broker' internationally, Nehru adopted a policy of non-alignment, refusing to join either of the two power blocs in the Cold War. He acted as a mediator in Korea, where he arranged a truce (p. 269), and in Vietnam, where he helped bring the various parties to Geneva in 1954 (p. 238). In 1955 he assisted in organizing the Bandung Conference of Afro-Asian peoples, which tried to create a Third World power group, and also supported China's claim to be the 'natural' leader of such a bloc. However, between 1959 and 1962 India's relations with China deteriorated: there were many clashes along the ill-defined border between the two countries, mainly in Ladakh, a barren and sparsely populated area of Kashmir. During the Indo-China war of 1962, Nehru was accused of having neglected India's defences. Meanwhile, his acceptance of US aid affected his reputation abroad, already besmirched by his forcible seizure of the Portugese colony of Goa in 1961.

India's relations with Pakistan were always uneasy, and particularly where they concerned Kashmir, a predominantly Muslim country with a Hindu Maharajah. When, in 1947, Pakistan invaded the state, the Maharajah asked for Indian help. The UN arranged a temporary truce, alloting the mountain region to Pakistan and the valleys to India. Nehru, a Kashmiri himself, wanted the state to be incorporated in India and refused the UN's proposal of a plebiscite to determine the people's wishes. Instead, Nehru held an election in the Indian-held region, won by his supposed ally, Sheikh Abdullah; when Abdullah declared Kashmir independent, Nehru imprisoned him.

The UN division of Kashmir led to disputes over the waters of the Indus River. West Pakistan was dependent on this river, and its four great tributaries, for her water supply, hydro-electricity plants and irrigation schemes. These rivers rise in India or in Indian-held Kashmir, and the Indians proposed to build a canal to carry waters to irrigate a desert area west of Delhi. In the wake of Pakistani protests, negotiations were held (1951–60) which led to the Indus Water Treaty for the sharing of the rivers. At the same times the World Bank organized massive foreign loans for the building of storage dams and irrigation canals.

In 1964 Nehru and Ayub of Pakistan were to meet to try to solve the Kashmir problem. Nehru died before this meeting could take place, leaving this, and other problems, for his daughter to solve.

## Indira Gandhi's India, 1966–84

When Nehru died in May 1964, the speedy accession of Lol Shastri was a proof that democracy had taken firm root. Shastri, imprisoned by the British for his part in civil disobedience campaigns, had served under Nehru and been responsible for the implementation of the anti-discrimination laws, which brought him into opposition with the right-wing traditionalists of Congress. It was to try to placate these critics that, in 1965, he went to war with Pakistan over Kashmir. The war eventually ended in 1966, when Prime Minister Kosygin of the Soviet Union arranged a meeting between Shastri and Ayub at Tashkent, where they agreed to end the fighting, but failed to produce a permanent solution to the Kashmir problem.

Shastri died in January 1966, and Congress chose Nehru's daughter, Indira Gandhi, as their new leader, a surprising choice by the male-dominated party. However, she led Congress to electoral victories in 1967 and 1971, continued her father's economic and reforming policies, and saw India become a net exporter of food.

Between 1967 and 1971 she fought the 'Syndicate' of party bosses who dominated Congress and sought to control her. She formed a powerful left-wing group, forced the rebels to declare themselves, and led her Congress (Indira) Party to victory in 1971. She was equally forceful in dealing with the threat from the communists who won control of West Bengal in 1967; rioting there and in neighbouring states led her to introduce decrees allowing direct, presidential rule 'in times of disorder'.

India's fourth Economic Development Plan aimed to increase national wealth by six per cent a year, providing some 18 million new jobs and raising the average income by 25 per cent. The plan was only a partial success: in 1966 inflation forced the government to devalue the currency to help exporters, and to bring in the foreign earnings needed to pay for development. In 1967 a drought in some states led to thousands dying of starvation. In 1971, while India was coping with the influx of Bengali refugees (p. 196), the coast of Orissa was hit by a huge tidal wave, which swept up the Bay of Bengal, killing thousands and leaving hundreds of thousands homeless.

Like her father, Indira Gandhi was a socialist: she nationalized the banks and, after the 1971 elections, the insurance companies. In that election her Party gained a hundred more seats and seemed stronger than ever. This helped when India and Pakistan went to war in 1971 (p. 196) but may have caused her to adopt a more forthright family planning policy. She allowed her son, Sanjay, to take charge of a programme which advocated male vasectomy; this he tried to enforce in some regions, while also trying to compel women to adopt some form of artificial method of birth control. Mrs Gandhi's opponents used Sanjay's hard-line policy and ruthless tactics as excuses for an attack on her government.

In 1975 the High Court found Mrs Gandhi guilty of corrupt practices and disqualified her from holding office for six years. She ignored the judgement and declared a state of emergency, which lasted until 1977. She gave herself power to rule without parliament, to arrest and imprison thousands of opponents without trial and to impose both her socialist policies and Sanjay's family planning programme upon the people. In 1977 she called fresh elections, during which her party faced an electoral alliance made up of Congress opponents led by Morarji Desai, Jagjivan Ram, leader of the 'untouchables' and one of her former ministers, as well as others who disliked her authoritarian rule. The alliance won enough seats for Desai to form a government, which collapsed, however, in 1979.

Indira Gandhi then returned to power as leader of the largest group in parliament. She faced a major problem in the Punjab, where Sikh extremists, led by San Jarnad Sing Bhindranwale, called for the creation of a separate Sikh state, Khalistan. Negotiations with the extremists and with more moderate Sikhs, failed to produce a solution, and in 1983 armed Sikhs took control of the Golden Temple in the Sikh holy city of Amritsar. Mrs Gandhi was unwilling to allow either 'separatism' or terrorism to gain ground in India, and the army drove the extremists from the Golden Temple. This led many moderate Sikhs to adopt an anti-Gandhi line. In 1984 she was murdered by one of her Sikh guards, leaving behind the India which she had helped to make a more prosperous India (Document 12.3).

## Rajiv Gandhi's India

Sanjay had been groomed as his mother's potential successor, but he died in 1980, and the Nehru mantle fell to the reluctant Rajiv Gandhi, an

airline pilot who had shown little interest in politics. Elected leader of
the Congress Party, he became Prime Minister of the world's largest
democracy.

In December 1984 he called national elections in which he was
supported by the intellectuals (opposed to his mother's autocratic
methods and Sanjay's ruthlessness), as well as by the growing number
of middle-class Indians who were the beneficiaries of the changes that
have taken place since 1947 (Document 12.2). As Nehru's grandson
Gandhi was also supported by the millions who looked, naturally, to
the 'dynasty' for leadership.

Maintaining his mother's socialist policies in some fields, he has
pursued his own course in others. Taxes have been cut and imports
liberalized; the prosperous are more content than ever. He has tried to
curb the corruption which affects much of India's economic and
political life while acknowledging that, in a largely feudal country
where the 'family' rather than the 'state' is seen as central, it may be
many years before he has much success.

He has tried to solve the Punjab problem by handing over power to a
government of the Sikh religious party, the Akali Dal, which is
opposed by the extremist followers of Bhindranwale, killed in the
attack on the Golden Temple. These have again taken control of the
Temple, and it remains to be seen whether the majority of Sikhs will
support the Akali moderates or the extremists.

Rajiv Gandhi has also had to contend with the problem created by the
Tamil minority in Sri Lanka, where, since 1984, the rebels have waged a
guerrilla war against the Sinhalese government. Some 40,000 Tamils
have already fled to India, which they see as their supporter. Gandhi
seeks to persuade the Sinhalese to adopt political rather than military
solutions to the problem, offering to use his own leverage over the
Tamils, who are 'kith and kin' to India's own 40 million Tamils. If there
is no political solution, he may be forced to intervene in defence of
Tamil interests.

Rajiv Gandhi has maintained India's place as a leading 'liberal' Third
World country, and in 1986 was one of the Commonwealth's
outspoken critics of South Africa's *apartheid* policy. Unimpressed by
the moderate stance taken by Reagan and Thatcher, he called for
mandatory sanctions against the Botha government. Reluctant he may
have been in 1984; by 1986 he seemed to fit naturally into the Nehru
mould.

### Pakistan, 1947–72

'We are a nation of a hundred millions, with our distinctive culture,
language and literature, art and architecture . . . [and] our distinctive
outlook on life.'

Jinnah to Gandhi, September 1944

Gandhi denied Jinnah's claims in 1944, arguing that Indian Muslims were as much Indians as were the Hindus: Pakistan had no historic roots, nor, despite the Muslim League, had it any distinctive social or economic policies. Jinnah *was*, in a sense, Pakistan (Document 12.1), an unreal state that had more than its share of problems.

Some of these were shared with India: Pakistan had mass illiteracy and a low *per capita* income, as well as food shortages and economic inequality. Other problems were peculiar to Pakistan, its two parts separated by 1000 miles, the peoples of the two regions divided in race and language. The death of Jinnah in 1948 and the assassination of the first Prime Minister, Liaquat Ali Khan in 1951 were disasters which further affected the state's development. Successive governments failed to cope with the eight million refugees who flocked to Pakistan from India; corrupt and self-seeking politicians failed to implement Five Year Plans aimed at economic and social improvement. They have also failed to solve the Kashmir problem. More importantly, in the long run, the people in the east, who produce rice and jute (Pakistan's main export), and speak Bengali, felt that they were maltreated by the Urdu-speaking people of the west, who have dominated the army, civil service and national life generally.

As the politicians squabbled, democracy became discredited. In October 1958 General Ayub Khan took power as President of the Republic. He removed corrupt politicians and civil servants, and introduced a programme of economic development. Land reform saw restrictions on the size of estates, with surplus land taken from wealthy landowners for redistribution among the peasants. Within six months refugees had been rehoused, and a series of dams and hydro-electric schemes were under way. Production of jute, carpets and leather goods was expanded, communications were improved and educational provision was enlarged, while agreement with India was reached over the Indus waters (p. 192), although not over Kashmir.

In 1965 Ayub won a sweeping victory in presidential elections, although he was less popular in the east than in the west. His government was blamed, unfairly, for the floods and famines which affected the east in the late 1960s, and his popularity slumped. To regain support, Ayub announced a scheme for 'the return to democracy'. A period of 'basic democracy' allowed local councils to be elected, which would later return MPs to Parliament. While voters and politicians came to terms with this new system, Ayub proposed to retain control of central government. However, in 1969 opponents combined to call for his overthrow. These included landlords angry at his land reforms, politicians released from gaol seeking a return to the pre-Ayub system, Muslim leaders demanding a more fundamentally Islamic state, and communists complaining that Ayub favoured the landowners who, on the other hand, thought he favoured the poor. In West Pakistan, Zulfikar Ali Bhutto, a leading landowning politician, accused Ayub of corruption, of ignoring the needs of the west and of seeking to maintain his personal rule.

In March 1969 the army commander, Yahya Khan, forced Ayub to resign. A new military government imposed martial law and promised that 'when the country was ready', democracy would be restored. Yahya kept his word, and elections were held in December 1970. In the west, Bhutto's People's Party won a large majority, while in the east, Sheikh Mujibur Rahman's Awami League won all but two of the seats. This meant that the League would have a majority of seats in Parliament and that, for the first time, Bengalis would control Pakistan's affairs.

Democracy, however, had no roots in Pakistan. Bhutto refused to accept the electoral result, and announced that his Party would boycott Parliament. Yahya tried to get the two sides to negotiate, but Bhutto insisted that the League accept the west's 'divine right' to rule. Mujibur would not agree to this overturning of the election result, and faced with Bhutto's intransigence he announced (March 1971) that East Pakistan was now the independent Republic of Bangladesh. Yahya, hoping to preserve the union, arrested Mujibur and sent troops to the east to restore law and order, and rule by central authority. Bengali refugees fled to India to escape the savagery of the West Pakistan forces, imposing a strain on Indian resources as eight million people clamoured to be fed and housed.

Indian and Pakistani forces clashed along the border, and fighting broke out in Kashmir. Indian troops went to the help of Bangladeshi 'rebels' and in December 1971 Yahya had to submit. Bhutto became President of West Pakistan, while Mujibur, released from gaol, took control of Bangladesh. Mrs Gandhi wanted a peaceful solution to the problem and had the support of the Soviet Union, although China (which had aided Pakistan) and the USA (which used Pakistan as a client state) would have preferred a strong and united state. In 1972 a conference held at Simla agreed that all troops, Indian and Pakistani, would withdraw from occupied territory. India agreed to repatriate 900,000 Pakistani prisoners-of-war, and maintain the status quo in Kashmir.

The autocratic and ambitious Bhutto refused to accept this agreement: his 'country' had been humiliated by the defeat and could not afford to lose East Pakistan's valuable trade. He denied the existence of Bangladesh, which was admitted to the British Commonwealth in 1972 – whereupon Pakistan left.

## Zia's Pakistan

'The despot who rides a hungry tiger.'

*The Times*, 2 January 1986

'The people of Pakistan want a deliverance. The Pakistan People's Party is going to show them the way.'

Benazir Bhutto, July 1986

Bhutto tried, but failed, to frame a constitution for the former West Pakistan, now simply Pakistan. Many people blamed him for the loss of the east and for the humiliating defeat by India. The economy declined further as China withdrew her aid, and floods affected the Indus valley in 1973. Muslim fundamentalists accused Bhutto of being too westernized; landowners feared his attempt to gain popular support, while left-wingers accused him of increasing autocracy. His inefficient, corrupt and ruthless government became increasingly unpopular. Then in mid-1977, the newly-appointed Chief of Staff, General Zia led a cou p. Bhutto was arrested, but quickly freed, as Zia announced that elections would be held within 90 days so that a civilian government could take over. However, Bhutto called for an even speedier end to martial law, and threatened the fragile peace. Zia re-arrested him, cancelled the elections and obtained the Supreme Court's support for the continuation of martial law. Bhutto was accused of implication in the murder of a political opponent; he was tried, and, in spite of world wide appeals, hanged on 4 April 1979. Other opponents of Zia were arrested, imprisoned or exiled, and most parties boycotted the elections held in November 1979, which Zia used as an excuse to continue in power. The Soviet invasion of Afghanistan in December 1979 turned Pakistan into a front-line state, needed by the USA; economic and military aid from the US enabled Zia to develop the economy and so provide some semblance of stability.

In February 1981 opposition parties formed the Movement for the Restoration of Democracy. Bhutto's widow, and his daughter, Benazir, were among the leaders. In March 1981 Zia launched a new constitution which provided for a nominated (not elected) parliament. At the same time, he put the Bhutto women under house arrest, seeking to limit the MRD's ability to campaign. In August 1983 he announced plans for 'a controlled return to democracy', and the MRD launched a country-wide campaign against his military government.

In September 1983 elections were held for local councils; these, claimed Zia, proved that the country was on the path to democracy. In December 1984 a referendum confirmed him in office for a further five years, and in February 1985 elections were held for a national Parliament. However, as no parties were allowed to campaign, the Assembly was 'party-less', while the Senate was packed with Zia's men. In December 1985 Zia announced the end of martial law, which led to the restoration of some civil rights, the closing of martial law offices, the abolition of martial courts and the repeal of most of the martial law orders. However, many of these had been written into the new constitution and can be repealed only by a two-thirds vote in Parliament – an unlikely prospect at present.

Zia has allowed political parties to undertake campaigns to win new members and drum up support for the elections promised for the 1990s. Such parties must accept Zia's concept of a new Pakistan; they must submit their accounts to a government registrar, and promise not to 'defame or bring into ridicule' the army or the judiciary. The People's Party, led by Bhutto's daughter, may find it impossible to keep within the boundaries set by Zia, who accuses her of getting aid from India, Libya and the Soviet Union, and of using too vigorous language in her attacks on his government. It remains to be seen whether Zia will win his confrontation with the daughter of the man who appointed him Chief of Staff in 1976.

## Bangladesh

'An American journalist was embarrassed to find that his bill for dinner was more than the average Bangladeshi's annual income.'

*The Times*, 8 December 1985

'What Ershad is trying to restore is certainly not democracy. He is trying to legitimize the power he illegally captured.'

Begum Zia, Opposition leader

The 1971–2 war caused much destruction in an already poor and overpopulated country, in which raging inflation, food shortages and frequent floods made matters worse. After the war there was increased racial conflict as Muslims fought Hindus, and Bengalis fought Biharis. While a small group of rich landowners and merchants survived, starvation was a constant threat for millions of landless peasants. The Awami League government was incapable of coping with the many problems of this new state, in which fifteen political parties vied for popular support.

Mujibur's assassination in August 1975 seems, in hindsight, to have been almost inevitable. The restless nature of this impoverished country was illustrated by the assassinations of his successors in 1975, 1976 and 1977, when General Ziaur Rahman emerged as military ruler. An upsurge of Muslim fundamentalism, coupled with Muslim anger at the Soviet invasion of Afghanistan in December 1979, made his rule an uneasy one, dependent on economic and military aid from the USA and Britain, and on subsidies from the oil-rich Muslim states of the Gulf.

In 1979 Ziaur called elections, hoping that 'normalcy' might be restored. The fifteen parties put forward 65 candidates in the presidential elections, and there was little chance of political stability in a country which badly needed it if investment were to be encouraged, inflation tackled and an attempt made at economic and social reform.

In March 1982 General Ershad seized power and imposed martial law, promising (of course) a return to civilian rule 'when the time was ripe'. Mujibur's daughter, Sheikh Hasina, led the remnants of the Awami League and worked to create an alliance of the fifteen parties opposed to martial law. By 1985 the opposition had won the support of jute-mill workers, engineers, and professional workers, who took industrial action in support of demands for a return to civilian rule.

In May 1985 local government elections were allowed, but only on a non-party basis, which produced village councils with a vested interest in supporting Ershad and his proposed 'partyless' future government. In May 1986 elections were held for a national parliament, and Ershad formed the Jatiyo (National) Party to express his views. The elections were marred by violence and ballot-rigging, the leaders of the Awami League protesting at the return of a Jatiyo-dominated Parliament. Ershad argued that the opposition's boycotting of the opening of Parliament, and their threats to call a strike as part of their anti-government campaign, proved the need for continued martial law. It remains to be seen whether this poor country will take even the first steps away from military rule.

## Documentary evidence

The initial partition of India was arranged by the last Viceroy, Earl Mount-batten of Burma (Document 12.1), who found it harder to negotiate with the Muslim Jinnah than with Hindu leaders. The subsequent partition of Pakistan in 1971–2 illustrated one weakness of Jinnah's policy, which seemed to have ignored the poverty of his part of the sub-continent. This poverty has continued (Document 12.2), whereas India has made some economic progress (Document 12.3).

## Document 12.1

*Mountbatten on Indian leaders, 1947*

'Far and away the most outstanding man in India, revered by millions of Muslims and Hindus alike, was Mahatma Gandhi. At my first meeting he didn't talk any business at all. We just chatted. We spent two hours in this way and the Press could hardly believe that we had not been deciding the fate of India. Well, perhaps we had – indirectly. Gandhi's political power was on the wane. He was a modern-day saint and saints cannot thrive for ever in a political atmosphere. At our next meeting he proposed as a solution to India's problems that I ask Jinnah to form an administration, even though he must have realized that this would give the Muslims virtual control. Anything rather than see India divided, or have a civil war. Of course it was quite impractical. I told him he must first get the support of the Congress Party and this he naturally failed to get.

Pandit Nehru was already a friend. My first meeting with him had been almost a year before, when he visited Singapore when I was still Supreme Commander South-East Asia. He knows now that he would get a fair deal from me. With Nehru the trust I was trying to build up with the leaders was already there – and more . . . friendship.

Patel was another tremendous figure. Inside Congress he was just about as eminent as Nehru . . . on internal politics. He was the man who dispensed patronage in the Party – as Home Minister he controlled the jobs. At one of our early meetings Patel and I had a stand-up row. He was used to getting his own way. He was astonished to find that he had to give way to me; but he did. From then on our relationship improved, until in the end we also became firm friends.

The man whom I had real difficulty in getting through to was Jinnah. If it could be said that any single man held the future of India in the palm of his hand in 1947 that man was Jinnah. To all intents and purposes Jinnah *was* the Muslim League and if the dream of Pakistan ever did come true it would be Jinnah who brought it to life and fashioned it. I tried the same technique with him that I had used with Gandhi, no business at the first meeting, just talk. He was surprised by this, but after a while he softened up a bit. But after that interview I said: "My God, he was cold!" '

(From the TV film, '*The Life and Times of Earl Mountbatten of Burma*')

## Document 12.2

*Poverty in the Indian sub-continent, 1979–80*

'India, Pakistan and Bangladesh have a combined population of over 88 million, including half of the poorest people in the world who face, every day, the problem of mere survival, when, in the words of the *Brandt Report*

> work is frequently not available, or, when it is, pay is very low and conditions often barely tolerable. Homes are constructed of impermanent materials and have neither piped water nor sanitation. Electricity is a luxury. Health services are thinly spread and in rural areas only rarely available within walking distance. Primary schools, where they exist, may be free and not too far away, but children are needed for work and cannot be easily spared for school. *Permanent insecurity is the condition of the poor.* There are no public systems of social security in the event of unemployment, sickness or death of the wage-earner in the family. Flood, drought or disease affecting people or livestock can destroy livelihood without hope of compensation.'

(*North-South: A Programme for Survival*, Pan Books, 1980)

## Document 12.3

*Signs of progress in Rajiv Gandhi's India, 1985*

'I asked the prime minister if he did not now see India as a capitalist country . . . free enterprise as the way forwards. No, he said, India was still socialist "in the sense that the government must work for the poor [and] that must change as the poor become less poor, as the training and capabilities of the people increase". Thirty-five years ago, he said, agriculture had comprised almost 100 per cent of the national product, there was almost no industrial infra-structure. Today, India had a "tremendous capability" in technology, engineering and management. State enterprise had started in India because the state was the only source of capital investment other than foreign companies. "We were suspicious about foreign investment and we still are to some extent. But now we have our own strength. If we were still weak maybe we would still be suspicious."

So private enterprise was doing well? Look at agriculture, said the prime minister, "a three-fold increase in productivity since Independence and it's been in private hands throughout". But wasn't one of the results also a disparity between the rich and the poor? "Yes and no. If you mean do we have very, very poor people in India, of course we do. And we do have a new rich, yes. But what you've got to see is the band of our population that our rich covers in the middle class. One tends to forget that India has a very substantial middle class which didn't exist 30 years ago. And one of the incredible things is that from 1980 to 1984 we've been able to reduce the percentage of people living below the poverty line, from 51 per cent to 37.5 per cent. Now that's a 14 per cent drop, and it's 14 per cent of 740 million, not 14 per cent of the 1980 population (680 million). That's what we've done in four years."

The rise of the Indian middle class has passed largely unnoticed by the outside world, but the consumption figures are quite stunning. In 1980 India made and sold 250,000 motor bikes and scooters; this year the figure was a million. In 1980 it made 35,000 cars; this year 100,000. In 1975 it made 100,000 TVs; this year 2.5 million. The stock market raised about £66 million in fresh shares in 1980; this year £1650 million. Figures like these lend a new meaning to the word "development". How far the wealth has trickled from its little islands of urban prosperity is a more troublesome question. Many Indian economists say that India has a greater absolute number of poor people than ever, and the cliché about the rich getting richer and the poor poorer can be proved statistically. A middle position argues that some poor have grown poorer, others the same, others again richer, with the last category in the majority. In a large and complex country, which adds 15 million to its population every year, statistics can be difficult to trust.

I asked about the new technology which he is keen to import. Was it such a good thing when labour was so cheap and in over-supply? And what was the point, say, of a computerized railway freight service when it was politically impossible to sack the 5000 clerks the computer would replace? Yes and no, he said. First, they had so many employed in the state sector "and we have no intention of sacking any of them". Second it was important to bear in mind that the older processes were less efficient. "I mean the railways make a tremendous loss. It means that many millions of rupees are removed from an anti-poverty programme or a dam or a power station. So the chap who is really paying is not the richer but the poorest whose programmes are cut."

The argument might be Thatcher's and in terms of their natural economic inclinations no prime ministers of India and Britain have been as close since Nehru and Attlee.'

('The Blooding of Rajiv Gandhi', *Sunday Times Magazine*, October 1985)

## FURTHER READING

ADANS, J. and IQBAL, S., *Exports, Politics and Economic Development: Pakistan, 1970–1982*, Westview, 1983

CAMPBELL-JOHNSON, A., *Mission with Mountbatten*, Hale, 1951

CHAMBERLAIN, M. E., *Decolonization*, Blackwell, 1985 (for the Historical Association)

CHAUDHURI, P., *Indian Economy: Poverty and Development*, Crosby Lockwood, 1979

FELDMAN, H., *Pakistan*, OUP, 1979

GOPAL, S., ed., *Jawaharlal Nehru: An Anthology*, OUP, 1980

HART, H. C., *Indira Gandhi's India*, Westview, 1976

JOHNSON, B., *India*, Heinemann, 1979

LEWES, P., *Reason Wounded: an experience of India's emergency*, Allen and Unwin, 1979

MARR, D., *Asia: The winning of Independence*, Macmillan, 1981

MELLOR, J. W., ed., *India: A Rising Power*, Westview, 1979

MOORE, R. J., *Escape from Empire: The Attlee government and the Indian problem*, OUP, 1983

STEPHENS, IAN, *Pakistan: Old Country, New Nation*, Penguin, 1964

WOLPERT, S., *A new history of India*, OUP, 1977

# 13
# Japan

### Rehabilitation

'The new Japan has a great opportunity to exert an influence in Asia by
. . . conduct and example, a great liberating influence.'
John Foster Dulles, 1951

In 1945 Japan was prostrate, its emperor deprived of his 'divine' status,
its cities and transport system devastated. Along with 15 million
unemployed was a US army of occupation.

Today, it has rebuilt its great industries, become the world's leader in
new technology, and a major force in international trade. It is one of the
Group of Five (with the USA, UK, West Germany and France) whose
ministers' decisions affect currency values, interest rates and international economic development.

In theory, between 1945 and 1951 Japan was the responsibility of an
Allied Council in Tokyo and the Far Eastern Commission in Washington. In fact, Japan was 'ruled' by General MacArthur, the Supreme
Commander, to whose autocratic methods Japan owes a great deal. He
introduced policies aimed at disarmament and demilitarization; he
organized the trials of war criminals, introduced a new constitution, as
well as administrative and social reforms, and tried to alter the cultural
and industrial pattern of the country.

MacArthur wanted to break the power of the *zaibatsu*, those huge
industrial combines whose leaders had once exerted a great influence on
Japanese politics. The old names and institutions disappeared. However, by 1986, six groups (Mitsubishi, Mitsui, Sumihoto, Fuyo, Sanwa
and Dai-Ichi Kangya) had linked together, each combining many
firms, banks and trading houses, while another ten groups link
suppliers and subsidiaries of a big firm or bank (Document 13.1). It is,
apparently, impossible to alter Japanese cultural and trading patterns.

MacArthur also wanted to end the power of the militarists, who in
the 1920s and 1930s had forced their expansionist policies on the

Emperor and politicians. Japan was forbidden an army, although this was ignored during the Korean War (p. 269) when a National Police Reserve, and Self-Defence Forces, were created. Even with these, some 250,000 men, defence spending has taken only about one per cent of GNP and around six per cent of government budgets. Japan has no nuclear capability, but is more of a 'great power' than some nuclear nations, such as Britain, France and India, because she spends more of her GNP on civilian, rather than military, investment.

MacArthur set Japan on the road to democracy. Under the constitution he presented in 1947, Japan has two Houses of Parliament, both directly elected. The franchise was extended to every adult, women being allowed to vote for the first time. The government is responsible to Parliament and not, as in the past, to the Emperor. While the latter was cut down to human size, some 200,000 people were barred from public life because of their recent history, and under the constitution, no officer in the armed services could become Prime Minister; there was to be civilian, not military, rule. There was to be no state religion, so that the nation would be free from the aggressive nationalism once associated with military leaders under the influence of traditional *samurai* doctrines.

Between 1945 and 1951 MacArthur instituted a series of economic reforms which had long-term beneficial effects. Two million peasants were given their own land, which led to increased agricultural output, a speedy end to postwar shortages, and greater political stability: nothing succeeds like possession, in damping down revolutionary fires. The elimination of big landowners at one end of the economic spectrum was matched by the encouragement given to workers to form trade unions, which were allowed to call strikes.

In Germany, the Allies quickly turned to the rebuilding of a war-torn economy (p. 267). In Japan, too, the Americans' attitude was soon coloured by their anti-communism. With the Korean War (p. 269) Japan became an essential provider of weapons (her industrial recovery being war-fuelled), and a base for US forces, which added to Japanese revenue and stimulated a variety of consumer-type industries. The speedy growth of the economy by 1953 was due to the determination, discipline and abilities of the people, and the autocratic government of MacArthur. A central planning organization regulated priorities and allocated resources, while the free-wheeling capitalist and competitive system continued to flourish. Economic growth was aided too by the cooperation between Japan's new leaders and the US authorities.

In 1951, as if in recognition of Japan's contribution to the Korean War effort, the USA and Japan signed the Treaty of San Francisco which formally ended the war and led to the withdrawal of US forces of occupation from the mainland, although they remained on Okinawa until 1972. By the Security Treaty (1960) the USA guaranteed the defence of Japan, whose rehabilitation was internationally recognized when, in 1956, she became a member of UNO.

## Political development, 1952–86

'Support for the Liberal Democrats is attenuated by apathy reinforced by scandals.'

*The Economist*, 7 December 1985

Japan's postwar political stability might be envied by many countries, and has played a part in her economic progress. No coups, as in Africa; no right-left switches, as in Britain; instead, an almost constant government has been maintained by the conservative Liberal Democrats. Politicians have been able to take the long view on economic and other issues, not constrained, as are British and US politicians, by thoughts of the next election. Economists, industrialists and central planners have been able to make, and stick to, decisions which bear fruit only in the long term.

The Liberal Democrats are not a homogeneous party, but rather a coalition of factions, each led by 'a strong man' who may or may not be a senior Minister. At the time of writing there are five main factions, the largest still led by Tanaka (p. 206), and the fourth largest by the current Prime Minister, Nakasone. The convention in the party is that no one occupies the Premiership for more than four years, so most Prime Ministers have had to be content with only one two-year term; competing rivals in the hierarchy want their turn at the top. In July 1986 Nakasone called elections some eighteen months before he needed to. One reason for this electoral gamble was his wish to get a third term as Prime Minister; if he had done badly at the polls, his chances would have been nil. However, his party won its most complete victory in thirty-one years of continuous rule, capturing 304 seats in the Lower House (a gain of fifty), and 142 in the Upper House (a gain of six). Nakasone claimed that he had never expected 'this kind of outcome. This voice of the nation, this voice of heaven, this voice of God.' It was impossible for his rivals to deny him the unprecedented third term in October 1986.

One of the reasons for the continued success of the LDP has been its ability to steal the opposition's clothes; when the growth of environmental concern led to the development of demand for anti-pollution measures, the government (which had presided over the system which produced the pollution) smoothly adopted the environmentalist cause. Division in the opposition ranks has helped the LDP, some calling for a Japanese army and a more vigorous foreign policy, others, more attuned to the electorate, decrying such strident militancy and arguing that defence spending would have to be at the expense of industrial investment. Some opposition spokesmen have called for a revival of Japanese nationalism, based, in part at least, on *samurai* legends; most of their colleagues fear a revival of militant nationalism, mindful of what it led to in the recent past. Given such divisions within the opposition it has been relatively easy for the LDP, presenting an apparently united face, to maintain itself in power.

It has done so in spite of financial scandals surrounding some of its leaders. In 1976, for example, Tanaka, leader of the largest faction, was found guilty of accepting bribes from the Lockheed Aircraft Company when he was Prime Minister in 1973. That hurt the party for a decade or so, the voters angered that 'a party of crooks' should be in charge of national affairs. Tanaka resigned from the LDP – but, ironically, continues to be a major power-broker in the game of political musical chairs.

*The Economist's* comment at the head of this section refers to voter apathy. In part this is caused by the almost constant success of the LDP faced with a divided opposition; in part it is due to voters' satisfaction with their country's economic performance: why change a winning team? However, apathy may be due to awareness of the 'wheels-within-wheels' political system, which seemingly denies the simple voter any real influence. The Japanese have learned that any ambitious, reform-promising politician has no chance of success unless he joins one of the factions and finds, additionally, some 'interest' (farming, forestry, transport, construction or electronics) to finance him. Even such a well-heeled politician has to accommodate himself to factional interests and to inter-factional arrangements. Gaining credibility as a silent supporter of a 'boss' and as a good coordinator counts for more than a reputation as an awkward innovator. This process either emasculates the rising politician or makes him a prisoner of various in-party and intra-party interests. Voters' cynical apathy may be easy to understand.

This system has allowed the bureaucracy to gain enormous power, so that, in effect, it runs Japan. Bureaucrats at various ministries control import licences and foreign exchange arrangements; officials at the Ministry of International Trade and Industry (MITI) persuade Japanese firms to share ideas, something which, in any event, companies have been willing to do. It is MITI officials who have persuaded firms to cooperate in basic, long-term research, of the kind which individual firms might not have considered viable. The bureaucracy has been helped by the Japanese tradition that civil servants retire in their fifties to take jobs in private industry; each new set of bureaucrats finds itself talking to members of the preceding set of bureaucrats, now turned industrialists, and both share an understanding of the officials' roles and the nation's needs. With government policy under their control, and with industry and commerce easily manipulated, the bureaucrats have played a major part in Japanese development. This may make voters apathetically cynical; however, they cannot deny that the system has worked effectively and in their interests.

## Economic development, 1952–86

'What will Japan do with its wealth?'

*The Economist*, Survey of Japan, 1973

By 1973, the last year before oil-price increases distorted world trade, Japan, the most industrialized nation in Asia, was one of world's trade leaders. The 'Japanese miracle' was evident in the growth of its shipbuilding, electronic and motor-vehicle industries, and in the continued rise in the level of exports (pp. 209–12). The International Trade Fair, EXPO 70, was both an advertisement for, and evidence of, Japan's success.

The 'Japanese miracle' has been even more astonishing than the 'economic miracle' experienced by West Germany. Between 1950 and 1973, Japan had an annual increase in GNP of 10.5 per cent; in 1973 her rate of economic growth was even greater than that of the USA and EEC countries. This speedy growth has continued:

*Real GNP: % change on previous years*

|       | 1980 | 1981 | 1982 | 1983 | 1984 | 1985 |       |
|-------|------|------|------|------|------|------|-------|
| USA   | −1   | 2.3  | −2   | 3.4  | 6.3  | 2.3  |       |
| Japan | 4.9  | 4.0  | 3.0  | 3.1  | 5.8  | 5.0  | (IMF) |

In 1985 Japan's GNP was the third largest in the world, exceeded only within the USA and the Soviet Union.

There was no natural base for this postwar development. Japan has few primary resources, virtually no oil, uranium, aluminium or nickel; she has very little coal, iron ore, copper or natural gas, and produces only half of her requirements of lead and zinc. Almost totally dependent on foreign materials, Japan nonetheless rebuilt her cities, transport systems and social fabric. The shortage of essential primary products became even more significant as Japan undertook industrial expansion; it is not surprising that the politico-bureaucratic system strove to obtain supplies of primary products either by participation in speculative exploration, or by acquiring some form of control over countries with these basic products.

To pay for essential imports, Japan had to quickly develop her export trade. In the 1950s and 1960s she had chronic trade deficits, her import needs outstripping her export capacity. In the 1980s we have come to see Japan as an exporting giant (pp. 209–12), and to view Japan's growth as export-led. Even in the 1960s and 1970s it was not so; the 1970s recovery was backed by domestic demand and by investment, with exports coming late in the day as stimulation. Companies became successful by competing at home; their later overseas success was due to their exploitation of the economies of scale created by their domestic situation. Domestic demand fuelled the export drive and not, as many think, vice versa.

Japan overcame her initial problems in a variety of interconnected ways. Government and bureaucrats ensured that non-essential imports were kept to the minimum, so that scarce foreign currency paid for essential raw materials and foreign technology. Land reform (p. 202) helped ensure an adequate supply of home-grown and import-saving food. Government, bureaucrats and industrialists joined in programmes of investment in industry and commerce. The diversion of a large share of GNP to investment meant that consumers were kept short of certain goods – housing, transport, clothing and the like. The cultural tradition of discipline and acceptance of decisions from on high meant that such shortages were accepted as inevitable in postwar Japan. The Japanese learned, over a period of ten or more years, that they could not spend all their income on consumer goods; so they became accustomed to a high level of savings, which provided industry and government with financial resources. This high propensity to save is still a feature of Japan, and can be contrasted to the US, with its high propensity to consume:

*Gross savings as % of GNP*

|       | 1980 | 1981 | 1982 | 1983 | 1984 |
|-------|------|------|------|------|------|
| USA   | 15   | 16   | 13   | 13   | 14   |
| Japan | 31   | 31   | 39   | 39   | 31   |

Since the Japanese GNP is almost as great as that of the USA, it is clear that the Japanese save, in total as well as in share of GNP, much more than Americans. This helps to explain their low propensity to import and the low level of budget deficits, in both of which they differ from the USA.

One cause of Japan's 'economic miracle' is the 'tribal' nature of Japanese business, creating a sense of mutual obligations, with loyalty owed to colleagues and compatriots. About one-quarter of Japanese companies have a system of 'jobs-for-life' for workers, ensuring loyalty in return for security, although such privileges do not exist for the majority. The 'tribal' theory with its concept of loyalty to compatriots does help to explain the linking, under one umbrella, of groups of firms, banks and trading houses (p. 203) who feel obliged to buy from and support one another (Document 13.1). 'Tribalism' also helps to explain the willingness of competing companies to share ideas, and even secrets, often at the instigation of the bureaucracy (p. 206).

The low level of defence spending is another cause of economic growth. Free from the pressures of the 'military-industrial complex' of which Eisenhower complained (p. 88), and lacking the Soviet-style 'metal eaters' (p. 76), Japan has been able to concentrate on industrial rather than military investment.

# The exporting giant

'The OPEC of the 1980s.'

*The Economist*, 7 December 1985

In the 1950s and 1960s Japan imported as little as possible, apart from essential raw materials and foreign technology. In the 1970s her development ensured that she became a major user of world resources. It was estimated that in 1981 Japan used one-tenth of the world's exports, and more than one-tenth of its oil. The problems associated with such needs will be considered on pp. 216–18.

During the 1960s, Japan's imports of raw materials (excluding oil and other energy sources) took up 3 per cent of her GNP. In 1984, however, things were different; imports of raw materials took up only 1.6 per cent of Japan's GNP, a figure lower than that of the four biggest EEC countries, West Germany, France, the UK and Italy. Japan's consumption of imported energy had also fallen, from nearly 7 per cent of the GNP to less than 5 per cent, again lower than the European 'four'. Conservation played a part in this fall; more importantly, Japan had developed high-tech electrical goods industries, requiring less energy and raw materials than the earlier industrial leaders, chemicals production, shipbuilding, steel-making and car manufacture.

While the imports bill fell as a percentage of GNP, Japan's exports rose sharply. One reason for this was the development of high technology, especially electronics. Today, electronic gadgets are essential to even low-tech products, and Japan has a lead in the worlds' fastest growing industries. Markets for most of her exports (the USA, EEC and China) have grown more rapidly than world trade as a whole. Government-guided projects in the 1970s ensured basic research for very large-scale integrated circuits, and support for Japan's computer industry. The sharing habits of 'tribalism' (p. 206) and the able leadership of secret-sharing and vertically-integrated groups (p. 203) helped Japanese firms to make great strides into the manufacture of computers, integrated circuits and telecommunication machinery. In Britain and other western countries, the venture into 'the brave new world' of computers was led by small firms or by government-aided firms, which had too little support and too little self-assurance. Japan's success is due, in part, to a national willingness to allow big firms to become even bigger, and to encourage the already strong to become yet stronger.

The export drive has been helped, until recently, by the relatively cheap *yen*, which made imports relatively expensive and exports relatively cheaper than they would otherwise have been. In 1986 the yen has been strengthened against foreign currencies – in September 1985 there were 270 yen to the US dollar, but there were about 150 to the dollar in July 1986. There is no sign that this has adversely affected Japan's trading position.

The low level of domestic consumption and the high level of domestic savings have shielded industry and government from the need to seek financial aid from overseas countries and bankers. Japan has no need of high interest rates to attract funds to support a trading and budget deficit.

There are several significant features of Japan's export-led boom. More than one-third of all her exports go to the USA, her largest trading partner, with Japan taking about 20 per cent of all US exports. Since 1982 Japan has supplied the goods for the US deficit-led boom. This linking of two leading economies (so that they have become almost one economy) creates problems. What happens if the US market slows down? For how long will the US government resist growing demands for protection against Japanese goods? Will the world continue to support a US trading deficit – including the $37 billion deficit with Japan? In 1984 the US needed an inflow of $43 billion of long-term capital; Japan has exported some $50 billion of such capital, much of it to the USA. How will such overseas investments be affected by future US policies on tax reform and financial liberalization? Remembering Japan's position *vis-à-vis* the USA after 1945, it is ironic to note the financial dependence of the USA on Japan in the 1980s.

Communist China is Japan's fourth biggest trading partner, while Japan is easily China's largest. Optimists see China as an alternative base for export-led Japanese growth if markets in the US and EEC decline. They see an inevitable link between the two giants of the Asian economy, which ignores the traditional Chinese suspicion of Japan, memories of wartime atrocities and communist antipathy to capitalism.

In 1962 Japan made a five-year commercial agreement with China on a barter basis, in spite of US hostility to China at that time. In view of China's relative poverty, this was, in reality, more of a token for the future than a major step of immediate significance. In the 1970s, and in the wake of détente, Japan has expanded her trade with China. In Deng's 'communist-capitalist' China (p. 109) there are increasing openings for this expansion. Since 1974, exports to China have grown from $2 billion (1974) to over $12 billion (1985), while imports from China have a grown from $1 billion to just over $8 billion. This growth was not uninterrupted; in 1971–2, 1976 and 1981–2 China cut back on imports, its economy unable to stand the strain of almost continuous deficits. There is no guarantee that there will not be similar restrictions in the future. Japan may well see China as a useful market but too unreliable to be the base for the long-term planning beloved of Japanese firms and bureaucrats.

In 1974 Japan imported 99.5 per cent of her oil, and 50 per cent of that from the Middle East. Following the oil-price increases of 1973, she looked elsewhere for supplies. In 1984 oil imports from China made up 40 per cent of all Chinese exports to Japan. Supplies were also sought from other Asian countries. Since most known oil supplies had already been developed by European or US companies, Japan's ability to invest in oil exploration is limited, but she has financed exploration in Indonesia, New Guinea and Australia. She has also made large non-oil investments in Malaysia, Thailand and the Philippines, and helped the growth in the economies of the ASEAN countries (Chapter 14).

In the 1950s and 1960s, Japan's growth was stimulated by domestic demand. In 1983 exports accounted for all the economic growth of that year, and in 1984 for two-thirds of the growth. Industrialists, trade union representatives and politicians in the USA, the EEC and elsewhere complain as Japanese goods make inroads into their domestic markets, causing unemployment, bankruptcies and trade deficits, leading to a rising demand for protection against Japanese goods. Japan agreed to impose self-regulating limits on some of her exports: car firms, for example, limited the volume of their imports into the UK and other EEC countries.

Overseas companies and governments complain that while their markets are relatively open to Japanese imports, the Japanese market is not so accessible to foreign goods. In spite of much received wisdom and anecdotal 'evidence', failure to break into the Japanese market is not due to Japanese trickery, protectionism or chauvinism (Document 13.1). There are, it seems, other reasons for western failure. Exporters in the EEC and USA fail to design specifically for the Japanese market, trusting that the Japanese will amend their cultural pattern to fit western tastes. Too many foreigners refuse to learn the language and customs of a proud people, and are less able to understand their tastes or to communicate with potential customers. Having failed to match Japanese export efforts, the deficit-facing countries want Japan to alter her economic policy in the interests of foreigners. 'If only Japan would run a bigger budget deficit . . . further revalue the *yen* . . . impose restrictions on its exporters . . . compel firms to use a quota of imports . . .' and so on.

Japanese commentators point out that until 1986 the dollar-yen rate depended more on US high interest rates than on Japanese policy, and that those high rates were required to finance US trading and budget deficits. The US could, they argued, change things either by cutting interest rates or simply devaluing the dollar, either unilaterally against the *yen* or multilaterally against a basket of currencies. This happened in 1986, and one waits to see if the fall in the value of the dollar has gone far enough (at 150 or so *yen* to the dollar) and whether this, or a larger fall, will affect the trading position.

More critical Japanese point to the failure of US and EEC workers to produce at the same rate as Japanese workers, who do not have the same greedy propensity to consume even if they do not produce. A minority of Japanese commentators agree with the vast majority of foreign critics in advocating a Japanese reflation which would ease trade pressure if,

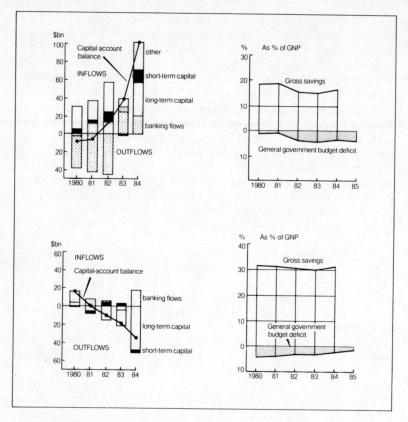

**13.1** These illustrations reflect the changing natures of the economies of the US (a–b) and Japan (c–d) between 1980 and 1985. This process of change has continued

additionally, the people could be persuaded to consume more imports or domestic products which rely upon imports. In the wake of the 1986 election, Nakasone promised to bring in a mildly expansionist and reflationary budget; not all Japanese agree with this policy, which runs contrary to traditional domestic management – a balanced, low budget, and a low level of taxation. There is, in fact, no agreement on how to lessen Japanese influence on other countries' economies.

## The financial giant

'Japan's economic and financial clout could eventually rival the power held by Britain in the 19th century and by the US after World War II.'
*Times*, 10 March 1985

In the nineteenth century Britain used its trading surpluses to finance

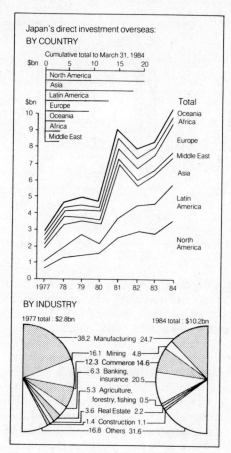

Japan's direct investment overseas:
BY COUNTRY

Cumulative total to March 31, 1984

BY INDUSTRY

1977 total : $2.8bn

1984 total : $10.2bn

- 38.2 Manufacturing 24.7
- 16.1 Mining 4.8
- 12.3 Commerce 14.6
- 6.3 Banking, insurance 20.5
- 5.3 Agriculture, forestry, fishing 0.5
- 3.6 Real Estate 2.2
- 1.4 Construction 1.1
- 16.8 Others 31.6

**13.2** Japan's balance of payments surpluses have enabled her to become a major investor overseas (Fig. 13.3), which is one of the reasons for her improving invisible income

overseas investment, sometimes in old colonial territories, sometimes (as in Africa) in newly-acquired regions, and sometimes in non-colonial countries. After World War II, the US used its surpluses to finance similar expansion by American firms and, to the ultimate cost of US economic power, to finance military activities (as in Vietnam) and to support allies (via NATO, SEATO and the rest). In the 1980s Japan is set to be the new 'economic imperialist'.

Figure 13.1 shows the capital accounts of the USA and Japan, and Figure 13.2 Japan's direct investment overseas (i) by countries and (ii) by industries. Almost everywhere, Japanese multinational corporations are building factories, buying companies and training foreign

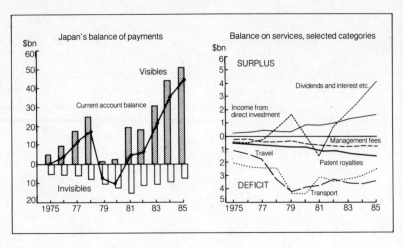

**13.3** Japan is on the road to being the world's leading industrial giant

workers to work for them. Japanese capital takes the form of loans, portfolio investments and buildings; although they buy foreign bonds, the Japanese prefer to buy companies or build them up from scratch. America has been a major area of investment: Matsushita, Toyota, Nippon Kokan and other 'tribal giants' (p. 203) now control some 500 industrial plants in the USA, manufacturing products ranging from electronics and cars to zip-fasteners and steel. US firms which once regarded themselves as world leaders are now happy to combine with a Japanese partner: General Motors–Toyota, Nippon Kokan–National Steel, Toshiba–Westinghouse, are three such US–Japanese combines. By forming such associations, Japan hopes to lessen the call for protectionism; Japanese industrial plants in the US are a response to American politicians' demands that, because Japan's exports have caused unemployment in the US, it is up to Japan to create more jobs.

Japan has helped finance the US national debt; Japanese investors poured $25 billion into US securities in 1985, about one-seventh of the $185 billion federal budget deficit. This pushed up the value of the dollar, and weakened the yen, as Japanese investors chased high US interest rates. This further increased the deficit on US trade as cheaper Japanese goods flooded the US market (providing the dollars needed for the Japanese bond-buying) and worsened the US deficit as interest payments were made.

Japan also exports capital, in the form of loans and grants, to its ASEAN neighbours. In 1984 there was a $240 million loan made to the Philippines, to help with its $26 billion foreign debt problem; $300 million in loans and grants went to Thailand; Japanese investment in Malaysia, Indonesia and South Korea, which strengthened these countries' economies, led to increased trade and prosperity throughout the Pacific region. Such Japanese expansion has to be handled circumspectly because of peoples' fears of exploitation by Japanese multinationals, and the lingering hostility which is a relic of World War II.

For many years, Japan's trading surplus was matched by a big deficit on invisible trade – services, tourism, investment income and so on (Figure 13.3). In April 1985 Japan had its first monthly surplus on this invisible account: since then it has gone back into deficit, but at a lower level than before. This improvement in the invisible account is due to the returns (interest and dividends) from Japan's overseas investments. In 1980 Japan earned a net $854 million from such investment; by 1984 that had more than quadrupled to $4.2 billion, a figure that was exceeded by August 1985. There can be little doubt that this part of Japan's current account will keep growing, as Japan continues to invest more abroad than foreigners invest in Japan.

## Can it go on?

'There may be calls for protectionism against Japanese investments. Our companies will want to remain dominant on their own turf.'
New York City Chemical Bank, *Time*, 18 March 1985

Japan's great success faces her with a problem: exports have to grow more quickly than imports if she is to maintain her current prosperity. The consequent surging increases in trade surpluses can only be avoided by major structural changes. If, for various reasons, Japan is unable to make such changes, the rest of the world may seek to exclude Japanese goods from their markets.

There is also the continuing question, pondered in Japan as well as overseas, of the relationship between trade surpluses and foreign policy. Nakasone has indicated that he would like to rewrite Japan's constitution (p. 204) to allow a stronger army; he would also double defence spending and adopt an independent but pro-western foreign policy. These issues divide not only the LDP but Japanese opinion as a whole, some fearing a growth of militant nationalism (Nakasone wants to revive the status of the Emperor and to promote a new nationalism in Japanese schools) and the hostility of Japan's Asian neighbours.

The link between the economies of Japan and the US pose two diverse problems for Japan. The first is crystallized in the question: *what happens if the US fails to limit its deficits?* In 1985–6 efforts were made to tackle the deficit problem, but, to date, rhetoric has been greater than substance. If the US fails, many economists believe that a continued fall in the value of the dollar (already evident in 1986) might force the US to adopt a tight monetary policy at home with even higher interest rates, limitations on credit expansion, cuts in government spending and increased US tariffs. Since the US takes some 35 per cent of Japanese exports, the result of such US policies would be catastrophic for Japan, and, indirectly, for ASEAN too.

There is a second question: *what happens as the dollar–yen relationship changes?* In the last quarter of 1985, the Finance Ministers of the five leading industrial countries acted together to force down the value of the dollar, thereby increasing the relative value of the yen. This appreciation has continued throughout 1986, causing Japanese export prices to rise. In theory this should lead to a fall in the volume and value of Japanese exports, cuts in exporters' profits, a deceleration of Japanese economic growth and a fall in her balance of payments' surplus. It is not surprising that Japanese exporters have criticized the upward re-valuation of the *yen*: they fear being priced out of the world's markets.

Of more immediate concern is the evidence of growing hostility towards Japan from her ASEAN neighbours. A Filipino historian writes of the danger of Filippinos becoming known, not as 'little brown Americans', but as 'little brown Japanese'. In August 1985 Malaysia's Prime Minister accused Japan of practising 'economic colonialism', and the President of South Korea, in Tokyo to seek Korean access to Japanese technology, complained that Japan was willing to invest her capital but not her expertise; Japanese firms, he said, were unwilling to share their developments with Korean firms. Japan has become the victim of its own success. Disliked in 1945 because of its militarists, it has come under recent attack because of its economic activity, even when that activity spurs other peoples' development, often financed by Japanese capital.

## Documentary evidence

Western governments and manufacturers complain that Japan makes it difficult to import goods into the world's leading manufacturing country. How far is this true? The OECD Economic Survey of Japan, August 1985, provides some insights.

### Document 13.1
*Japanese imports*

'Is Japan more closed to imports than other countries? The question is an old one, but nobody ever believes the answers.
*Tariffs* are not a block. In 1983 Japan's average tariff rate was 4.5% for dutiable goods and 2.5% for all imports, lower than in America or Europe. Even in textiles the tariff of 13.8% is lower than America's 22.7% and about the same as Europe's.
*Quotas* are not a problem in industry. There are five, including one for leather goods and a big one for coal, compared with six in America and 27 in France, three in Germany and one in America.
*Subsidies* are middling. Subsidies to private and public firms in Japan were steady at about 1.5% of GDP in 1982, higher than in America (0.5%) but well below the EEC (2.8%). Most of these subsidies are to Japan National Railways (which loses $20 million a day) and to the few remaining coal mines. No

important industrial sector in Japan is receiving large subsidies. Research and development? In 1983, 22.2% of RAD spending came from public funds compared with 45% in America, 42% in Germany and 50% in Britain.

*Non-tariff barriers* have a special place in foreigners' demonology about Japan, mainly because they are unmeasurable and also because they exist. Undoubtedly over-zealous customs men have made importing tough and domestic firms have had things rigged in their favour. For the most part, however, it is a question of whether foreign firms are willing to adapt products and practices to a market of 120 million people. Since 1981 Japan has made a series of moves to make importing easier, including bringing standards and certification rules closer in line to international methods.

*The yen* is not manipulated to boost exports and impede imports. Manipulation was abandoned in the early 1970s and finally buried by the abolition of exchange controls in 1980.

*Distributing* is cumbersome for the Japanese and importers alike as there are many levels of wholesalers and because small stores have been protected from supermarkets. In Japan there are 13 shops for every 1000 people compared with six in America and West Germany, 11 in France. By value, wholesale sales are five times retail sales in Japan, compared with one to two times in America and Europe. Like the language, this can be overcome by study.

*Groups* are a harder obstacle. Six groups link together batches of firms, banks and trading houses; another ten combine suppliers and subsidiaries of a big firm, for example Matsushita or a bank. They account for a quarter of all Japanese firms' sales. As long as prices are not exorbitant, members of the group feel obliged to buy from each other. This does block outsiders, whether Japanese or foreign. Japanese business relationships can be conservative and for good reason. Customers like reliable supplies, especially if they want to save money on stocks. This makes it hard but not impossible to prise a buyer away from his existing suppliers. It takes perseverance and proof that deliveries will keep flowing. Naturally this is easier for a factory just down the road than for one halfway round the world which is subject to dock and railway strikes. This tends to mean that importers have to pass a stiffer test because they are less easily trusted.

Do Japanese customers resist foreign goods? This is impossible to prove. In many cases it is difficult to tell the difference, and Japanese firms buy stacks of things made in Japan by foreign firms or imported. Two factors probably do affect purchases. Some foreign goods are sold as premium items with high profit margins but correspondingly low volume. Also, established firms' sales forces may be better than newcomers at handling distribution and persuading retailers to give shelf space to their products and to promote them.

*Trade rules* The central problem is one of exchange rates, relative competitiveness, prices and savings. American and European trade negotiators have long admitted that even if all Japanese barriers to trade were removed, it would make little difference to the trade figures. Politicians are less easily convinced because their constituents' jobs are being exported to Japan. It is easier to win votes by criticizing Japan, its exporters and its remaining barriers than to make the painful economic adjustments needed to solve the imbalance. This does not mean that Japan can sit on a moral pedestal and do nothing. It, too, must tackle the economic problem. Surplus countries have to be the most open in their dealings and are the least able to plead domestic problems to justify barriers.

Into this category falls the protection of Japanese agriculture, textiles firms, sawmills, leather firms, oil refiners, insurers, lawyers and even, to some extent, steel. All this must go if Japan's overseas markets are to stay open.'

(*OECD* Economic Survey of Japan, August 1985)


## FURTHER READING

ALLEN, G. C., *A short history of modern Japan*, Allen and Unwin, 1981

BURKS, A., *Japan: A Postindustrial Power*, Westview, 1984

GIBSON, M., *The rise of Japan*, Wayland, 1972

HOLLERMAN, L., *Japan and the United States: Economic and Political Adversaries*, Westview, 1983

NOBUTAKE, I., *Japan: The new superstate*, Freeman, 1974

STORRY, R., *A history of modern Japan*, Penguin, 1975

THUROW, L., ed., *The management challenge: Japanese views*, MIT Press, 1985

ZEPKE, N., *The Hundred Year Miracle*, Heinemann, 1977

# 14

# ASEAN

## South-East Asia

'. . . the Pacific Basin, with the world's most thrusting economies scattered round its rim, is set to take over the focal role that was held by the Mediterranean some 400 years ago.'

*Sunday Times* survey, 1985

There are 34 countries 'round the rim' and another 23 island states within the Pacific Basin, the 2.4 billion people living there (about half the world's population) producing around half of the world's GNP. Some of these countries are world powers in their own right: the USSR (Chapter 5), the USA (Chapter 6), China (Chapter 7) and Japan (Chapter 13) have major interests in the Basin and wield great influence there.

'South-East Asia' describes the countries lying between India (Chapter 12), China, Australasia and the open sea (Fig. 14.1). Before 1939, all of these, except Thailand, were ruled by foreigners. During the war, Japan incorporated most of them in 'the Great Asia Co-Prosperity Scheme'. The defeat of the colonial powers was a major spur to nationalism in former colonies, which was further aided by US perceptions of the Atlantic Charter (p. 38). After the war, the Dutch were driven from Indonesia, and the French from Indo-China (Chapter 15); the British ceded independence to Malaya and Singapore, as the US did to the Philippines.

In 1967 Thailand, Malaysia, Singapore, Indonesia and the Philippines formed the Association of South-East Asian Nations (ASEAN) in order to combat poverty, disease and other social ills, to improve their commercial and bargaining position, and to keep foreign powers at bay. The ASEAN states were, and still are, conscious of the 'foreigner', of the threat of Chinese expansion, of Japanese 'yen imperialism', of Soviet ambitions and of how these conflicting interests have led to 'war by proxy' in, for example, Vietnam.

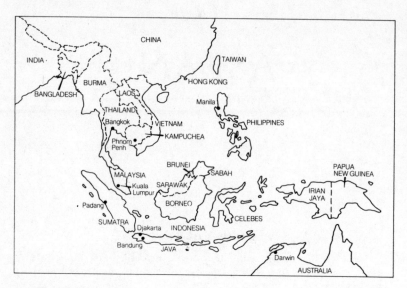

**14.1** The ASEAN nations

During the 1970s and early 1980s these ASEAN states enjoyed high economic growth: Singapore's growth was described as 'a miracle', the growth of Thailand and Indonesia as 'almost miraculous'. Much of this growth was due to expanding world trade. As the USA and Japan developed their economies, the ASEAN states enjoyed the spin-off effects. In 1983, for the first time, US trade with East Asia outstripped America's traditional trade with Europe.

However, falling prices for oil and other primary products in the mid-eighties led to a slower rate of growth, and the ASEAN states face a future made even more uncertain by doubts about China's policies, and by the continuing unrest in and around Vietnam (Chapter 15).

## Indonesia

'Dutch authority over the Indies is willed by God.'
                              Dutch Catholic spokesman, May 1946

The 13,000 or so islands of the Dutch East Indies were conquered by Japan in 1941–2. In 1939 they had provided half of the world's natural rubber and pepper, and a start had been made on developing their valuable oil deposits. Holland exploited the East Indies in its own interest, governing with the aid of traditional chiefs, who retained limited power, and suppressing any sign of local nationalism. In 1927 a Javanese engineer, Sukarno, founded the Indonesian Nationalist Party, with some support from a small local middle class, but none from the religious-minded chiefs or the exploited masses. Sukarno spent thirteen years in gaol while the Dutch persuaded the islanders that he wanted only Javanese control of the scattered islands.

Having defeated the Dutch, the Japanese released Sukarno, and allowed him and his INF party some administrative and political power in return for support in recruiting a local 'Volunteer Force' to defend Indonesia against the threat of Allied invasion; Sukarno was allowed to make radio broadcasts and became well-known among the islanders.

Following the Japanese surrender (15 August 1945), Sukarno declared Indonesia independent (17 August), armed his 'Volunteer Army' with Japanese weapons and published a constitution. The British landed in Indonesia in September to administer the colony until Dutch officials came from Europe. Fighting between British and Indonesian forces led Mountbatten to advise the Dutch to negotiate with Sukarno when they arrived in Java. Reluctantly, they saw that they might not be able to regain their pre-war control because of their domestic economic weakness, combined with the anti-imperialism of the USA and British unwillingness to back military action against the 'rebels'. Negotiations with the INF led to an agreement by which Java, Madun and Sumatra became a nationalist-governed Republic, and a Federation of the United States of Indonesia was established consisting of that Republic, along with Borneo and 'the Great East' of the other islands.

The Dutch set up puppet governments, hoping to gain control of the Federation. This angered Sukarno, whose efforts to gain international recognition for his Republic annoyed the Dutch. In July 1947 the Dutch attacked the Republic and captured parts of Java and Sumatra, while Sukarno appealed to the UN. Australia and newly-independent India helped organize UN-led negotiations, which in January 1948 produced an agreement giving Holland the right to rule in Indonesia until an election was held. The Dutch organized their own plebiscite, set up governments in many islands and a Federal Government without a single member from Sukarno's Republic. In September 1948 Stalin took advantage of the confusion to order a communist rising against the Republic. The rising was put down, and then followed by a second Dutch attack (December 1948); Jakarta, the capital of Java, was bombed and many Republican leaders were captured.

The Dutch success was short-lived. The UN called for a cease-fire, and the US cut off all economic aid to war-ravaged Holland. The Dutch were forced to agree to a conference at the Hague, where on 1 August 1949 Holland agreed to the establishment of a Republic of the United States of Indonesia (the whole of the former colony) as part of a Netherlands–Indonesia Union in which the Republic was an equal partner. The Queen of Holland was Head of the Union, eventually dissolved in 1954.

The Dutch remained hostile to the Republic and maintained control in West Irian, part of New Guinea (Fig. 14.1). In 1957 Sukarno expelled all Dutch citizens from Indonesia and confiscated their property. He promoted anti-Dutch opinion in West Irian and forced the UN to take control there in 1962: In 1963 it was handed over to Indonesia, in a final victory over the former colonial masters.

In 1963 the increasingly autocratic Sukarno opposed plans to incorporate the British colonies of Sarawak and Sabah within a new Federation of Malaysia. Indonesian guerrillas fought Malaysian forces in Sarawak and Sabah; Singapore, and various towns in Malaya, were bombed, and parachutists landed. The UN condemned Sukarno, who withdrew from the Organization in 1965. However, in 1966 Sukarno put an end to this 'war', in the face of domestic problems.

The 1950 constitution provided for a democratic government, but until 1955 the provisional parliament was appointed and not elected. In 1955 each of the four major parties won roughly the same number of seats in the first election. Sukarno claimed that this would lead to political instability, and that western democracy could not be transplanted to Indonesia. In 1956–7 there were clashes between Javanese officials and people of the smaller islands, resentful of the intrusive 'big brothers'. At the same time, right-wing Islamic groups fought with the communists, and the already unstable government became almost unworkable. In 1960 Sukarno dissolved parliament and set up a National Front with a People's Consultative Congress (which he rarely consulted) and a Supreme Advisory Council (whose advice he never followed).

The Soviet Union gave Sukarno technical aid to develop the state's oil and gas resources, viewing Indonesia as a counter-balance to Chinese influence in the region. Sukarno used the threat of a communist takeover to ensure the army's support, and persuaded his political opponents that, if he was overthrown, a 'communist versus army' struggle would harm the country's prospects. In September 1965 a false report of his death led to a communist rising in which army generals were killed. In a counter-coup, the army killed over 500,000 communists and jailed another 1.5 million, firmly establishing its control over Sukarno, who was overthrown in March 1957. His successor, General Suharto, has maintained a ruthless autocracy with vast numbers of potental opponents retained in detention.

Suharto enjoyed the benefit of the economic boom of the 1970s, which followed the increase in oil prices and the development of natural gas resources, offsetting the fall in rubber prices (Figure 14.2a). During this decade, the economy grew by an average of seven per cent a year. With some 170 million people, Indonesia is the world's fifth most populous country. Scientific farming has made it self-sufficient in terms of its food needs, with Java (where two-thirds of the population live) a major rice exporter.

However, the economy has now run into trouble. In the mid 1980s

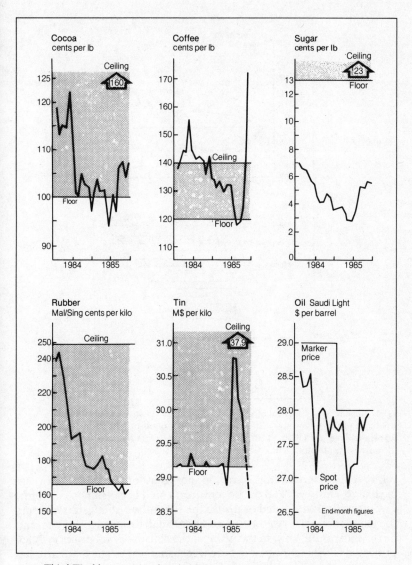

**14.2a** Third World countries, often dependent on one primary product, suffer when the prices of commodities fluctuate wildly. Members of ASEAN are particularly affected by the changes in prices of rubber, tin and oil

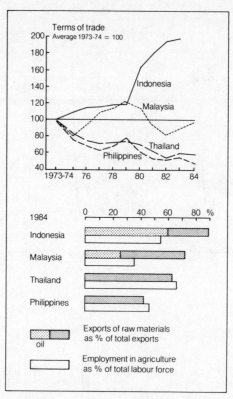

**14.2b** In spite of a good deal of progress, many ASEAN states are still over-reliant on primary products. The fortunate position of oil-producing Indonesia was short-lived: the fall in oil prices since 1984 has brought her into the less fortunate state already occupied by Malaysia and Thailand

oil revenues (providing some 70 per cent of the state's foreign exchange) slumped, and the government could not maintain economic growth at the rate needed to absorb the 1.8 million youngsters entering the job market each year. In 1982 GDP growth dropped to 2.2 per cent; in 1985 it was nil, and, in the wake of the collapse of oil prices in 1986, projected GNP is expected to be lower than it was in 1985. Suharto has tried to make up for the shortfall with budget cuts, increased prices for fuel and a push for non-oil exports, fearing that economic decline would aggravate racial and religious tensions. Some of the millions of unemployed youngsters may join one or other of the anti-Suharto groups. There are Islamic traditionalists who, on small islands and in villages, resent the 'westernization' following industrial development which leads to a decline in Islamic morality; in 1965–6 feudal Muslim landowners allied themselves with the anti-communist forces, preferring rule by the dictatorial Sukarno. In the event of continued economic failure, landowners and fundamentalists may find themselves allied with discontented but agnostic youngsters in towns and cities who have become angered at the corruption of the government which has allowed Suharto to pocket billions of dollars through shady business deals, and his wife, Madame Tien, to gain the nickname of 'Madame Tiene per cent'.

## Malaysia

'We looked to the west for a long time . . . no longer a suitable model. People there want a good life without facing the realities of a world they no longer control. If we were to imitate them we would find ourselves in a mire.'

Mahathir Muhamed, Prime Minister of Malaysia, 1982

In 1941 Britain ruled over a patchwork of Malayan states: a Crown Colony (Penang and Singapore); Federated Malay States, whose rulers exercised power under British control; and a group of northern states which were 'protected', not federated. Japanese occupation (1942–5) saw the growth of a Chinese-led resistance movement in which the Malayan Communist Party took the lead.

Although Japan surrendered in August 1945, Britain could no longer claim that invincibility which had been psychologically important in pre-war days. With a Labour government in power in Britain, and Mountbatten doing his anti-colonial best in Burma and Indonesia, the postwar administration accepted the need for constitutional change. In 1946 it put forward an experimental Union of Malaya, rejected by local people because of its overcentralization and its continuation of colonial traditions. In 1948 Britain created the Federation of Malaya for the ten states of Malaya, giving Singapore separate status (p. 226). Some Chinese resented the Malays' dominant position within the Union, and, stimulated by Stalin in his 1948 campaign against the West (p. 267), began a guerrilla war. In June 1948 the administration announced a state of emergency and organized resistance to the Malayan Races Liberation Army, led by the communist Chen Ping. The war, at its most intense between 1950 and 1953, and clearly won by 1957, did not end officially until 1960.

The defeat of the guerrillas was due to a combination of military and political actions. Helicopters were used to take well-trained troops to attack guerrilla bases; 'new villages', easily protected, housed the local people so that the guerrillas were unable to find sanctuaries; and the sale and supply of food to rural areas was carefully supervised. On the political side, the British brought forward plans for full independence, while, on the other hand, Malays failed to see what benefit would come from communist rule.

While the state of emergency was still ongoing, the Federation of

Malaya was given full independence within the Commonwealth in August 1957. Its first Prime Minister, Tunku Abdul Rahman, persuaded the leaders of the Chinese population to cooperate not only in negotiations leading to independence, but also in the subsequent government of the Federation. In 1963 the Federation expanded, and changed its name to Malaysia, to include Singapore, Sabah, Sarawak and Malaya itself. Singapore seceded in August 1965 (p. 227), by which time Malaysia was under attack from Indonesia (p. 222). That intermittent war ended in 1966, but was followed by a dispute with the Philippines, who also claimed sovereignty over Sabah. That dispute lasted from 1968 to 1972, and only in 1977 did Marcos renounce Filipino claims to Malaysian territory.

In spite of Abdul Rahman's influence, many Malays feared that the Malayan Chinese would continue to dominate the economic life of the Federation. They controlled its tin and rubber resources – which gave the Malaysian people one of the highest living standards in southern Asia. Malayan discontent with this 'exploitation' led to serious race riots, and, in May 1969, to the suspension of parliamentary govern-ment – which lasted until February 1971. Relations between the two racial groups eased as Malaya enjoyed continuing economic growth, due to the expansion of world trade in general, and of US and Japanese trade in particular, combined with the success of Singapore, and the willingness of multinationals to invest in Malaysia (Document 14.1). The fall in world prices for Malaysia's main exports (tin and rubber) led to a decline in revenue (Figure 14.2a) after 1980, while further falls in 1984–5 made it increasingly imperative for Malaysia to pursue a policy of industrialization, to reduce their reliance on these primary products. In 1980 Malaysia had earned 72 per cent of her foreign revenue from primary products; in 1985 she got only 56 per cent of a larger foreign income from such sales – a sign of an improving situation.

Ever since 1957, Malaysia has suffered from attacks by the remnants of Chen Ping's communist guerrillas, based in Thailand and supported by China and the Soviet Union. Malaysian politicians have been very conscious of the threat from the north, where, with the communist victory in Vietnam, they saw the 'Domino Theory' (Document 15.1) become a reality with the fall of Cambodia (p. 245). It is not surprising that Malaysia is uneasily aware of the conflicting interests of the great powers in the ASEAN region.

## Singapore

'The five ASEAN countries are not able to provide the industrial dynamo on their own.'

Singapore Foreign Minister Rajaratnam

In 1946 Singapore, a separate colony, was set on the road to independence. In its first elections (March 1948) the mainly Chinese electorate voted six representatives onto the Legislative Council, dominated by ex officio and nominated members. A Progressive Party and a Labour Party were formed, and helped educate the people politically. In spite of the Emergency (p. 225), a second election was held in March 1951 and half the population went to the polls. Twenty-two candidates fought for nine seats; six were won by the Progressives, and three by Labour. In 1955 a new constitution led to fresh elections for twenty-five seats within an Assembly in which the elected members had a majority; the Governor's Executive Council consisted of three ex officio and six elected members from the Legislature.

In 1954 young radicals formed the People's Action Party (PAP), aimed at speeding up constitutional progress, which they hoped to achieve by peaceful means, although they were willing to cooperate with communist agitators. In 1955 the PAP won three of the four seats it contested and, refusing to join the government side, formed an Opposition to David Marshall's Labour Front government. He resigned in June 1956 when independence talks collapsed. His successor, Lim Yew Hock, got that concession from Britain, and in March 1959 the Legislative Assembly was dissolved to make way for a 51-member Parliament. The PAP fought all the seats and won over half of the total vote, in an election in which voting was compulsory. The PAP leader, Lee Kuan Yew, became Prime Minister and has been in power ever since, having won all the seats in several elections. Modern Singapore is very much the creation of Lee Kuan Yew and the PAP.

Abdul Rahman of Malaya had been concerned at the pro-communist policies of the PAP, and did not think that, in power, Lee would be able to control the communists. As an anti-communist measure, Rahman invited Singapore to join an enlarged Malaysia (p. 226); Lee had always believed that Singapore could not exist independently of Malaya and welcomed the invitation. Extremists in the PAP opposed him, left the Party and formed the Barisan Sosialis – a communist front. In a referendum in 1962 the voters approved the concept of the Federation, which came into being in August 1963.

Throughout 1964, Singapore was threatened by Indonesia (p. 222). Anti-government riots were organized by Indonesian saboteurs with communist support. Nor was this the only threat to the Federation. The Malays were particularly afraid of Chinese dominance, and their fear increased because three-quarters of Singapore's population is Chinese. Malay politicians were aware that energetic and able Ministers from the PAP might gain political control of the Federation, which would be the less Islamic as a result of Chinese presence. For economic, political and religious reasons the Federation came under strain, and in September 1965 Singapore seceded, to become an independent nation.

Before and after 1965, Singapore enjoyed a seemingly continuous 'economic miracle'. Its growth rate exceeded even that of Japan in the decade 1962–72, and because of the sustained growth rate its per capita income in 1985 was $6620, nine times that of India. The government has played a major role in this growth, but some western critics claim that Lee has followed a communist-style path; certainly the government controls development through its Development Bank, its trading companies and its national airline. Lee, however, has been a vigorous enemy to communism, and has no sympathy with its political philosophy (Document 14.2). The government has also aided development by providing the political stability which made foreign investment more likely. As the *Sunday Times* noted in 1985; 'It is as the natural home of the growing banks and Asian financial markets that *politically stable* Singapore stands to score more heavily' (italics added).

In some ways the government has adopted a Keynesian policy, but it has also followed the principles of *laisser-faire* economics. Taxes are kept low and inequalities accepted, in a system which encourages the pursuit of self-interest and self-enrichment (Document 14.2). It has been helped by a responsible trade union movement, whose leaders recognized, until very recently, the danger of industries decamping to neighbouring low-wage economies if Singaporeans priced themselves out of the market.

Multinational companies are encouraged to invest in the island state (Document 14.1), with local investment and development following on behind, although the government remains conscious of an over-reliance on foreign capital.

Some people think that it was 'natural . . . [and] inevitable' that Singapore should have developed, given its location on international trade routes. This is to ignore the disadvantages from which the island suffers; it has no mineral resources, too little space and few if any raw materials, as well as too little water and few energy resources. The 'location' argument also begs the question of why Suez or Panama haven't developed at this rate.

Singapore benefitted from the world boom in the 1960s and 1970s, which reinforced the effects of the state's political stability. However, in 1985 the GNP plunged from an 8.2 per cent growth in 1984 to a minus 1.7 per cent fall in 1985, with a minus 4.5 per cent rate being registered for the final quarter of that year. The recession is made visible in the empty hotels and offices, shops and boutiques, and abandoned building projects. Oil-refining has dropped because Indonesia and Malaysia have built their own refineries; the fall in world prices for tin, rubber and other primary products has brought a slump in commodities trading and banking, and lowered the need for many service industries.

During the boom years, companies outbid each other for qualified employees, and wage rates rose by an average of 20 per cent a year for three successive years up until 1984. These high costs hinder Singapore's efforts to compete with low-wage Taiwan and Hong Kong. In February 1986 a special committee recommended methods of stimulating the economy. Their solution included cuts in corporate taxes, reductions in mandatory savings schemes, and no net increases in wages for two years. It remains to be seen how far the island state will manage to recover, and how well it will cope with the hazards of life in the region, which has more than its fair share of foreign problems.

## Thailand

'Muang Thai – "the land of the free".'

Thailand, known as Siam until 1939, is the only ASEAN state not to have once been a colony. It formed a buffer zone between British-controlled Burma and the French-held Indo-China. The Thai people, while assimilating Chinese immigrants, some 12 per cent of the population, remain conscious of their uncertain position in a region in which the major powers and Vietnam struggle for influence. As a member of SEATO (p. 270) Thailand puts itself firmly in the western bloc along with Pakistan and the Philippines, and looks to the USA for defence purposes.

Until 1973 a series of 'strong men' ruled, and, until 1962, they supervised an economy based on the export of rubber, tin, teak and rice. In 1985 Thailand was the world's largest rice exporter, with 40 per cent of its foreign earnings coming from this trade.

In 1964 the USA set up bases in Thailand for use during its war in Vietnam. The influx of US troops, and the influence of their spending, strained the economic and cultural life of the state. In 1973 there were serious riots against the corrupt and inefficient government, which led the military to take over, installing an interim civilian government, and convening a constituent assembly which issued a democratic constitution in October 1974. Elections were held in January 1975 and a predominantly civilian government set out to clean up public life, tackle inflation and undo the harm done by the US presence, which diminished as US troops left when the Vietnam war ground to a halt.

A Chinese-packed 'Patriotic Front' had guerrilla bases among the Meo people along the Thai–Laos border. In 1976 they were strengthened by communist successes in Vietnam, the uncertainties in Kampuchea (Chapter 15), and the unwillingness of the US to support Thai attempts to deal with the guerrillas. The Thai military intervened again (1976) to replace the civilian government with one in which the forces were more influential. This military-civilian government viewed the Vietnamese invasion of Kampuchea (1979) as dangerous communist expansion, threatening the independence of Laos, and ultimately of Thailand. Thailand then persuaded its ASEAN partners to unite in a plea for the right of the Cambodian people to settle their future without foreign intervention. There is no evidence that the Soviet Union and China took heed, nor is there any reason to believe that these powers, or Vietnam, will respect Thailand's wish to be independent.

## The Philippines

'Let history judge harshly on this; until every Filipino . . . has been liberated from ignorance, poverty and disease, I shall have failed you.'
President Marcos, 1981 Presidential campaign

In 1898, following the Spanish–American War, the Philippines were ceded to the USA, which acknowledged the Filipinos' rights to self-government and independence. In March 1934 the US Congress ruled that the islands would become independent in 1946, until when the 'Commonwealth' enjoyed a form of autonomy under the supervision of a US High Commissioner. The Japanese conquered the islands in 1942, but they were retaken by July 1945. The US ceded sovereignty in July 1946, when the Republic of the Philippines came into being.

From the outset it faced a number of problems. Most serious was the Hukbalahap Movement, centred on Luzon in the north, a left-wing group based on the Anti-Japanese People's Liberation Army, which had carried out successful operations in the jungle during the war. After July 1946 it fought the Filipino government, much as Chen Ping fought the British in Malaya (p. 225). By 1950 the 'Huks' controlled Luzon, and 'governed' more than half a million people. The USA, with its naval bases in the islands, and its involvement in the anti-communist Korean War (1950–3), helped the government to stamp out the 'Huks', whose pro-communist threat was ended in 1954.

However, a pro-Maoist Communist Party of the Philippines was founded in central Luzon at Christmas 1968, aiming to replace the old Philippines Communist Party, which was led by middle-class intellectuals. Organizing a New People's Army, and following Mao's example (p. 103), they penetrated and politicized many of the islands' 40,000 villages, raiding government-protected towns and attacking government forces and officials on the way. At the time of Marcos's overthrow (February 1986), the rebels had the support of many non-communists opposed to his unjust and tyrannical rule; his forces had used terrorist tactics against the rebels, which succeeded only in arousing liberal and Church opposition in the predominantly Catholic islands.

The Republican government also faced, and faces, unrest among the predominantly Muslim population of the southern islands. Filipino Muslims have been affected by the spread of Islamic fundamentalism, which has had major success in Iran (p. 142), and which Muslims see as an excuse to oppose a government which has no sympathy with them. It remains to be seen whether the post-Marcos government will be able to make peace with this violent group.

In 1946 the islands, and especially their capital, bore all the marks of a recent savage war. While the 'Huks' fought in the north, other, smaller, groups were formed by gang leaders willing to take advantage of an inexperienced government to enrich themselves. Gang wars, robberies and murders were common, while the mass of the population remained unhappy at the corruption which allowed ministers and officials to enjoy a high standard of living amid great poverty.

From the outset the government was in the hands of the Nationalists, a right-wing Party enjoying the support of the Catholic Church, which was concerned by the threat from the 'Huks'. The Minister of Defence, Magsaysay, who was credited with the defeat of the 'Huks', was elected President in 1953, and had popular support for his planned 'war on poverty'. This failed, however, and the rich continued to enjoy an American standard of living, while the majority lived much as they would have done in any Third World Country.

In 1962 the Filipino government claimed Sabah (Figure 14.1), broke off relations with Malaya, and refused to recognize the new state of Malaysia. This 'confrontation' further disrupted the economy, and slowed the faltering drive to eradicate poverty. In 1965 Marcos, a member of the Liberal Opposition in the Senate, left his party, joined the Nationalists and won the 1965 Presidential election, promising economic and social reform and 'the protection and extension of civil rights, and the enhancement of professional ethics in politics.'

One response to his election was the formation of the new Communist Party. Perhaps as a result of his anti-communist drive, Marcos was re-elected in 1969, by people more concerned with the communist threat than with his failure to bring in economic and social reform. This continued failure led to demonstrations by students and workers; in September 1970 troops fired on students marching on the Presidential Palace, which led to criticism by Liberal politicians such as Senator Benigno Aquino. Priests affected by the 'liberal' views of the Second Vatican Council, and some sections of the press, were also critics of Marcos. In September 1972 Marcos imposed what he called 'humane martial law', to combat student unrest and communist rebellion. Many thousands, including Aquino, were arrested, but in a referendum the majority of voters agreed to a new constitution giving the President unlimited powers during the period of martial law. This was not ended until June 1981, by which time Marcos's New Society Party had swept the polls at elections for an interim parliament (April 1978). Marcos retained the Presidency at the 1981 elections, ignoring widespread criticism that the election had been rigged.

The war against the northern communists and southern Muslims led to a growth in the size and the influence of the army, on which Marcos became increasingly reliant. In spite of the outspoken opposition of the Catholic leader, Cardinal Sin, Marcos's party won a 2–1 majority in parliamentary elections in May 1984 and he was able to ignore the criticism which followed the murder of the Opposition leader, Aquino, and the judicial decision to free army leaders who had been charged with organizing it.

In September 1985 the Supreme Court ruled 7–5 in favour of Marcos's decision to call a sudden election, which some considered unconstitutional since his presidency had eighteen months yet to run. By the time of the Presidential elections (February 1986) the islands' economy was in decline. One reason for this was the continuing northern war, in which, during 1985, some 45,000 rebels, soldiers and civilians were killed without the government showing any signs that it could win the battle. The uncertainty of this costly 'war' helped explain the decline in the economy, which contracted by 5.5 per cent in 1984 and another 3.5 per cent in 1985. Companies were unwilling to invest in the restless islands where, even officially, unemployment was put at 7 per cent. Filipinos used to find work in the prosperous Middle East, but that road to prosperity was closed in the wake of the fall in oil prices after 1984. Filipinos returning from the Gulf not only added to the numbers of unemployed; they also provided additional support for left-wing and liberal critics of a government which failed to provide economic and social reform.

Marcos's failure was highlighted by, and worsened by, the state's overseas debt. The Philippines is now one of the world's chronic debtors, owing approximately $25.5 billion. Interest payments on this debt take up more than half of all foreign earnings, and the IMF has imposed harsh conditions for the stand-by loans needed to maintain the economy.

In the Presidential elections of February 1986, despite government attempts to control and fix the voting, Cory Aquino, widow of the murdered Senator, defeated Marcos. Unwilling to cede power, Marcos was finally forced to resign following the threat of US military intervention. It is too soon to say how the new, democratically elected President will cope with the myriad problems facing her government. These include division among her supporters, some of whom might prefer a military government led by a 'strong man'; underground resistance by some of Marcos's well-placed supporters in the scattered islands; the continued war by the Communists and Islamic groups; the run-down economy burdened with a huge overseas debt; and the difficulty of attracting essential foreign capital and multinational expertise. In the 1950s the Philippines' economy grew faster than any other in South-East Asia. Under Marcos it had the slowest economic growth of any non-communist country in the region. Only time will tell what it does under Aquino.

### Documentary evidence

Singapore has become one of the 'superstars' in the world's economic league.

Some western critics claimed that its long-serving Prime Minister, Lee Kuan Yew, ran a communist-like state. In fact, his free enterprise system encouraged multinational companies to help the island's growth (Document 14.1), while he opposed demands for economic and social egalitarianism (Document 14.2). Singapore, more than any other member of ASEAN, is of great strategic importance. The Soviet Union uses the British-built naval base to maintain its supervision of affairs in the Indian Ocean and the South China Seas (Document 14.3).

## Document 14.1

*'Socialist' Singapore and its multinationals*

'Our experience of multinationals in Singapore has benefitted our workers and business executives. We recognize that multinational corporations come to make money, but if we control basic economic policies, we can use them for our own progress. They have brought us capital, technology, expertise and markets. On our own, we could not have developed these fast enough to provide employment as well as generate economic growth. Their operations supplement and complement Singapore entrepreneurship. Out of this development, our own multinational corporations have been an asset rather than a liability.'

(The Singapore Minister of Labour, quoted by Josey)

## Document 14.2

*Lee Kuan Yew on perceptions of equality*

'Some socialists wrongly believe that since poverty is caused by exploitation, then, when exploitation ends, so would poverty. To eradicate poverty, ignorance has to be eradicated and obscurantism banished, and the have-nots have to be educated, trained, disciplined and made into hard and useful members of a modern industrial community. Only in communist countries in Asia are there people who still believe that pristine faith and dogma and fervour can solve all the problems of modernization and industrial development . . . the younger generation in Asia is no longer stirred by the simple slogans of an egalitarian society: more and more the young are showing that they want to be equal in order that they can strive to be unequal. What they want is not to be equal throughout life but to have equal opportunities so that those whose ability and whose application are better than the average can become more equal than the others.'

(Lee to the Socialist International, quoted by Josey)

## Document 14.3

*The Russians and Singapore's naval base*

'The Russians do not have Singapore as a naval base, but the next best thing: what are described by Western defence experts as "huge Russian fishing fleets" in the Indian Ocean and South China Sea, their duties being not only to fish but also to act as a vast floating naval base and infrastructure to monitor surface and underwater "teeth" units of the Russian navy out of sight beyond and beneath the horizon. Some of the trawlers are equipped with the world's most

sophisticated surface, underwater and air-attacking gear. It is estimated that
bunkering and storage facilities enjoyed by the trawlers at Singapore may form
a vital part of this Russian navy's lifeline which could enable it to go into action
whenever ordered.'

(Donald Wise, in *The Far Eastern Economic Review*)


# FURTHER READING

ANDAYA, B. W. and L. Y., *A history of Malaysia*, Macmillan, 1982
BROINOWSKI, A., ed., *Understanding ASEAN*, Macmillan, 1982
CALDWELL, M., *Indonesia*, OUP, 1968
CHARLTON, M. and MONCRIEFF, A., *Many Reasons Why*, Scolar Press, 1978
JOSSEY, A., *Singapore: Its Past, Present and Future*, Andre Deutsch, 1980
LONDON, B., *Metropolis and Nation in Thailand*, Westview, 1979
MARR, D., *Asia: The Winning of Independence*, Macmillan, 1981
OSBORNE, M., *South-East Asia*, Allen and Unwin, 1979
PARK, J. K., ed., *Korea and Indochina: Towards Inter-Regional Co-operation*,
    Westview, 1981
STEINBERG, D. J., *The Philippines*, Westview, 1982
YU, G. T., ed., *Intra-Asian International Relations*, Westview, 1978

# 15

# Vietnam and her neighbours

### A significant region

'The Vietnamese victory appears to be very impressive.'
Prince Sihanouk of Kampuchea, on the Vietnamese invasion,
March 1985

In 1945 no one could have foreseen that French Indo-China would become an important factor in international politics, while few would have heard of 'Vietnam'. Forty years later, almost everyone has read of the area, and TV has brought its wars into our homes.

The region provides an opportunity to examine the intransigence of French imperialists and the way in which people on the spot can frustrate plans made by far-away politicians. The methods by which guerrilla troops defeated better-armed and larger forces provided lessons for the Algerian rebels (p. 120), while the USA and the Soviet Union fought a 'war by proxy' as the USA developed the 'Domino Theory' (Document 15.1) which helps explain US involvement in the region. The US withdrawal from Vietnam in 1973 proved that even a technologically advanced state could not guarantee victory over locally-supported guerrillas, especially if its own people were divided on the issue of participation. After the US withdrawal, China invaded Vietnam, to find that the Soviet-supported state was not only well able to defend itself, but also capable of becoming an aggressive power in its own right. Its invasion of Kampuchea has led Thailand and Malaysia to fear that there may be great truth in the once-despised 'Domino Theory'.

### French intransigence, 1945–50

'. . . the Provisional Government, representing the whole Vietnamese people, declare that . . . we break off all relations of a colonial character with France.'

Ho Chi-minh's 'government', August 1945

In 1939, French Indo-China consisted of a colony (Cochin-China) centred on Saigon, two Vietnamese protectorates (Tonkin and Annam, where Bao Dai was Emperor) and two larger protectorates (Cambodia and Laos). In these five regions, run for the benefit of France, Asiatics were literally second-class citizens; they could not form trade unions or political parties; a minority were allowed a French-style education enabling them to work for the colonial administration, but they could take only the less important jobs, and at lower salaries than Europeans doing the same work.

Leading nationalists had formed the Vietminh movement, which in 1939 was led by Ho Chi-minh and Vo Nguyen Giap. Ho (1890–1968) had lived and worked in London, Paris and Moscow before returning to found the Indo-Chinese Communist Party in 1930. Giap (born in 1912) was a history teacher and qualified lawyer who had been imprisoned for his nationalist activities. His sister was executed, and his wife died after two years in gaol.

After May 1940 France allowed Japan to take control of Indo-China: Ho and Giap led guerrillas against both French masters and Japanese invaders, with the support of various nationalist groups (of which only Ho's was avowedly communist). Like Mao, the guerrillas won peasant support by giving them land in areas which they controlled. In March 1945 Japan officially took over, uniting Cochin-China, Tonking and Bao Dai's Annam in one region (Vietnam), and governing Cambodia and Laos as two separate states. Emperor Bao announced the abrogation of treaties with France, asserted Vietnamese independence and proclaimed his willingness to cooperate with Japan as part of 'Greater East Asia'. His collaboration allowed the guerrillas of the Vietminh to claim the role of true Viet nationalists, and, on the Japanese surrender (15 August 1945), Bao handed the seals of office to the Vietminh leaders, officially recognizing them as the legal authority over the whole country. Ho promptly declared Vietnam an independent country, and included representatives of every nationalist group within his 'provisional government'.

In October 1945 French officials returned to Saigon, dismissed the nationalist 'government', occupied Saigon and tried to regain control of the whole country. Guerrilla terrorist attacks in the French suburbs of Saigon persuaded them to hold talks with Ho, who wanted an independent Vietnam, linked to France much as the Dominions were linked to Britain in the Commonwealth. In March 1946 local negotiations led to agreement on an independent North Vietnam as part of a Federation of Indo-China. Between June and September 1946, while Ho was in Paris to finalize the agreement, many of his supporters accused him of collaboration with the French, who foolishly rejected Ho's plan for Vietnamese independence.

At the end of 1946, the French tried to destroy Ho's 'government'; Haiphong was bombed, and, in retaliation, French officials in Hanoi were attacked by guerrillas. The French tried to win Vietnamese support by persuading ex-Emperor Bao to accept the Presidency of a new Vietnam, the state which they would not cede to Ho's nationalists. The French, however, could not get even the malleable Bao to accept the merely nominal power behind which they would continue to rule. He refused to accept this inferior status, and while the French bickered with Bao, Ho and Giap were extending their guerrilla war. Having refused to collaborate, as Bao seemed to be doing, they gained increasing support among all sections of the Vietnamese people.

### France loses Indo-China, 1950–4

'. . . to impress upon the free nations the international character of the conflict started by the Viet Minh which was endangering the future of South-East Asia and to stress the need to organize a common effort to cope with the present threats [and] to establish a durable peace.'

French National Assembly, Agenda, 22 November 1950

In 1950, while trying to defeat Ho, the French allowed King Sihanouk to enjoy some power in Cambodia. Prince Sonvanna Pouma was given similar power in Laos, as was Bao Dai in Vietnam. At this point, the French found that their 'war' was being subsumed into the Cold War (Chapter 17), as a result of Mao's success in China, Soviet and Chinese aid to Ho. US perceptions of the communist nature of Ho's forces, and French appeals for aid against this 'communist' threat, led to the proposal of the Domino Theory, which later formed the basis of US foreign policy (Document 15.1).

Local French officials and army leaders expected a quick victory, with their stronger and better-armed forces. Certainly, the French controlled the cities and towns where they left large forces. However, they failed to capture the countryside and the mountains, where the guerrillas set up their bases with the support of the peasants, and from where they by-passed French block-houses to make night attacks on property and people in the towns.

By 1953 the French had lost 38,000 men in a war costing 600 billion francs a year, more than the total French investment in Vietnam. Politicians began to wonder whether it was worth continuing an expensive, and apparently unwinnable war. General Navarra, a new French commander, decided to bring Giap's forces to a pitched battle, confident of his ability to win. In November 1953 he took Dien Bien Phu, deep inside Vietminh territory, and built up a garrison supplied by air from Hanoi. Giap's men built up forces in the surrounding hills, carrying huge guns on bicycles through the jungle. In March 1954 the Battle of Dien Bien Phu began. Giap's men captured French outposts and guns for use against the beleaguered garrison. France asked for increased US aid, and Dulles talked of the value of dropping 'one or two atomic bombs', which alarmed western leaders, notably Eden of Britain, who sought to end the war.

Preliminary negotiations began in the summer of 1953, and saw the rulers of Cambodia and Laos denounce their agreements with France and demand complete independence. Eden persuaded the Soviet Union, the USA and France to meet in Geneva in May 1954 to settle Indo-Chinese affairs. The conference opened on the very day on which Dien Bien Phu fell to the guerrillas.

Britain and the Soviet Union cooperated to persuade a reluctant Dulles and a war-weary Mendès-France to accept a settlement in which France withdrew completely from Indo–China. Cambodia and Laos were to become independent, and Vietnam was to be divided along the 17th parallel into a communist-controlled north and a 'free' south under Bao Dai. Elections were to be held throughout Vietnam in 1956 to allow the formation of a government for the whole country. The USA, fearing a communist victory, refused to sign this part of the agreement, while Vietnamese nationalists, now controlled by Ho's communist party, rejected the division of their country – particularly when the USA refused to agree to national elections. Many of Ho's guerrillas inside South Vietnam formed the Viet Cong, and prepared to continue the fight for a united Vietnam.

## Eisenhower, Dulles and Vietnam, 1952–60

'The Americans lacked a clear aim from the start [but were] committed to the Saigon regime.'

*The Times*, 20 April 1985

The US policy in these years was a result of Eisenhower's experience in NATO at the onset of the Cold War (p. 268). McCarthyite hysteria in the USA (p. 90), Dulles's belief in the 'Domino Theory' (Document 15.1), his fear of Mao's China, and his rejection of neutralism, which was to turn him against Nasser in 1956 (p. 121), were other contributory factors.

The USA had aided France, and been a signatory to the Geneva Agreement. Dulles, becoming increasingly angry with Bao Dai, whom he thought 'soft on communism', supported a coup in October 1955 in which the Catholic 'strong man', Ngo Dinh Diem, became President of South Vietnam. Dulles hoped that he would prevent a communist takeover. In fact, his government became increasingly unpopular. The Buddhist majority resented the tyrannical nature of his rule, his refusal to hold elections and the ruthless behaviour of the army. Diem attacked, imprisoned and executed both religious leaders campaigning for a Buddhist state, and left-wingers seeking reform.

Ho's supporters in the south set up the National Liberation Front as the political arm of the anti-Diem forces; its military wing was the Viet Cong, a guerrilla army supplied by Ho, China and the Soviet Union.

Eisenhower promised to aid Diem 'through military means' if he undertook 'needed reform'. For the eleven million peasants in the

Mekong Delta the land question was of prime importance. Two million were landless, and most of the remainder were subsistence farmers paying high rents to absentee landlords whom they identified with Diem's government, which made no attempt at 'needed reform', in contrast to Ho's policy of handing land to the peasants when he gained control of an area. It is little wonder that the communists won 'the hearts and minds' of the people, while Diem became increasingly unpopular.

The US also gave economic aid to Laos, where Souvanna Phouma was threatened by the Pathet Lao communist movement, led by his half-brother, the ex-Prince Souphananouvong, and by the plotting of US-supported army officers seeking power for their own corrupt ends.

## The Kennedy–Johnson years, 1961–8

'. . . the security of all South East Asia will be endangered if Laos loses its neutral independence.'

Kennedy, March 1961

'Over the war and all Asia is another reality: the deepening shadow of Communist China. Vietnam is part of a wider pattern of aggressive purpose.'

Johnson, July 1964

Obviously, Kennedy and Johnson subscribed to the 'Domino Theory'. In March 1961 Kennedy used it to defend his decision to send aid to Laos. Later (March 1962), he sent 500 US marines to bases in Thailand, while the Seventh Fleet was despatched to the South China Sea as a warning to China. In spite of this, however, a new Soviet-backed government was formed in Laos, which included the leader of the Pathet Lao.

Eisenhower had sent 'military advisers' to help Diem's forces, and in October 1961 Kennedy sent about 16,000 more, plus equipment and helicopters, urging Diem to adopt the 'safe village' policy which had helped to defeat the Malayan communists (p. 225). Kennedy also formed his 'Green Berets', a special force which it was hoped would defeat the enemy in the jungle. Throughout 1962 and 1963 Kennedy was advised that Diem was winning the civil war against the 23,000 Viet Cong and their 100,000 irregular guerrillas. In October 1963, however, he was told that the autocratic and non-reforming government of the Catholic Diem could not win this war, which was threatening to involve the USA in 'a quagmire'. Diem was murdered by members of a CIA-backed group, which then put a military government in power. In return, Kennedy promised to step up the volume of aid, and increase the degree of US involvement. Some of his friendlier critics suggest that, had he lived, he would have diminished US participation. This cannot now be proved one way or the other.

Johnson, who became President on Kennedy's assassination

(November 1963), accepted the 'Domino Theory', but as, an uneasy successor to the charismatic Kennedy he was, in any case, almost incapable of withdrawing from Vietnam. A humiliation would not be the best start to a Presidency devoted to the achievement of a 'Great Society' (p. 92). In Vietnam, the communists gained control over more than half of the country's 43 provinces, while Diem's successors fought among themselves and failed to produce an effective government.

In August 1964 two US destroyers were fired upon in the Tonking Gulf, and Johnson persuaded Congress to pass the 'Tonking Gulf' resolution, which allowed him to 'wrap himself in the flag' and escalate US participation in the war. North Vietnam was bombed in the hope that this would cut Ho's aid to the Viet Cong; over the next seven years, North Vietnamese cities suffered more than German cities had during World War II; Johnson stepped up the numbers of US servicemen involved and soon 500,000 Americans were engaged in the fight to defeat the far smaller and less well-equipped guerrilla armies which faced them.

Mass media coverage of the war resulted in people becoming 'semi-brutalized', as Viet Cong terrorism and US retaliation with weapons, including napalm, came to form part of regular TV viewing. Few of Johnson's advisers accepted that the war could not be won (Document 15.2); many agreed that 'one more, bigger, effort' would bring victory (Document 15.3). Public opinion, initially roused to support the anti-communist war, slowly became disillusioned as liberal commentators, Johnson's main critics, stressed the success of the Viet Cong.

In January 1968 the guerrillas launched an offensive to coincide with the Vietnamese Tet Festival, in which they captured 80 per cent of towns and village and laid siege to the US Embassy in Saigon. Although most of this land was later recaptured, the immediate success of the Viet Cong was highlighted by the media as evidence of America's inability to win the war. A great increase in support for the anti-war movement meant that it became a focal point for other anti-Johnson forces, including blacks (p. 93), students (p. 93) and liberals.

US planes used Thai bases from which to launch attacks on the North; northern aid to the Viet Cong passed along routes through Laos and Cambodia (Fig. 15.1a). In spite of themselves, Vietnam's neighbours were involved; communist forces in Laos and Cambodia kept open the Ho Chi-minh trail to the south, before taking their own internal action.

In March 1968 public pressure forced Johnson to halt the bombing of North Vietnam. The increasing violence of the anti-war demonstrations also forced him to announce that he would not seek re-election in November 1968. He retired, another war victim.

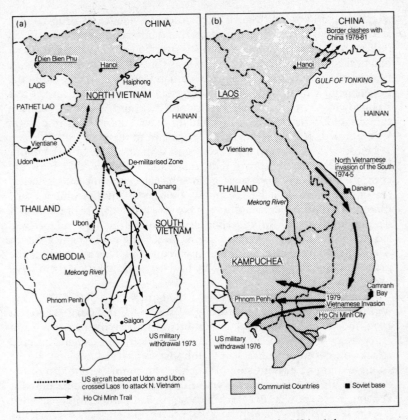

**15.1a** After the French had been driven from Indo-China, the USA tried to halt communist progress in the region. In spite of massive technological superiority and the influx of over 500,000 servicemen, the attempt ended in failure and the withdrawal of the US from Vietnam in 1973

**15.1b** The once-derided 'Domino Theory' seemed to have been proved by the appearance of communist governments in Kampuchea and Laos once Vietnam had been united under the Ho Chi-minh government. However, Sino-Soviet hostility (Fig. 15.2) deepened as Vietnam appeared to operate as a Soviet satellite, allowing the Soviet navy to use US-built bases at Danang and Camranh Bay

## The Nixon years, 1969–74

'Extrication from Vietnam is the necessary pre-condition of the US Army as an institution.'

Presidential adviser, McGeorge Bundy, May 1971

The US Army failed to deliver the expected victory, despite the fact that in 1969 there were 500,000 US servicemen, 50,000 South Koreans and 750,000 South Vietnamese engaged in a battle against 450,000

Viet Cong and 70,000 North Vietnamese. Evidence of drug-taking, atrocities such as the My Lai massacre, and unrest amongst officers, all indicated that army morale was badly affected by the war. Nixon also had to take other considerations, such as the dollar's weakness (p. 94), into account. Congress began to demand an end to the 'imperial Presidency' which had allowed Truman to wage war in Korea, Kennedy to permit the ill-fated attack on Cuba, and, above all, Johnson to escalate US participation in Vietnam. The Tonkin Gulf resolution was repealed, and demands made for an end to the war.

Nixon was anxious to hold talks with China and the Soviet Union, aimed at détente and arms reduction, and he knew that both the communist powers had their own internal economic and political reasons for wanting such talks. In July 1969, at Guam (Document 15.4), Nixon called on America's allies to take up a greater share of the cost of defending 'freedom'. In Vietnam, implementing the 'Nixon Doctrine' led to a policy of Vietnamization: US personnel trained South Vietnamese forces to defend their own country. This allowed for the gradual withdrawal of US forces; by mid-1971 about half of them were back home.

At the same time, Nixon restarted the bombing of the north, along with the Ho Chi-minh trail through Laos and Cambodia, where, in 1970, the neutralist Sihanouk government had been overthrown by an army coup which put General Lon Nol in power. The General ordered attacks on communist bases in Cambodia, which led not only to the strengthening of peasant support for the communists, but also to the danger of his own overthrow; Nixon's bombing of Cambodia aimed at keeping him in power. In March 1971 South Vietnamese forces invaded Laos to try to destroy communist bases there, but were driven back in a disastrous retreat. Neither Vietnamization nor US bombing could prevent the growth of communist power and influence.

In March 1972 the Viet Cong launched a major offensive in the south, threatening government forces near Hue, around Kintum and Saigon. The US increased the volume of their aid to the South Vietnamese, but like Chiang's men in 1948 (p. 103), they had little stomach for the fight. Nor did the heavy bombing of the north, or the mining of the harbour at Haiphong, halt the North Vietnamese drive. By the end of 1972 the Viet Cong controlled the entire western half of South Vietnam.

In January 1973 the USA and North Vietnam agreed a cease-fire following long negotiations in which South Vietnam's President Thieu was only a reluctant participant. The 17th parallel was accepted as a dividing line between North and South Vietnam; areas in the south, controlled by the Viet Cong, would now come under a Communist Provisional Revolutionary Government. All US troops were withdrawn following this agreement, which was seen as a humiliation for the USA. North Vietnam had won, partly because of Soviet aid but mainly as a result of the southern peasants' support for the Viet Cong.

The Peace Agreement was seen to be meaningless when North Vietnam almost immediately invaded the South. Nixon was powerless to act, even if he had wished to, because, in August 1973, Congress had passed the War Powers Act, overriding his veto. This act stated that within 48 hours of committing US forces abroad, the President had to report to Congress on the circumstances and proposed scope of his actions. Any forces then had to be withdrawn within 90 days unless Congress authorized a longer period. While this was still a matter of negotiation, Nixon ordered the bombing of the Khmer Rouge forces in Cambodia; Congress retaliated by threatening to cut off funds for the army, and forced Nixon to end the bombing in August 1973.

North Vietnam quickly overran a series of South Vietnamese strongholds. In May 1975 Saigon fell, and in 1976 Vietnam was united under a communist government. The Socialist Republic of Vietnam joined the UN in 1977, in spite of initial US opposition, and in 1978 joined COMECON (p. 45), its membership sponsored by the Soviet Union but criticized by some east European governments.

## 1975–86

'Vietnam . . . the Asian Prussia . . .'

*The Times*, 20 April 1985

'If the Khmer Rouge under Pol Pot come to power they would kill all the educated people . . . a step towards barbarism.'

Lon Nol, April 1975, quoted in *The Times*, 27 November 1985

In the 1960s and 1970s many perceived China as Ho Chi-minh's main supporter, and the beneficiary of his success. It is now clear that the Soviet Union was Vietnam's main supplier, and the principal beneficiary of the emergence of a united and militant-nation forming part of the Soviet 'southern pincer' against China (Figure 15.2). The 'northern pincer' had been the cause of the Battle of Damansky Island in the Ussuri River (1969), the movement of Soviet armed divisions (1974) and SS–20s (1979) to the frontier between Mongolia and China, and the construction by both powers of complex electronic equipment to aid their mutually hostile surveillance of each other's missile bases. The Soviet invasion of Afghanistan (1979) was meant to ensure the western arm of that 'northern pincer', whose eastern army is based on the Soviet port of Vladivostok. Soviet naval forces from that 'northern pincer' have linked with Vietnam-based sections of the 'southern pincer', using Vietnamese ports as bases from which to strengthen Soviet influence in the Pacific and Indian Oceans.

Chinese leaders saw the dangerous role which Vietnam might play in the encircling of China. From 1978 onwards there have been border clashes between Chinese and Vietnamese forces (Figure 15.1b). China offered refuge and support to Sihanouk after he was driven from Cambodia by Lon Nol's military coup, and also supplied arms to the

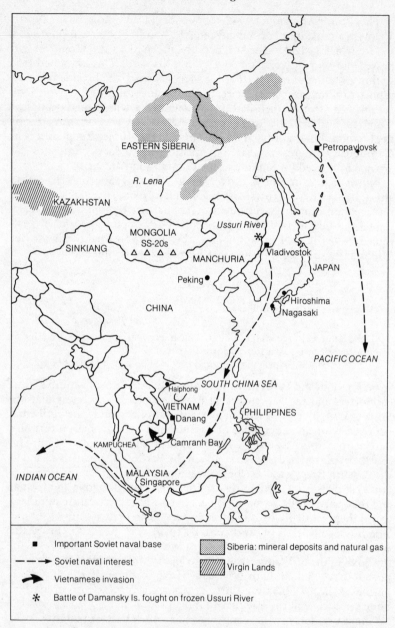

**15.2** Soviet and Chinese interests clash along the border and in Vietnam, which compels the Soviet Union to maintain defensive and offensive forces in the Far East

communist Khmer Rouge movement, opposed to Lon Nol.

The Khmer Rouge had the support of nationalists opposed to US efforts to use Cambodia as a military base, many of them peasants who gained from the Khmer's land reforms in areas they controlled, or former supporters of Sihanouk – royalists, traditionalists and neutralists – who saw the Khmer as less evil than a US-backed Lon Nol, whose government became increasingly repressive.

In April 1975 the Khmer launched an attack on the capital, Phnom Penh, and drove Lon Nol into exile, installing Sihanouk as head of state. Sihanouk was a mere puppet for a régime which, under Pol Pot, imposed a full-scale Marxist régime on 'Democratic Cambodia', now renamed Kampuchea. Lon Nol had been right: Pol Pot proved to be even more fanatical than Mao, more ruthless than Lenin and more efficient than Stalin. The population of the capital was driven into the countryside to work in the fields as part of its political education: war was declared on intellectuals, teachers, nationalists, artists and other potential opponents of the frightful régime, including anyone even suspected of being 'western educated'. Sihanouk was forced to resign in 1976 when Pol Pot's policies were in full swing. By 1979 some 3 million of Kampuchea's 7 million people had been killed, while another two million had died in the famine which swept the country.

Border clashes between Vietnamese and Kampuchean forces east of the Mekong River led to open warfare in the winter of 1977–8. In November 1978 the Soviet Union signed a Treaty of Friendship and Cooperation with Vietnam, and supported an invasion of Kampuchea some two weeks later, sending tanks, artillery and SAM missiles, and transferring fifty patrol boats from the Pacific Fleet to the Vietnamese Navy. Aided by 5000 Soviet and hundreds of Cuban 'advisers', the Vietnamese hoped for a quick victory. However, their forces are still bogged down in Kampuchea, facing a tripartite coalition of guerrilla groups nominally headed by the ever-present Sihanouk and including a reborn Khmer Rouge, no longer led by Pol Pot, and a Khmer People's National Liberation Front headed by a former Prime Minister Son Sann. These guerrillas have been driven into Thai bases, from where they launch sporadic attacks on the Vietnamese-backed government, which is unwilling to negotiate with Sihanouk. He has the diplomatic support of the ASEAN nations, who fear the spread of fighting into Thailand: they, too, have a 'Domino Theory'.

Under the 1978 Treaty, the Soviet Union won major concessions from Vietnam: its fleet uses huge US-built naval bases at Danang and Camranh Bay for operations in the South China Sea and the Indian and Pacific Oceans which strengthen the 'southern pincer' against China, and further alarm the ASEAN states.

Following the unification of Vietnam in 1976, millions of people fled the country rather than face government by the communists. Many took flight in a variety of vessels, and the 'boat people' found refuge in some western countries; others fled to Thailand which had been the HQ for US air operations in South-East Asia, and housed the surveillance facilities for monitoring movements in the region. In 1976, following the Vietnamese conquest, Thailand persuaded the US to withdraw all of its personnel – which led to a decline in US economic investment too. Thailand has had to face the problem of unemployment, as well as the continued threat of a Vietnamese attack on rebel bases across the Kampuchea–Thai border. The withdrawal of the US from Vietnam has not led to the peace and harmony which many western 'liberals' claimed would follow the success of Ho Chi-minh.

## Documentary evidence

George Kennan (Document 17.1), one of Truman's advisers, feared the development of overheated US opposition to communism. Dulles, Eisenhower's Secretary of State, accepted the 'Domino Theory' (Document 15.1) and began the US involvement in Vietnam which, under Kennedy and Johnson, increased in spite of diplomats' warnings that the war could not be won (Document 15.2). US military leaders insisted that with more power the US could defeat the rebels (Document 15.3). By the 1970s it was clear that the US was not going to win, and Nixon extricated his country from the mire of Vietnam. In the process he developed a new theory of foreign policy (Document 15.4); his 'Nixon Doctrine' made it clear that the US would no longer be the sole torch-bearer for freedom.

## Document 15.1

*The 'Domino Theory', 1952*

'*Objective*
To prevent the countries of South-East Asia from passing into the communist orbit, and to assist them to develop their will and ability to resist communism from within and without . . .
*General considerations*
Communist domination of South-East Asia would critically endanger United States security interests. The loss of any of the countries of South-East Asia to communist aggression would have critical psychological, political and economic consequences. In the absence of effective and timely counteraction, the loss of any single country would probably lead to relatively swift submission to communism by the remaining countries of this group. Furthermore alignment with communism of the rest of South-East Asia and India, and in the longer term of the Middle East (with the probable exception of at least Pakistan and Turkey) would in all probability follow; such widespread alignment would endanger the stability and security of Europe.'

(1952 Policy Statement by US on Goals in S. E. Asia)

**Document 15.2**

*George Ball, Under-Secretary of State, on the war that cannot be won, 1964*

'(1) *A Losing War.* The South Vietnamese are losing the war to the Viet Cong. No one can assure you that we can beat [them] or even force them to the conference table on our terms, no matter how many white, foreign (US) troops we deploy. No one has demonstrated that a white ground force of whatever size can win a guerrilla war in jungle terrain in the midst of a population that refuses cooperation to the white forces (and the South Vietnamese) and thus provides a great intelligence advantage to the other side.

(2) *The Question to Decide.* Should we limit our liabilities in South Vietnam and try to find a way out with minimal long-term costs? The alternative – no matter what we may wish it to be – is almost certainly a protracted war involving an open-ended commitment of US forces, mounting US casualties, no assurance of a satisfactory solution, and a serious danger of escalation . . .

(3) *Need for a Decision Now.* So long as our forces are restricted to advising and assisting the South Vietnamese, the struggle will remain a civil war between Asian peoples. Once we deploy substantial numbers of troops, it will become a war between the US and a large part of the population of South Vietnam, organized and directed from North Vietnam, and backed by the resources of both Moscow and Peking. The decision you face now is crucial. Once large numbers of US forces are committed to direct combat, they will begin to take heavy casualties in a war they are ill-equipped to fight in a non-cooperative if not downright hostile countryside. Once we suffer large casualties, we will have started a well-nigh irreversible process. Our involvement will be so great that we cannot, without national humiliation, stop short of achieving our complete objectives. Of the two possibilities, I think humiliation would be more likely than achievement of objectives – even after we have paid terrible costs.'

(*Pentagon Papers*, p. 459)

**Document 15.3**

*The military demand for more power, 1967*

'Commander, US Military Assistance Command, General Westmoreland, analyzed the strategy under the present program of 470,000 men for the President. He explained his concept of a 'meatgrinder' where we would kill large numbers of the enemy but in the end do little better than hold our own, with the shortage of troops still restricting [him] to a fire brigade technique chasing after enemy main force units when and where it could find them. He then predicted that 'unless the will of the enemy is broken or unless there was an unravelling of the Vietcong infrastructure the war could go on for 5 years.' If our forces were increased that period could be reduced although not necessarily in proportion to increase in strength, since factors other than strength had to be considered. For instance, a non-professional force, such as that which would result from fulfilling the requirement for 100,000 additional men by calling reserves, would cause some degradation of normal leadership and effectiveness. Westmoreland concludes by estimating that with a force of 565,000 men, the war could well go on for three years. With a total of 665,000 men it could go on for two years.'

(*Pentagon Papers*, p. 580)

# Document 15.4

*The 'Nixon Doctrine', 1970*

'The post-war era of American foreign policy began in 1947 with the Truman Doctrine and the Marshall Plan . . . the world has changed dramatically since [then]. We now deal with a world of stronger allies, a community of independent developing nations, and a Communist world still hostile but now divided. Others now have the ability and the responsibility to deal with local disputes which once might have required our intervention. Our success will depend not on the frequency of our involvement in the affairs of others, but on the stamina of our policies. This will best encourage other nations to do their part, and most enlist the support of the American people.

This is the message of the doctrine I announced at Guam – the 'Nixon Doctrine'. Its central thesis is that the US will participate in the defence and development of allies and friends, but that America cannot – and will not – conceive all the plans, design all the programs, execute all the decisions, and undertake all the defence of the free nations of the world. We will help where it makes a real difference and is considered in our interests. America cannot live in isolation if it expects to live in peace. We have no intention of withdrawing from the world. The only real issue before us now is how we can be most effective in meeting our responsibilities, protecting our interests and thereby building peace. A more responsible participation by our foreign friends in their own defence and progress means a more effective common effort towards the goals we seek. Peace in the world requires us to continue our commitments, but a more realistic American role in the world is essential if American commitments are to be sustained over a long pull. In my State of the Union Address, I affirmed that 'to insist that the other nations play a role is not to retreat from responsibility; it is a sharing of responsibility'. . . . We will view new commitments in light of a careful assessment of our own national interests and those of other countries, of specific threats to those interests, and of our capacity to counter those threats at an acceptable risk and cost.'

*(Keesings Contemporary Archives*, 1970)

## FURTHER READING

BRAESTRUP, P., ed., *Vietnam: Ten Years after the Paris Peace Accords*, University Press of America, 1984

DUIKER, L. J., *Vietnam: A Nation in Revolution*, Westview, 1984

DUIKER, W., *The Communist Road to Power in Vietnam*, Westview, 1981

HODGKIN, T., *Vietnam*, Macmillan, 1981

KARNOW, S., *Vietnam: a history*, Penguin, 1984

ZASLOFF, J. J. and BROWN, M., *Communist Indochina and US foreign policy*, Westview, 1978

# 16

# The United Nations Organization

## Wartime origins

'. . . they desire to bring about the fullest collaboration between all
nations in the economic field, with the object of securing for all improved
labour standards, economic advancement and social security.'

The Atlantic Charter

Although at their meeting in August 1941, Churchill and Roosevelt did
not specifically name an international body, it was clear that their stated
aims required some postwar successor to the ill-fated League of
Nations. In January 1942 26 Allied Nations signed an agreement in
Washington accepting the principles of the Atlantic Charter with its
promise of a 'brave new world'. When Churchill, Roosevelt and Stalin
met in Teheran, in November 1943, they specifically agreed on the
setting up of a new international organization. To that end, a
conference was held at Dumbarton Oaks, near Washington, in
August–November 1944, at which Allied delegates agreed the basic
framework of the proposed organization, whose charter was accepted
by the Allied leaders at the Yalta Conference in February 1945 (p. 33).

Representatives from some fifty nations approved the Charter at San
Francisco in June 1945. With 111 Articles, this was a more substantial
document than the Covenant of the League of Nations, and, unlike that
document, it was independent of peace treaties and therefore could not
be regarded as a 'covenant of victory'. The Charter came into effect on
24 October 1945 (United Nations Day). With 51 initial members, by
1960 the UNO had increased its membership to 100, and by 1970 to
127. At the time of writing it has 150 member states. This growth is to a
large extent a result of decolonization (Chapters 8–12), as a result of
which many Asian and African states, as well as the West Indies, have
become independent. These 'new' states share a good deal in common:
all have struggled against colonialism, and their poor economies
frequently depend upon foreign aid. Although this Afro-Asian bloc

relies on trade with the West, it has tended to vote with the Soviet Bloc
at the UN. Nehru, and later Nasser, termed these 'new' nations a
'Third World' of 'unaligned states'. Hard-line westerners, such as
Dulles of the USA, interpreted this 'neutralism' as support for the
Soviet Union.

From the outset the UNO differed radically from the League. Russia
and the USA were founder members of UNO, whereas the USA had
never joined the League, and the Soviet Union only committed itself
late in the day. Voting in the Assembly is by a simple majority, no
nation having the veto enjoyed by League members, although the
permanent members of the Security Council have that power during
Council debates. None of the postwar treaties referred to the UNO;
each post-1918 treaty included references to the League. None of
UNO's members has withdrawn permanently, although some have
walked out temporarily: the Soviet Union absented itself for a time in
1950 when the USA refused to allow Mao's China to take the Chinese
seat. France also left, in 1958, after a hostile UN resolution concerning
her war with the Algerian 'rebels' (Chapter 8). In 1965 Indonesia
withdrew during her war with Malaysia (pp. 222–4). All these states
later resumed their places at UNO. In the 1930s, on the other hand,
Japan, Germany and Italy all withdrew permanently from League
membership.

## Aims

'The purposes of the United Nations are:
. . . to maintain international peace and security . . . to save succeeding
generations from the scourge of war. . . .
. . . to develop friendly relations among nations based on respect for the
principles of equal rights and self-determination of peoples . . . to
reaffirm faith in fundamental human rights. . . .
. . . to achieve cooperation in solving international problems. . . .
. . . to promote better standards of life in larger freedom . . .
. . . to be a centre for harmonizing the action of nations in the attainment
of these common ends. . . .'
          *The Charter of the United Nations Organization*, 26 June 1945

The Soviet Union and its satellites signed this 'liberal' Charter even as
Stalin was imposing Soviet control over eastern Europe, where there
would be no 'self-determination' for Poles and others (p. 34), and little
regard for 'fundamental human rights' as they are understood in
western countries. The Charter may have been, at one level, merely an
idealistic signpost to an unattainable future; on the other hand it
realistically stated the need for economic, social, educational and
cultural progress throughout the world, especially in underdeveloped
countries.

To accommodate the interests of states concerned for their
sovereignty, the Charter agreed (Article 2) that the UN would have no

right to interfere in member states' internal affairs, save to enforce measures approved by the Security Council. It also recognized the rights of nations to form regional organizations, such as the EEC and NATO, aimed at economic improvement or at local collective action against aggression.

The Charter makes several references to human rights, and in 1948 the General Assembly approved the *Universal Declaration of Human Rights*, a document which illustrates the progressive nature of these, and the seemingly impossible tasks imposed on whoever is supposed to have the reciprocal duties arising from these rights. Postwar history does not show that either the Charter or the Declaration made much difference to the lives of the bulk of the world's population, who still have no 'right to work . . . free choice of employment . . . favourable conditions of work . . . right to equal pay . . . supplemented by other forms of social protection . . .'.

More practically, the Charter gave the Security Council the powers to raise armed forces to be used for the resistance of aggression, and to maintain peace. This provision has been called into play from time to time, and for many it is then that the UNO is seen to work. Too few people are aware of the prosaic but significant work done by the myriad of UN agencies.

## Structures

The basic structure of the UNO is similar to that of the League of Nations, but the rules under which its various bodies work aim to make it more effectively efficient than the League.

*The General Assembly* consists of representatives from each member state, which may send five delegates but have only one vote. It meets once a year, in September, but special sessions may be called in times of crisis by the members themselves or by the Security Council. It chooses its own President, controls its own agenda, elects the non-permanent members to the Security Council, appoints members to Councils and Committees whose work it supervises. It debates and makes proposals about international problems, and considers the UN budget and each member's contribution.

Most decisions require only a simple majority, although the Assembly may decide that a particularly serious issue needs a two-thirds majority. In November 1950, by 50 votes to 5, it passed the 'Uniting for Peace' resolution which ruled that if the Security Council was rendered inoperative by a permanent member's use of the veto, the Assembly could act and even recommend the use of armed force. This suggests that a two-thirds majority in the Assembly could overrule a veto in the Council, but this has never been put to the test, nor has the Charter been amended to incorporate this decision.

*The Security Council* can, in moments of crisis, meet almost immediately. Initially it consisted of eleven members, five of them permanent (China, France, Britain, the USA and the USSR), and the other six elected by the Assembly for two-year terms. In 1965 the number of non-permanent members was increased to ten.

Until 1971, the 'China' seat was occupied by representatives of Chiang Kai-shek. Even after Mao had become ruler of China, the US used its veto to prevent a communist delegate taking China's seat in the Council. In 1971, as part of the 'thaw' in US–Chinese relations, the Nixon government agreed to allow communist China to replace Chiang's Taiwan (Formosa) in the Council.

The Council implements decisions made by the Assembly, and deals with crises as they arise, by whatever means seem appropriate. It may call on members to take economic sanctions against an aggressor, and, when necessary, ask them to provide armed forces to operate as a UN militia. Council decisions require at least nine of the fifteen members to vote in favour, and these must include all five permanent members, each of whom has a veto and can prevent action being taken.

*The Secretariat* looks after administrative work, prepares minutes and translations into the five official UN languages (English, Russian, French, Chinese and Spanish), and provides other information needed by delegates to the Assembly, the Council and Committees.

The *Secretary-General* is appointed by the Assembly for a five-year term on the recommendation of the Council. He has much greater power and influence than his League predecessor, and may bring issues before the Council whenever he wishes. Disagreement among the permanent members has sometimes led to difficulties in appointing a Secretary-General, but the major powers have always agreed that whoever is appointed has to come from one of the lesser powers, and until 1972 none of those appointed had previously been a career diplomat. Trygve Lie of Norway (1946–52) was a lawyer-turned-politician who supported UN action in Korea (p. 256–7 and Document 16.2), and was in other ways too pro-western for Soviet tastes. When it was clear that the Soviet Union would veto a proposal to re-appoint him, he resigned. Dag Hammarskjold of Sweden (1952–61), an economist and civil servant, helped to make the post both more important and better known. He played a major role in the crises in Suez in 1956 (p. 122), and in the Congo (p. 159 and Document 16.3). He died in a mysterious air crash while trying to bring peace to the Congo. U Thant of Burma (1961–71), formerly a teacher, often expressed anger at the UN's failure to act decisively and fairly, and accepted a second term only with great reluctance. Kurt Waldheim of Austria (1971–81), had worked in the Austrian Foreign Ministry and represented his country at the UN before. Against China's wishes he became yet another European Secretary-General. His period in office was dominated by the almost continual crisis in the Middle East (pp. 133–8) and Cyprus, while the relative helplessness of the Organization was revealed by the Soviet Union's invasion of Afghanistan in December 1979 (p. 145), and its inability to act to free the US hostages held in Iran in 1980 (p. 142). Waldheim's hope of a third term in office was denied to him by Chinese opposition. He then gained greater notoriety when, during the presidential elections in Austria in 1986, he was accused of having been involved in Nazi terror campaigns in the wartime Balkans. Perez de Cuellar of Peru is the current Secretary-General. He tried, but failed to find a peaceful solution to the Falklands crisis in 1982, and has had to cope with the increasingly serious financial crisis facing the UN, and with the effects of the US withdrawal from UNESCO (p. 255).

*The International Court of Justice* sits in the Hague, not at the UN headquarters in New York. It consists of fifteen judges of different nationalities, each elected for three-year terms by the Assembly and Council acting jointly. Member states which bring issues to the Court have to agree beforehand to accept its findings. It has had some successes, settling a frontier dispute between Belgium and Holland, and a disagreement between Britain and Norway over fishing limits. Its power is obviously restricted by some states' decision not to appear before it; Britain, for example, excludes disputes with Commonwealth members from its jurisdiction; and the Soviet Union refuses to allow the Court to rule on events in eastern Europe. The Court had also found itself facing both ways over the issue of Namibia (p. 178). In 1965 it ruled in favour of South Africa in a dispute over that country's mandate, but in 1971 changed its mind and voted in favour of an end to South African occupation of the territory.

*The Trusteeship Council* replaced the League's Mandates Commission in preparing mandated territories for independence. By 1970 its work was almost completed; most of the territories taken from Germany after the First World War, and from Italy and Japan after the Second, had achieved their independence. There remained some trust territories in the Pacific Islands and New Guinea, administered by Britain, Australia, New Zealand and the USA.

The Council has been an improvement on the League's Commission; people in trust territories have the right of appeal to the Council, and many hundreds of such appeals have been heard by the Council or by the General Assembly. Council inspectors visit trust territories at least once every three years, ensuring that they are being administered in accordance with UN wishes and aims. However, it has failed notably in respect of South West Africa (Namibia) (p. 178).

## The Economic and Social Council

'The profound difficulties of the rich are their excuse for doing next to nothing about the infinitely more real problems of the poor.'
Lady Jackson, at UNCTAD, Chile, 1972

The Economic and Social Council consists of 27 members elected by the Assembly, one-third of them retiring each year. It supervises the work of he UN in economic, social, educational, health and similar fields. It has set up commissions to deal with drugs, trade, population and the status of women. While trying to rationalize, it has appointed four regional commissions – for Europe, Latin America and Africa, and for Asia and the Far East.

The Council also supervises the work of 30 other commisions and specialized agencies which aim to improve the lot of mankind. It is possible to group these under four headings:

1 *Inherited*   Some UN agencies were simply inherited from the League of Nations. The *International Labour Organization* (ILO) was founded in 1919 and continues to operate under UN auspices, producing agreement on such matters as the proper inspection of labour conditions in agriculture, paid holidays, minimum wages, youth employment and training schemes for industrial development. The *Universal Postal Union* (UPO) was directly inherited from the League, while the *International Telecommunications Union* (ITU) is the logical successor to the League's Organization for Communications and Transit.

2 *Relief*   The United Nations Relief and Rehabilitation Agency (UNRRA) was set up in 1943 to provide relief (mainly supplied by the USA) to countries liberated from German occupation, and it formally came to an end in 1949. The *United Nations Relief and Works Agency* was set up in 1950 to provide for Arab refugees from Palestine (p. 116), supplying basic food, clothing and shelter, and later, schools and medical services in refugee camps. The *United Nations International Children's Fund* (UNICEF), founded in 1946 to help children left in difficulties by the war, is now concerned mainly with the welfare of children in underdeveloped countries, and with the relief of children suffering as a result of disasters such as famines, floods and earthquakes.

3 *Economic and social cooperation*   A main aim of UNO (Document 16.1) has been furthered by agencies such as the *Food and Agricultural Organization* (FAO), which was set up in 1945. It aims to raise living standards by encouraging improvements in agricultural production, the sharing of information and the provision of technical assistance, sometimes with the help of other agencies such as the *World Bank* and the *World Health Organization* (WHO). The WHO was set up in 1948 to combat disease, and promote cooperation and knowledge in health matters; to fight epidemics, promote child and maternal welfare and generally improve living standards. Its most celebrated successes have been the virtual elimination of smallpox, and the reduction in the incidence of malaria.

4 *Economic development*   This was one of the aims of the Atlantic Charter (p. 249) and of the UN's own charter (Document 16.1). Disagreement between US and British experts on proposals for the liberalization of trade meant that a planned International Trade Organization did not come into being, although, in 1948 the *General*

*Agreement on Tariffs and Trade* (GATT) was established to promote the removal of tariff barriers. Financial cooperation and economic development were the bases for the formation of such agencies as the *International Monetary Fund* (IMF) (p. 36) and the *International Bank for Reconstruction and Development*, better known as the *World Bank* (p. 37). An affiliated agency, the *International Finance Corporation* (IFC) was set up in 1956 to promote loans to encourage private enterprise, especially in underdeveloped countries. Many of the loans to governments have been wasted on grandiose schemes, or have been misused by politicians in developing countries. Moreover, the interest charges on these loans have been a heavy burden, especially as world prices for primary products have fallen.

In 1964, under pressure from poorer countries, the *United Nations Conference on Trade and Development* (UNCTAD) was set up to coordinate demands by poorer countries for 'fairer' treatment at the hands of the wealthier. The findings of the Brandt Commission and of a British Commonwealth Commission (*The North-South Dialogue: Making it Work*, 1982) indicated the continued failure of UN member states to fulfill the optimistic expectations of the authors of the Charter.

The *United Nations Educational, Scientific and Cultural Organization* (UNESCO) was established in 1946 to wage war against illiteracy, and promote international cooperation between artists, scientists and scholars in all fields, in the belief that the best way of avoiding war was to educate people in the ways of peace. This agency has become steadily more politicized as Afro-Asian countries have gained majorities in its Assembly and governing body. Their left-wing and autocratic attitudes have annoyed many western delegates, and it was not surprising that, after many protests, the US withdrew its membership in the 1980s, leaving the agency much the poorer. Britain and other western states are currently considering their positions but may follow the US example and resign.

### Peace-keeping in a divided world

'. . . in exercise of the right of collective self-defence recognized by Art. 51 of the UN Charter . . .'

*NATO Treaty*

'. . . in the exercise of the right to collective self-defence in accordance with Article 51 of the UN Charter . . .'

*Warsaw Pact*

Both power blocs claim loyalty to the UN Charter, but both have played their own roles in denying the UN a right to interfere in events which affect them particularly. The Soviet Union ignored the UN during the crises in Hungary (1956), Czechoslovakia (1968) and Afghanistan (1979), and the USA has ignored or defied the UN over racial conflict in America and its policies in Nicaragua. While it is fair to

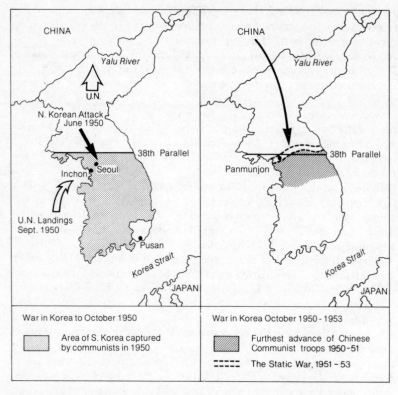

**16.1** The Korean War (1950–3) appeared to form a part of Stalin's anti-western campaign; it was the cause of China's initial excursion into world affairs, and an excuse for the anti-liberal hysteria which swept the USA

claim that the UN has been more successful than the League in its peace-keeping role, it has often been rendered ineffective by self-interested major powers.

In 1946 the UN helped to arrange the independence of *Indonesia* (Chapter 14), and played a vital role in 1961–2 when Holland and Indonesia both claimed West New Guinea (West Irian). Although U Thant's initial appeal for negotiations was ignored, it was a UN force which organized the transfer of the territory to Indonesia in 1962, after a short war.

In 1947 the problem of *Palestine* was passed on to the UN by Britain (p. 115). Although its proposal for the partition of the mandate was rejected, the UN's declaration enabled the Jewish settlers to set up the state of Israel. While unable to prevent a series of Arab–Israeli wars (Chapter 8), the UN did useful work in caring for Arab refugees, as well as arranging cease-fires and providing supervisory forces whenever the warring parties agreed a truce.

*The Korean War* (1950–3) was the one occasion when the UN acted decisively in a crisis involving a great power, but only because that power (the Soviet Union) was temporarily absent from the Security Council. When South Korea was invaded by North Korean troops (see Fig. 16.1), the Security Council condemned the Soviet-supported North and called on member states to help the South. While Britain (Document 16.2) and other members sent troops, the UN forces consisted mainly of US personnel.

By the time the warring parties had agreed on a cease-fire in 1953, the Assembly had passed the 'Uniting for Peace' resolution (p. 251), while Soviet complaints had forced Trygve Lie's early retirement and replacement by Hammarskjold (p. 232). He was Secretary-General when British, French and Israeli forces attacked *Egypt* in 1956 (p. 122). Supporters of the UN claim that it was the Council's condemnation (in the face of British and French vetoes) and the Assembly's hostility which forced the aggressors to withdraw, allowing the UN to try to negotiate a peaceful settlement over the Canal, and to send a UN Emergency Force to separate the Israelis and Arabs. However, Britain and France were probably more affected by military threats from the Soviet Union and by economic pressure from the USA, where Eisenhower was involved in the presidential election (p. 122).

Soviet support for the UN condemnation of Britain and France contrasted sharply with its own cynical, and simultaneous, invasion of *Hungary* (p. 47) and its vetoing of a Council resolution calling for the withdrawal of its forces. This combined with its refusal to cooperate with an Assembly committee set up to investigate the Hungarian 'problem'. Almost as cynical was the behaviour of the USA; its unwillingness to threaten the Soviet Union contrasted sharply with its treatment of Britain and France (Figure 16.2).

Between 1960 and 1964 the UN was involved in the *Congo* (p. 159 and Document 16.3) where a UN force of over 20,000 tried to restore order and a UN Congo Fund was set up to help the recovery and development of the war-torn country. The Soviet Union, France and Belgium refused to pay their share of the costs of this operation, because of their opposition to the way in which the situation was handled by the UN and by Hamarskjold, who was killed while flying on a UN mission in the Congo.

The UN is still involved in *Cyprus*, a British colony which became independent in 1960. In 1963 a civil war broke out between the Greek majority of the island's population and the Turkish minority. In March 1964 a UN peace-keeping force restored an uneasy peace, which was broken in 1974 when the Greeks tried to unite the island with mainland Greece. Turkish troops, sent to protect the Turkish Cypriots, seized the north of the island as an enclave from which all Greeks were expelled.

**16.2** In November 1956, *Punch* showed a stern-looking UN General-Secretary Hammarskjold punishing the 'culprits' in the attack on Egypt: the pugnacious Ben Gurion, of Israel, and Eton-jacketed Selwyn Lloyd, of Britain, have the French leader between them. A triumphant Nasser looks on, while Khrushchev takes advantage of the 'teacher's' concern over Suez to beat Hungary into submission

UN forces again arranged a cease-fire, and are still in Cyprus policing the frontier between Greeks and Turks.

In 1948 the UN negotiated a cease-fire between India and Pakistan in *Kashmir* (p. 191), but in spite of the presence of a UN peace-keeping force in the region, war broke out in 1965, and the UN had to intervene again to arrange a precarious cease-fire.

In 1968 the Soviet Union vetoed a Council resolution condemning its invasion of *Czechoslovakia* (pp. 47–9). The ineffectiveness of the Organization in the face of a great power's refusal to cooperate was further illustrated by the Soviet vetoing of a Council resolution condemning the invasion of *Afghanistan* in December 1979 (p. 145). This resolution also called for the withdrawal of Soviet troops, but in 1986 they are still in Afghanistan. In spite of the UN Charter, might, sometimes, seems to be right.

### Power politics – forty years on

'The United Nations is in a mid-life crisis.'
US delegate, Okun, October 1985
'The UN is an umbrella which folds up every time it rains.'
Israeli Foreign Minister, Abba Eban

In their recent search for détente, and agreements on arms limitation and control, the superpowers have ignored the UN and held their own bilateral negotiations (Chapters 18 and 19). In pursuit of the development of human rights in the Soviet Union, western countries signed the extra-UN Helsinki agreements in 1972 (p. 286) ignoring the UN's initial work (p. 250). It is not surprising that the celebrations to mark the fortieth anniversary of the signing of the Charter were somewhat muted, and, indeed, marred by wrangling.

The USA has shown its distaste for the UN by withdrawing from UNESCO (p. 253), by refusing to submit to the jurisdiction of the International Court, and by threatening to slash its contributions to UN budgets. When the Secretary-General protested that the UN could not afford a US reduction of its $806 million contribution, Secretary of State Schulz brusquely replied, 'That's too bad. It's your problem.'

Contemporary US antipathy to the UN stems from several sources. It resents the Soviet Union's refusal to contribute towards the upkeep of peace-keeping forces, and the inability of the Organization to act when Soviet forces invade neighbouring countries. It has become disenchanted with an organization in which the increasing number of so-called 'non-aligned' countries have tended to gang up on the USA and its surrogates, particularly Israel; the reception in the Assembly of the gun-toting leader of the PLO, Arafat, in 1975 may be seen as a particularly grotesque example of Afro-Asian willingness to seek even unfavourable sticks with which to beat the US.

Then there is the failure of the UN to condemn international terrorism. in 1979 a motion condemning it was defeated by the Arab states and their supporters. In 1986 the USA took unilateral action against 'state-sponsored terrorism' and bombed military targets in Gaddaffi's Libya. Condemnation of this action by the Afro-Asians at the UN strengthened the US beliefs that the Organization is no longer what Trygve Lie had called 'a town meeting of the world', but has deteriorated into a centre for international squabbling. Brian Urquhart, Under Secretary-General for Special Political Affairs has written: 'There are moments when I feel that only an invasion from outer space will reintroduce into the Security Council that unanimity and spirit which the founders of the Charter were talking about.'

## Documentary evidence

In his address of welcome to the delegates to the 29th session of the UN General Assembly, President Ford drew attention to the economic and social aims of the UN and to the link between those aims and the preservation of peace (Document 16.1). He was speaking in the wake of the economic crises created by the rise in the prices of food and oil in 1972–4, an inflationary development which affected almost every country in the world, but which was particularly hurtful to developing and underdeveloped countries (see pp. 309–11). In this instance the UN was unable to act effectively. Not so in 1950 when, owing to the temporary absence of the Soviet delegate from the Security Council, the USA was able to push through a resolution that the UN should supply South Korea with military aid (largely US-provided) (Document 16.2). Dag Hammarskjold was Secretary-General during the long running crisis in the Congo (Document 16.3), which was the result of the Belgian desire to hang on to its 'financial stake' in the copper-rich province of Katanga (pp. 158–60). Note in extract *E* that Hammarskjold was reluctant to allow strong action by UN forces.

## Document 16.1

*The aims of the United Nations Organization*

'Today, I welcome you, the representatives of 138 nations . . . Since the UN was founded, the world has experienced conflicts and threats to peace. . . . Today, we have the opportunity to make the remainder of this century an era of peace and cooperation and economic wellbeing . . . we are all part of one interdependent economic system. The food and oil crises demonstrate the extent of our interdependence. Many developing nations need the food surplus of a few developed nations. And many industrialized nations need the oil production of a few developing nations. . . . Failure to cooperate on oil and food and inflation could spell disaster for every nation. . . . A global strategy for food and energy is urgently required. Four principles could guide a global approach: first, all nations must substantially increase production; second, all nations must seek to achieve a level of prices which not only provides an incentive to producers but which consumers can afford; third, all nations must avoid the abuse of man's fundamental needs for the sake of narrow national advantage; fourth, the nations of the world must assure that the poorest among us are not overwhelmed by rising prices of the imports necessary for their survival. . . . There is no limit to American determination to act in concert with other nations to fulfil the visions of the UN Charter: "to save succeeding generations from the scourge of war" and "to promote social progress and better standards of life in larger freedom".'

> (President Gerald Ford to the 29th session of the General Assembly, 18 September 1974)

## Document 16.2

*The UN and the Korean War, 1950*

'I am asking the House to support the Government in the action which is fulfilling our obligations under the Charter of the United Nations . . . in the circumstances which have arisen in Korea. I think it would be as well to set on record the facts of the situation and the actions which have been taken by the United Nations. . . . Korea became a fully independent state in 1895 as a result of the Sino-Japanese War. It subsequently fell under Japanese domination and was formally incorporated into the Japanese Empire in 1910. In 1945, when Japan was defeated, it was arranged that the Japanese north of the 38th Parallel should surrender to the Russians and those to the south to the Americans.

On 25th June, there started the invasion of South Korea by the armed forces of North Korea . . . it being alleged that South Korea attacked North Korea. Anything less likely, in view of the fact that North Korea was heavily armed and South Korea was not, could not possibly be imagined. . . . There could not be a greater affront to the United Nations, and any suggestion condoning such an action would, in my view, have struck at the whole basis of the United Nations, which as been set up in order to try to preserve the peace of the world. This was immediately recognized by the calling of an Emergency Meeting of the Security Council. . . .'

> (Prime Minister Clement Attlee to the House of Commons, 5 July 1950)

## Document 16.3

*The UN and the Congo crisis, 1960–1*

A.   *The Fundamental Law of the Congo, June 1960*
'The Congo constitutes, within its present boundaries, an indivisible and democratic state.'

B.   *An appeal by President Kasavubu and Prime Minister Lumumba, 13 July 1960*
'The Government of the Republic of the Congo request urgent despatch by the United Nations of military assistance . . . the Belgian action is an act of aggression against our country. We accuse the Belgian Government of having carefully prepared the secession of Katanga with a view to maintaining a hold on our country.'

C.   *The UN Security Council, 13 July 1960*
'The United Nations Security Council:
1 Calls upon the Government of Belgium to withdraw troops from the territory of the Republic of Congo.
2 Decides to authorize the Secretary-General to take the necessary steps . . . to

provide the Government (of the Congo) with such military assistance as may be necessary.'

D.   *The secession of Katanga*

'KATANGA INDEPENDENCE DECLARED: The masquerade of Katanga's 'independence' is becoming daily more pathetic. M. Tshombe, the self-styled president, is today more under the dominance of Belgian officials than he was . . . before Congo's independence. His régime depends entirely on Belgian arms, men and money. . . . The outline of Belgium's emergency policy for Katanga is now discernible. It is to protect the great Belgian financial stake here and hold a political bridgehead in the hope of a Congolese union amenable to Belgium and the West.'

(*Daily Telegraph*, 27 July 1960)

E.   *Can the United Nations act effectively?*

'The United Nations force is a temporary security force in the Congo with the consent of the Government to help to restore law and order. It cannot take the initiative in the use of armed force: it can only act in self-defence. The United Nations cannot interfere in the internal conflicts in the Congo.'

(Dag Hammarskjold, July 1960)

F.   *The Security Council's 'demands', 24 November 1961*

'The Security Council . . .

8  Declares that all secessionist activities against the Republic of the Congo are contrary to the Fundamental Law [Document 16.3a] and Security Council decisions and specifically demands that such activities which are taking place in Katanga shall cease forthwith.'


## FURTHER READING

CLARK, W., *From Three Worlds*, Sidgwick and Jackson, 1986
FITZSIMMONS, O., *Towards One World*, University Tutorial Press, 1974
GIBBONS, S. R. and MORICAN, P., *League of Nations and UNO*, Longman, 1970
HOGGART, R., *An idea and its servants; UNESCO from within*, Chatto and Windus, 1978
LUARD, E., *The United Nations: How it works and what it does*, Macmillan, 1979
WALDHEIM, K., *In the Eye of the Storm*, Weidenfeld and Nicolson, 1986

# 17

# The Cold War
# 1945–53

## Historic origins

'Secretary of the Navy Forrestal [said] that this difficulty over Poland could not be treated as an isolated incident – there had been many evidences of Soviet desire to dominate adjacent countries and to disregard the wishes of her allies.'

White House discussion, 23 April 1945: Truman, *Memoirs*

Wartime cooperation between the Soviet Union and the West was only a short break in the traditional Russian hostility to the outside world (p. 42). Soviet historians, and, since the mid-1960s, many 'liberal' western historians, have justified this suspicion of the West: the country has been frequently invaded (Document 2.2), often devastated, and, they claim, only rarely the aggressor, and, even then, more in defensive reaction than in an effort to conquer or expand.

Other western historians argue that Russia has always been expansionist. They show that the small state of the original 'Rus' increased its territory in every direction, under a series of Tsars whose ambitions had alarmed statesmen, diplomats and rulers as far apart as China (p. 275) and Britain, whose first twentieth-century alliance had been the anti-Russian Anglo-Japanese Alliance, 1902. It is worth noting that de Gaulle described Stalin as 'a latter-day Tsar' while Stalin's latest biographer sees his rule as 'the logical culmination of the Russian political tradition' – in both domestic and foreign affairs.

Long before Truman succeeded Roosevelt (12 April 1945), Stalin had shown a complete disregard, for wartime promises in the Atlantic Charter (p. 38) and the Anglo–Soviet Treaty of 1942 (p. 32). By his treatment of Poland and other 'liberated territories' he had shown that their would be no 'free election' in the 'liberated territories' no matter what the Yalta Agreement said (Document 2.2 and pp. 34–5). His defenders, both Soviet and western, argued then and later that he sought only a defensive *cordon sanitaire* to protect the Soviet Union from future attack. Stalin had in mind, they say, western aid given to the anti-Bolshevik Whites during the Civil War, the appeasement of anti-Bolshevik Hitler in the 1930s, the betrayal of his ally, Czechoslovakia, at the Munich Conference (1938) to which the Soviet Union was not invited, the delay in the opening of a Second Front during the recent War while the Soviet Union bore the brunt of German attack, and Anglo–US secrecy over the development of the atomic bomb.

Churchill, an anti-Bolshevik 'warrior' in 1919, and some US foreign policy makers such as Kennan and Dean Acheson, saw Stalin's policies not so much as 'Bolshevik expansionism', but rather as 'traditional Russian reaction'. They wanted a development of traditional western policies – anti-Russian alliances, strong diplomatic language and, in the last resort, the threat of action. Kennan (Documents 17.1 and 17.3) never wanted Truman to become a 'Cold War warrior' in an anti-communist 'crusade'.

Truman and other US policy-makers saw Stalin's takeover of Eastern Europe as part of the accepted Communist doctrine of world revolution, as advocated by Lenin and Trotsky, as well as home-grown US communists and, more recently, Khrushchev (p. 274) and Brezhnev (p. 287). Some historians argue that Truman's lack of historical understanding led him to follow a hard, anti-communist line which pushed the Soviet Union to become even more suspicious, and so make its own contribution to the deepening of the Cold War atmosphere.

## Cold War developments, 1945–7

'What is to happen about Russia? Like you I feel a deep anxiety . . . an iron curtain is drawn down upon their front.'

Churchill to Truman, May 1945

By the time the statesmen met at Potsdam (July 1945), Soviet troops occupied German territory east of the Oder–Neisse rivers and Stalin had made it clear that this was to form a part of postwar Poland, whatever was agreed at Yalta (Document 2.2). Truman had none of Roosevelt's wartime experience. He had never met Stalin, and he lacked Roosevelt's confidence that Stalin could be controlled (p. 32).

However, the US was uncertain about its role in the postwar world. Even as late as Christmas 1945, it was hoped that all US troops would be quickly withdrawn from Europe. British Foreign Secretary Ernest Bevin, who had once hoped that 'left would speak with left', had become increasingly angered at Soviet intransigence, and simultaneously became aware of Europe's incapacity to stand up to Soviet power. He wanted the USA to play an active part in the defence of postwar Europe, although, like Truman and Byrnes, he attacked Churchill for his 'Iron Curtain' speech (Document 3.1). Soviet policy-makers helped Bevin gain US support.

In 1946, while imposing his control over eastern Europe, Stalin tried to expand Soviet influence over Turkey and Iran. By the Anglo-Iranian–Soviet Treaty of 1942, Soviet troops were stationed in northern Iran to guard against a German invasion (Document 9.3). In 1946, the USSR tried to annex the Iranian province of Azerbijan. An Iranian appeal to the UN received world-wide publicity and Stalin withdrew his troops. However, in March 1946, Stalin argued that Turkey was a weak and anti-Soviet country, unable to prevent 'foreign control' over the Dardanelles; as 'a matter of our own security' he demanded a Soviet base in the Straits. Not surprisingly, this demand was rejected by Britain, which had fought Russia over this issue in the nineteenth century.

Britain was already facing Soviet power in Greece, where 60,000 British troops supported the royalist government against communist rebels, who received aid from Albania, Bulgaria and Yugoslavia. By February 1947, Britain could no longer afford this drain on her economic resources; she was already in the process of handing over her Palestinian mandate to the UN (p. 113) and it was no surprise when she declared that she wished to withdraw from Greece. Bevin appealed to the USA to take Britain's place there.

Kennan, and Under-Secretary of State Acheson, advised Truman that the USA should play a more active rule in world affairs (Document 17.1). Acheson told Congressional leaders that 'Soviet pressure on the Straits, Iran and northern Greece' made possible 'a Soviet breakthrough which might open three continents to Soviet penetration' (Fig. 17.1). Assured of Congressional support, Truman announced his 'Doctrine' on 12 March, promising US support for 'free peoples who are resisting subjugation by armed minorities or outside pressure.' Congress agreed to give military and economic aid to Greece and Turkey, so that communism might be 'contained'. This apparent 'blank check' (Document 17.1) alarmed Kennan and other US diplomats, but pleased Bevin and other Europeans fearful of Soviet power. This marked a major stage in the development of the Cold War.

Stalin and his ideological henchman, Zhdanov, saw this 'doctrine' and the Marshall Plan (Document 17.2) as the 'twin forks' of US imperialism, although the Plan offered aid to eastern as well as western European countries. Stalin forbade Soviet satellites from taking part in discussions on the Plan. By September 1947, 16 nations were antici-pating US aid, and by 1951 some $13 billion had poured into western Europe, fostering the recovery of agriculture and industry, and so ensuring both that markets were available for US goods, and that Soviet expansionism would be halted.

In September 1947 Stalin set up Cominform to draw together the

**17.1** The Soviet control of eastern Europe, 1944–7. At this time, Yugoslavia was still behind the 'Iron Curtain', Stalin was trying to gain control of the Dardanelles and Greece, and the USA was being drawn into European affairs – almost against its own will

various European communist parties, and tighten his grip over the satellites, whose governments were forced to adopt Soviet-style policies in agriculture and industry, trade with fellow Cominform states, and minimize links with other countries.

Yugoslavia refused to toe the Cominform line, and was expelled (p. 44). The Czech government toyed with the idea of accepting Marshall aid, and in February 1948 suffered the coup which imposed Stalinism upon them (Document 17.3 and p. 44). Few US leaders accepted Kennan's view that this was merely a defensive reaction to the Marshall Plan. US public opinion was increasingly influenced by the work of the UN–American Activities Commission, and by the trial of

Alger Hiss, as much as by evidence of a Soviet attempt to force the Allies out of Berlin in June 1948.

The hardening of US opinion was best illustrated by a Senate resolution of 11 June, prior to the Berlin blockade. This called for US support for the UN, condemned the Soviet's excessive use of the veto in the Security Council, and called on the US government to ensure the maintenance of peace 'by making clear its determination to exercise the right of individual and collective self-defence under Article 51 of the UN Charter . . .'. This resolution was introduced by a Republican, Arthur Vandenberg, once an opponent of US participation in the Second World War, and a leading critic of US involvement overseas in the postwar world. His introduction of this 'interventionist' resolution was a mark of the change in US attitudes in reaction to Soviet policies.

## The Berlin blockade, June 1948–May 1949

'. . . it wasn't until the Berlin airlift that American public opinion really wakened up to the facts of life . . . [and] . . . appreciated communist tactics.'

Attlee, *A Prime Minister Remembers*

In 1948 Stalin, thwarted in Iran and Turkey but successful in consolidating control over eastern Europe (now including Czechoslovakia), organized communist uprisings against the nascent government of Indonesia (p. 221) and the British in Malaya (p. 225). He also made the first postwar attempt to gain control of Berlin.

At Yalta and Potsdam it had been agreed that Germany and Berlin should be divided into four zones (Figure 2.1). While Stalin treated his zone as a satellite, using its resources for Soviet benefit, the western Allies organized the economic and political recovery of their zones. In February 1948 they agreed on the creation of a new state from their zones which, with Marshall Aid, were already enjoying an economic prosperity envied by people in the Soviet zones. In June 1948, in pursuit of further economic recovery, a new currency was introduced within the unified western 'zone', including West Berlin, where rationing and price controls were ended. The Soviet authorities refused to accept the new currency in East Berlin, and used this reform as an excuse to try to drive the Allies from Berlin, deep inside the Soviet sector.

On 1 April 1948 the Soviets had already imposed restrictions on travel between their zone and West Germany, which they saw as a threat, with West Berlin as 'a capitalist thorn in the communist body politic', through which refugees flooded to the West. On 24 June 1948, after the currency reform, Stalin ordered the blockading of all land routes from the West to Berlin, confident that the Allies would be driven out once the 2.4 million people ran short of food, coal and other essentials.

General Clay (Document 17.3) first proposed that he 'shoot his way' through the blockade. Instead, the Allies organized a massive airlift, and over the next ten months, 2 million tons of supplies were taken to the blockaded city via 277,728 flights into airfields in the Allied zone. That the Allies refused to bow to Soviet pressure was important; if the pressure had succeeded, Stalin might have used 'salami tactics' (p. 42) to gain control of other sections of Germany, slice by slice. Stalin called off the blockade in May 1949, by which time the Allies had learned to work together, and US opinion had further hardened; the Cold War atmosphere had become more bitter, and the North Atlantic Treaty Organization had been formed.

In March 1948 Bevin had helped to form a European Alliance through the Brussels Treaty (p. 58) but the Berlin blockade showed that Europe alone was incapable of withstanding Soviet pressure. Bevin wanted to get the Americans involved in the defence of western Europe, but had made no progress until July 1948, when the blockade had shown Vandenberg that 'America could no longer go on in isolation'. Negotiations led to the signing of the treaty which set up NATO (April 1949), in which the Brussells powers (Britain, France, Belgium, Holland and Luxembourg) were joined by the USA, Canada, Portugal, Denmark, Ireland, Italy and Norway. These countries agreed that an attack on any one of them was an attack on all, and placed their defence forces under a joint NATO command which would coordinate western defence policies.

## The Korean War, 1950–3

'The attack upon Korea makes it plain that communism has passed beyond the use of subversion to conquer independent states and will now use armed invasion and war.'

Truman, 27 June 1950

American public opinion, infected by McCarthyite hysteria (pp. 89–90) and alarmed by Mao's victory in China (p. 103), supported Truman's view that the attack on South Korea in June 1950 was a reaction to failure in Berlin, Indonesia (p. 221) and Malaya (p. 225), and was part of a plan for the advancement of world communism.

In August 1945 the USA and the USSR had jointly organized the surrender of Japanese forces occupying Korea, dividing the country along the 38th parallel, with Soviet troops controlling the north and US troops the south. A UN motion called for country-wide elections, the USA hoping that the larger population of 'its' south would ensure the return of a pro-western government. However, no national elections were held, and Korea became caught up in the Cold War. Instead, elections were held in the south, supervised by the UN. The independent Republic of Korea (South Korea) was set up in August 1949, with Syngman Rhee as President, and Seoul as the capital (Figure 16.1). In September the Soviet Union set up the Democratic People's

Republic of Korea (or North Korea) led by Kim Il Sung, with its capital at Pyongyang. Soviet and US troops withdrew, leaving a divided country with Rhee and Kim claiming the right to control the whole.

Rival troops clashed along the border, and Stalin, seeing North Korea as a surrogate client, provided Kim with tanks and other equipment for his 130,000-strong army. Seemingly without Moscow's approval (the Soviet delegate having absented himself from the UN), Kim ordered the invasion of the South on 25 June 1950. The USA pushed an anti-Kim resolution through the Security Council and equipped a UN army, which, under MacArthur, went to help the South Koreans who had been heavily defeated in the initial onslaught. MacArthur's army was soon penned in around the port of Pusan (Figure 16.1); he organized a bold amphibious landing at Inchon behind the North Korean lines and drove the invaders back over the 38th parallel.

With a view to uniting the country and holding free elections, Truman ignored the possibility of a truce, ordered the invasion of the north and disregarded a Chinese warning that they might intervene. By October 1950, MacArthur had captured two-thirds of the country, including Pyongyang, and reached the Yalu River, the border with China. In November the Chinese launched a massive attack; their 300,000 troops outnumbered and defeated the UN forces and by mid-January 1951 were across the 38th parallel and had captured Seoul. MacArthur argued that the atomic bomb should be dropped on China. Attlee flew to Washington to persuade Truman that this could spark off a Third World War: Truman agreed and MacArthur was sacked.

In June 1951 North Korean and Chinese forces had been cleared from South Korea and the Soviet Union proposed an armistice. While discussions went on, so too did the fighting, until agreement was reached in July 1953, and the frontier settled upon as roughly following the 38th parallel (Figure 16.1).

What had been achieved by this flare-up in the Cold War? China had become further convinced of US hostility; its leaders recalled US aid to Chiang during the Civil War, which ended in 1949 (Chapter 7); they feared the US fleet on duty between Taiwan and the mainland, there to prevent an attack on Chiang, which suggested the possibility of a US-supported invasion of the mainland. The invasion of North Korea after China's warning, and MacArthur's call for an atomic attack, were perceived in Peking as only the latest examples of US antipathy to communist China, whom the US veto kept from occupying the China seat in the UN.

China's military success against US troops encouraged her to act as a supporter of anti-western forces in Indo-China (Chapter 15), and then in other underdeveloped Third World countries in Asia, Africa and Latin America. The same military success alarmed the USA, now in

266    *The Cold War, 1945-53*

conflict with both communist giants. Having arranged the NATO alliance against Soviet advance in Europe, the USA formed the South-East Asia Treaty Organization in 1954 and supported the Baghdad Pact in 1955 and the Central Treaty Organization in 1959, although it didn't join either.

## A 'thaw'?

'. . . there are only two ways – either peaceful coexistence or the most destructive war in history.'

Khrushchev, 1956

In 1949 the Soviet Union exploded its first atomic bomb; in August 1953 its hydrogen bomb. Both sides in the Cold War were now equally matched. Khrushchev was right; the world had to learn to live in a nuclear-based 'peaceful coexistence', or face the horrors of nuclear war.

Khrushchev made his 'peaceful coexistence' remark during his anti-Stalin campaign of 1956 (p. 78). Stalin's death in March 1953 had major effects in eastern Europe (p. 45), and within the Soviet Union, where first Malenkov and then Khrushchev called for an increased output of consumer goods, even at the expense of military expansion. Stalin's death shortly followed the inauguration of Eisenhower, after a campaign in which he had promised to end the Korean War and 'bring the boys home'. The onset of the talks of Panmunjon was, for many, a sign that the worst days of the Cold War were over; Khrushchev seemed to be less of a hard-liner than Stalin, while Eisenhower appeared to be less of a 'Cold War warrior' than Truman. Perhaps the Cold War was over?

## Documentary evidence

On the death of Roosevelt on 12 April 1945, Truman became President of the USA when the war-time alliance with the Soviet Union was disintegrating. The idea of containing Soviet power in Europe was first clearly stated by George Kennan, a US diplomat who had served in Russia until 1946. In a memorandum presented to Truman in July 1947 he called on the US to adopt policies which would 'increase enormously the strains under which Soviet policy must operate . . .'. Truman's 'doctrine' of containment alarmed Kennan (Document 17.1): Soviet perceptions of that 'doctrine' and of the Marshall Plan (Document 17.2), led, according to Kennan (Document 17.3), to the Czech crisis and the attempt to drive the Allies from Berlin. This, in turn, led the Allies to form NATO. It is clear that there are grounds for historical debate as to the origins and development of the Cold War, and not everyone will accept Kennan's 'liberal' view that the Soviet Union was merely reacting to western 'aggression'.

## Document 17.1

*George Kennan's unease concerning Truman's policies*

'I was not alone in my awareness of the danger that the sweeping language of the message might be subject to misinterpretation. Mr Acheson was himself at pains to try to dispel among members of Congress the impression that what the President had said represented a blank check. . . . Nevertheless, the mis-apprehension conveyed was, as I see it, never entirely corrected . . . the conduct of our foreign policy would continue to be bedevilled by people in our government as well as in other governments who could not free themselves from the belief that all another country had to do to qualify for American aid was to demonstrate the existence of a Communist threat. Since almost no country was without a Communist minority, this assumption carried very far. And as time went on, the firmness of understanding for these distinctions on the part of our own public and government appeared to grow weaker rather than stronger. In the 1960s so absolute would be the value attached to the mere existence of Communist threat, that such a threat would be viewed as calling, in the case of South-East Asia, for an American response on a tremendous scale, without serious regard even to those main criteria that most of us in 1947 would have thought it natural and essential to apply.'

(G. F. Kennan, *Memoirs*, Hutchinson, 1968)

## Document 17.2

*Marshall on his Plan, 1947*

'The truth of the matter is that Europe's requirements for the next 3 or 4 years of foreign food and other essential products – principally from America – are so much greater than her present ability to pay that she must have substantial additional help, or face economic, social and political deterioration of a very grave character.

The remedy lies in breaking the vicious circle and restoring the confidence of the European people in the economic future of their own countries and of Europe as a whole. . . . Aside from the demoralizing effect on the world at large and the possibilities of disturbances arising as a result of the desperation of the people concerned, the consequences to the economy of the United States should be apparent to all. . . . Our policy is directed not against any country or doctrine but against hunger, poverty, desperation and chaos. Its purpose should be the revival of a working economy in the world so as to permit the emergence of political and social conditions in which free institutions can exist.

Any government that is willing to assist in the task of recovery will find full cooperation, I am sure, on the part of the United States Government. Any government which manoeuvres to block the recovery of other countries cannot expect help from us. Furthermore, governments, political parties or groups which seek to perpetuate human misery in order to profit therefrom will encounter the opposition of the United States. . . .'

(*Congressional Record*, 80th Congress, 5 June 1947)

## Document 17.3

*Kennan's criticisms of NATO*

'On the very day of my departure, the Czech crisis reached its height. The realization of what had occurred burst with great violence upon the American press. . . . The shock was heightened when on 11th March news was received of the mysterious death, either by murder or suicide, of Jan Masaryk, foreign minister of the Czechoslovak Republic . . . a friend of the West. His death dramatized, as few other things could have, the significance of what had just occurred in that country.

Of even greater importance, I believe, for its effect on American official opinion, was a telegram received from General Lucius Clay, in Berlin on 5th March. For many months, Clay wired, logical analysis had persuaded him that war with the Soviet Union was unlikely '*for at least ten years*'; but '*. . . Within the last few weeks, I have felt a subtle change in Soviet attitude which I cannot define but which now gives me a feeling that it may come with dramatic suddenness.*'

Washington, particularly the military establishment and the intelligence fraternity . . . overreacted in the most deplorable way to Clay's telegram and the Czech coup. A real war scare ensued, the intensity of which may be judged from the fact that on 16th March the CIA thought it necessary to hand to the President an estimate saying that war 'was not probable within sixty days. . . .'

In offering this brief summary of the March crisis of 1948, I must point out that both of the events that threw official Washington into such a dither – the consolidation of Communist power in Czechoslovakia and the attempt by the Russians to force the Allies out of Berlin – were defensive reactions on the Soviet side to the . . . Marshall Plan and to the preparations . . . to set up a separate German government in Western Germany. They represented Moscow's attempt to play, before it was too late, the various political cards it still possessed on the European continent.'

(G. F. Kennan, *Memoirs*, Hutchinson, 1968)

## FURTHER READING

ARNOLD-FORSTER, M., *The Siege of Berlin*, Collins, 1979

BALFOUR, M., *West Germany: A Contemporary History*, Croom Helm, 1983

BALFOUR, M., *The Adversaries: America, Russia and the World*, 1941–62, Routledge & Kegan Paul, 1981

BULLOCK, A., *Ernest Bevin: Foreign Secretary*, Heinemann, 1983

CARTER, D., *The Great Fear: The Anti-Communist Purge under Truman and Eisenhower*, Secker and Warburg, 1978

HALLE, L. J., *The Cold War as History*, Harper and Row, 1971

HAMMOND, P. Y., *Cold War and Détente*, Harcourt Brace, 1975

KAPLAN, L. S., *The United States and NATO: The Formative Years*, University of Kentucky Press, 1984

LA FEBER, W., *The Origins of the Cold War: a historical problem with interpretations and documents*, John Wiley, 1971

LA FEBER, W., *America, Russia and the Cold War, 1945–71*, 3rd ed., John Wiley, 1976

MURPHY, R., *Diplomat Among Warriors*, 1964

SMITH, W. B., *Moscow Mission, 1946–49*, Heinemann, 1950

STUECK, W., *The Weidemeyer Mission: American Politics and Foreign Policy during the Cold War*, University of Georgia Press, 1984

# 18

# International relations, 1953–74

## The spirit of Geneva, 1954–5

'The basic purpose of Communist strategy remain the same – the domination of the world by Communism, as represented by the USSR. The purpose remains, and will remain, constant through every change of leadership; only the tactics vary.'

J. Sejna, *We Will Bury You*, 1982

Jan Sejna, a member of the ruling Central Committee of the Czech Communist Party since 1954, fled from the country in 1968 because he feared that Dubcek's reforms would lead to Soviet military intervention (p. 48). Like the Soviet leaders, he must have viewed with cynical pleasure the western welcome for the 'thaw' after the death of Stalin in March 1953.

On p. 238 we noted that the fall of Dien Bien Phu on 7 May 1954 marked the total failure of French intransigence in Indo-China. On that same day, the foreign ministers of Britain, France, the USA, the Soviet Union and China met at Geneva, where, in July 1954 they agreed a settlement of Indo-Chinese affairs (p. 238). This further success of 'International Communism' angered US Secretary of State Dulles, who wanted to do more than just 'containing Russia' (Document 18.1). Dulles believed in the 'Domino Theory' (Document 15.1), and had wanted to use the atomic bomb against North Vietnam. However, the Geneva Agreement was welcomed in the West as a sign that the communist powers could be brought to negotiations at the conference table.

In July 1955 Khrushchev, providing more evidence of 'the thaw', visited Belgrade to make peace with Tito (p. 78). He then went to Geneva to meet the Prime Ministers of Britain and France, and the President of America. This was the first meeting between the leaders of the USA and USSR since Potsdam some ten years before. The conference was held in a friendly atmosphere, giving fresh evidence of 'the Geneva Spirit', a relaxation of the Cold War tensions, although it failed to achieve anything of substance.

In February 1956, following his attack on Stalinism (p. 78), Khrushchev visited countries in western Europe. In April 1956 he and Bulganin visited Britain, where, in spite of a row with the leaders of Britain's Labour Opposition, he presented 'an acceptable face' of Soviet Communism. People who had lived through the Cold War period and who had feared the outbreak of war over, for example, Berlin, welcomed Macmillan's claim that 'there ain't gonna be no war.'

## The Eisenhower years, 1953–60

'I wish I could say tonight that a lasting peace is in sight.'
From Eisenhower's Farewell Address, 17 January 1961

At the 20th Party Congress, Khrushchev announced a 'revision' of Soviet foreign policy. War was not inevitable; coexistece was desirable; in the age of the hydrogen bomb, there would be no winners. However, in May 1958, at a Warsaw Pact meeting in Moscow, he outlined the tactics needed to gain a socialist victory in the struggle between 'states having different social systems'. He had earlier boasted to a gathering of western diplomats, 'We will bury you': Soviet aims had not changed; as Sejna wrote, 'only the tactics vary'.

The crushing of the Hungarian rising in 1956 (p. 47) showed that Stalin-like, Khrushchev would maintain Soviet power. Meanwhile, in spite of Dulles's statements on 'liberation' (Document 18.1), the USA did nothing to support the Hungarian rebels other than to table a condemnatory resolution at the UN. Almost simultaneously at the UN, the USA and USSR had cooperated to condemn the Anglo–French action in Suez (p. 122); the decline in the prestige of these two powers in the Middle East seemed to be as welcome in the USA as in the USSR. However, in 1957, alarmed at the evidence of growing Soviet influence in the Middle East, Eisenhower called for Congressional action (Document 18.2). Updating the 'Truman Doctrine' (p. 265), he promised that the USA would ensure peace with justice throughout the world and was prepared to get involved, both economically and militarily. Only Lebanon welcomed the offer of US aid (Document 18.2); influenced by Nasser, other Arab countries rejected the offer and, in some cases, organized the overthrow of pro-western governments. In 1958 the US marines landed in Lebanon to prevent yet another coup (p. 123) in a region where the influence of Nasser and the USSR had grown since 1956.

Pursuing his policy of wooing western opinion, Khrushchev went to the USA in 1959 to address the UN Assembly and meet Eisenhower at Camp David, where both agreed to hold a summit meeting in 1960 to consider the problems of Berlin and disarmament. Macmillan, the British Prime Minister, welcomed the idea of a summit, hoping to play an active role on the world stage. Dulles, de Gaulle of France and Adenaeur of West Germany, warned of the need to guard against Soviet attempts to gain control of West Berlin (p. 279).

The summit was finally arranged, to be held in Paris, in May 1960. Khrushchev knew that leaders of the Soviet forces as well as Party hardliners opposed holding talks with the USA, in view of Dulles's hawkish position (Document 18.1) and Eisenhower's 'Doctrine' (Document 18.2). If Khrushchev was rebuffed by the USA, or, worse still, if he appeared to concede anything, opposing factions within the Politburo might gain control. Before the conference he told western journalists that he intended to sign a treaty with East Germany, and force the West to grant it diplomatic recognition. As soon as the summit began he announced that a US U–2 'spy' plane had been shot down over Russia, and that he was no longer prepared even to discuss the German problem with the untrustworthy Americans. He cancelled the summit as well as the invitation previously extended to Eisenhower to visit Moscow. Back home, Khrushchev claimed a 'triumph': he had shown up the Americans whose behaviour 'delayed progress' to peaceful coexistence.

## China and the Soviet Union, 1945–64

'The atomic bomb is a paper tiger.'
Mao in the *People's Daily*, 31 December 1962

As in Russia's relations with the West, there is a continuum in Sino–Russian relations. China resented the Russian occupation of the Amur Valley in the seventeenth century, and attempts to conquer Mongolia in the nineteenth. Earlier in the twentieth century, the two powers had clashed over the mineral-rich area of Sinkiang, bordering on Kazakhstan. In the 1920s there was a division between the Soviet concept of communism (based on the industrial worker) and Mao's peasant-based revolution. In 1949 Stalin could do little other than welcome the victory which established communist rule over China, although he had provided little aid for Mao in his struggle against the US-backed Chiang.

Following Sino–Soviet cooperation in the Korean War (p. 269), Stalin sent technicians and materials to aid China's industrialization (p. 104), although, the Chinese claimed, he sent more aid to India, and never shared his atomic secrets with China, which continued to resent the way in which Stalin had stripped Manchuria of its industrial goods in 1945 and 1946.

After Stalin's death, relations between the two powers deteriorated. Mao, who had formerly accepted Stalin as Communism's 'elder statesman' now claimed this title for himself and resented Soviet efforts to hold China in some form of tutellage. He was angered by Khrushchev's denunciation of Stalin, his plea for coexistence, and by his claim that an atomic war would destroy both the capitalist west and communist east. Mao argued that the US had not won the Korean War in spite of her atomic weapon.

He attacked Khrushchev's efforts to provide higher living standards for the Soviet people, and dismissed Khrushchev's argument that, 'You cannot put theory into your soup or Marxism into your clothes. If after forty years of Communism, a person cannot have a glass of milk or a pair of shoes, he will not believe that Communism is a good thing . . .'. Mao condemned this as 'revisionism', a backsliding from the purity of Marxist–Leninism. This was a 'goulash Communism', and he wanted 'permanent revolution'. Although Mao had received Soviet aid for his 'Great Leap Forward' in 1958 (p. 105), the Chinese version of the commune was radically different from the Soviet model (p. 106).

There was a public quarrel between leaders of both countries at the Soviet's 22nd Party Congress in 1960. Following this, Khrushchev cut off Soviet economic aid to China, while Mao condemned the decision to hold talks with the US Presidents in 1960 and 1961, accused Khrushchev of stupidity and cowardice in the Cuban affair in 1962 (p. 278), and refused to take part in the negotiations leading to the Test Ban Treaty of 1963 (p. 279). In 1964 China exploded her own nuclear bomb, and could now claim equality in this respect with the Soviet Union.

In 1964 Khrushchev planned a meeting of the world's communist leaders, where he would urge them to throw China out of the 'communist club'. He was alarmed by the support which Rumania and Albania, in particular, gave to Mao's claim to world leadership. However, before he could put his anti-Mao plan into operation, Khrushchev himself was overthrown (p. 80) and the Sino–Soviet split remained, to trouble Brezhnev.

## The Cuban crisis, 1962

'This build up of communist missiles is a deliberate provocative change in the *status quo* which cannot be accepted by this country.'
           President Kennedy, 22 October 1962

'Your rockets are in Turkey.'
           Khrushchev to Kennedy, 23 October 1962

The Cuban crisis had its origins in the overthrow of the US-backed, corrupt government of ex-army sergeant Batista, who had exiled or executed his enemies, misused dollar aid from the USA, stolen government funds and led Cuba into bankruptcy. During 1958 and 1959 some Cubans fought a guerrilla war led by Fidel Castro, who took power when Batista fled to the USA in 1959. The USA ended its aid to Cuba, and persuaded other western governments and the IMF not to give Cuba the loans needed to put her house in order. Castro asked communist governments for aid, and, in retaliation, set about the nationalization of US-owned industries. This confirmed US suspicions

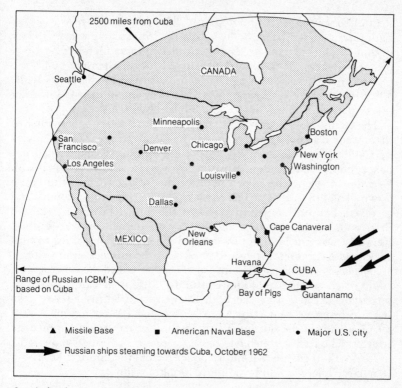

**18.1** A sketch map which helps to explain US fears of Cuba-based Soviet missiles

that Castro was a 'communist stalking horse', another of those successes of 'International Communism', (Document 18.1 and 18.2), operating at a distance of only some 90 miles from the US mainland.

The US government allowed Batista's supporters to train in preparation for an invasion of Cuba, and increased pressure on Castro by refusing to buy Cuban sugar. The Soviet Union agreed to buy the sugar, and also to provide economic aid and technical assistance, which, for the US government, was yet further proof that Cuba was becoming a Soviet satellite.

In 1961 Kennedy took charge of Eisenhower's plan for an invasion of Cuba. In April 1961 he authorized the attack on Cuba in which 1500 Cuban exiles went ashore at the Bay of Pigs. The mission was a disaster; the invasion force surrendered after three days. Fearing further attacks, Castro accepted military aid from the Soviet Union which installed ballistic missile bases on the island. In February 1962 the Warsaw Pact countries were told that in the event of a nuclear war these bases would be used to launch rocket attacks on the US.

In October 1962 aerial photographs showed that Castro was armed with Intermediate Range Ballistic Missiles, threatening every US city within a radius of 2500 miles (Figure 18.1). On 22 October Kennedy ordered a naval blockade of Cuba, to 'halt this offensive build up'; Castro argued that the weapons were defensive in character, while Khrushchev claimed that they were less threatening than US missiles based in Turkey, bordering on the Soviet Union.

The two leaders kept in contact by letter and telephone; neither of them wanted a nuclear war. Kennedy was supported by Macmillan and de Gaulle, who was, nonetheless, angry because Kennedy had not consulted Europe's leaders. Khrushchev was also under pressure, from Kremlin 'hawks' who hoped to force the young Kennedy to climb down. The US maintained its naval blockade; ships were stopped and searched, and only innocent cargo let through. Khrushchev realized that, with the US air force and Polaris submarines on war-footing, Kennedy was not bluffing; he ordered missile-carrying ships to turn back, and on 27 October agreed to remove the missiles from Cuba.

This crisis, which showed that in a bi-polar world the superpowers could reach decisions without consulting Europe or China, was also important because it caused both Kennedy and Khrushchev to take steps to improve contact between Moscow and Washington. A new telephone link ('the hot line') was established to provide immediate contact. The letters which had passed between the leaders indicated a mutual will to ensure that future policies would be more defensive in character. There would be no more 'brinkmanship'.

## The German problem, 1960–72

'. . . after 1945 the East–West confrontation overshadowed Germany and divided Europe. We cannot redress this division, but we can strive to lessen its worst effects, seeking a regulated form of peaceful coexistence.'
Chancellor Willy Brandt, 6 June 1970

West German foreign policy had been controlled, from 1949 to 1963, by Chancellor Adenauer. One prong of that policy was summed up in the 'Hallstein Doctrine', promulgated by the Federal Foreign Minister, Hallstein, in December 1955. This stated West Germany would regard diplomatic recognition of East Germany as an unfriendly act, as it would amount to an acceptance of the division of Germany. The second aim of Adenauer's policy was to reunite Germany; in 1955 he visited Moscow to examine the possibilities of Soviet agreement to re-unification, but, while he established diplomatic relations with the Soviet Union, he accomplished little else, partly because a third aim of his policy was the placing of West Germany firmly in the western bloc – as confirmed by her membership of NATO, and his involvement with the creation of the EEC.

Adenauer antagonized the Soviet Union and her satellites by insisting that only West Germany had the right to represent 'Germany', and that East Germany was not a sovereign state. We have seen (p. 275) that Khrushchev threatened to sign a bilateral treaty with East Germany in May 1960, and so force the West to recognize Ulbricht's state. In the event he did not do so. However, following the failure to reach agreement over Berlin with Kennedy, when they met in Vienna in 1961, Khrushchev ordered the building of the Berlin Wall, ending any hope of reunification.

In 1966 the dominant Christian Democratic Union was forced to form a 'Grand Coalition' with the opposition Social Democratic Party, whose leader, Willy Brandt, former Mayor of West Berlin, became Foreign Minister. By the time that he became Chancellor in a SDP-led coalition, Brandt had held discussions with the Soviet Union and the leaders of Warsaw Pact countries, in the hope of finding a settlement to solve the problems presented by the division of Germany. The negotiations were not easy; East Germany feared that improved relations between West Germany and Warsaw Pact states might leave her isolated; Poland, with former German territory now part of western Poland, feared for the future of these lands if Brandt succeeded in his negotiations, while the Stalinist government saw that any weakening of the threat from West Germany would undermine the Polish people's need for Soviet protection. The Soviet Union feared that Brandt's proposed *détente* might isolate East Germany, split the Warsaw Pact and reduce eastern European dependence on the defensive power of the Soviet Union. Brandt, too, had to educate West Germans to accept the postwar *status quo* and the need for a new relationship with East Germany.

In 1969 Brandt opened talks with Poland on the subject of the frontier and the German minorities living in the once disputed areas around the Oder-Neisse. At the same time, he had to assure the Soviet Union that he was not seeking to undermine Soviet power or policies in eastern Europe. In August 1970 he signed a non-aggression treaty with the Soviet Union which recognized the existing frontiers in Europe, including the frontier between the two Germanys. In November 1970, the Polish–West German Treaty was finalized and by December 1973 Brandt had signed treaties with every Warsaw Pact country.

These many-sided discussions took place while the USA, under Nixon, was negotiating with China and the Soviet Union. The new 'thaw' and the much vaunted progress towards *détente* (Chapter 19) helped speed Brandt's progress. In September 1971 a new four-power agreement on Berlin was signed, the first since 1947; in October 1971 Brezhnev, convinced of the genuine nature of Brandt's search for peaceful solutions to the problems of Central Europe, forced the East Germans to negotiate with Brandt on access and traffic between the two Germanys. After an agreement on these issues had been signed (June 1972), Brandt continued negotiating with the East Germans with a view to the signing of a treaty in which the two states would recognize each other's membership of rival alliances (NATO and the Warsaw Pact) and which would lead to the admission of both Germanys to the UNO. This Basic Treaty was signed in December 1972, and both Germanys entered the UNO in September 1973.

These various negotiations and treaties had rid Europe of almost all the problems which had previously strained relations and been a major cause of the Cold War. If the 'German problem' could thus be resolved, it could be hoped that other problems might be solved. The road to Helsinki and to *détente* was now open.

## Arms and disarmament, 1945–73

'A new golden age has arrived. The world is moving towards generations of peace.'

*Washington Post*, October 1972

Few subjects received more attention in the postwar world than the arms race and the failure of the superpowers to agree on arms limitation, let alone disarmament. The Soviet Union spent more than its economy could afford as it tried to catch up with the USA, which responded with yet greater spending, in an effort to maintain its lead. Kissinger spoke for many when he complained, 'What in the name of God is "strategic superiority"? What is the significance of it politically, militarily, operationally? What do you do with it?'

In 1946 the UNO set up the Atomic Energy Commission, and in 1947 a Conventional Armaments Commission. The Soviet withdrawal from both led the UN to merge them into a Disarmament Commission (1952), in the hope that this might lead to a new approach. In spite of much talking, this Commission (reconstituted in 1959 and in 1962) failed to reach any agreement, but in 1966 it optimistically sponsored a Disarmament Commission at Geneva.

When the 'spirit of Geneva' (p. 273) promised a new atmosphere, Eisenhower proposed his 'open skies' plan (1956), under which the powers would allow 'spy planes' from other countries to overfly their territory to verify the size of opposing military forces. The Soviet Union, suspicious of any policy emanating from the USA, rejected this plan. In October 1957 Rapacki, the Polish Foreign Minister, put forward a plan under which Poland, Czechoslovakia, East and West Germany would become 'nuclear free' zones, in which there neither the manufacturing nor in the stockpiling of nuclear weapons would be permitted; joint inspection by NATO and Warsaw Pact states would ensure compliance with the plan. The USA and Britain rejected this scheme which, they argued, ignored the size of Soviet conventional forces.

Talks on the problem of detecting nuclear explosions opened in Geneva in October 1958, by which time Britain had exploded its first hydrogen bomb (May 1957), and the USA had become vulnerable to potential attack from rocket-launched nuclear weapons. In spite of East–West hostility over Berlin (p. 279) and the election of Kennedy in 1960 as Eisenhower's successor, these talks went ahead, leading to the Nuclear Test Ban Treaty, signed in Moscow in July 1963 by the USSR, the USA and Britain. It had taken the three powers over five years to agree on the banning of nuclear tests, both in the atmosphere and under water. Critics pointed out that this treaty was more concerned with pollution than disarmament or arms control, and that neither France (with its own hydrogen bomb) nor China (developing the bomb which was exploded in 1964) signed the treaty.

After further long discussions, the three signatories of the 1963 treaty signed the Non-Proliferation Treaty (1968) in which they agreed not to transfer nuclear weapons to other states; this desirable end was endangered by the fact that, again, neither China nor France signed. Nor did the Treaty say anything about weapons' development by the three Powers. Britain's economic decline made it unlikely that she would long remain an independent nuclear power; it was the USA and USSR which took part in a grisly arms race which forced the public to learn new words and acronyms as they heard of 'second strike forces' made of Minutemen, ICBMs and Polaris submarine-launched missiles, which could be 'knocked out' by ABMs, which, however, might be overcome by MIRVs. An already bemused public was further baffled by the conflicting claims of both sides over the number and efficacy of the other's weapon systems. It was difficult enough to follow the simple figures of weapon-numbers. But these hid more than they revealed, and begged many questions: how many warheads were carried by each of the 1000 or so ICBMs? What tonnage of explosive power was in each warhead? How accurate were these weapons? How many would be knocked out by an enemy's 'first strike', and how many would survive as a 'second strike' against an aggressor?

Inability to answer these questions, coupled with mutual suspicion, led to the continuation of the arms race, the situation summed up in the acronym MAD, 'Mutual Assured Destruction'. Many wondered, with Kissinger, what could be done about this capacity to overkill. Certainly it did not help the US to victory in Vietnam. Politicians in the USA and USSR became increasingly concerned at the cost of the arms race, a major factor in the USA's budgetary and trading deficits, and in the USSR's continuing economic weakness. It is not surprising that both powers wished to find some way of cutting back on missile development.

Negotiations took place against a favourable background: Brandt's *Ostpolitik* was defusing the German situation; Nixon was anxious to improve relations with China; Brezhnev, fearing a US–China rapprochement, wanted a *modus vivendi* with the USA; the USSR had, by 1972, achieved a degree of superiority in terms of numbers of weapons systems and was less fearful of coming to an agreement than she had been when the USA was manifestly the superior power. Not that Brezhnev was prepared to cede much. In November 1968 he justified the Soviet invasion of Czechoslovakia (p. 48) with the 'doctrine' that the socialist community had the right to intervene in any fellow socialist country when internal and/or external forces hostile to Communism threatened to restore a capitalist-style system.

On 20 January 1969, as Nixon was being inaugurated, the USSR announced that it would be prepared to negotiate a mutual limitation of strategic delivery vehicles. In February the USA responded positively, and, after both sides worked out their bargaining positions, negotiations began in November 1969, continuing until 1972, first at Helsinki, and later in Vienna. During these three years the economies of both the USA (p. 94) and the USSR (p. 80) continued to decline, putting further pressure on the negotiators to reach agreement.

In November 1972 both sides signed the two agreements which make up SALT I. One, of unlimited duration, restricted each power to only two complexes of Anti-Ballistic Missiles, one to cover their respective capitals, the other to cover a single complex of ICBM launch silos. The second agreement, the Interim Agreement on the Limitation of Strategic Arms, was to last until October 1977, and would ensure that the level of missile numbers would remain at the 1972 level. This provided the USSR with a quantitative superiority, which the USA felt was outweighed by her qualitative superiority. Both sides connived at the ambiguity and uncertainty of parts of this treaty, which did not mention modernization of weapons, the replacement of old by new systems, or the enlargement of missile sites to take larger, and heavier, weapons. It is not surprising that as the ink dried on SALT I, accusations were being made that one side or the other was in breach of the agreement. Nor did the signing of SALT I lead to a lessening of activity elsewhere. In 1975 the USSR with the aid of its Cuban satellite intervened in Angola and elsewhere to increase its influence worldwide.

However, the world saw SALT I as the start of a new 'golden age' in which, wrote Alistair Buchan, 'peace had descended on the world'. What the world could not know, in 1978, was that in 1973 OPEC countries would take concerted action on oil supplies and prices and so create a new international economic crisis which would affect the prospects for peace and mutual agreements.

## Nixon's diplomatic revolution, 1969–73

'We judge by different standards. We talk of compromise; they talk principles. We exalt stability; they believe in struggle.'
            Kissinger, 29 February 1972, after Nixon's first visit to China

Nixon won his Congressional seat in 1948, after accusing his liberal Democrat opponent of being a subversive, indistinguishable from a communist. An active participant in the UN–American Activities Committee, Nixon claimed credit for the imprisonment of Hiss (p. 89), and was a leading critic of Truman and Acheson, whose policies, he claimed, had helped Mao to victory in 1949 (p. 103). As Eisenhower's Vice-President, he had supported the Dulles 'doctrine' (Document 18.1).

That as President he should work for a Sino–US rapprochement (Document 18.3), and put limits on US willingness to act internationally (Document 15.4), as well as sign SALT I (p. 282) and seek friendly relations with the Soviet Union, points to a major shift in his personal attitudes as well as in US policy.

Nixon was helped by external developments, and by communist perceptions of his decision to withdraw from Vietnam (p. 243). One factor on his side was the deepening hostility between China and the USSR; there were border clashes in August 1969 as both countries claimed lands north of the Rivers Amur and Ussuri; there was heavy fighting on Damansky Island in the middle of the Ussuri and along the long Sinkiang section of the 4000 mile-long border between the two countries, during which the Soviet Union threatened to use nuclear weapons against its communist rival. Eastern European newspapers, moreover, reported the imminence of a Soviet air strike against Chinese nuclear installations at Lop Nor. In September 1969 when Kosygin flew to attend the funeral of Ho Chi-minh in Hanoi, his plane was routed the long way round to avoid Chinese territory. Following the funeral, Kosygin and Premier Chou En-laid met on many occasions but failed to heal the breach. In spite of Mao's contempt for the 'paper tiger' of atomic weapons, China knew that it did not have the strategic retaliatory power to match that of the Soviet Union. It was this realization which brought Mao to accept the need for *détente* with the USA.

In March 1971 the US lifted restrictions on travel to China; and in June it scrapped the embargo on trade. In July Kissinger went to Peking (Document 18.3), and Nixon announced that he would visit China in May 1972.

The Soviet Union was also engaged in its own *détente* with the USA. In May 1972 Nixon flew to Moscow to sign SALT I (p. 282), and, later, on US television, announced that 'mankind has outgrown the rigid armour of the Cold War which it once had to bear.' *Détente* had become a reality; the world appeared to be justified in its optimism concerning a peaceful future.

## Documentary evidence

George Kennan had feared that US foreign policy would, mistakenly, become too 'hawkish' (Document 17.1). The development of the 'Truman Doctrine' in

1947 (Document 17.3) bore out his fear while the emergence of the 'Domino Theory' (Document 15.1) and Dulles's hardline policy (Document 18.1) saw US policy develop a crusading character. There was a more practical basis to Eisenhower's call for a vigorous US policy in the Middle East in 1957, the need for which was caused, in part at least, by the decline in Anglo–French prestige in the region after the débâcle of the Suez crisis of 1956, when US policy had helped ensure the failure of Anglo–French policies there. Nixon had been party to the Dulles–Eisenhower policies; however, as President he took a much less 'hawkish' line. His own 'Doctrine' (Document 15.4) promised a withdrawal of the US from the front-line, while his rapprochement with China (Document 18.3) may, in hindsight, prove to be the one item for which he will be best remembered.

## Document 18.1

*Dulles calls for a 'rolling back' policy, 1953*

'I have no objection to saying in open session that we shall never have a secure peace or a happy world so long as Soviet communism dominates one-third of all the peoples that there are, and is in the process of trying to extend its role to many others. . . .

We must always have in mind the liberation of these captive peoples. Now liberation does not mean a war of liberation. Liberation can be accomplished by processes short of war. . . . A policy which only aims at containing Russia where it now is, is, in itself, an unsound policy; if our only policy is to stay where we are, we will be driven back. It must be and can be a peaceful process, but those who do not believe the results can be accomplished by moral pressure, by propaganda, just do not know what they are talking about.'

(Secretary of State, John Foster Dulles, to the Senate
Foreign Relations Committee, 15 January 1953)

## Document 18.2

*The Lebanon crisis and the Eisenhower 'Doctrine', 1957*

'The Middle East has reached a new and critical stage in its long history. All this instability has been heightened and manipulated by International Communism. Russia's interest in the Middle East is solely that of power politics. Considering her announced purpose of communizing the whole world, it is easy to understand her hope of dominating the Middle East. The region contains about two-thirds of the presently known oil deposits of the world and it normally supplies the petroleum needs of many nations in Europe, Asia and Africa. These things stress the immense importance of the Middle East. If the nations of the area lose their independence, if they were dominated by forces hostile to freedom, that would be both a tragedy for them and for many other free nations whose economic life would be subject to near strangulation. Western Europe would be endangered just as though there had been no Marshall Plan, no NATO.'

(Congressional Record, 85th Congress, 1st Session, 1957)

'Resolved. . . .
That the President be authorized to cooperate with any nation in the general area of the Middle East desiring assistance. . . .

*Section 2* The President is authorized to undertake military assistance programmes with any nation desiring such assistance. . . .
*Section 3* . . . authorized to use, during the balance of the fiscal year 1957 for economic and military assistance . . . not to exceed $200,000,000.'

(Department of State Publication, 7107, 85th Congress, March 1957)

## Document 18.3

*Nixon's 'diplomatic revolution' in relations with China, July 1971*

'There can be no stable peace without the participation of China. That is why I have undertaken initiatives in several areas to open the door for more normal relations between our two countries. I sent Dr Kissinger to Peking during his recent world tour. The announcement that I shall now read is being issued simultaneously in Peking and in the USA:

'Premier Chou En-lai and Dr Kissinger held talks in Peking from July 9 to 11, 1971. Knowing President Nixon's desire to visit China, Premier Chou has extended an invitation to President Nixon to visit China at an appropriate date before May 1972. President Nixon has accepted the invitation with pleasure. The meeting between the leaders of China and the USA is to seek the normalization of relations between the two countries and to exchange views of concern to the two sides.'

No question of Asian policy has so perplexed the world in the last 20 years as the China question, and the related question of representation in the UN. Basic to that question is the fact that each of two Governments claims to be the sole Government of China. The USA will support action at the General Assembly calling for seating the People's Republic of China.'

(President Richard M. Nixon, July 1971)

### FURTHER READING

BEGGS, R., *The Cuban Missile Crisis*, Longman, 1971

BRANDT, W., *A Peace Policy for Europe*, 1969

BROWN, A. and GRAY, J., *Political Culture and Political Change in Communist States*, Macmillan, 1977

BROWN, A. and KASER, M., *The Soviet Union since the fall of Khrushchev*, Macmillan, 1979

BUCHAN, A., *The End of the Post-War Era*, Weidenfeld and Nicolson, 1974

CALLO, D., *The German Problem Reconsidered*, 1978

DAVISHKA, K. and HANSON, P., eds., *Soviet East European Dilemmas*, Heinemann, 1981

DE PORTE, A. W., *Europe between the Superpowers*, Yale, 1979

EDMONDS, R., *Soviet Foreign Policy, 1963–73* OUP, 1975

GARVER, J. W., *China's Decision for Rapprochement with the USA, 1968–71*, Westview Press, 1983

GARVEY, T., *Bones of Contention: An Enquiry into East–West Relations*, Routledge and Kegan Paul, 1978

GROSSER, A., *The Western Alliance*, Macmillan, 1980

HANSON, P., *Trade and Technology in Soviet-Western Relations*, Macmillan, 1981

KAISER, R. G., *Russia*, Secker and Warburg, 1976

KHRUSHCHEV, N. S., *Khrushchev Remembers*, Penguin, 1974

KISSINGER, H., *The White House Years*, Weidenfeld and Nicolson, 1982

KISSINGER, H., *Years of Upheaval*, Weidenfeld and Nicolson, 1979

LAQUEUR, W. and RUBIN, B., eds., *The Human Rights Reader*, New American Library, 1979

MCCAULEY, M., ed., *The Soviet Union since Brezhnev*, Heinemann, 1983

MAYALL, J. and NAVARI, C., *The End of the Post-War Era: Documents on Great Power Relations, 1968–75*, CUP, 1980

PIPES, R., *Soviet Strategy in Europe*, Macdonald and Jane's, 1976

RIGBY, T., et al., eds., *Authority, Power and Policy in the USSR*, Macmillan, 1980

RUBINSTEIN, A. Z., *Soviet Foreign Policy since World War II: Imperial and Global*, Prentice-Hall Int., 1983

SHORT, P., *The Dragon and the Bear: Inside China and Russia Today*, Abacus, 1982

URBAN, G. R., *Détente*, Temple Smith, 1977

# 19
# Détente, 1973–86

## Definitions and methods

'*Détente* is a process of managing relations with a potentially hostile
country in order to preserve the peace while maintaining our vital
interests.

Kissinger to the US Congress, April 1973

In 1972–3 there were good grounds for optimism, in view of Brandt's
*Ostpolitik*, SALT I, Nixon's visit to Peking, and the continued US
withdrawal from Vietnam. However, 'hawks' in both the USA and
USSR criticized their leaders' retreats from the more hardline stances of
the Cold War. In June 1973 Brezhnev, seeking to reassure his critics,
affirmed the continuing nature of 'the class struggle of the two
systems', while arguing that this need not 'threaten wars, dangerous
conflicts and an uncontrolled arms race'. In the USA, too, Kissinger
insisted that the USA would not be neutral in 'the age-old antagonism
between freedom and tyranny', while arguing that 'other imperatives'
imposed limits on the USA's ability 'to produce internal changes in
foreign countries. Consciousness of our limits is recognition of the
necessity of peace.'

Some critical westerners saw Brezhnev's 'programme for peace' as a
trap for over-eager statesmen and politicians. The more optimistic, like
Kissinger, claimed that 'a web of interests' would create both a climate
of better understanding and an interdependence that would ensure
stable and peaceful relations, USA–USSR trade deals and US aid for
Soviet economic development, along with cultural and scientific
exchanges, would provide Soviet citizens with a glimpse of what might
be, while rising expectations would produce pressure for reform and
democratization.

## Helsinki, 1975

'The participating states will promote and encourage the effective

exercise of civil, political, economic, social, cultural and other rights and freedoms, all of which derive from the inherent dignity of human persons and are essential for his free and full development.'
                                        Article VII, Helsinki Agreement, 1975

During the SALT negotiations, Brezhnev proposed a European Security Conference. Nixon, however, wanted to concentrate on the winding-down of the Vietnam War. The European powers, hesitant in their response to Soviet overtures, insisted that the USA and Canada had to be participants in such a Conference.

The Conference on Security and Cooperation in Europe (CSCE) opened in Helsinki in July 1973 and went on, in Helsinki and Geneva, until the 'Final Act' was signed in Helsinki on 1 August 1975. Not a legally binding document, it had no force in international law, although the signatories agreed to 'adopt' its terms. There was no machinery for enforcement, or for monitoring the degree to which the nations 'adopted' it, although there were provisions for periodic reviews of the implementaion of its terms.

The USSR gained by the Conference's recognition of the frontiers agreed by Brandt's *Ostpolitik*; the post-Hitler arrangements received the seal of international approval. Brezhnev wanted an agreement on military bases and troop levels, while the western powers wanted a Soviet agreement on a wider definition of 'security', to include 'mutual understanding', and declarations concerning governmental and non-governmental contacts between peoples for economic, social and technical cooperation, and, more significantly, for cooperation in 'humanitarian fields'. Under this heading, the western powers insisted on articles concerning 'human rights'; the Soviet Union tried to limit these clauses to 'discussions between "systems" ' while the western powers insisted that they be extended to 'individuals' and 'individual states' which could be criticized if they failed to live up to the promises made.

Western cynics noted that Stalin had signed the Atlantic Charter (p. 38) and the UN Charter on Human Rights (p. 251), and asked why, given postwar history, people expected the Soviet leopard to change its repressive spots because of a non-binding and non-enforcable agreement. Moreover, they claimed that the Soviet Union had gained recognition for their gains made in Europe since 1944; where now was Dulles's promise of 'rolling back' communism (Document 18.1)?

More optimistic westerners saw the Helsinki Agreement as significant, since the Soviet government had signed a document which might be used against it in future disputes over human rights. They claimed that the updating of the UN Charter brought the issue of Human Rights to the attention of a generation to whom the Universal Declaration of 1948 was mere history. Furthermore, in keeping with Kissinger's belief in 'a web of interests', they claimed that the 'linkage' of the economies of East and West would bring about the hoped-for 'rising expectations' in the East, the forerunner to demands for social, economic and political reform.

However, to Brezhnev and his colleagues, the Agreement was merely 'a scrap of paper'. For Soviet leaders it consisted entirely of a military core, leading to lower military expenditure allowing economic, social and political benefits for the various power groups in the Soviet leadership. Other parts of the *détente* package were, in Soviet eyes, only peripheral, and acceptable only if beneficial to the USSR. US Senator Jackson's attempts to amend a proposed US–USSR trade deal with clauses concerning Soviet treatment of Soviet Jews led to the Soviet cancellation of the deal.

Nor did the signing of the Agreement change anything in the Soviet Union or eastern Europe. Dissidents were still harassed: the Czech government attacked the members of the Charter 77 group set up to monitor Czech adherence to the Agreement; the Soviet government increased its pressure on Sakharov and other dissidents.

The Watergate scandal (p. 93) led to Nixon's fall. It also increased Congress's perceptions of its role and powers. In 1975 Democratic President Carter, under pressure from a more hardline Congress, affirmed 'America's commitment to human rights as a fundamental tenet of our foreign policy.' Brezhnev condemned this as an attempt at 'interference with our internal affairs'. It is small wonder that the first review of the Agreement (Belgrade, 1977) took place in a climate of animosity, and consisted largely of charge followed by counter-charge. The next review (Madrid, 1981) saw the West condemning the Soviet invasion of Afghanistan as further evidence of its refusal to adhere to the Agreement. Representatives of the Helsinki powers failed to reach an agreement when they met at Ottawa (June 1985), Belgrade (November 1985) and Berne (May 1986). These three meetings were concerned with the promises made at Helsinki to promote contacts between East and West. The Ottawa talks ranged widely over the human rights field; at Budapest the focus was on cultural links, at Berne on personal contacts. Each meeting followed the same course: the Soviet and east European governments were reproached for their failure to honour their 1975 promises, while they in turn condemned the criticisms as an outrageous interference with their internal affairs.

Although they quarrelled in Madrid in 1981, there was an agreement, under Soviet pressure, to call a special CSCE Conference on disarmament. This opened in Stockholm in January 1984, and ended without any agreement in September 1985. This failure, coupled with other evidence of Soviet intransigence, led many to wonder whether it was worth going on any longer with the weary and unrewarding 'Helsinki process' which, in eleven years, had produced so little.

The failure on disarmament should have surprised no one, because talks on Mutual and Balanced Force Reductions (MBFR) have been going on since 1973 with similar lack of success. These talks had their origins in NATO proposals (1968) which Brezhnev had agreed to during his talks with Nixon in Moscow (May 1972), although he insisted that the MBFR talks took place separately from the CSCE talks. In January 1974 NATO and Warsaw Pact delegates met in Vienna. The Soviet delegates took a hard line from the start, refusing to reveal the size of Warsaw Pact forces and making clear their insistence on the retention of military superiority in Central Europe. In view of this less-than-flexible approach on the one side and, on the western side, the realization that, after Helsinki, the Soviet Union had no real interest in *détente* as understood in the West, it is not surprising that 'the bored delegates have done little more than design a club tie' after some 12 years of negotiations.

However, in September 1986 the ESC powers provided the *détente* process with a fillip when, almost without warning, they reached an agreement which confirmed earlier agreements (that NATO and Warsaw Pact states would inform the other side before undertaking military manoeuvres) and, more significantly, consented for the first time to on-site inspection of manoeuvres and facilities by representatives of the other side. Western commentators noted that the Soviet Union was now willing to allow western observers to overfly the Soviet Union and eastern Europe (albeit in Warsaw Pact 'planes) to make their checks. This was taken as evidence that Gorbachev was winning the battle in the Soviet Union for a more open society, and of a Soviet desire for agreement on other arms' issues.

## SALT II, 1974–86

'I'm prepared to go the extra mile in seeking an interim framework of truly mutual restraint.'

President Reagan, April 1986

In 1981 Francis Pym, the British Defence Minister, defined *détente* as an attempt to 'identify and build on areas of common interest with the aim of establishing understanding and confidence. Arms control agreements and trade . . . of genuine benefit to both sides are examples.' Pym supported Kissinger's 'web of interests' theory, although he pointed out that success 'depends on the Soviet Union accepting that it must behave with restraint, and accepting that *détente* applies to all areas of international relations, not just to Europe'. He appreciated the Soviet Union's use of arms talks as a mere 'tactic' (p. 273) without any change in long-term strategical objectives.

In the winter of 1972–3 negotiations opened for SALT II, which the re-elected Nixon hoped would lead to a review of the needs of the world as a whole. This optimism disappeared in the wake of the Watergate scandal and Nixon's resignation in August 1974. However, even if Nixon had been unscathed by scandal, there would have been major difficulties in the new negotiations. The 'interim agreement' of

1972 had not yet been converted into a permanent treaty – largely because of technological development. The Soviet Union had built a new generation of MIRV missiles (SS–17–19) which fitted into the quantitative limits set by SALT I, but which were of longer range, more accurate and of greater megatonnage than the weapons they replaced. Meanwhile the SS–20, a mobile launcher, threatened the US fixed-silo Minuteman, the US 'second-strike' weapon. The USA, for its part, had developed the 'cruise' missile which did not fit into any SALT I category. While the USA claimed that this sonic-speed weapon with its pinpoint accuracy over ranges exceeding 2000 miles was, in SALT I terms, a 'tactical' weapon and not a 'strategic' one, the Soviet Union saw it as a major threat to their existing systems. While the USA developed the B–1 intercontinental bomber, and new warheads to increase the accuracy and penetration of Minutemen, and worked on the Trident SLBM to replace Polaris, the USSR produced the Backfire bomber capable of inter-continental strategic missions.

These post-SALT I changes took place against a critical background. Brezhnev had agreed (May 1972) not to try 'to obtain unilateral advantage' at the expense of the USA. However, intervention in Angola had won more influence for the USSR in the strategically significant southern Africa. And this in spite of a Nixon–Brezhnev agreement (July 1974) to reduce the number of ABM sites from two to one, the start of negotiations on the banning of the underground testing of nuclear weapons with yields above 150 kilotons and the promise of a meeting at Vladivostok in November 1974 to review SALT I and prepare the ground for SALT II.

Following Nixon's fall, it was Ford who met Brezhnev in November 1974, watched by a power-conscious Congress less prepared to be 'smooth talked' into accepting presidential policy, and by a US public critical of Soviet violations of human rights and of her intervention in Angola. This new attitude in the US was illustrated by Senate approval for the Jackson amendments to a proposed US–USSR trade deal (p. 289). Kissinger tried to halt this 'blackmailing attempt' to control US–USSR relations, but in the post-Watergate climate, Congress would not be denied. The Soviet Union cancelled the deal, in spite of which Kissinger, travelling ever hopefully, went to Moscow (January 1976), seeking an agreement on the number of new and more sophisticated weapons developed since 1972. These negotiations were still under way when Carter became President in January 1977. The growth of Soviet power was revealed in a study produced by the International Institute for Strategic Studies:

*Historical changes of strength, 1963–76 (mid-years)*

|      | USA   |       |                      | USSR  |       |                      |
|------|-------|-------|----------------------|-------|-------|----------------------|
|      | ICBMs | SLBMs | Long-range bombers   | ICBMs | SLBMs | Long-range bombers   |
| 1963 | 424   | 224   | 639                  | 90    | 107   | 190                  |
| 1964 | 834   | 416   | 630                  | 190   | 107   | 175                  |
| 1965 | 854   | 496   | 630                  | 224   | 107   | 160                  |
| 1966 | 904   | 592   | 630                  | 292   | 107   | 155                  |
| 1967 | 1054  | 656   | 600                  | 570   | 107   | 160                  |
| 1968 | 1054  | 656   | 545                  | 858   | 121   | 155                  |
| 1969 | 1054  | 656   | 560                  | 1028  | 196   | 145                  |
| 1970 | 1054  | 656   | 550                  | 1299  | 304   | 145                  |
| 1971 | 1054  | 656   | 505                  | 1513  | 448   | 145                  |
| 1972 | 1054  | 656   | 455                  | 1527  | 500   | 140                  |
| 1973 | 1054  | 656   | 442                  | 1527  | 628   | 140                  |
| 1974 | 1054  | 656   | 437                  | 1575  | 720   | 140                  |
| 1975 | 1054  | 656   | 432                  | 1618  | 784   | 135                  |
| 1976 | 1054  | 656   | 387                  | 1527  | 845   | 135                  |

(*Source: International Institute for Strategic Studies*)

## The military balance 1977–8

Carter, with 'human rights' a central plank in his electoral platform, made it clear that further *détente* depended on Soviet willingness to comply with agreements reached in 1972 and 1975. He published a letter he had sent to Sakharov, the leading Soviet dissident; received another, Bukovsky, at the White House; and condemned the Czech attacks on the members of Charter 77. The shift in US policy was publicized when the Secretary of State, Vance, went to Moscow in March 1977. Calling for 'the first truly disarmament-orientated' scheme as part of the SALT negotiations, he proposed a lowering of the number of strategic delivery vehicles, along with a ceiling on the number of MIRV missiles and on modifications for existing ICBMs. He also proposed the abandoning of the plan for deploying mobile missiles, and the prohibition of the production of 'cruise' missiles and Backfire bombers. Many 'hawks' in the US industrial-military complex hoped that these proposals would be rejected. So, too, did equally powerful groups in the USSR, where Vance's proposals seemed to aim at seeking a unilateral advantage via the destruction of half of the Soviet's rockets, deemed to be 'too heavy' or 'too effective'.

Behind the public rhetoric, negotiations went on until May 1977, when a 'three-tier framework' was agreed, within which there would be a SALT II agreement to last until 1985, a separate agreement (to run for three years) on the Backfire bomber and 'cruise' missiles, and a third agreement on 'a statement of principles', pointing the way to further reductions in strategic arms. SALT II was signed in Vienna on 18 June 1979. In what Carter called 'the most detailed, far-reaching and comprehensive treaty' the following weapons were allowed within each country:

|  | USA | USSR |
|---|---|---|
| ICBMs | 1054 | 1398 |
| ICBMs/MIRVs | 550 | 608 |
| SLBMs | 656 | 950 |
| SLBMs/MIRVs | 496 | 144 |
| Heavy bombers | 573 | 156 |

This treaty was presented to the Senate in June 1979, where, in spite of Carter's plans, it met a hostile reception, reflecting US anger at Soviet violations of the 1975 Agreement on human rights and its aggressive policies in Africa and Asia (where it supported Vietnam's invasion of Kampuchea, see p. 245). Carter's inability to free the US hostages held by Iranian radicals at the Embassy in Teheran was a further source of anger. The Soviet invasion of Afghanistan in December 1979 (p. 145) served to illustrate the Soviet pursuit of long-term aims, as well as their total disregard for the 1975 Agreement and for US opinion. Carter's response to that invasion did little to assuage US anger. As if in proof of Mao's claim that the atomic weapon was only 'a paper tiger', the nuclear-strong USA countered Soviet aggression by boycotting the 1980 Moscow Olympic Games, by restructuring the cultural exchanges, in which Kissinger laid such store, by suspending credits to the Soviet Union and by banning the export of high technology to the USSR. It was notable that Carter did not ban the sale of US grain to the Soviets; he feared the anger of US farmers in an election year.

None of this deterred Soviet leaders, who went ahead with the Olympic games and used western criticism as an excuse to call for greater loyalty on the part of the 'besieged' Soviet people, whose nationalism and traditional anti-westernism was reinforced during 1980. Nor did the accession of the hardline Reagan lead to clarification of US attitudes towards SALT II. 'Hawks' within his administration wanted to abandon the treaty, claiming that the USSR had violated its terms. 'Liberals' in the government argued that if the US honoured the treaty, it would enable her to wring more exacting arms-control concessions from the USSR.

In May–June 1986 Reagan sent out contradictory signals; while he agreed to the dismantling of two Poseidon submarines, to make room for a new Trident submarine within the limits of the 1979 Treaty, he pacified his hard-line supporters by announcing that, if the USSR did not rectify its admitted violations of the treaty, he might ignore its limitations. Reagan has said that he will 'go through with it' unless the Soviets mend their ways, cut down their missile build-up, move to correct their Treaty violations and start to negotiate seriously. In July

1986 the Soviet response to this hard line was to agree to a meeting of US and USSR SALT negotiators in Geneva. The optimism which greeted this apparent 'liberalism' on Gorbachev's part was short-lived, for the Soviet delegates walked out of the Conference within days of its opening. Few observers expect the Soviet Union to be willing to accept Reagan's demands, so it seems that SALT II will lapse.

## New attitudes in the West, 1980–6

'their evil Empire . . .'.

Reagan on the USSR, 1983

'. . . the ill-fated Yalta Conference . . . spheres of influence . . . the wound that runs through the heart of Europe.'

Vice-President Bush, 1983

In May 1979 Margaret Thatcher became Britain's first woman Prime Minister. Soon her critical comments on Soviet failure to live up to the Helsinki and other recent agreements had earned her, in Iron Curtain countries, the nickname of 'The Iron Lady'. During the winter of 1979–80, US attitudes also changed: some of Carter's administration became increasingly critical of the Soviet Union, while public opinion was reflected in Reagan's successful campaign to become the Republican nominee for the Presidency, during which he called for a more combative and unyielding policy towards the USSR.

Reagan became President in January 1981. In November US–USSR talks opened in Geneva on the limitation of Intermediate Nuclear Forces (INF) in Europe. There was no linkage of trade or human rights in these arms talks: the Soviet Union made no promise to 'exercise restraint' elsewhere. Nor, perhaps surprisingly, did the USA call off the talks when Soviet pressure led to the declaration of the anti-Solidarity state of emergency in Poland.

Brezhnev offered 'very substantial reductions' in Soviet intermediate range missiles if the West renounced the deployment of Pershing and 'cruise' missiles. Reagan, on the other hand, proposed a 'zero option': both powers would dismantle their long-range theatre force systems. Neither were realistic proposals, but the Soviet one did take account of its superiority in weapons numbers, something they had previously denied.

While these talks drifted on, each side working out its negotiating position, Reagan ordered the reinstatement of plans to manufacture the neutron bomb, which would kill or immobilize humans while leaving buildings intact. He also ordered the manufacture of the B–1 bomber, which Carter had cancelled in his search for *détente*.

When the US deployed Pershing and 'cruise' missiles, the USSR called off the INF talks. However, when it became clear that Reagan was not to be deflected from his 'hawkish' line by walk-outs, the talks were resumed; Soviet delegates hinted that if the USA deployed its new missiles in the West, the USSR would deploy SS–20 missiles in Warsaw Pact countries.

In January 1984 these INF talks seemed to have finally collapsed as the Soviet delegates walked out, accusing Reagan of refusing to negotiate seriously. However, in March 1986 arms negotiators from the USA and USSR met in Geneva to re-open negotiations on three 'baskets' of arms issues – the INF discussions being one of those 'baskets'. Reagan's hardline policy may be seen to have succeeded: the new weapons have been installed in Europe, and yet the Soviet delegates returned to the talks. Critics who argued that US policies would both deter and anger the USSR ignored both Soviet domestic problems and Gorbachev's need for *détente*, in addition to the traditionally favourable Russian response to shows of strength.

The second of the 'baskets' considered in 1986 involved the follow-up to SALT II. In June 1982 Reagan called for a resumption of talks, but suggested that in view of the US public's antipathy to SALT II, a new acronym should be found. Thus the negotiations were labelled Strategic Arms Reduction Talks, or START, perhaps a happy augury for a fresh beginning. These talks opened in October 1983, but, like the INF talks, they were called off in January 1984, to be re-opened, like the INF talks, in March 1986, only to be halted again, like the SALT II talks, when the Soviet delegates walked out in July 1986 (p. 294).

## The Strategic Defence Initiative (SDI)

'. . . Star Wars . . .'.

US comment on SDI, 1984

In 1983 Reagan unveiled a plan for a new basis to western security. The SDI, immediately dubbed 'Star Wars', envisages a situation in which both the USA and the USSR have defensive shields made up of a combination of space technology and developments in the use of laser beams, allowing the destruction, in space, of incoming ballistic missiles. Such a protective system would render ineffective all existing offensive systems.

The USSR and the USA had been researching Strategic Defence in the 1970s; the USSR had, in fact, developed radar and missile systems as the basis for a nationwide ABM system (banned under SALT II), and had done more sophisticated research involving lasers and particle beams. However, the USSR feared that superior US technology would allow the USA to overtake Soviet efforts. Party leaders and economists also worried that Soviet military leaders would demand the expenditure needed to ensure êquality with their US counterparts. Andropov, and later Gorbachev, were too fully conscious of the inability of the decaying system to produce what the military might demand.

Gorbachev also feared that 'Star Wars' might happen quickly: the USA had produced the Apollo moon programme to give the USA a lead in space exploration, in spite of the USSR's initial success with the first *sputnik*. Gorbachev overlooked the technical and technological difficulties associated with SDI, which is still in the research stage, and it is still possible that development will take place at a pace which the Soviet system might match. He also ignored US Congressional opposition to SDI at a time of rising budget deficits and federal overspending. There is no guarantee that Congress will vote the money to fund the research, for if Congress votes to cut the budget deficit, this will affect the defence programme, and work on SDI will be slowed down, if not cancelled.

'Star Wars' was the third 'basket' under discussion in Geneva in 1986. For the USSR, it was the 'touchiest' issue on which it wished to concentrate negotiations, hoping to 'knock out' SDI at an early stage. The USA, on the other hand, would have preferred to concentrate on the first two 'baskets' (p. 294 and p. 295), leaving consideration about SDI for future negotiations.

## Sino–Soviet rapprochement?

'It is not clear where Gorbachev is going. We hoped to normalize Sino–Soviet relations. So far we have had no positive response.'
                                        Deng Xiaoping, *Time*, 4 November 1985

Not all Chinese leaders welcomed friendlier relations with the USA and a continuation of hostility to the USSR. Some would have preferred a restoration of friendship with the other communist giant. In spite of the bitterness of the cross-border fighting and the public rhetoric ('Mao is another Hitler'), leaders of the USSR also sought to heal the division. When Andropov became Soviet leader he appreciated the cost of maintaining 500,000 Soviet troops and one-third of the USSR's arsenal of missiles along the Sino–Soviet border. He, and other Soviet realists, would have preferred to have stationed these in the west.

Under Andropov's guidance, talks opened with Mao's successors, and have continued. However, as Deng pointed out in November 1985, there are serious obstacles to progress. The first stumbling-block is Soviet support for the Vietnamese invasion of Kampuchea (p. 243). China, defeated by Vietnam, perceives her as a Soviet satellite in an area which China claims as her own 'sphere of influence'. Vietnam allows the Soviet Pacific Fleet to use bases at Danang and Camranh Bay for operations in the surrounding seas and oceans (Figure 15.2); given the Soviet long-term aim of world conquest, the link with Vietnam is of major strategic importance, and agreement with China over the Soviet role in this region is unlikely.

'Second,' said Deng, 'Afghanistan'. China sees the Soviet occupation of Afghanistan as an attempt to gain power in yet another country bordering on China. Afghanistan is also potentially another base for Soviet missiles. In the summer of 1986 Gorbachev tentatively suggested that, as part of a USA–USSR deal, the Soviet Union might disengage itself from a costly and seemingly unwinnable war. The offer to withdraw some 7500 troops (July 1986) may be a token of Soviet will to negotiate further; if it is not, and is a final offer, then agreement with China (and the USA) may be far off.

'Third,' noted Deng, 'reduction of missiles and troops on the Sino–Soviet border', which are seen by China as a threat 'not only to China but all of Asia'. The USSR, however, sees them as necessary defensive forces, given the build-up of China's military strength, her friendship with the USA, and her traditional hostility to Russian advances into the Far East (p. 275). Deng claimed: 'we bring this up at every meeting with the Soviets and we realize that removing all three at the same time might be difficult. So far we have had no positive response.'

## The Reagan–Gorbachev summits, 1985–6

'America is back, standing tall.'

Reagan, electioneering, 1984

'. . . for the first time we are not only pointed in the right direction towards reduction and elimination of nuclear weapons; we have begun to move down that road.'

Reagan, 30 July 1986

During the 1984 Presidential Election campaign, Reagan argued that the US had a strategic advantage over the USSR: new nuclear-armed bombers, new Trident submarines and thousands of 'cruise' missiles were on their way. Within hours of Gorbachev's accession to power in March 1975, Reagan invited him to the USA 'at a mutually convenient time'. In view of his 'hawkish' reputation and the aggressive language he used with reference to the Soviet system, Reagan's commitment to 'summitry' dismayed and puzzled some of his hardline supporters. Some expected that he would be 'turned off' by the shooting of a young US major on duty in East Berlin, where the Soviet authorities had left him unattended as he died. Instead, Reagan argued that this event made it even more necessary to hold a summit meeting, to prevent the same thing happening again. Some claimed that Reagan was so 'mesmerized by talk of arms control and summitry' that he was 'too paralyzed to respond even to murder'. 'Historians may conclude that it was during this administration that the US conclusively lost the Cold War', said one, in what many will see as an extravagant claim.

The first Reagan–Gorbachev summit was held in Geneva in November 1985. Reagan's critics argued that 'Gorbachev was laughing all the way to the summit', since, they claimed, he had nothing to lose and everything to gain, whereas Reagan had nothing to gain unless the Soviet Union agreed to genuine and balanced arms reduction.

Certainly Gorbachev's hand was the weaker: after more than 60 years of communism, Soviet economic performance is now acknowledged, even by Gorbachev, to be lamentable. The standard of living for the majority of the Soviet people is barely increasing; there are shortages of the most simple foodstuffs, an extraordinary decline in life expectancy and an increase in the incidence of certain diseases. A society whose leaders survive only by ruthless central control of the content and flow of information is now facing a West that is beginning to reap the incalculable benefits of the information revolution. However much Gorbachev may want to improve living standards for his people, the Marxist system which created him is unable to accommodate the political relaxation necessary for real economic growth, or the creation of an information revolution, and remain recognizably the same. The system cannot allow developments which would provide Soviet citizens with free access to computers; this would give them access to western systems, and ideas.

Gorbachev also appreciates the cost of trying to match the US in terms of military spending. In 1985 Soviet military expenditure consumed 16 per cent of a relatively smaller GNP, while US expenditure took less than 6 per cent of its larger GNP. If Soviet military leaders have their way, and Gorbachev allows spending on 'Star Wars' technology, the standard of living of the Soviet people will fall even lower. Gorbachev would prefer to cut military spending, to allow increased industrial, agricultural and social expenditure.

At their Geneva meeting the two leaders arrived at no great decisions, other than that they would meet again in the USA in 1986. Subsequently, Gorbachev announced that if the USA continued with its 'Star Wars' development, there would be no fresh talks. However, while the USA went on with its SDI research, US–USSR talks continued, and, in spite of some temporary doubts, arrangements were finalized for a second summit. To smooth the path to that meeting, Reagan used conciliatory language about Gorbachev ('a modern man') and arms control ('my determination [is] to keep the momentum going'). In letters to Reagan, Gorbachev has proposed an extension of the ABM treaty for 15–20 years, which he claimed would ban the deployment of a space-based 'Star Wars' system. Reagan countered by suggesting a delay of five to seven years for deployment in space. Since, in fact, the USA is unlikely to be ready to deploy SDI weapons for at least 10 years, agreement seems to be close on this issue. However, Reagan has insisted that 'we will not bargain away SDI, because it is a promising area of technology that could release the world from the threat of ballistic missiles. We must continue our SDI programme.' And, for his part, Gorbachev has declared that the USSR will match US spending. 'However much it costs our people to spend on defence, never have I heard anyone saying, "Let us abandon defence and move everything to consumer goods".' Coming from anyone other than the man who has clawed his way to the top in the Soviet system, this would seem to be a naive remark. From Gorbachev, it is, perhaps reluctantly, a statement of intent; it is impossible to say, before the second summit, how that intent will be affected by decisions reached with Reagan.

## Documentary evidence

Before Reagan and Gorbachev met in Geneva in November 1985, many commentators feared that the Soviet leader would outsmart the US President (Document 19.1), although they perceived that the Soviet Union had, in reality, the weaker position. After the summit, there was a greater appreciation of Reagan's abilities and successes; few Presidents had been as popular in the USA or as effective abroad (Document 19.2).

## Document 19.1

*The domestic effects of international relations, 1985*

'Reagan goes to Geneva with several disadvantages. That the summit is taking place at all is a great propaganda coup for Gorbachev. It wrong-foots Reagan because it tends to confirm the Russians' contention that they are to be considered entirely equal to the Americans by western public opinion.

And Reagan has much to lose. He could be forced by Gorbachev's exploitation of western opinion into shackling SDI. He could be forced into abandoning attempts to modernize America's strategic forces, which are ancient compared to the Soviets, and which Congress is increasingly reluctant to fund . . . leading to increasing instability and increasing fear of the Soviet Union.

Those western commentators who are asking if the Americans and the Soviets will reach some kind of arms agreement are asking the wrong question. Instead they should ask if Gorbachev will succeed in limiting American SDI or American strategic arms so much that the Soviet Union can retain superpower status through military equivalence. If this happens, the discomforts of the East–West competition are likely to continue for many years. . . . The Soviet Union will increasingly realize that to compete effectively with the West, it must either change its political system or manage to sap the political will of the West, with adventures such as Afghanistan and with the psychological assault that fear of Soviet arms engenders, so that the West, too, experiences political, social and economic decline. If Reagan emerges from the summit with an acceptance of his offer to share SDI, Gorbachev will be forced to choose one of two paths. He can watch his country fade into secondary status as a world power in a world where all countries will be protected by SDI from most of the effects of a full-scale attack. Or he can begin the fundamental changes to the political system in the Soviet Union that would permit the free flow of ideas, information and capitalist activity that alone could create the economic growth necessary to superpower status and genuine competition with America.'

(David Hart, *The Times*, 15 November 1985)

## Document 19.2

*Reagan's world leadership, December 1985*

'Reagan is now clearly the world's pre-eminent leader. He has five successful years as President under his belt, too long to dismiss as mere luck. The derisive labels of "amiable dunce" and "the Tefflon President" lie discredited. The vaunted foreign people-eaters, such as Canada's Trudeau, West Germany's Schmidt and now the Soviet Union's Gorbachev, have marched one by one into Reagan's presence. None has managed to devour him [but have] emerged with varying degrees of respect and affection. The lions of the liberal-policy élite of Washington have retreated into a sullen silence. "They harbour a resentment of Reagan because he is not following their prescription on how to run the world. Worse, he is successful."

In every scene played out in Geneva he had a slight physical advantage. "But it was never threatening," said one who was there. "Reagan radiated good will."

"I know Communism," Reagan told an aide before he sat down with Gorbachev. "I've followed it for 30 years." He would not, he vowed, make it a Mike and Ronnie show, nor a hugging and kissing acquaintance. Yet, when the Soviet boss showed up, Reagan, directing him to the stairs, touched him gently on the arm . . . body language for civility not intimacy. It is part of Reagan's nature to like people. He came out of a good private session with Gorbachev and told an aide, "Sometimes I've got to remind myself just who he is and what he represents." Reagan seems to have succeeded in that also.'

(Hugh Sidey, *Time*, 9 December 1985)

*Author's note, May 1987.* While the pessimism concerning the possibility of arms agreements now seems to have been misplaced, the optimism concerning Reagan's position seems to have invited nemesis in the shape of the Irangate hearings.

## FURTHER READING

BERTRAM, C., *Prospects of Soviet Power in the 1980s*, Macmillan, 1980

BYRNES, R., ed., *After Brezhnev – Sources of Soviet Conduct in the 1980s*, Frances Pinter, 1983

CARLTON, D. and SCHAEF, C., eds., *The Arms Race in the 1980s*, Macmillan, 1982

GEORGE, A. L., et al., *Managing US–Soviet Rivalry*, Westview Press, 1983

HAMMOND, P. Y., *Cold War and Détente*, Harvester Press, 1975

HOLM, H. H. and PETERSON, N., *The European Missiles Crisis*, Frances Pinter, 1983

KINCARDE, W. H. and BERTRAM, C., *Nuclear Proliferation in the 1980s*, Macmillan, 1982

KISSINGER, H., *Nuclear Weapons and Foreign Policy*, Westview Press, 1984

RUBIN, B., et al., *Human Rights and US Foreign Policy*, Westview Press, 1979

SCHIAVONE, G., ed., *East–West Relations: Prospects for the 1980s*, Macmillan, 1982

STANLEY, T., et al., *US Foreign Economic Strategy for the Eighties*, Westview Press, 1983

TOKES, R., ed., *Dissent in the USSR*, Johns Hopkins UP, 1976

SHARP, J. M. C., ed., *The Warsaw Pact: Alliance in Transition*, Macmillan, 1984

VOLTEN, P. M. C., *Brezhnev's Peace Programme*, Westview Press, 1983

# 20

# The Third World

## Definitions

'Everyone has the right to a standard of living adequate for the health and
well-being of himself and of his family . . . food, clothing, housing . . .
medical care and necessary social services, and the right to security in the
event of unemployment . . . or other . . . circumstances beyond his
control.'

Article 25 of the UN Declaration of Human Rights, 1948

Western commentators may be accustomed to writing in social or
economic terms about the hundred or so Third World countries which
have a pitifully low standard of living. However, many Third World
leaders want their countries to be accorded a wider, political, importance. In 1955 four such leaders called for 'a non-aligned alternative' to
dependence on either the USSR or the USA. These were Sukarno of
Indonesia, Tito of Yugoslavia, Nehru of India and Nasser of Egypt.

In April 1955 Sukarno hosted a gathering of leaders of twenty-nine
African and Asian states at Bandung, where they explored the prospect
of non-alignment and Afro–Asian cooperation. Tito, expelled from the
Cominform in 1948 (p. 44), was the only European leader invited to
Bandung, and he hoped to united the developing countries with Soviet
satellites in a non-aligned front. Nehru welcomed the call for 'a non-
aligned and neutralist attitude' towards the Cold War and the chance of
creating a united front against 'colonial oppression'. He helped define
Third World objectives: an Afro–Asian representative on the UN
Security Council; Palestine for the Arabs; nuclear disarmament; human
rights. He claimed that Bandung heralded a new era: 'It would be
misreading history to regard Bandung as an isolated occurrence and not
part of a great movement in human history.'

Nasser saw Egypt as the link between three continents and hoped to
play a major role as the leader of the Third World, although Nehru
championed the claims of China, whose Chou En-lai was a conciliatory

delegate at Bandung. However, the rapidly intensifying rivalry of India and China in Asia weakened the effectiveness of the conference, which was further weakened by fighting between other members elsewhere in Asia and Africa.

Tito hosted the first Non-Aligned Foreign Ministers Conference in Belgrade in 1961 at the height of the Berlin crisis. If Sukarno had had his way, this conference would have produced only a chorus of familiar anti-western tunes, which might have won Soviet praise but would have forfeited all chance of it gaining recognition as a truly independent force in world affairs. It was saved from this fate by Khrushchev, who, on the eve of the conference, ended the nuclear moratorium agreed in 1958 (p. 276). Tito, Nehru, U Nu (Burma) and Mrs Bandaranaike (Sri Lanka) insisted that the conference condemn the Soviet action.

In June 1965 a follow-up to the Afro–Asian Bandung Conference opened in Algeria, but had to be abandoned because of the conflict between representatives of Chinese and Soviet interests, and because of the overthrow of the Algerian government led by Ben Bella. This was effectively the end of the Afro–Asian 'movement'. However, leaders of the non-aligned countries continued to meet, their numbers increasing as more countries gained their independence. There were eighty-five countries represented at the 1978 Belgrade Conference, where Tito repeated his definition of non-alignment: 'Our movement is anti-bloc in its commitment. It does not visualize the future of the world as resting on the balance of the bloc powers or on the supremacy of one bloc over the other.' This brought Tito and the Indian delegates into conflict with Castro of Cuba, whose forces helped Angola and Mozambique to gain their independence and who wanted the non-aligned states to move towards communism. In 1979 Tito flew to Havana to meet Castro, where he condemned his pro-Soviet policies. After Tito's death (1980), this view was put by, among others, Singapore's Foreign Minister, who condemned Castro: 'The leadership of our movement by a country so openly committed to promoting the interests of its superpower patron has seriously eroded our credibility and effectiveness in international affairs.'

Since then Nehru's daughter and grandson, as successive presidents of the group, have sought to erase most of the pro-Soviet marks left by Castro's presidency. In September 1986 some 108 states were represented at the Harare Conference, where the main thrust of the debate was towards the creation of a united front against South Africa, the last vestige of colonialism in Africa and Asia. The 'non-alignment' of the group was shown by its rejection of Gaddaffi's call for the adoption of a more vigorously anti-US stance; most leaders jeered at his claim that the group was pro-Zionist, pro-US and not anti-imperialist.

The political effectiveness of the Third World in international affairs may be debatable. There can be no doubt that in economic terms they are a world apart from the rich world of the North (Figure 20.1), and

THE BRANDT REPORT, 1980

WILLY BRANDT 1957–66 Mayor of West Berlin ; 1966–9 Minister of Foreign Affairs;
1969–74 Federal German Chancellor.
In 1971 he received the Nobel Peace Prize for his Ostpolitik —his strenuous efforts to promote harmony
between the superpowers (détente) by recognizing the permanence of Europe's post-war frontiers.

This map is drawn on the PETERS PROJECTION. Devised by Dr Arno Peters of the University of Bremen, it highlights the division between the wealthy worlds of the superpowers and the relative poverty of the majority of people living in the Third World. The twenty-two countries that attended the 1981 Cancun Summit in Mexico are indicated by numbers on the map:

| THE RICH | | THE POOR | | | |
|---|---|---|---|---|---|
| 1 The United States of America | 5 United Kingdom | 9 Bangladesh | 13 Ivory Coast | 17 Guyana | 21 China |
| 2 France | 6 Canada | 10 India | 14 Algeria | 18 Nigeria | 22 Yugoslavia |
| 3 Federal German Republic | 7 Sweden | 11 Tanzania | 15 Brazil | 19 Saudi Arabia | |
| 4 Japan | 8 Austria | 12 Philippines | 16 Mexico | 20 Venezuela | |

**20.1** The North-South divide

since they are not part of the 'second' world of Communism, they may be seen as a Third, poor, world. It is on this aspect of their affairs that the rest of this chapter concentrates. Not all of them are equally poor or equally underdeveloped: some, such as Brazil and Mexico, have become known as Developing Countries (DCs), while others, like Tanzania and Zambia, remain Less Developed Countries (LDCs). It is possible that some may soon move out of their Developing stage and, like several ASEAN states (Chapter 14), become Developed Countries.

## Becoming aware of the Third World

'. . . mankind never before had such ample technical and financial resources for coping with hunger and poverty.'
The Brandt Report, *North-South: A Programme for Survival*, Pan, 1980

The Atlantic Charter (p. 38) promised that 'all States' and 'all nations' would collaborate in trade and economic matters for the benefit 'of all'. From the outset, the UN sponsored many agencies and commissions aimed at providing assistance for less developed nations (p. 255). Former colonial powers, such as Britain and France, had special knowledge of conditions in the underdeveloped world, and provided various forms of assistance to their former colonies. In 1950, for example, British Commonwealth Foreign Ministers met in

Colombo to draw up the Colombo Plan, aiding the development of
South- and South-East Asia. They set up a council to organize various
forms of training and research, and to fund economic development and
the provision of better health services. The plan received support from
non-Commonwealth countries, notably Japan, and from UN agencies.
Over the years its scope was extended to provide scholarships for the
education of Third World Commonwealth countries, which were also
given help by experts of all kinds, such as teachers, doctors, engineers.
In 1959 a Commonwealth Assistance Loans scheme was established to
promote agricultural, industrial and social development.

Many private agencies, founded in western countries, focus attention
on, and provide aid for, the Third World. Germany, perhaps because of
a wish to wipe out memories of Hitler, has been especially generous in
this regard. In Britain itself, OXFAM, CAFOD, War on Want and
other agencies have helped channel aid to Third World countries,
deriving their funds from contributions, donated by people and firms
affected by propaganda and appeals of these and similar agencies.

In spite of such private aid, and the work of UN, as well as
intergovernmental loans and grants, the LDCs continue to lag behind
the developed world in terms of their economies and their ability to
provide people with reasonable standards of living. While some
westerners complain of the poverty to be found in, for example, our
inner cities, such relative deprivation is a world apart from the real
poverty and hunger found in Asia (Document 12.2), Latin America
(Document 20.1) and much of Africa. We will examine some of the
reasons for the growing disparity between the rich 'North' (to use
Brandt's terms) and the poor 'South' (Figure 20.1). In 1964, under
pressure from Third World States, UNCTAD was set up (p. 255) to
coordinate the demands of poorer countries for 'fairer treatment at the
hands of the wealthier'. UNCTAD drew attention to many problems,
such as the change in the prices of primary goods on which most poor
countries depend for foreign revenue, together with the high cost of
much western aid and the 'compound interest' process of growth
which, seemingly inevitably, condemns the poor to remain that way. If
both a developed and an underdeveloped country have the same annual
growth rate (say, 4 per cent), then within 25 years the gap between
them will become even larger, as this table shows:

*National Income, assuming 4% annual growth*

|         | Developed country | Underdeveloped country |
|---------|-------------------|------------------------|
| Year 1  | 100               | 60                     |
| Year 25 | 268               | 160                    |

In 1973 Third World leaders met in Algiers to concentrate their
protest at the failure of the developed world to give sufficient attention
to their continuing plight. Some wanted to organize a system by which

**20.2** 'Don't you feel comforted by the thought of all the benefits it'll bring to future generations?' One cartoonist's view of the gap between North and South

the prices of raw materials would be increased, to the benefit of poorer countries. However, the leaders failed to agree on what might be done, and in view of the subsequent fate of efforts to regulate the prices of tin, coffee, sugar and other commodities, it is probable that no such system can be devised (Figure 14.2a). Even OPEC found it impossible to maintain their own high prices, which were imposed on the world in the 1970s by this powerful cartel.

In 1977 Willy Brandt (p. 303) was chosen to head a commission set up to examine ways of closing the gap between rich and poor countries. The UN supported the commission, whose members came from rich and poor nations alike. The work of UN agencies was considered, and issues such as population growth, food supplies, health and related environmental problems were studied. The Brandt Report, *North-South: A Programme for Survival* (1980), drew attention to the chaos that would result from 'mass hunger, economic disaster, environmental catastrophe and terrorism'. It deplored world spending on arms (Figure 20.2), and the crisis of starvation, with 12 million under-fives dying of starvation in 1979 (the 'Year of the Child'), and called for a vast redistribution of economic resources from the rich 'North' to the poor 'South'. (Fig. 20.2). In July 1981 delegates from rich countries met in Ottawa to consider Brandt's proposals but decided only to call a world summit of 'North' and 'South' in Cancun, Mexico. There, 22 leaders representing two-thirds of the world's population met in October 1981. Nothing of substance emerged from this 'summit', and in October 1982 a group of Commonwealth experts produced a report, *The North-South Dialogue: Making it Work*, drawing attention to the rich nations' failure to respond to the crisis facing the underdeveloped Third World. This, too, received little attention, and in a world affected by the oil-price induced recession, the rich nations became even more introverted and even less concerned with the plight of the poor. This was highlighted in 1985–6, when it seemed that only private agencies and individuals were concerned with the famine in Ethiopia and the Sudan. Pop stars, sportsmen and others organized varieties of Live Aid to raise famine relief funds. It seemed that the EEC (with mountains of wheat, and butter) and the USA (with one-third of its farms deliberately forced out of production) were unwilling, or unable, to act.

## Third World problems

Many Third World countries are 'one product' nations, meaning that they rely for employment, taxation and foreign earnings on a single commodity. Copper accounts for 95 per cent of Zambia's exports; cocoa for 84 per cent of Ghana's, Brazil is heavily dependent on its coffee crop, as is Malaysia on its output of tin and rubber. The prices which these countries get for their products vary with the level of output and of world demand. The supply of a commodity may be high in a good year and low in a bad one. If world demand goes down (for various reasons) when supplies are large, prices fall sharply, and so does the income of the Third World country.

In times of war (for example, 1950–3) prices of raw materials rise sharply, only to fall equally quickly with the return of peace. Similarly, when a drought wipes out half a crop, prices soar, consumption falls, farmers replant, and reap a big harvest just as the fall in demand has gathered pace – and prices are slumping. Nobody welcomes this 'boom-bust' cycle. Rich and poor nations have cooperated in the past to draw up agreements about the output of commodities in the search for relatively stable prices. Such agreements came under strain in the years after the 1973 increases in oil prices, when the rich world's industrial output fell by ten per cent and commodity prices as a whole by 24 per cent. In the recovery period of 1975–7, world industrial output rose by 15 per cent, and commodity prices by 67 per cent. In 1976 rich and poor countries alike voted for the UNCTAD proposal to set up 18 agreements regulating prices and supplies of raw materials and food.

Until 1985 a relative stability on the commodity markets helped underdeveloped countries to plan their futures. However, in 1985 and 1986, there was a sharp fall in commodity prices as the producing nations tried to sell ever-larger amounts of output to a shrinking market. OPEC is an outstanding example of the failure of even a powerful cartel to control prices and output. But there were similar failures in other commodities. Between 1984 and 1985 cocoa prices fell from 120 cents a pound to 80, sugar from 7 cents a pound to 2.5 cents, rubber from 240 cents a kilo to 160, and tin from $31 a kilo to 20. Oil, as may be better known, quickly fell from $30 a barrel to $10 in 1986.

Even when commodity prices remain stable at relatively high prices, Third World countries still have low *per capita* income. In 1982 the per capita income (in US dollars) of various nations was as follows: USA, 6670; West Germany, 6260; Britain, 3590; Zambia, 520; Ghana, 430; Uganda, 240; India, 140; Bangladesh, 100; Somalia, 90. The poverty of some Third World countries may be due to the poor quality of their technical expertise and equipment, an over-production of their principal commodity, or the climatic conditions. The result of a low income is often a low level of private investment, since few people have money to save, and a lack of money for public investment, since governments can collect only a low volume of taxation from already poor people. Thus, too little is spent on infra-structure (roads, education, health services etc.), and this further impedes economic development. Restricted consumer spending provides little encourage-ment for private merchants or entrepreneurs while, overall, a low standard of living prevails in all Third World countries (Documents 12.2 and 12.3).

The economic policies of richer nations have made things worse for developing and underdeveloped countries. Demand for Malaysia's natural rubber declined with the development of synthetic rubber; other 'synthetics' such as rayon, nylon and various plastics affect the demand for raw materials such as wool, copper, cotton, tin and zinc.

Some developing countries now produce industrial goods to compete with products manufactured in the richer countries. This is one result of aid provided by the latter which ought to be welcome, because it raises incomes and living standards within the developing countries. However, most industrialized nations resent such competition, and try to prevent imports from developing countries by upholding tariffs, quotas and even total bans. The growth of western protectionism is a major problem, about which Third World countries can do little apart from appeal to UNCTAD or some such agency.

Perhaps the worst problem facing Third World countries is the rapid growth in their populations. In the richer, developed, nations, populations rise slowly, if at all. The US population is rising by about one per cent a year, and those of most European countries by less than that, in spite of sharp falls in death rates. Birth rates have fallen even more sharply, partly as a result of the changing role of women in western society, their greater expectations with regard to living standards, as well as a greater knowledge of and willingness to use contraceptives and, as a last resort, the Abortion Act or its equivalent.

In Asia, on the other hand, although death rates are as high as in the West, and infant mortality rates much higher, the population is increasing by some 2 to 3 per cent a year. Death rates have fallen, with the introduction of western scientific and medical knowledge, improved food production, sanitary and educational reforms, and a rise, however, small, in family income. Such an increase in population creates problems – feeding, housing and employing an increasing population, and paying for the imports needed to feed, clothe and employ them can be a great strain on any nation. Any rise in *per capita* income may be negligible as increased production fails to match the growth in population.

African populations have tended to increase even more sharply than those of India and Asian countries, as economic development, and a slowly rising living standard, have encouraged larger families. Urbanization has increased job opportunities and access to housing, both of which have stimulated increases in the number of marriages, and so led to increased birth rates. Such population increases puts a growing pressure on food supplies in a world which reads of the USA's 'grain mountain' and the EEC's 'mountains' of meat, wheat and other products. It might seem a simple matter to transfer this 'unwanted' food to the hungry Third World. Unfortunately, economic systems are never that simple. Among the questions that have to be asked are: Can the poor pay for the food? If not, will western taxpayers agree to pay for the food to be transferred? If they do, how would the transfer affect the incomes of local farmers?

In western societies there is often a long-term acceptance of some form of family limitation. In Third World countries large families are still seen as desirable, and there are strong religious objections to the artificial methods of birth control accepted in the west. Moreover, it has proved difficult to educate largely illiterate peoples in the methods of family planning. In India, Mrs Gandhi and her son, Sanjay, tried to make sterilization compulsory, and this was one reason for her fall from power in 1977 (p. 193).

The 'slippage' in the relative positions of rich and poor countries (p. 304) is due, in part, to this population problem, but it is also a result of difficulties connected with the provision of, and use of, development aid.

## International development aid

Third World countries need foreign aid if they are to progress. Unable to finance their own development (p. 307), they need help to create an economic infrastructure which developed countries take for granted, including power supplies, dams, and generating stations. Electricity is a luxury (Document 12.2) when there is a shortage of power for industrial and agricultural purposes. A good transport system is often desperately needed: in September 1986 relief for the victims of the Lake Nios disaster near Cameroon's northwest border was hindered by the absence of highways in even this populated area. This is but one example of a lack of infrastructure, illustrating the consequent problems facing farmers, industrialists and governments in Third World countries. Commonly, there are too few schools and too few teachers. In 1976, when it was the world's leading oil producer, Saudi Arabia reported that 75 per cent of its population was illiterate. Similar figures are to be found in Bangladesh (Document 12.2) and Peru (Document 20.1).

If money has to be spent on importing food, a balance of payments problem will arise, and a Third World country will be unable to pay for the imported capital goods needed for its development. If these countries are to feed their populations they need, among other things, agricultural colleges, machinery and improved storage facilities.

Industrial progress, now enjoyed by India (p. 200) and by ASEAN states (Chapter 14), means better job prospects, higher incomes, better living standards and greater spending by the government on social welfare schemes. To achieve this, Third World countries need help with buying the necessary equipment and building the necessary factories, as well as with managing and operating the new industries.

We have seen that the UNO (p. 255) and the Commonwealth (p. 303) provide various forms of aid, as do many western nations, which make government-to-government loans and grants. Third World countries welcome the grants, since these carry no interest and do not have to be repaid. Most aid comes in the form of loans from govern-ments, UN agencies and commercial banks. These have to be repaid (over, say, ten or twenty years), and carry an interest charge adjusted every six months in line with changes in world interest rates.

In the 1970s western banks had to cope with an influx of money from oil-producing, mainly Arab, countries. They had to pay interest on these deposits, and tried to recoup that interest (and make profits) by lending out the money. Many Third World countries were persuaded to take out loans which, in the 1980s, they were unable to repay, because of a fall in their foreign earnings. Their position was worsened by the upward move in interest rates: in 1972 these stood at about 5 per cent; in the 1980s they reached 15 per cent for a time, vastly increasing the cost of a loan.

Third World countries accept loans, hoping that they will be able to meet the interest and repayment charges from increased export earnings. In the 1980s many found that their exports failed to match their expectations. Nigeria, Mexico and Venezuela all suffered from falling oil prices. Other countries have suffered from the general fall in primary product prices (p. 307); members of ASEAN complain (Figure 14.2a), but their position is much healthier than that of, say, Zambia or Ghana or any of the 'one-crop' economies (p. 306).

Many nations who provide aid insist that the money has to be spent within their own borders, limiting the freedom of the developing country while helping the economy of the donor country. The USA and the USSR often use aid as a weapon in their foreign policy wars, as a reward to recipients following the 'party line'. Thus South Korea is a US satellite and North Korea a recipient of Soviet aid. This type of 'help' frequently takes the form of military 'advice', which does little for a nations economic development, and may indeed be detrimental to progress.

Too many recipient countries have wasted much of their aid on arms or on glamorous projects such as huge sports stadia, massive government-office complexes and status-making airports. In September 1986 Zimbabwe spent over £200 million hosting the meeting of Non-Aligned states, providing luxury villas and lavish entertainment for visiting delegations. Many Third World Countries have spent aid on prestigious industrial development which, in the event, their social infrastructure could not sustain: shortages of trained personnel makes it increasingly difficult to operate sophisticated industries. At the same time, and sometimes seemingly deliberately, they have ignored traditional industries, including farming: it seems as if 'independence' is often synonomous with 'urbanization'. In September 1986 experts from the FAO met African agricultural ministers to draw up a document, *African Agriculture – The Next 25 Years*, outlining a strategy for Africa to *regain* the capability to feed itself. The document points out that if current trends continue only four African countries will be able to feed themselves in 25 years time, while the rest will have to import 100 millions tons of cereal a year, the cost of which would far exceed the revenue earned from African exports of tea, coffee, cotton, cocoa and other products. It revealed that few African countries spend more than 10 per cent of their budgets within the agricultural sector, and that less than 20 per cent of foreign aid is used in this area. Since the population of Africa will double over the next 25 years, agricultural output will have to be vastly increased if there are not to be famine, political instability or international tension. While governments promise new policies in accordance with the FAO findings, the fact remains that between 1980 and 1986 food production per head in Africa fell by nearly 20 per cent. It will require a great deal of education, of both ministers and people, to reverse this trend.

A Third World country's development may be helped by the work of multinational firms. The opening of a Ford car plant, an Esso refinery or an ICI chemical plant provides employment and increased incomes. However, many such firms use their economic power to try to control government policy. Before the formation of OPEC, Middle Eastern countries suffered in this way, as have many Latin American countries such as Chile. It remains true, nonetheless, that the only thing worse than having multinationals in a country is having none.

In the 1980s the developed world suffered from the recession induced by increased oil prices. This was one of the causes of the fall in commodity prices which hampered Third World development. During such recessions, poorer countries need aid more than ever, but it is at just these times that western countries reduce it, and restrict imports from developing Third World countries. In spite of a general rhetorical acceptance of the Brandt Report, there has been little, if any, transfer of resources from the rich countries (which get richer every year) to the poor (which grow, if at all, only slowly). Instead, in 1985 there was a transfer of capital resources from the poor to the richer countries: the total of repayments and interest charges on outstanding loans was *five times* greater than the total of foreign aid to third World nations.

## Oil and the Third World, 1973–86

In Chapter 9 we saw how oil prices changed in the 1970s and 1980s, and how these changes affected the economies of what some refer to as 'The Fourth World' of rich, but underdeveloped, OPEC countries. In Chapter 10 we saw how the development of Nigeria was successively helped then hindered by these changes.

Most Third World countries are not oil producers, but importers, and had to pay high prices for their oil in the 1970s and early 1980s. Families in poor countries spend a higher proportion of their small incomes on oil than do families in richer countries; it is their fuel for cooking, lighting and heating. With increased oil prices, there was a fall in already poor living standards, as people had less money to spend on other products.

Rising oil prices led to increases in the cost of almost every industrial product. This, as we have seen, harmed the industrialized world, since it led to a drop in overall demand, and so to unemployment. But rising prices harmed Third World countries to an even greater extent; they had to pay more for their imports, including machinery and other goods needed for development; foreign aid bought less than had been expected, and development was slowed down.

The fall in the volume of world trade, and the rise in unemployment in richer countries, led to a fall in demand for Third World primary products further worsening those countries' balance of payments positions and lowering living standards for individual families. It might seem that these countries and families would gain from the recent sharp fall in oil prices. At one level they have, as import bills have fallen, and families spend a smaller proportion of their income on oil and oil-based products. However, demand for the countries' own products is still low, as the industrialized world remains in recession and adopts protectionist and import-saving policies. The collapse in commodity prices in the mid-1980s is both cause and proof of the plight of the Third World.

Nigeria was not the only oil-producing country to suffer in the 1980s. Venezuela, a founder member of OPEC, has an economy which 'floats on oil', accounting for 90 per cent of its exports. Falling oil prices in 1985–6 led to an economic crisis within Venezuela, which had borrowed 'in the expectation of plenty' to finance various forms of development. Mexico is perhaps the best, or worst, example of an oil-rich country which has had to borrow to finance development, and is now in deep trouble. In 1974, with a rising income from oil exports, Mexico not only spent that revenue on development, but borrowed heavily from western banks, trusting in permanently rising oil prices to finance these debts. In 1978–80, with further increases in oil prices, Mexican optimism and western eagerness to lend seemed justified. In 1980–2, however, recession led to a rise in interest rates (making it more expensive for Mexico to service her debt) and inflation rocketed, increasing the costs of imports linked to Mexican development. The Mexican government had to cope with the effects of inflation, a soaring budget deficit (the result of its vast spending on social and economic development) and increasing unemployment as the oil industry was forced to cut production in the face of falling demand. With rising deficits on her balance of payments, in 1983 Mexico's government was forced to ask the IMF for assistance, which was given on condition that Mexico adopted an austerity programme to help lower the volume of her imports, while raising export levels. The effect was a sharp rise in unemployment, increased political tension and, because the government refused to cut its social spending, a sudden growth in domestic inflation and a fall in the value of the *peso*. In 1982 $1 exchanged for 100 *pesos*; in 1985 $1 bought 500 *pesos*.

The falling value of the *peso* made it increasingly difficult for Mexico to meet its foreign obligations. In 1982–3 Mexico, along with many other debtor countries, persuaded western banks and agencies to renegotiate interest charges and to reschedule debt repayments. Western banks had little option but to agree: if they refused, Mexico might have defaulted on her overseas payments, forcing western banks to wipe loans to Mexico off their balance sheets as 'bad debts'. The financial chaos which would have followed in the West made this an unacceptable alternative. In 1983-4 western banks lent Mexico (and others) the money needed to meet interest charges, thus further increasing the size of the debt and future servicing charges, and merely putting off the day when reality will have to be faced.

In 1985 the US Treasury Secretary, James Baker, produced the 'Baker Plan', a 'Program for Sustained Growth', aimed at promoting economic growth in developing countries. This programme would force these countries to adopt 'market-oriented policies', strengthening the private sector, encouraging tax and trade union reforms, and opening up markets to private investors. Mexico and other debtor countries have accepted some parts of this package, but have also called for an immediate reduction in interest rates to help ease their position.

In 1986 Mexico hosted the World Cup Finals while suffering from the effects of an earthquake, a 65 per cent inflation rate, a fall in trade surplus from $13 billion (1984) to $8 billion (1985), a budget deficit of 10 per cent of GDP (twice the figure agreed with the IMF in 1983) and a declining *peso*. With a government unwilling to make further cuts in its spending, and workers unwilling to accept further cuts in depressed living standards, Mexico illustrates the problems facing many debtor countries. Whatever the outcome of the 'Baaker Plan', the crisis will continue, and this will affect not only people in Third World countries but also many western banks, who will not welcome the announcement by Mexico's Finance Minister that 'foreign loan obligations cannot take precedence over the needs of the people'. Our interdependent world faces the probability of a major financial crisis.

## Documentary evidence

The Atlantic Charter (1941) and the UN Charter on Human Rights (1948) were concerned, among much else, with the creation of a world in which all peoples would enjoy a fairer share of the 'good life'. The Brandt Report (1980), the Commonwealth Report, *North-South Dialogue: Making it Work* (1982) and other subsequent reports make it clear that the gulf between the richer and poorer nations is, if anything, greater than it was forty years ago. Terrible poverty may be seen in Bangladesh (Document 12.2), Peru and in sub-Saharan Africa. This poverty, and the increasing gap between rich and poor nations, has many causes, not least of which is the population explosion within Third World countries (Document 20.1).

## Document 20.1

*The Population Explosion, 1971*

'In the course of some 200,000 years, the species of Homo Sapiens multiplied to reach the present figure of about 3 billion. It will doubt that figure in less than forty years. Many experts think that by AD 2000 world population will rise to 7.4 billion if birth and death rates remain constant at the 1960 level. The *annual* population increase in world population is estimated to be more than 65 million. [*In fact, it was 80 million in 1974.*] Compare this with the UK's total population (1971) of 54.7 million. The *daily* population increase is estimated to be about 180,000 [*in fact it was 215,000 in 1975*], equivalent to the entire population of the London Borough of Barking, or Sunderland. On this reckoning, every second there are nearly four extra people added to the world's population. In the developed regions the rate of annual population increase is moderate, for example 0.7 per cent p.a. in the UK. In the developing areas the population is soaring . . . Brazil, 3.1 per cent; Botswana, 3.4 per cent; Costa Rica, 4.3 per cent; Malaysia, 3.3 per cent; Mali, 3.9 per cent. The Indian population increased only by 2.1 per cent between 1951 and 1961, but that added 81 million to the population. By AD 2000 the peoples of the less developed areas of the world will have doubled their numbers. Their populations will probably be about 6 billions. Birth control is essential to stabilize the rate of growth of the world's population, and to bring balance in the age range in national populations. Family planning techniques, however, cannot be a substitute for the determination to provide adequate food, decent housing and educational opportunities for the population in developing countries. Over the past century the birth rates have declined amongst communities where the standard of living has risen considerably and where more educational opportunities have been made available. People then chose to limit their familes. . . .'

(Christian Aid: *Facts and figures about the Population Explosion*, 1971)

## FURTHER READING

BHAGWATI, J. N., ed., *The New International Economic Order: The North-South Debate*, Massachusetts Institute of Technology Press, 1977

BOLLING, L. R., *Private Foreign Aid*, Westview, 1982

CASSEN, R., *Does Aid Work?*, OUP, 1986

CLARK, B. A. et al., eds., *The North-South Dialogue: Making it Work*, Commonwealth Secretariat, 1982

HARRISON, P., *Inside the Third World*, Penguin, 1979
                *The Third World Tomorrow*, Penguin, 1980

MORTIMER, R. A., *The Third World Coalition in International Politics*, Westview, 1984

MORTON, K. and TULLOCH, P., *Trade and Developing Countries*, Croom Helm, 1977

MURRAY, T., *Trade Preferences for Developing Countries*, Macmillan, 1977

NYERERE, J., *Freedom and Unity*, OUP, 1969

SCHUMACHER, E. F., *Small is Beautiful*, Blond and Briggs, 1973

UN Report, *The Population Debate* (2 vols), UN New York, 1975

# Index